# Perspectives on the L2 Phrasicon

SECOND LANGUAGE ACQUISITION

***Series Editors:*** **Professor David Singleton**, *University of Pannonia, Hungary* and Fellow Emeritus, *Trinity College, Dublin, Ireland* and **Associate Professor Simone E. Pfenninger**, *University of Salzburg, Austria*

This series brings together titles dealing with a variety of aspects of language acquisition and processing in situations where a language or languages other than the native language is involved. Second language is thus interpreted in its broadest possible sense. The volumes included in the series all offer in their different ways, on the one hand, exposition and discussion of empirical findings and, on the other, some degree of theoretical reflection. In this latter connection, no particular theoretical stance is privileged in the series; nor is any relevant perspective – sociolinguistic, psycholinguistic, neurolinguistic, etc. – deemed out of place. The intended readership of the series includes final-year undergraduates working on second language acquisition projects, postgraduate students involved in second language acquisition research, and researchers, teachers and policymakers in general whose interests include a second language acquisition component.

All books in this series are externally peer-reviewed.

Full details of all the books in this series and of all our other publications can be found on http://www.multilingual-matters.com, or by writing to Multilingual Matters, St Nicholas House, 31-34 High Street, Bristol BS1 2AW, UK.

SECOND LANGUAGE ACQUISITION: 148

# Perspectives on the L2 Phrasicon

## The View from Learner Corpora

Edited by
**Sylviane Granger**

MULTILINGUAL MATTERS
Bristol • Blue Ridge Summit

DOI https://doi.org/10.21832/GRANGE4856
Library of Congress Cataloging in Publication Data
A catalog record for this book is available from the Library of Congress.
Names: Granger, Sylviane, editor.
Title: Perspectives on the L2 Phrasicon: The View from Learner Corpora/ Edited by Sylviane Granger.
Description: Bristol, UK; Blue Ridge Summit, PA: Multilingual Matters, 2021. | Series: Second Language Acquisition: 148 | Includes bibliographical references and index. | Summary: 'This is the first book to investigate the field of phraseology from a learner corpus perspective. It includes cutting-edge studies which analyse a wide range of multiword units and extensive learner corpus data to provide the reader with a comprehensive theoretical, methodological and applied perspective onto L2 use in a wide range of situations' – Provided by publisher.
Identifiers: LCCN 2021010571 (print) | LCCN 2021010572 (ebook) | ISBN 9781788924856 (hardback) | ISBN 9781788924863 (pdf) | ISBN 9781788924870 (epub) | ISBN 9781788924887 (kindle edition)
Subjects: LCSH: Language and languages – Study and teaching – Foreign speakers. | Phraseology – Study and teaching. | Second language acquisition.
Classification: LCC P53.6123 .P48 2021 (print) | LCC P53.6123 (ebook) | DDC 418.0071 – dc23
LC record available at https://lccn.loc.gov/2021010571
LC ebook record available at https://lccn.loc.gov/2021010572

British Library Cataloguing in Publication Data
A catalogue entry for this book is available from the British Library.

ISBN-13: 978-1-78892-485-6 (hbk)

**Multilingual Matters**
UK: St Nicholas House, 31-34 High Street, Bristol BS1 2AW, UK.
USA: NBN, Blue Ridge Summit, PA, USA.

Website: www.multilingual-matters.com
Twitter: Multi_Ling_Mat
Facebook: https://www.facebook.com/multilingualmatters
Blog: www.channelviewpublications.wordpress.com



The policy of Multilingual Matters/Channel View Publications is to use papers that are natural, renewable and recyclable products, made from wood grown in sustainable forests. In the manufacturing process of our books, and to further support our policy, preference is given to printers that have FSC and PEFC Chain of Custody certification. The FSC and/or PEFC logos will appear on those books where full certification has been granted to the printer concerned.

Typeset by Riverside Publishing Solutions.
Printed and bound in the UK by the CPI Books Group Ltd.
Printed and bound in the US by NBN.

# Contents

**Contributors** vii

**Part 1: Introduction**

1 Phraseology, Corpora and L2 Research 3
*Sylviane Granger*

**Part 2: The Learner Phrasicon: Synchronic Approaches**

2 The Functions of N-grams in Bilingual and Learner Corpora: An Integrated Contrastive Approach 25
*Signe Oksefjell Ebeling and Hilde Hasselgård*

3 Exploring Learner Corpus Data for Language Testing and Assessment Purposes: The Case of Verb + Noun Collocations 49
*Henrik Gyllstad and Per Snoder*

4 The Passive and the Lexis-Grammar Interface: An Inter-varietal Perspective 72
*Gaëtanelle Gilquin and Sylviane Granger*

**Part 3: The Learner Phrasicon: Developmental Approaches**

5 Phraseological Complexity as an Index of L2 Dutch Writing Proficiency: A Partial Replication Study 101
*Rachel Rubin, Alex Housen and Magali Paquot*

6 Automatically Assessing Lexical Sophistication Using Word, Bigram, and Dependency Indices 126
*Kristopher Kyle and Masaki Eguchi*

7 Adjective + Noun Collocations in L2 and L1 Speech: Evidence from the Trinity Lancaster Corpus and the Spoken BNC2014 152
*Vaclav Brezina and Lorrae Fox*

8 Development of Formulaic Knowledge in Learner Writing: A Longitudinal Perspective 178
*Taha Omidian, Anna Siyanova-Chanturia and Stefania Spina*

9 Tracing Collocation in Learner Production and Processing: Integrating Corpus Linguistic and Experimental Approaches 206
*Marco Schilk*

**Part 4: Postface**

10 Phrasicon, Phrase, Phraseology 235
*David Singleton*

**Index** 245

# Contributors

**Vaclav Brezina** is Senior Lecturer at the Department of Linguistics and English Language and a member of the ESRC Centre for Corpus Approaches to Social Science, Lancaster University. His research interests are in the areas of applied linguistics, corpus design and methodology, and statistics. He is the author of *Statistics in Corpus Linguistics: A Practical Guide* (CUP, 2018) and a co-author of the *New General Service List* (*Applied Linguistics*, 2015). He has also designed a number of different tools for corpus analysis, such as #LancsBox, BNClab, LancsLex and Lancaster Stats Tools online.

**Signe Oksefjell Ebeling** is Professor of English Language at the University of Oslo, Norway. Her research interests include corpus-based contrastive and learner language analysis on topics such as verb semantics, phraseology and idiomaticity. Her previous publications include *Patterns in Contrast* (2013), co-authored with Jarle Ebeling, several co-edited volumes on contrastive linguistics, and a number of papers on contrastive analysis and contrastive interlanguage analysis. She was, with Hilde Hasselgård, editor of the international journal for contrastive linguistics *Languages in Contrast* for six years (2014-2019). She is currently on the editorial board of *Languages in Contrast* and the *International Journal of Learner Corpus Research*.

**Masaki Eguchi** is a PhD student in the Department of Linguistics and a member of the Learner Corpus Research and Applied Data Science Lab at the University of Oregon. His research interests include the teaching and learning of words and multiword units in second language contexts. He is particularly interested in triangulating corpus, psycholinguistic, and classroom research. He is also interested in the use of advanced quantitative research methods and statistics in applied linguistics research.

**Lorrae Fox** is a PhD student in the Department of Linguistics and English Language and is a member of the ESRC Centre for Corpus Approaches to Social Science, Lancaster University. Her doctoral research investigates phraseological competence in L1 and L2 spoken English, focusing on collocations, and how corpus methods can be used to inform language testing. Other research interests include second language acquisition and language teaching.

**Gaëtanelle Gilquin** is Professor of English Language and Linguistics at the University of Louvain. Most of her research has been carried out within the frame of learner corpus research. She is also interested in the links between learner corpus research and contact linguistics, and how Learner Englishes and New Englishes can share certain features. She is co-editor (with Sylviane Granger and Fanny Meunier) of the *Cambridge Handbook of Learner Corpus Research* and is the author of a number of publications dealing with corpus linguistics.

**Sylviane Granger** is Professor Emerita of English Language and Linguistics at the University of Louvain. In 1990 she launched the first large-scale learner corpus project, the International Corpus of Learner English, and since then has played a key role in defining the different facets of the field of learner corpus research. Her current research interests focus on the analysis of phraseology in native and learner language and its integration into reference and instructional materials. She has written widely on these topics and gives frequent invited talks to stimulate learner corpus research and to promote its use in second language acquisition research and foreign language teaching. Her book publications include the *Cambridge Handbook of Learner Corpus Research* (2015) and *Twenty Years of Learner Corpus Research: Looking Back, Moving Ahead* (2013), both co-edited with Gaëtanelle Gilquin and Fanny Meunier.

**Henrik Gyllstad** is Associate Professor of English Language and Linguistics at the Centre for Languages and Literature, Lund University. His overall research focus is on language testing and assessment, bi- and multilingualism, and psycholinguistics. More specifically, he is interested in test development and validation, lexical processing and representation, vocabulary, phraseology and formulaic language. He co-edited (with Andy Barfield) the volume *Researching Collocations in Another Language: Multiple Interpretations* (2009). His work has appeared in journals such as *Applied Linguistics*, *ITL International Journal of Applied Linguistics*, *Language Learning*, *Language Testing* and *Studies in Second Language Acquisition*, and in *The Routledge Handbook of Vocabulary Studies* (2019).

**Hilde Hasselgård** is Professor of English language at the University of Oslo, and specializes in corpus-based and functional linguistics. Her most recent publications are mainly within corpus-based contrastive studies and Learner Corpus Research. She has also published on English grammar, most notably *Adjunct Adverbials in English* (2010). She has co-edited volumes such as *Cross-linguistic Perspectives on Verb Constructions* (with Signe Oksefjell Ebeling, 2015) and *Time in Languages* (Benjamins). She is on the editorial board of *Languages in Contrast* and the *International Journal of Learner Corpus Research* and is Vice President of the Learner Corpus Association.

**Alex Housen** is Professor of English Linguistics and Applied Linguistics in the Department of Linguistics & Literary Studies and currently Dean of the Faculty of Linguistics and Literary Studies at the Vrije Universiteit Brussel, Belgium. His research focuses on linguistic, cognitive and social factors in second language acquisition, bilingualism, and bilingual and second language education. His recent research deals with language complexity and cognitive mechanisms in SLA. His publications have appeared in various journals and edited volumes. He co-authored and co-edited several books, including *Bilingualism: Beyond Basic Principles* (with J-M. Dewaele & Li Wei, 2003), *Investigations in Instructed Second Language Acquisition* (with M. Pierrard, 2005) and *Dimensions of L2 Performance and Proficiency – Investigating Complexity, Accuracy and Fluency in SLA* (with F. Kuiken & I. Vedder, 2012). He has also worked as a consultant on bilingual and language education for the Soros Foundation, the United Nations Development Programme and various ministerial agencies across the world.

**Kristopher Kyle** is Assistant Professor in the Linguistics department and the Director of the Learner Corpus Research and Applied Data Science Lab at the University of Oregon. His research interests include second language acquisition and the assessment of second language speaking and writing. He is especially interested in applying natural language processing and corpora to the exploration of these areas. He and colleagues have developed and released a number of learner corpus analysis tools including the Tool for the Automatic Analysis of Lexical Sophistication (TAALES) and the Tool for the Automatic Analysis of Syntactic Sophistication and Complexity (TAASSC).

**Taha Omidian** is a PhD student at Victoria University of Wellington, New Zealand. He specializes in the use of corpus linguistic and computational methods to explore systematic patterns in language data. His research interests include corpus linguistics, computational linguistics, quantitative linguistic research methods, English grammar, register variation, vocabulary, phraseology, language learning, language for specific purposes, multilingualism, and academic writing.

**Magali Paquot** is FNRS Research Associate at the Centre for English Corpus Linguistics, Institut Langage et Communication, University of Louvain. She is co-editor in chief of the *International Journal of Learner Corpus Research* and a founding member of the Learner Corpus Research Association. Her research interests include second language acquisition, learner corpus research, phraseology, complexity and cross-linguistic influence.

**Rachel Rubin** is a PhD student in the Department of Linguistics and Literary Studies at the Vrije Universiteit Brussel and the Centre for English Corpus Linguistics at the University of Louvain, where she is working on an FWO-funded project investigating lexicogrammatical complexity in L2 Dutch. Her research interests include second language acquisition, learner corpus research, natural language processing, complexity, and phraseology.

**Marco Schilk** is Senior Lecturer for English Linguistics at the University of Hildesheim. His research interests include applied linguistics, corpus linguistics and psycholinguistics. A main focus of his work is on lexico-grammatical variation in ESL and EFL varieties/variants of English from a corpus linguistic and psycholinguistic perspective. He has published widely in those areas. His books include *Structural Nativization in Indian English* (2011) and *Language Processing in Advanced Learners of English* (2020).

**David Singleton** is Emeritus Fellow, Trinity College Dublin, where he was, until his retirement from that institution, Professor in Applied Linguistics. Thereafter he held a professorship at the University of Pannonia, Hungary. He served as President of the Irish Association for Applied Linguistics, as Secretary General of the International Association of Applied Linguistics and as President of the European Second Language Association. His publications include titles on cross-linguistic influence, the lexicon, the age factor and multilingualism. In 2015 he received the EUROSLA Distinguished Scholar Award and in 2017 was awarded Honorary Membership of AILA.

**Anna Siyanova-Chanturia** is Senior Lecturer in Applied Linguistics at Victoria University of Wellington and Guest Professor in Linguistics and Applied Linguistics at Ocean University of China. Her research interests include psychological aspects of second language acquisition, bilingualism, usage-based approaches to language acquisition, processing and use, vocabulary and multiword expressions, quantitative research methods (corpora, eye movements, EEG/ERPs): She is co-editor (together with A. Pellicer-Sanchez) of *Understanding Formulaic Language: A Second Language Acquisition Perspective* and co-author (together with P. Durrant, S. Sonbul and B. Kremmel) of forthcoming *Research Methods in Vocabulary Studies*.

**Per Snoder** is Senior Lecturer in Language Education at Stockholm University, Sweden. He defended his PhD thesis, *L2 Instruction and Collocation Learning*, in 2019 and continues to do research with clear applications for L2 learners and teachers, notably the researcher-teacher collaboration project *Word Up!* together with F. Meunier and T. Nilsson. His research interests also include mapping adolescent L2 learners' vocabulary size and depth.

**Stefania Spina** is Full Professor of Linguistics at the University for Foreigners of Perugia. She works in the area of applied linguistics, and her main research interests include learner corpus research (the acquisition of Italian as a second language, with a focus on phraseology) and corpus linguistics (register variation, academic Italian and the discourse of Italian media).

# Part 1: Introduction

# 1 Phraseology, Corpora and L2 Research

Sylviane Granger

## 1 Introduction

Phraseology is undoubtedly one of the linguistic fields that have undergone the most dramatic changes in recent years. From being a somewhat peripheral area in both linguistic theory and practice, it has come to occupy a much more central position in language studies in general and foreign language learning and teaching in particular. This development is largely due to the 'corpus revolution' (Rundell, 2008), which has provided researchers with automated tools and methods with which to extract and explore multiword units. As a result, the scope of phraseology has expanded considerably. Although its home base is still primarily lexical, phraseology stands at the interface of other fields, in particular morphology, grammar and discourse (Granger & Paquot, 2008). Increased attention is currently being paid to a wider range of units, many of which – such as collocations, lexical bundles and lexico-grammatical patterns – tend to display a high degree of semantic compositionality. These units are more frequent than semantically non-compositional units such as idioms, which were long considered the core units of phraseology and commanded the lion's share in L2 (i.e. foreign or second language) learning and teaching. The main objective of this volume is to show how a specific type of corpus, the learner corpus, which can be broadly defined as an electronic collection of language use data produced by foreign or second language learners, can contribute to the study of the L2 phrasicon, i.e. the learners' stock of phraseological units.

This chapter is structured as follows. Section 2 describes the two main approaches to phraseology: the classical approach, which established phraseology as a field in its own right, and the new perspectives offered by corpus phraseology. Section 3 offers an overview of studies of the L2 phrasicon, with a particular focus on those that rely on learner corpus data. Section 4 lays out the structure of the volume and provides a brief description of each chapter.

## 2 Phraseology

Phraseology has traditionally been viewed as a subfield of lexicology dealing with the study of word combinations rather than single words. Defined by Cowie (1994: 3168) as 'the study of the structure, meaning and use of word combinations', phraseology was first recognized as a discipline in its own right by Eastern European researchers in the 1950s/1960s. In this 'classical tradition' (Cowie, 1998: 2) and its later extensions, a certain number of linguistic criteria are deemed essential for a word combination to qualify as a phraseological unit. Depending on their degrees of semantic non-compositionality (i.e. non-deducibility of the meaning of the whole word combination from its parts), syntactic fixedness, lexical restriction and institutionalization, different categories of phraseological unit have been set up and placed on a cline from the most variable and transparent to the most fixed and opaque. One of the main preoccupations of linguists working within this tradition has been to distinguish one type of phraseological unit from another (e.g. collocations vs idioms or full idioms vs semi-idioms), and especially to distinguish the most variable and transparent multi-word units from free combinations (*read a book*), which only have syntactic and semantic restrictions and are therefore considered to fall outside the realm of phraseology (Cowie, 1998: 4–7). This work has resulted in the identification of very fine linguistic distinctions between units, which are extremely valuable but often based on criteria that involve a large element of subjectivity. In addition, excessive concern with a strict delimitation of the field of phraseology results in the exclusion of potentially relevant units on the grounds that they are fully free and hence of no interest in an L2 teaching perspective. For example, Howarth (1998: 164) excludes *to blow a trumpet* from the field of phraseology as it is a 'free combination', i.e. a combination that is not lexically restricted; both words are used in their literal sense and *to blow* can be used with a large number of nouns. However, for French learners, for example, the use of the verb *to blow* with the noun *trumpet* is far from self-evident, as in French the corresponding verb *souffler* cannot be used transitively (**souffler une trompette*). The preposition *dans* ('in') is required (*souffler dans une trompette*); alternatively, a different verb can be used: *jouer de la trompette* ('play the trumpet'). This example shows that what may appear at first sight to be free can in fact involve some degree of conventionality.

Corpus linguistics, the linguistic framework within which the new approach to phraseology is situated, relies on large amounts of authentic data in electronic format and makes use of powerful software tools to speed up and enhance data extraction and analysis. The domain that has benefited most from this approach is lexis, which by reason of its sheer size cannot possibly be investigated comprehensively on the basis of intuition alone or small data samples. Besides their capacity to process large amounts of data, computers have the added advantage of being particularly apt at exploiting the syntagmatic dimension of lexis, i.e. how words pattern with surrounding words. There is nothing easier for a computer than to extract words or sequences of words, count them and sort them so as to uncover co-occurrence and recurrence patterns of use. As a result, corpus linguistics has given new vitality to lexical studies and resulted in a complete overhaul of the theory and practice of phraseology. A key figure in this approach is John Sinclair, whose pioneering lexicographic work (1987) turned phraseology on its head. The new approach to phraseology he initiated, referred to as the distributional or frequency-based approach (Evert, 2004; Granger & Paquot, 2008; Nesselhauf, 2005), consists in identifying phraseological units not top-down but bottom-up, on the basis of quantitative criteria. This corpus-driven approach generates a wide range of word combinations, which do not all fit into predefined linguistic categories. It has opened up a 'huge area of syntagmatic prospection' (Sinclair, 2004: 19) encompassing not only phraseological units in the traditional sense but also word combinations which are 'syntactically and semantically compositional, but which occur with markedly high frequency (in a given context)' (Sag *et al.*, 2002: 3). Such units, traditionally regarded as peripheral or falling outside the limits of phraseology, have recently revealed themselves to be pervasive in language, while many of the most restricted units – in particular, figurative idioms and proverbs – which were considered to be the phraseological units par excellence have proved to be very infrequent (Moon, 1998: 83).

Unlike proponents of the classical approach to phraseology, Sinclair and his followers are not preoccupied with setting clear boundaries to phraseology, as they view the tendency for words to form 'semi-preconstructed phrases that constitute single choices', the so-called 'idiom principle' (Sinclair, 1991: 110), as central to language. In this view of language, grammar and lexis are seen as intrinsically intertwined. Sinclair (2000: 191) challenges the separation of a grammatical component, 'which produces patterns of organization', from a lexical component, 'which produces items that fill places in the patterns'. For him, this age-old distinction 'may not be fundamental to the nature of language, but more a consequence of the inadequacy of the means of studying language in the pre-computer age' (2000: 192).

As is apparent from the title of his seminal book, *Corpus, Concordance, Collocation*, the phraseological units to which Sinclair devoted the most attention were collocations. In the new approach he has initiated, significant collocation is 'regular collocation between items, such that they occur more often than their respective frequencies and the length of the text in which they occur would predict' (Jones & Sinclair, 1974: 19). Words that appear significantly more frequently on either side of the node, usually in a window of four words on either side, are considered to be significant collocations. Several statistical tests (mutual information, t-score, etc.) are used to determine the degree of significance of the association. This method does full justice to the graded nature of collocations. Instead of being categorized in a binary manner as collocational or non-collocational (i.e. free) combinations, word combinations can be shown to display a wide range of strengths of association. As pointed out by Sinclair *et al.* (2004: 72): 'there is no hard and fast distinction between a casual and regular collocation, simply different degrees of probability'. This automatic extraction method is a very powerful heuristic. The downside is that the output is a mixed bag of phraseological units which, in the classical approach, would fall into different categories (compounds, collocations, idioms, etc.). Each approach clearly has its advantages and its disadvantages, and which one to choose depends on the objectives of the study. The two approaches can also be combined. For example, it is possible to use the quantitative approach to extract significant collocations in the Sinclairian sense and then to apply linguistic criteria to classify the resulting units into meaningful linguistic categories.

Unlike collocations, which were already studied in the classical tradition albeit in a different framework, lexical bundles are a completely new type of phraseological unit, which can only be extracted by means of computer technology. First introduced by Doug Biber and colleagues (Biber *et al.*, 1999; Conrad & Biber, 2004), lexical bundles are fully corpus-driven sequences of words that recur most frequently in a given register, such as *from the point of view of* in formal writing and *I tell you what* in informal speech. While collocations consist of two words that can be found at some distance from each other (*a <u>daunting</u> <u>task</u>*; *the <u>task</u> was truly <u>daunting</u>*), lexical bundles can be made up of a much larger number of words, but these need to be contiguous and to appear in exactly the same form. The word sequences *it can be said that*, *it can however be said that* and *it could be said that* are three different bundles. As is the case with statistical collocations, the extraction of lexical bundles also generates a mixed bag of linguistically defined phraseological units, including compounds and compound-like units (*on the other hand*), collocations (*a significant number*), and speech-act formulae (*thank you very much*). For a range of applications, particularly pedagogical applications, it makes sense to subcategorize them, as they may involve different types of processing and therefore necessitate different teaching methods. But because it casts its net wide, lexical bundle extraction is a powerful discovery procedure which has brought to light aspects of phraseology that had hitherto remained off limits.

## 3 Phraseology in L2 Research

Research into the L2 phrasicon can be subdivided into two main approaches: one that studies the acquisition and processing of phraseological units by foreign or second language learners (henceforth referred to as L2 learners[1]) on the basis of highly controlled elicitation and experimental data, and the other that studies the actual use of these units by L2 learners on the basis of L2 natural language use data in electronic format. The first has prevailed in second language acquisition (SLA) research while the second is rooted in the emergent field of learner corpus research (LCR) (Granger *et al.*, 2015). As the focus of this volume is on the LCR approach, I will limit the description of the SLA approach to some of its key features in terms of objectives, data and methods and use it as a backdrop to bring into focus the distinctive contribution made by LCR. For more comprehensive surveys of the SLA approach, the reader is referred to the excellent volumes edited by Schmitt (2004) and Siyanova-Chanturia and Pellicer-Sánchez (2019).

### 3.1 The SLA approach

The SLA approach aims to investigate how learners acquire and process phraseological units, usually referred to in this approach by the term 'formulaic sequences', defined psycholinguistically as multiword units that present a processing advantage for learners because they are stored whole in their lexicon or because they are highly automatized (Myles & Cordier, 2017: 10). Among the questions raised are the following: To what extent are formulaic sequences stored and processed as unitary wholes? Is L2 processing similar to L1 processing? How does L2 processing develop across time? What factors influence L2 processing? To answer this last question, the effect of a range of variables is investigated, such as learners' differences in terms of age (Glass, 2019), aptitude and attitude/motivation (Schmitt *et al.*, 2004) and socio-cultural integration (Dörnyei *et al.*, 2004), and characteristics of the formulaic sequences, such as transparency (Gyllstad & Wolter, 2016) or proximity, i.e. adjacent vs non-adjacent units (Vilkaitė & Schmitt, 2019). Learners' knowledge and processing of formulaic sequences is tested through psycholinguistic measures such as reaction times, eye-tracking and electrophysiological measures. Multiple-choice tests and productive measurement tests (e.g. cloze tests) are also widely used. As the focus is on acquisition, several studies adopt a longitudinal design, which consists in observing a limited number of learners (Dörnyei *et al.*, 2004) or sometimes just one (Bell, 2009) at certain intervals over a period of time. This approach, which highlights 'the immensely rich data that can be gathered by looking at the behavior of individual subjects, in depth, over time' (Barfield & Fitzpatrick, 2009: 155), has brought to light considerable individual variability in the acquisition of formulaic sequences. However, as pointed out by Gass and Selinker (2001: 31), it also raises doubts about the generalizability of the findings as it is 'difficult to know with any degree of certainty whether the results obtained are applicable only to the one or two learners studied, or whether they are indeed characteristic of a wide range of subjects'.

In quite a number of SLA studies the main focus is on idioms, i.e. opaque or semi-opaque, usually figurative, units. For example, Karlsson's (2019) book-length study deals exclusively with 'classical idioms' such as *spill the beans*. Spöttl and McCarthy (2004: 196) focus expressly on 'opaque or semi-opaque chunks which might present a processing challenge to the learner' (see also Cieślicka, 2015 and Hubers, 2020). In many cases, the term 'formulaic sequence' is claimed to be used as an umbrella term to refer to a wide set of multiword strings, but a look at the units investigated shows that the majority represent a specific subset. For example, Underwood *et al.*'s (2004: 169–172) list is mainly made up of figurative idioms, while seven of the ten sequences targeted in Bishop's (2004) study are phrasal or phrasal-prepositional verbs. Some researchers, however, focus explicitly on one specific subtype, particularly collocations, which are attracting increasing attention in the field (Barfield, 2009; Glass, 2019; Vilkaitė & Schmitt, 2019; Wolter, 2009). To identify the formulaic units, a highly varied set of sources is used, including dictionaries of idioms or collocations, reference corpora of native language use such as the *British National Corpus* (BNC) or the *Cambridge and Nottingham Corpus of Discourse in English* (CANCODE), existing corpus-driven lists (e.g. Martinez & Schmitt, 2012) and/or lists of units investigated in previous scientific publications.

## 3.2 The LCR approach

The second approach to the L2 phrasicon emerged within a relatively new corpus-based research strand, learner corpus research (Granger *et al.*, 2015), which relies on large electronic collections of language use data produced by L2 learners. As the use of learner corpora is not yet standard in L2 studies, it seems useful to start this section with a brief presentation of their distinctive features.

Learner corpora, which at first only contained L2 English data but now cover a wide range of L2s,[2] have the following characteristics:

- They are large, in terms of numbers of both words and learners.
- They contain (near-)natural language use data.
- The data collection relies on strict design criteria.
- The data consists of written or spoken continuous discourse.
- The data is in electronic format and is therefore analysable with the help of automatic software tools and methods.

*Size* is a defining feature of corpora in general. As stated by Sinclair (1995: 21), '[t]he whole point of assembling a corpus is to gather data in quantity'. Learner corpora therefore tend to be counted in hundreds of thousands or even millions of words and involve hundreds or thousands of learners, but in view of the difficulty of collecting high-quality L2 data, they can never hope to reach the considerably larger sizes achieved by L1 corpora. Size matters in L2 studies. Many SLA studies end with a caveat on the small size of the data set and point to the need to replicate the study on a larger scale. In this respect, learner corpora clearly have a role to play. The *language use data* is collected with as few constraints as possible on learners' output. Admittedly, it is rarely possible to collect fully natural data, but open-ended tasks such as written compositions or oral interviews, which are extremely popular in LCR, leave learners free to use their own wording to express their thoughts, in contrast with the experimental data and constrained productive tasks that are often used in SLA studies. Lack of constraint comes at a cost, however. In reference to speech, Read and Nation (2004: 33) highlight the 'tension between the control and manipulation of key variables needed to obtain interpretable results and the desirability, in the interests of external validity, of recording speech which is as natural and unmonitored as possible'. Learner corpora are not totally uncontrolled, however. To qualify as learner corpus data, learner language needs to be collected on the basis of *strict design criteria*. For example, each essay contained in the *International Corpus of Learner English* (Granger *et al.*, 2020) is accompanied by 21 variables which can be used to compile homogeneous data sets. These metadata involve both learner variables such as age, gender, mother tongue background and knowledge of other foreign languages, and task variables such as medium, genre, topic, length and task conditions. In accordance with one of the key requirements of corpus-hood, learner corpora contain *continuous discourse* rather than decontextualized sentences. This important feature opens up interesting perspectives for L2 studies that go well beyond linguistic features at sentence level to cover a wide range of textual and rhetorical components of language use. Last, but definitely not least, learner corpora are in *electronic format* and this, as pointed out in Section 2, opens up exciting perspectives, particularly for phraseological research. In addition to the possibilities afforded by software tools in terms of extraction and sorting of phraseological units, learner corpora can benefit from automatic annotation thanks to part-of-speech taggers, which can help identify phraseological units containing different combinations of parts of speech (POS), and parsers, which go one step further by allowing the identification of phrase structure (NP, VP, etc.) and dependency relations (head, modifier, etc.).

The LCR approach to the L2 phrasicon aims to answer research questions such as the following: What distinguishes L2 use of phraseological units from L1 use? Do native speakers use more phraseological units than L2 learners? Does the use of phraseology by L2 learners vary across languages and language varieties? Are there differences between learner populations from different language backgrounds? Does the use of phraseology vary with proficiency and, if so, how? What kinds of difficulty do phraseological units present for learners? Do some types of unit present greater difficulty than others? To answer such questions the method that is most commonly used is contrastive interlanguage analysis (CIA) (Granger, 1996, 2015), which consists in (1) comparing learner corpora with one or more reference corpora of native (or expert) language use, and/or (2) comparing different learner varieties with each other. The first type of comparison makes it possible to uncover typical features of interlanguage – not only errors, but also instances of under- and overrepresentation of words, phrases and structures. The second is a good method for assessing the influence of the many variables that play a part in SLA, such as task effects and the learner's mother tongue or level of proficiency. Another popular method is computer-aided error analysis (CEA), a way of annotating and analysing learner errors that is more rigorous and standardized than Error Analysis (Corder, 1967, 1971). It is mainly used in an applied perspective, i.e. to contribute to the design of pedagogical tools and methods tailored to learners' attested needs (Dagneaux *et al.*, 1998; Granger, 2003; Lüdeling & Hirschmann, 2015).

In the LCR approach, phraseological units are identified on the basis of their degree of co-occurrence and recurrence. As the criteria used are usually quantitative, the two types of unit that are most commonly analysed are collocations and lexical bundles, both of which are very frequent, whereas figurative idioms such as *spill the beans* are very infrequent. They involve a high degree of semantic compositionality and therefore present little difficulty for reception but are particularly challenging for production. As learner corpora contain language use data, they are ideal resources for identifying and analysing these productive difficulties. The following sections contain a brief introduction to the LCR approach to collocations and lexical bundles. For more comprehensive overviews, see Paquot and Granger (2012), Ebeling and Hasselgård (2015) and Granger (2019).

Collocations in learner corpora can be identified in two different ways. Specific words or word combinations can be extracted automatically and their collocations identified manually using the standard semantic, syntactic and lexical criteria of the classical approach to phraseology (see Section 2). As shown by Nesselhauf's (2005: 25–40) study of verb + noun collocations, this approach yields very interesting results, but the identification procedure is complex, time-consuming and inherently subjective. Most researchers today use quantitative criteria to extract statistical collocations, i.e. pairs of words that occur in close vicinity to each other with a frequency greater than chance. The statistical measures that are most commonly used are mutual information (MI) and t-score (for an overview of statistical measures, see Gablasova *et al.*, 2017). As pointed out in Section 2, one of the main advantages of this method is that it does justice to the graded nature of collocations: words are more or less tightly associated, and association scores provide a fine-grained picture of this continuum. In addition, different statistical methods bring out different types of association. MI tends to highlight word combinations made up of low-frequency words (e.g. *vicious circle*), and t-score brings out those composed of high-frequency words (e.g. *young people*). Durrant and Schmitt (2009) extracted these two measures from a large reference corpus and assigned the corresponding scores to each combination of adjective/noun + noun in a learner corpus and a comparable L1 corpus. On that basis they were able to conclude that '[a]dvanced non-native phraseology differs from that of natives not because it avoids formulaic language altogether but because it overuses high-frequency collocations and underuses the lower-frequency, but strongly-associated, pairs characterised by high mutual information scores' (2009: 175). In a study relying on a similar methodology but involving a wider range of word combinations, Granger and Bestgen (2014) established the same pattern in a comparison of intermediate and advanced learners, thus demonstrating strong links between statistical collocations and language proficiency.

Lexical bundles have also been studied extensively in LCR. The most important contribution of lexical bundle research lies in its links with discourse studies. It has shown that registers are characterized by a whole stock of recurrent sequences that 'are important building blocks of discourse, associated with basic communicative functions. In general, these lexical bundles serve as discourse framing devices: they provide a kind of frame expressing stance, discourse organization, or referential status' (Biber *et al.*, 2004: 400). Within LCR, lexical bundle research has mainly centred on academic writing, which is highly routinized, particularly for the expression of text organization (*on the other hand, this is due to*) and stance (*this would suggest that, it is clear that*). To identify lexical bundles, recurrent sequences of *n* words that meet a specified frequency threshold (e.g. 20 occurrences per million words) and dispersion (e.g. occurring in at least three different texts) are extracted from the learner corpus. The structure and function of the units extracted are subsequently analysed and compared with lexical bundles extracted from native (or expert) reference corpora and/or other learner corpora. For example, Ädel and Erman (2012) investigated the use of four-word lexical bundles in linguistics papers written in English by L1 speakers of Swedish and a comparable corpus of native English writing, and compared the results with those obtained by Chen and Baker (2010) in their study of lexical bundle use by L1 Chinese learners. Staples *et al.* (2013) compared the quantity and quality of lexical bundles across three proficiency levels (low, intermediate and high) and found that the number of lexical bundle tokens decreased with proficiency. The fact that collocations and lexical bundles vary with proficiency level opens the door to new indices of proficiency, alongside the traditional single-word lexical measures and syntactic measures. These phraseological measures have been proved to be better indicators of the quality of texts than single word measures (Bestgen, 2017; Paquot, 2018) and therefore hold great potential for language testing and automatic assessment.

Some converging trends emerge from learner-corpus-based studies of collocations and lexical bundles (for more details see Granger, 2019). First, intermediate to advanced learners (the group targeted in most LCR studies) prove to make abundant use of phraseological units, but their repertoire is more restricted than that of their L1 counterparts and they tend to use this restricted set with a very high degree of recurrence. They cling on to some 'phraseological teddy bears' (Hasselgård, 2019), i.e. units that they feel most comfortable with. Second, learners' L2 phrasicon is heavily influenced by their L1 phrasicon, leading to both positive and negative transfer. This is probably due to the fact that collocations and lexical bundles, unlike idioms, are not particularly salient, and learners, not being aware of their formulaicity, tend to transfer them literally into the L2. L1 effects, which rarely feature as a key variable in the SLA approach, are at the heart of many LCR studies. Multi-L1 corpora such as the *International Corpus of Learner English* (Granger *et al.*, 2020) contain data from a large number of mother tongue backgrounds. As a result, they are an ideal resource for establishing whether a given phraseological unit is specific to an L1 population and therefore most probably L1-induced, or shared more generally by several L1 populations and therefore most probably developmental. A third trend concerns the development of phraseological use. Although longitudinal studies are less frequent in LCR than in SLA, the few that exist suggest that the development of phraseological competencies is slow. As a result, researchers often fail to observe any significant development, especially in studies that cover a short period of time.

It is clear from this brief presentation that the SLA and LCR approaches to the L2 phrasicon present a number of significant differences in their respective objectives as well as the data and methods used to achieve them. However, their agendas are highly complementary and it is regrettable that there has been so little contact between the two fields, as evidenced by the limited awareness of their respective publications and the small number of cross-references. Reading in each field, one cannot help being struck by the mutual relevance and, in some cases, the great similarity of the findings. For example, the 'teddy bear' effect observed in LCR finds an echo in the 'lexical security blankets' observed by Karlsson (2019: 261) in her study of idioms based on a controlled writing task.

## 4 Overview of the Book

The general objective of this volume is to demonstrate how learner corpus data processed with corpus analysis tools and methods can contribute to enriching our knowledge of the L2 phrasicon. The studies rely on a range of learner corpora, mainly of L2 English, but also of L2 Dutch (Chapter 5, Rubin *et al.*) and L2 Italian (Chapter 8, Omidian *et al.*). Following the general trend in LCR, the focus is on phraseological units used in writing rather than speech, with the exception of one study (Chapter 7, Brezina and Fox). Also typical of LCR research in general, the learners range from intermediate to advanced, although one study (Chapter 8, Omidian *et al.*) widens the scope by covering beginner-level learners. As regards the types of phraseological unit, apart from two studies that respectively explore lexical bundles (Chapter 2, Ebeling and Hasselgård) and lexico-grammatical patterns (Chapter 4, Gilquin and Granger), the dominant types covered in the volume are collocations, in particular verb-direct object, noun-adjective and verb/adjective-adverb collocations. A range of phraseological indices, investigated independently or in combination with other lexical and syntactic indices, prove to be particularly good indicators of language proficiency. Several studies rely on advanced statistical methods, in particular multifactorial approaches drawing on different types of regression modelling techniques, to assess the impact of learner and task variables on the size and quality of the L2 phrasicon, thereby responding to a call for a higher degree of statistical sophistication in LCR (Gries, 2015). Although the book does not focus on teaching, the findings have clear applied relevance as they can help identify which phraseological units to teach a particular L1 population at a particular proficiency level.

The volume is structured as follows. The chapters are subdivided into two main sections, devoted respectively to cross-sectional and developmental approaches to the L2 phrasicon. This is an unusual subdivision in SLA. The commonly used subdivision is between cross-sectional studies, which compare samples of learner writing or speech gathered from different categories of learner at a single point in time, and longitudinal studies, which track the same learners over a given time period. In this framework, pseudo-longitudinal studies, i.e. studies based on data 'collected from groups of learners of different proficiency levels at a single point in time' (Ellis & Barkhuizen, 2005: 97), are classified among cross-sectional studies. In the current volume, however, they are classified, together with longitudinal studies, under the umbrella term 'developmental'. The reason is that, although the pseudo-longitudinal design does not provide any information on the development of the same learners over time, 'a longitudinal picture can be constructed by comparing the devices used by the different groups ranked according to their proficiency' (Ellis & Barkhuizen, 2005: 97). In the same vein,

Jarvis and Pavlenko (2008: 37) observe: 'pseudo-longitudinal designs are also related to longitudinal methodology in the sense that they include language users at successive levels of language ability'. As both types of study deal with the development of proficiency, and there are clear signs that the two designs can be fruitfully combined (see, for example, Bestgen & Granger (2014) and Omidian *et al.*, Chapter 8, this volume), it seems justified to group them and to include in the cross-sectional part only synchronic studies that do not incorporate the proficiency dimension.

The first chapter in the cross-sectional section, 'The Functions of N-grams in Bilingual and Learner Corpora: An Integrated Contrastive Approach', co-authored by Signe Oksefjell Ebeling and Hilde Hasselgård, focuses on the functions of lexical bundles. The study relies on the Integrated Contrastive Model, which consists in combining a contrastive interlanguage analysis of learner and native data with a contrastive analysis of the two languages involved. It investigates the use of lexical bundles in a bilingual corpus of English and Norwegian published research articles in linguistics. With a view to assessing the impact of L1 transfer, the results are compared with a previous study by the same authors, which contrasted the use of lexical bundles in research articles written by Norwegian learners of English and novice native English speakers. A quantitative analysis of the main discourse functions expressed by the bundles yielded inconclusive and to some extent contradictory results. However, a qualitative analysis of the lexicalizations used by the L2 learners provided clear evidence of L1 transfer.

The impact of the learners' L1 is also very much in evidence in the next chapter, 'Exploring Learner Corpus Data for Language Testing and Assessment Purposes: The Case of Verb + Noun Collocations', co-authored by Henrik Gyllstad and Per Snoder. The perspective here is decidedly an applied one: the aim is to assess to what extent learner corpus data can inform the testing and assessment of learners' phraseological skills. The focus is on verb-noun collocations extracted from the Swedish and Italian subcorpora of the *International Corpus of Learner English*. The L2 collocations are analysed in terms of their frequency and strength of association in reference corpora of English and Italian with a view to investigating differences in collocability and assessing the impact of cross-linguistic influence. The chapter contains concrete illustrations of how learner-corpus-based insights can be implemented in a range of test formats.

The third and last chapter in this section, 'The Passive and the Lexis-Grammar Interface: An Inter-varietal Perspective', co-authored by Gaëtanelle Gilquin and Sylviane Granger (Chapter 4), explores the use of the *be*-passive by learners of English as a foreign and as a second (EFL/ESL) language. Often presented as a purely grammatical structure in L2 studies, the passive is shown here to be a structure that straddles grammar and lexis. The passive forms of 20 verbs extracted from 8 subcorpora (4 EFL and 4 ESL) of the *International Corpus of Learner English* and a comparable native speaker corpus are investigated in terms of passive frequency, lexical preferences and phraseological patterns. The results point to a general underuse of the passive as compared to the native baseline, but with significant differences across learner populations as regards passive ratio and phraseological patterning. Contrary to expectations, the degree of exposure to English along the EFL–ESL continuum did not appear to have a significant impact on passive use.

The developmental section opens with 'Phraseological Complexity as an Index of L2 Dutch Writing Proficiency: A Partial Replication Study', co-authored by Rachel Rubin, Alex Housen and Magali Paquot (Chapter 5). The chapter replicates on the basis of a corpus of L2 Dutch two previously published studies of L2 English by the third author. Those studies established that phraseological indices of language complexity, computed on the basis of the mean MI scores of three types of dependency relations (verb-direct object, noun-adjective and verb/adjective-adverb), were significant predictors of language proficiency. The replication study aims to assess the cross-linguistic validity of these indices by applying them to a corpus of L2 Dutch writing produced by B1 (lower intermediate) and B2 (higher intermediate) learners. Entering the phraseological indices alongside more traditional lexical and syntactic indices in a multifactorial regression model, the authors are able to confirm the results obtained for L2 English. The phraseological indices prove to have strong predictive power, while the standard single-word-based lexical indices do not emerge as significant.

Also centred on the predictive power of phraseological indices, the next chapter, 'Automatically Assessing Lexical Sophistication Using Word, Bigram, and Dependency Indices', co-authored by Kristopher Kyle and Masaki Eguchi (Chapter 6), investigates the relative importance of word, adjacent bigram and dependency bigram indices in predicting the holistic scores of argumentative essays from the Test of English as a Foreign Language. The authors rely on the same dependency bigrams as those used by Rubin, Housen and Paquot, complemented with subject-verb relations, but use three association measures (MI, t-score and Delta-p), thereby opening the way to interesting comparisons between the measures. Using a linear regression model, they establish that the best predictors of holistic scores are three of the dependency bigrams (noun-adjective, verb-direct object and verb-adverb) but only one word-level index (contextual distinctiveness). The results suggest that dependency bigrams may be better indicators of phraseological competence than adjacent bigrams.

'Adjective + Noun Collocations in L2 and L1 Speech: Evidence from the Trinity Lancaster Corpus and the Spoken BNC2014', co-authored by Vaclav Brezina and Lorrae Fox (Chapter 7), stands out as the only chapter in the volume focused on learner speech. A large corpus of L2 English speech is used to investigate intermediate and advanced learners' use of adjective-noun collocations, and the results are compared in terms of frequency and strength of association with an L1 baseline corpus, the Spoken British National Corpus 2014. The results showed a proficiency effect on the proportion of modified nouns and the collocation strength measured with the log Dice, and an L1 effect on collocation strength whatever the measure (frequency, MI score, log Dice). However, no differences were found between the lower and higher intermediate levels (B1 and B2) and the higher intermediate (B2) and advanced levels (C1/C2), which offers further confirmation that the development of phraseological skills tends to be slow. The study also revealed large individual differences between learners.

While the preceding three chapters in the developmental section relied on a pseudo-longitudinal design, the chapter co-authored by Taha Omidian, Anna Siyanova-Chanturia and Stefania Spina, 'Development of Formulaic Knowledge in Learner Writing: A Longitudinal Perspective' (Chapter 8), adopts a longitudinal approach. The study traces the development of the use of verb-noun collocations by Chinese learners of Italian over a six-month period. Three dimensions of phraseological knowledge are investigated (exclusivity, phrase frequency and phrasal diversity), each computed by a different collocation measure. Conducting linear mixed effects regression analyses, the authors assessed to what degree these measures varied with time, proficiency level and prior language exposure. One particularly interesting result was that time was found to be a significant predictor of only one dimension (phrasal diversity), while proficiency had a significant effect on all three dimensions. As in the preceding chapter, the study shows that learners vary considerably in their acquisition of phraseological knowledge.

Marco Schilk's chapter, 'Tracing Collocation in Learner Production and Processing: Integrating Corpus Linguistic and Experimental Approaches' (Chapter 9), closes the section. It is one of the very rare studies that rely on the conjoined use of learner corpus data and experimental data, a design that has often been advocated in recent years but has so far found little resonance among the L2 research community. The author relies on verb-noun collocations from a previously published learner-corpus-based study of German learners of English and uses them as prompts for a combined eye-tracking/electroencephalography analysis with two groups (intermediate and advanced) of L1 German learners. The experiments comprise three types of collocation: native-like, interference-based and incongruous. The results show that the two learner groups profit cognitively from typical native-like collocations but differ in their processing of interference-based collocations, of which advanced learners appeared to show a greater awareness.

The volume closes with a postface by David Singleton. He links up the research reported in the volume with his own research on the acquisition and processing of the L2 lexicon, expresses some thoughts on the thorny construct of frequency, and shares some personal reflections on ideas discussed in individual chapters.

All the chapters in the volume shed some light on important facets of the use of phraseological units by L2 learners and offer an important complement to studies focused on the processing of these units. Process and use are two sides of the same phraseological coin. While it is undeniably essential to understand how phraseological units are processed by L2 learners, it is equally important to investigate what L2 learners do with their phraseological competence in actual performance. It is important to bear in mind, however, that it is still early days for L2 phraseology research. Although we are now in possession of a sizeable body of research, it must be acknowledged that there are as yet few truly conclusive results. There are several reasons for this. First, studies have focused on a wide range of different phraseological units, and what goes for one type of unit does not necessarily go for another. Second, even studies that deal with the same type of unit may vary in the definitions they rely on and/or the methods used to identify and analyse those units. Third, there are numerous variables that affect both processing and use, and studies differ in the variables they choose to focus on. SLA studies have tended to investigate variables such as age and aptitude, which have so far been neglected in LCR, while LCR studies, as evidenced by the contents of the current volume, have paid particular attention to other variables, in particular the learners' L1 and their proficiency level, which have been less in evidence in SLA. In this as in many other respects, the SLA and LCR approaches are complementary, and I am convinced that the field could make a great leap forward if strong synergies were developed. As observed by Myles (2015: 330), there are still many LCR studies that lack 'the theoretical frameworks which would enable rigorous interpretation or explanation of the data'. The explanatory power of LCR would be greatly increased by insights from studies relying on elicitation and psycholinguistic methods. But experimental studies also stand to gain from a rapprochement with LCR. As rightly noted by Schmitt and Underwood (2004: 173), although corpus studies do not give us access to the mental processes that underlie the acquisition and processing of phraseology, performance data from L2 learner studies 'can go some way towards illuminating their acquisition'. There are various ways in which LCR data and methods could be of benefit to process-oriented studies. As shown by Schilk (Chapter 9 of this volume), learner-corpus-extracted phraseological units can be used as prompts for experimental studies. Large learner corpora can also be used as reference corpora in experimental studies, or studies involving a limited number of learners, in order to assess the generalizability of the findings across

L2 corpora comprising many learners with different L1 backgrounds. A few researchers have also demonstrated the benefit of data triangulation by combining mental processing and language use data (e.g. Siyanova & Schmitt, 2008; Vetchinnikova, 2019). As the synergies between SLA and LCR are currently growing (cf. Le Bruyn & Paquot, 2020), we can hope to see more of these types of study in the future, to the benefit of L2 phraseology research, which is only beginning to reveal its true potential.

## Notes

(1) The term 'L2 learners' refers to both learners who learn the target language through instruction in a country where the target language is not used in everyday life and learners who acquire the target language mainly through exposure in a country where the target language is the predominant language in everyday life. This does not in any way imply that we find the distinction irrelevant for phraseological studies. Quite the opposite: the distinction is very likely to have a major impact on the learners' phrasicon but has unfortunately been the subject of very few studies to date.

(2) A list of learner corpora can be found on the following webpage maintained by the Centre for English Corpus Linguistics of the University of Louvain: https://uclouvain.be/en/research-institutes/ilc/cecl/learner-corpora-around-the-world.html.

## References

Ädel, A. and Erman, B. (2012) Recurrent word combinations in academic writing by native and non-native speakers of English: A lexical bundles approach. *English for Specific Purposes* 31, 81–92.

Barfield, A. (2009) Exploring productive L2 collocation knowledge. In T. Fitzpatrick and A. Barfield (eds) *Lexical Processing in Second Language Learners* (pp. 95–110). Bristol: Multilingual Matters.

Barfield, A. and Fitzpatrick, T. (2009) Taking stock. In T. Fitzpatrick and A. Barfield (eds) *Lexical Processing in Second Language Learners* (pp. 154–158). Bristol: Multilingual Matters.

Bell, H. (2009) The messy little details: A longitudinal case study of the emerging lexicon. In T. Fitzpatrick and A. Barfield (eds) *Lexical Processing in Second Language Learners* (pp. 111–127). Bristol: Multilingual Matters.

Bestgen, Y. (2017) Beyond single-word measures: L2 writing assessment, lexical richness and formulaic competence. *System* 69, 65–78.

Bestgen, Y. and Granger, S. (2014) Quantifying the development of phraseological competence in L2 English writing. *Journal of Second Language Writing* 26, 28–41.

Biber, D., Conrad, S. and Cortes, V. (2004) *If you look at…*: Lexical bundles in university teaching and textbooks. *Applied Linguistics* 25 (3), 371–405.

Biber, D., Johansson, S., Leech, G., Conrad, S. and Finegan, E. (1999) *Longman Grammar of Spoken and Written English*. Harlow: Pearson Education.

Bishop, H. (2004) The effect of typographic salience on the look up and comprehension of unknown formulaic sequences. In N. Schmitt (ed.) *Formulaic Sequences. Acquisition, Processing and Use* (pp. 227–244). Amsterdam & Philadelphia: Benjamins.

Chen, Y.-H. and Baker, P. (2010) Lexical bundles in L1 and L2 academic writing. *Language Learning and Technology* 14 (2), 30–49.

Cieślicka, A. (2015) Idiom acquisition and processing by second/foreign language learners. In R. Heredia and A. Cieślicka (eds) *Bilingual Figurative Language Processing* (pp. 208–244). Cambridge: Cambridge University Press.

Conrad, S. and Biber, D. (2004) The frequency and use of lexical bundles in conversation and academic prose. *Lexicographica* 20, 56–71.
Corder, S.P. (1967) The significance of learners' errors. *International Review of Applied Linguistics in Language Teaching* 5, 161–70.
Corder, S.P. (1971) Idiosyncratic dialects and error analysis. *International Review of Applied Linguistics in Language Teaching* 9, 147–60.
Cowie, A.P. (1994) Phraseology. In R.E. Asher (ed.) *The Encyclopedia of Language and Linguistics* (pp. 3168–3171). Oxford: Oxford University Press.
Cowie, A.P. (1998) Introduction. In A.P. Cowie (ed.) *Phraseology: Theory, Analysis, and Applications* (pp. 1–20). Oxford: Oxford University Press.
Dagneaux E., Denness, S. and Granger, S. (1998) Computer-aided error analysis. *System: An International Journal of Educational Technology and Applied Linguistics* 26 (2), 163–174.
Dörnyei, Z., Durow, V. and Zahran, K. (2004) Individual differences and their effects on formulaic sequence acquisition. In N. Schmitt (ed.) *Formulaic Sequences. Acquisition, Processing and Use* (pp. 87–106). Amsterdam & Philadelphia: Benjamins.
Durrant, P. and Schmitt, N. (2009) To what extent do native and non-native writers make use of collocations?' *International Review of Applied Linguistics in Language Teaching* 47 (2), 157–177.
Ebeling, S.O. and Hasselgård, H. (2015) Phraseology in learner corpus research. In S. Granger, G. Gilquin and F. Meunier (eds) *The Cambridge Handbook of Learner Corpus Research* (pp. 207–230). Cambridge: Cambridge University Press.
Ellis, R. and Barkhuizen, G. (2005) *Analysing Learner Language*. Oxford: Oxford University Press.
Evert, S. (2004) The statistics of word cooccurrences: Word pairs and collocations. PhD thesis, Institut für maschinelle Sprachverarbeitung, University of Stuttgart.
Gablasova, D., Brezina, V. and McEnery, T. (2017) Collocations in corpus-based language learning research: Identifying, comparing, and interpreting the evidence. *Language Learning* 67 (S1), 155–179.
Gass, S.M. and Selinker, L. (2001) *Second Language Acquisition: An Introductory Course*. Mahwah, NJ: Lawrence Erlbaum.
Glass, C. (2019) *Collocations, Creativity and Constructions: A Usage-based Study of Collocations in Language Attainment*. Tübingen: Narr Francke Attempto Verlag.
Granger, S. (1996) From CA to CIA and back: An integrated contrastive approach to computerized bilingual and learner corpora. In K. Aijmer, B. Altenberg and M. Johansson (eds) *Languages in Contrast. Text-based Cross-linguistic Studies* (pp. 37–51). Lund Studies in English 88. Lund: Lund University Press.
Granger, S. (2003) Error-tagged learner corpora and CALL: A promising synergy. *CALICO* 20 (3), 465–480.
Granger, S. (2015) Contrastive interlanguage analysis: A reappraisal. *International Journal of Learner Corpus Research* 1 (1), 7–24.
Granger, S. (2019) Formulaic sequences in learner corpora: Collocations and lexical bundles. In A. Siyanova-Chanturia and A. Pellicer-Sanchez (eds) *Understanding Formulaic Language: A Second Language Acquisition Perspective* (pp. 228–247). Abingdon: Routledge.
Granger, S. and Paquot, M. (2008) Disentangling the phraseological web. In S. Granger and F. Meunier (eds) *Phraseology: An Interdisciplinary Perspective* (pp. 27–49). Amsterdam & Philadelphia: Benjamins.
Granger, S. and Bestgen, Y. (2014) The use of collocations by intermediate vs. advanced non-native writers: A bigram-based study. *International Review of Applied Linguistics in Language Teaching* 52 (3), 229–252.
Granger, S., Gilquin, G. and Meunier, F. (eds) (2015) *The Cambridge Handbook of Learner Corpus Research*. Cambridge: Cambridge University Press.
Granger, S., Dupont, M., Meunier, F., Naets, H. and Paquot, M. (2020) *The International Corpus of Learner English. Version 3*. Louvain-la-Neuve, France: Presses Universitaires de Louvain.

Gries, S.Th. (2015) Statistics for learner corpus research. In S. Granger, G. Gilquin and F. Meunier (eds) *The Cambridge Handbook of Learner Corpus Research* (pp. 159–181). Cambridge: Cambridge University Press.
Gyllstad, H. and Wolter, B. (2016) Collocational processing in light of the phraseological continuum model: Does semantic transparency matter? *Language Learning* 66 (2), 296–323.
Hasselgård, H. (2019) Phraseological teddy bears: Frequent lexical bundles in academic writing by Norwegian learners and native speakers of English. In M. Mahlberg and V. Wiegand (eds) *Corpus Linguistics, Context and Culture* (pp. 339–362). Berlin: De Gruyter Mouton.
Howarth, P. (1998) The phraseology of learners' academic writing. In A.P. Cowie (ed.) *Phraseology: Theory, Analysis, and Applications* (pp. 161–186). Oxford: Oxford University Press.
Hubers, F. (2020) Two of a kind: Idiomatic expressions in native speakers and second language learners. Doctoral thesis, Radboud University, Nijmegen, The Netherlands. http://hdl.handle.net/2066/215818.
Jarvis, S. and Pavlenko, A. (2008) *Crosslinguistic Influence in Language and Cognition.* New York & London: Routledge.
Jones, S. and Sinclair, J. (1974) English lexical collocations: A study in computational linguistics. *Cahiers de Lexicologie* 24 (1), 15–61.
Karlsson, M. (2019) *Idiomatic Mastery in a First and Second Language.* Bristol: Multilingual Matters.
Le Bruyn, B. and Paquot, M. (eds) (2020) *Second Language Acquisition and Learner Corpora.* Cambridge: Cambridge University Press.
Lüdeling, A. and Hirschmann, H. (2015) Error annotation systems. In S. Granger, G. Gilquin and F. Meunier (eds) *The Cambridge Handbook of Learner Corpus Research* (pp. 135–157). Cambridge: Cambridge University Press.
Martinez, R. and Schmitt, N. (2012) A phrasal expressions list. *Applied Linguistics* 33 (3), 299–320.
Moon, R. (1998) Frequencies and forms of phrasal lexemes in English. In A.P. Cowie (ed.) *Phraseology. Theory, Analysis, and Applications* (pp. 79–100). Oxford: Oxford University Press.
Myles, F. (2015) Second language acquisition theory and learner corpus research. In S. Granger, G. Gilquin and F. Meunier (eds) *The Cambridge Handbook of Learner Corpus Research* (pp. 309–331). Cambridge: Cambridge University Press.
Myles, F. and Cordier, C. (2017) Formulaic sequence (FS) cannot be an umbrella term in SLA: Focusing on psycholinguistic FSs and their identification. *Studies in Second Language Acquisition* 39 (1), 3–28.
Nesselhauf, N. (2005) *Collocations in Learner English.* Amsterdam & Philadelphia: Benjamins.
Paquot, M. (2013) Lexical bundles and L1 transfer effects. *International Journal of Corpus Linguistics* 18 (3), 391–417.
Paquot, M. (2018) Phraseological competence: A missing component in university entrance language tests? Insights from a study of EFL learners' use of statistical collocations. *Language Assessment Quarterly* 15 (1), 29–43.
Paquot, M. and Granger, S. (2012) Formulaic language in learner corpora. *Annual Review of Applied Linguistics* 32, 130–149.
Read, J. and Nation, P. (2004) Measurement of formulaic sequences. In N. Schmitt (ed.) *Formulaic Sequences: Acquisition, Processing and Use* (pp. 23–35). Amsterdam & Philadelphia: Benjamins.
Rundell, M. (2008) The corpus revolution revisited. *English Today* 24 (1), 23–27.
Sag, I.A., Baldwin, T., Bond, F., Copestake, A. and Flickinger, D. (2002) Multiword expressions: A pain in the neck for NLP. In A. Gelbukh (ed.) *Computational Linguistics and Intelligent Text Processing* (pp. 1–15). Third International Conference, CICLing 2002. Lecture Notes in Computer Science, vol. 2276. Berlin & Heidelberg: Springer.

Schmitt, N. (ed.) (2004) *Formulaic Sequences: Acquisition, Processing and Use*. Amsterdam & Philadelphia: Benjamins.
Schmitt, N. and Underwood, G. (2004) Exploring the processing of formulaic sequences through a self-paced reading task. In N. Schmitt (ed.) *Formulaic Sequences: Acquisition, Processing and Use* (pp. 173–189). Amsterdam & Philadelphia: Benjamins.
Schmitt, N., Dörnyei, Z., Adolphs, S. and Durow, V. (2004) Knowledge and acquisition of formulaic sequences: A longitudinal study. In N. Schmitt (ed.) *Formulaic Sequences: Acquisition, Processing and Use* (pp. 55–71). Amsterdam & Philadelphia: Benjamins.
Sinclair, J. (1987) *Looking Up: An Account of the COBUILD Project in Lexical Computing*. London & Glasgow: Collins ELT.
Sinclair, J. (1991) *Corpus, Concordance, Collocation*. Oxford: Oxford University Press.
Sinclair, J. (1995) Corpus typology – a framework for classification. In G. Melchers and B. Warren (eds) *Studies in Anglistics* (pp. 17–33). Stockholm: Almqvist & Wiksell International.
Sinclair, J. (2000) Lexical grammar. *Naujoji Metodologija* 24, 191–203.
Sinclair, J. (2004) Trust the text. In J. Sinclair and R. Carter (eds) *Trust the Text: Language, Corpus and Discourse* (pp. 9–23). London: Routledge.
Sinclair, J., Jones, S. and Daley, R. (2004) *English Collocation Studies: The OSTI Report*. London: Bloomsbury.
Siyanova, A. and Schmitt, N. (2008) L2 learner production and processing of collocation: A multi-study perspective. *The Canadian Modern Language Review* 64 (3), 429–458.
Siyanova-Chanturia, A. and Pellicer-Sánchez, A. (eds) (2019) *Understanding Formulaic Language: A Second Language Acquisition Perspective*. New York & London: Routledge.
Spöttl, C. and McCarthy, M. (2004) Comparing knowledge of formulaic sequences across L1, L2, L3, and L4. In N. Schmitt (ed.) *Formulaic Sequences: Acquisition, Processing and Use* (pp. 191–225). Amsterdam & Philadelphia: Benjamins.
Staples, S., Egbert, J., Biber, D. and McClair, A. (2013) Formulaic sequences and EAP writing development: Lexical bundles in the TOEFL iBT writing section. *Journal of English for Academic Purposes* 12 (3), 214–225.
Underwood, G., Schmitt, N. and Galpin, A. (2004) The eyes have it: An eye-movement study into the processing of formulaic sequences. In R. Schmitt (ed.) *Formulaic Sequences: Acquisition, Processing and Use* (pp. 153–172). Amsterdam & Philadelphia: Benjamins.
Vetchinnikova, S. (2019) *Phraseology and the Advanced Language Learner*. Cambridge: Cambridge University Press.
Vilkaitė, L. and Schmitt, N. (2019) Reading collocations in an L2: Do collocation processing benefits extend to non-adjacent collocations? *Applied Linguistics* 40 (2), 329–354.
Wolter, B. (2009) Meaning-last vocabulary acquisition and collocational productivity. In T. Fitzpatrick and A. Barfield (eds) *Lexical Processing in Second Language Learners* (pp. 128–140). Bristol: Multilingual Matters.

# Part 2: The Learner Phrasicon: Synchronic Approaches

# 2 The Functions of N-grams in Bilingual and Learner Corpora: An Integrated Contrastive Approach

Signe Oksefjell Ebeling and Hilde Hasselgård

## 1 Introduction

In a previous article we studied phraseological sequences (n-grams) in texts by Norwegian learners of English and native speakers of English in two academic disciplines: linguistics and business (Ebeling & Hasselgård, 2015a). The 100 most frequent n-gram types in the Varieties of English for Specific Purposes dAtabase (VESPA) learner corpus and the British Academic Written English (BAWE) corpus were functionally classified according to an adapted version of Moon's (1998) framework for analysing fixed expressions and idioms, distinguishing informational, situational, evaluative, modalising and organisational n-grams (see Section 2.4). This approach revealed differences between disciplines (e.g. significantly more modalising n-gram types in linguistics) and between L1 groups (e.g. significantly more evaluative n-gram types in native-speaker (NS) texts). This chapter adds a cross-linguistic dimension to the original study by analysing data from the Cultural Identity in Academic Prose (KIAP) corpus,[1] which is a multilingual, comparable corpus of research articles (Fløttum *et al.*, 2006).

After presenting the results from the previous contrastive interlanguage study, we will perform a contrastive analysis of n-grams in English and Norwegian in order to diagnose, in line with the Integrated Contrastive Model (Granger, 1996), the extent to which the phraseology of the Norwegian learners' interlanguage may be influenced by their native language. The 100 most frequent 3- and 4-gram types for the contrastive analysis will be extracted from the English and Norwegian linguistics sections of the KIAP corpus, and the functional classification will be carried out as in Ebeling and Hasselgård (2015a). The focus is restricted to one discipline (linguistics) in order to narrow the scope slightly and to avoid problems of corpus comparability within the business material (Ebeling & Hasselgård, 2015a: 91). Such an analysis will also enable a comparison of n-gram use between student and 'expert' academic writing, and in this way throw light on the extent to which the L1 and L2 apprentice academics match what may arguably be called the target usage of their discipline (albeit not necessarily the learning target of each student). The proposed combination of corpora is hoped to differentiate between features of novice writing and L1 influence in the learners' interlanguage. More precisely, our research questions are the following:

(i) What discourse functions do recurrent 3- and 4-grams have in English and Norwegian published linguistics articles? What are the cross-linguistic similarities and differences?
(ii) To what extent can the cross-linguistic analysis explain the usage of n-grams by Norwegian learners of English?
(iii) To what extent are the same patterns and functions used across the dimensions of L1 and writer expertise (novice/expert)?

Based on previous research, we assume that the novice writers share some characteristics regardless of L1: e.g. the students may be expected to use organisational n-grams more often than the professional academics, and the Norwegian learners even more so than the English-speaking novice writers (Ebeling & Hasselgård, 2015a; Hasselgård, 2009; Leedham, 2015). Ebeling and Ebeling (2017) found significant differences in the distribution of functional types of 3-grams between English and Norwegian fiction; we may expect to find similar cross-linguistic differences in academic writing too.

This chapter is structured as follows. Section 2 gives an account of the material and method used, including an outline of the Integrated Contrastive Model (2.1), the corpora (2.2), the n-gram extraction method (2.3), and a brief description of the functional classification procedure (2.4). In Section 3 we present the previous interlanguage study in more detail, including important observations and results, before moving on to the contrastive analysis of n-grams in English and Norwegian linguistics research articles (Section 4). Section 5 is concerned with the novice (learners and native speakers) vs. expert comparison in the English data, while the discussion in Section 6 brings together the findings from the two types of contrastive analysis – the previous Contrastive Interlanguage Analysis and the new Contrastive Analysis – in accordance with the Integrated Contrastive Model. Some concluding remarks are offered in Section 7.

## 2 Method, Material and Classificatory Framework

### 2.1 The Integrated Contrastive Model

The overall methodological framework of this study is the Integrated Contrastive Model (ICM) (Granger, 1996; Gilquin, 2000/2001). The model combines two types of analysis: Contrastive Interlanguage Analysis (CIA) (Granger, 1996, 2015), in which a comparison is typically made between an interlanguage variety and reference language variety (Granger, 2015: 17), and Contrastive Analysis (CA), in which a comparison is made between two or more different languages (Johansson, 2007: 1). The underlying assumption is that a contrastive analysis can, at least partly, either predict or diagnose transfer-related interlanguage phenomena. As Granger emphasises: 'it is important to note that the terms "predictive" and "diagnostic" refer to mere hypotheses, which can be confirmed or refuted by corpus investigation' (Granger, 1996: 46). An ICM-based study may start from a cross-linguistic analysis to make predictions about interlanguage performance, or, as in our case, start from a contrastive interlanguage analysis and form hypotheses about (i) discrepancies between the interlanguage and the reference language variety and (ii) cross-linguistic differences between the learners' first and second language. These hypotheses then form the basis for the contrastive analysis based on a bilingual corpus (cf. Granger, 2018: 189). We concur with Gilquin (2000/2001: 101) that 'this presupposes a constant movement between the two disciplines [CA and CIA], but also and above all the availability of reliable CA and CIA data in the form of well-designed and representative bilingual and learner corpora'.

### 2.2 The corpora

The material for the original interlanguage study was extracted from the British Academic Written English (BAWE) corpus and the Varieties of English for Specific Purposes dAtabase (VESPA) corpus. The former contains proficient student writing from UK universities in a number of academic disciplines (Alsop & Nesi, 2009; Heuboeck *et al.*, 2008), while the latter contains student L2 English writing also from several academic disciplines. Both corpora thus include course work texts written by novice writers within their respective disciplines. In the 2015a study, texts from two disciplines were investigated: linguistics and business. Those culled from the BAWE corpus were all written by students whose L1 was English, while those from the VESPA corpus were written in English by students whose L1 was Norwegian (VESPA-NO).

The data for the contrastive analysis part of this study are culled from the KIAP (Cultural Identity in Academic Prose) corpus. KIAP is a comparable corpus of research articles in three languages (English,

**Table 2.1** Breakdown of data in terms of number of texts and words

| Corpora | Texts | Words |
|---|---|---|
| VESPA-NO (L2-EN) | 239 | 267,855 |
| BAWE (L1-EN) | 76 | 167,437 |
| KIAP-NO (L1-NO) | 50 | 269,913 |
| KIAP-EN (L1-EN) | 50 | 437,798 |

French and Norwegian) and three academic disciplines (economics, linguistics and medicine) (Fløttum *et al.*, 2006). For the purpose of the comparison with BAWE and VESPA we use the English and Norwegian linguistics sub-corpora. In other words, the contrastive analysis will draw on published texts written by professional linguists in their native language.

Table 2.1 gives a description of the corpora used in terms of number of texts and number of running words.[2] As can be seen, the corpora differ substantially in size, a fact that will need to be borne in mind when discussing the findings. Nevertheless, since we focus almost exclusively on the most frequent combinations of words, and on *types* rather than *tokens*, this difference in size should not influence the results too much.

The comparability of the corpora can be described in terms of Halliday's notions of field ('what is happening'), tenor ('who is taking part') and mode ('what part is the language playing') (Halliday, 1985: 12). The corpora are comparable along the dimension of field: they all come from the discipline of linguistics. However, VESPA and BAWE differ in tenor from KIAP regarding writer expertise (novice vs. expert) and readership (unpublished, implying a limited number of addressees vs. published, implying a greater number of readers). KIAP-NO differs from the others in mode by being written in Norwegian,[3] while VESPA-NO stands out by representing second-language writing.

## 2.3 Extraction of n-grams

To ensure comparability between the CIA and CA studies, we follow the procedure of the original study, using WordSmith Tools (Scott, 2016) to extract the top 100 3- and 4-grams with a frequency threshold of 5 and a range of 3. That is, all the extracted 100 3- and 4-grams are uninterrupted sequences of three and four words that occur at least five times in identical form in at least three different corpus texts (dispersion across individual writers was not checked).[4] Note that our operationalisation of n-grams is the same as Biber *et al.*'s for lexical bundles, i.e. 'recurrent expressions, regardless of their idiomaticity, and regardless of their structural status' (Biber *et al.*, 1999: 990), which occur above a set frequency threshold and across a minimum number of corpus texts (Biber *et al.*, 1999: 993). See also Ebeling and Hasselgård

**Table 2.2** Token frequency span of top 100 3-gram and 4-gram types in VESPA, BAWE and KIAP

| | Frequency span 3-grams | | Frequency span 4-grams | |
|---|---|---|---|---|
| | N (raw) | per 100k words | N (raw) | per 100k words |
| VESPA | 46–376 | 17–140 | 16–102 | 6–38 |
| BAWE | 20–165 | 12–99 | 7–32 | 4–19 |
| KIAP-NO | 23–166 | 9–62 | 7–62 | 3–23 |
| KIAP-EN | 50–238 | 11–54 | 14–117 | 3–27 |

(2015b: 209) for a survey of studies of lexical bundles in Learner Corpus Research. However, we have chosen to retain the term n-gram, as in our previous study (Ebeling & Hasselgård, 2015a).

Although the study focuses on n-gram types rather than tokens, it is useful to get a sense of token proportion. As shown in Table 2.2, the (token) frequency span of the top 100 n-gram types varies across the corpora, e.g. between 46 and 376 occurrences for English 3-grams produced by the Norwegian learners (VESPA) and between 14 and 117 for English 4-grams produced by professionals whose native language is English (KIAP-EN). (See also Appendix A, Tables A.1 and A.2 for lists of the most frequent 3- and 4-grams in the material.)

These discrepancies in number of occurrences demonstrate not only frequency differences relating to n-gram length but, potentially, also differences in corpus size and differences between the languages. In all the corpora the recurrence of 3-grams is generally higher than that of 4-grams, which is as expected: the shorter the n-gram the greater its chance of recurring in identical form. The largest corpus, KIAP-EN, to some extent shows that size matters, in that it has the highest frequency of 4-gram tokens as well as the most frequent 3-gram at rank 100 (with 50 occurrences) in terms of raw numbers. However, when tokens are normalised per 100,000 words, it can be seen that, relatively speaking, it is in fact the learners in VESPA who produce the most frequently recurring n-grams ranked 1–100. We can only speculate as to the reason for this, but it could be that Norwegian learners of English, as indicated in previous research (Hasselgård, 2019), draw on a smaller number of chunks that they use more frequently in the same way as they over-use high-frequency core vocabulary (Hasselgren, 1994; Ringbom, 1998). In other words, learners may be more repetitive than native speakers.[5]

Finally, we expected the token recurrence in KIAP-NO to be markedly lower than in the English language corpora because of what has previously been found in contrastive studies of fiction texts (Ebeling & Ebeling, 2017; Hasselgård, 2017): Norwegian is generally less recurrent than English, i.e. fewer sequences recur frequently in identical form. This may be due to several factors, including a relatively large number of accepted spelling/inflectional variants in Norwegian (e.g. *på den eine|ene sida|siden* 'on the one hand') and morphological and syntactic differences between English and Norwegian (for instance, Norwegian compound nouns are usually spelt as one word, and definiteness is marked by a word-final morpheme instead of a definite article, as in *the word order* = *ordstilling<u>en</u>*, or the Norwegian verb-second constraint which makes the English 4-gram *we have seen* correspond to both *vi har sett* and *har vi sett*, depending on the context). These differences notwithstanding, the token counts for the top 100 3- and 4-grams in Norwegian linguistics articles do not stand out in comparison with English.

## 2.4 Functional classification of n-grams

Moon's (1998) taxonomy for the classification of fixed expressions and idioms is central to our functional classification of n-grams. Our adapted version of Moon's original model (Ebeling & Hasselgård, 2015a), given in Figure 2.1, contains five broad categories: informational, situational, evaluative, modalising and organisational. Each category is exemplified in Figure 2.1 by a 3- or 4-gram. As seen to the left in the figure, the model is grounded in Halliday's three metafunctions of language (e.g. Halliday, 1994: 36). It may be noted that the categories correspond roughly to those found in, for example, Biber *et al.* (2004), i.e. referential, stance and discourse organisers (2004: 384). The model we have applied here is a bit more fine-grained, with three interpersonal categories (Moon, 1998: 218). These are distinguished as follows. Evaluative n-grams convey evaluations and attitudes apart from those that are modalising, i.e. that contain a modal expression. Situational n-grams 'relate to extralinguistic context' (Moon, 1998: 217). In Moon's study this category included, for example, greetings and other references to the speakers' surroundings. In our case it mostly consists of references to other texts, such as *in fletcher and garman* in Figure 2.1. Although it is challenging to apply the taxonomy to sequences that do not necessarily

| | Category | Function | Example |
|---|---|---|---|
| Ideational | informational | stating proposition, conveying information | *of the brain* |
| Interpersonal | situational | relating to extralinguistic context, responding to situation | *in fletcher and garman* |
| | evaluative | conveying speaker's evaluation and attitude | *is important to* |
| | modalising | conveying truth values, advice, requests, etc. | *we can see* |
| Textual | organisational | organising text, signalling discourse structure | *in this paper* |

**Figure 2.1** The functional classification model (adapted from Moon, 1998: 217)

constitute ‘complete structural units’ (cf. Biber & Conrad, 1999: 183), previous research has shown that the application of this model to the functional analysis of n-grams is both possible and fruitful (e.g. Ebeling, 2011; Ebeling & Ebeling, 2017; Ebeling & Hasselgård, 2015a). Indeed, and as pointed out by Conrad and Biber (2005: 58–59), n-grams (or lexical bundles, to use their term) that are ‘identified purely on frequency criteria do have strong functional correlates, indicating that speakers and writers regularly use them as basic building blocks of discourse’.

In our classification, we do not allow dual membership of an n-gram. In other words, each potentially functionally ambiguous n-gram has been assigned to one functional class only according to its most frequent use in the relevant corpus. For example, the n-gram *at the same time* was classified as organisational (see example (1)) since this function was more frequent in the material than the informational (temporal) use seen in example (2).

(1) *At the same time*, this grammatical feature is not treated very thoroughly by Tottie or Algeo … (VESPA-NO)
(2) In the example above, it seems that the process of treading water is happening *at the same time* as Bernard says he is sorry. (VESPA-NO)

## 3 Contrastive Interlanguage Analysis: Previous Study

Ebeling and Hasselgård (2015a) compared the use of recurrent word-combinations in texts written in English by L1 Norwegian (VESPA) and L1 English (BAWE) university students of linguistics and business. We investigated 3- and 4-grams extracted from the BAWE and VESPA corpora, classified functionally according to the model presented in Figure 2.1, to answer the following research questions:

(i) What discourse functions do the recurrent word-combinations have?
(ii) To what extent are the same patterns and functions used by learners and native speakers?
(iii) To what extent are the same patterns and functions used in both disciplines?
(iv) Is L1 background or discipline more decisive for the use of recurrent word-combinations and their functions? (Ebeling & Hasselgård, 2015a: 88)

The study uncovered a somewhat complex picture. The distribution of some of the functional categories of n-grams was shown to distinguish learners from native speakers in both linguistics and business. For example, in linguistics, the learners were found to use fewer evaluative and more organisational n-grams than the native speakers (see Table 2.3). In the business material (not included in Table 2.3) the

Norwegian learners were found to use more informational and fewer modalising n-grams than their native peers.

Some differences between the learners and native speakers were also observed regarding the form of the n-grams used. N-grams involving first-person pronouns were more frequent among the learners, a finding that substantiates previous research reporting that (Scandinavian) learners of English tend to be visible authors (e.g. Petch-Tyson, 1998; Paquot *et al.*, 2013). A prominent feature among the native speakers, by contrast, was the relatively frequent use of n-grams with non-personal projection (extraposition, e.g. *it is evident that; it is important to*) as well as n-grams including complex noun phrases (e.g. *of the language; the extent to which*). Finally, passive verb phrases, such as *been found to, has been suggested that*, were also more frequently used by the native speakers.

Regarding research questions (iii) and (iv), we found that there were more (statistically significant) differences across disciplines than across L1 groups, as attested by, for example, more overlapping n-grams between the corpora in linguistics than in business and by more evaluative and modalising n-grams in linguistics compared to business across L1 backgrounds. It was concluded that, despite the differences noted across L1 groups, 'the Norwegian learners – particularly the linguistics students – are in fact advanced users of English who are to a great extent able to adapt to disciplinary conventions' (Ebeling & Hasselgård, 2015a: 102).

The final section of the previous study suggested some avenues for further research, one of which was to compare the output of the apprentice academics represented in BAWE (native speakers of English) and VESPA (learners of English) to published academic writing in order to examine the extent to which they match the usage of experts in the field. This is, to a large degree, what the present study aims to do. Within the framework of the Integrated Contrastive Model, we follow the same research structure as the 2015a study to perform a contrastive analysis of functional types of n-grams in English and Norwegian research articles in linguistics. The results from the previous CIA of the BAWE and VESPA linguistics n-grams will then be reassessed in the light of the fresh CA based on the KIAP corpus, representing professional writing in linguistics by native speakers of English and Norwegian. As mentioned above, there are two motivations for keeping to one academic discipline: to limit the scope (and complexity) of the comparison so that a clearer picture may emerge and because there are greater problems of corpus comparability in the business/economics sections of BAWE, VESPA and KIAP than in the linguistics sections.

We thus seek to establish to what extent the Norwegian learners of English may be influenced by their L1 and to shed some light on how apprentice academics compare with professionals with regard to n-gram use. Table 2.3 (Ebeling & Hasselgård, 2015a: 95) and the observations

**Table 2.3** Learners' (VESPA) and native speakers' (BAWE) use of n-gram types according to function

| | 3-grams | | | 4-grams | | |
|---|---|---|---|---|---|---|
| | BAWE | VESPA | p-value | BAWE | VESPA | p-value |
| Informational | 46 | 57 | 0.1571 (p > 0.05) | 42 | 49 | 0.3942 (p > 0.05) |
| Situational | 1 | 0 | | 4 | 0 | 0.1297 (p > 0.05) |
| Evaluative | 24 | 8 | 0.003814 (p < 0.01) | 29 | 15 | 0.02648 (p < 0.05) |
| Modalising | 16 | 9 | 0.1995 p > 0.05 | 11 | 14 | 0.6689 (p > 0.05) |
| Organisational | 13 | 26 | 0.03222 (p < 0.05) | 14 | 22 | 0.1976 (p > 0.05) |
| | 100 | 100 | | 100 | 100 | |

in the following paragraph can provide a starting-point and basis for the discussion in Section 5.

Table 2.3 gives an overview of the distribution of the top 100 3- and 4-gram types according to their function in the BAWE and VESPA linguistics assignments. A test of equal proportions was carried out pairwise for each of the functional classes (`prop.test` in R), producing a p-value in each case. Cells with statistically significant results are shaded in grey. These show that the native speakers use more evaluative 3- and 4-gram types and fewer organisational 3-gram types than the Norwegian students. It is also worth mentioning that both the BAWE and VESPA n-grams are most typically informational, accounting for +/-50% of all n-gram types. Moreover, in BAWE the second-most frequent functional type is evaluative, while in VESPA it is organisational. A relatively similar distribution is found for modalising n-grams, while situational ones are marginal in both L1 groups.

To investigate whether these differences can be attributed to the influence of Norwegian, we now turn to a similar analysis of n-grams in published academic writing in L1 English and L1 Norwegian (Section 4). This analysis will also enable us to compare novice and professional writing to assess the extent to which students have acquired the functional phraseology of the field in terms of n-gram use (Section 5).

## 4 Contrastive Analysis

### 4.1 Comparing n-grams across L1s: English vs. Norwegian

In the following we present the discourse functions of the top 100 3- and 4-gram types in the English and Norwegian linguistics articles from KIAP before discussing some of the salient word-combinations included in some of these functional classes.

**Table 2.4** English and Norwegian n-gram types according to function in published articles

| | 3-grams | | | 4-grams | | |
|---|---|---|---|---|---|---|
| | KIAP-EN | KIAP-NO | p-value | KIAP-EN | KIAP-NO | p-value |
| Informational | 75 | 64 | 0.1246 ($p > 0.05$) | 57 | 39 | 0.01612 ($p < 0.05$) |
| Situational | 0 | 0 | | 2 | 1 | |
| Evaluative | 2 | 19 | 0.0002237 ($p < 0.001$) | 15 | 29 | 0.02648 ($p < 0.05$) |
| Modalising | 2 | 4 | 0.6785 ($p > 0.05$) | 8 | 13 | 0.3562 ($p > 0.05$) |
| Organisational | 21 | 13 | 0.1876 ($p > 0.05$) | 18 | 18 | 1 ($p > 0.05$) |
| | 100 | 100 | | 100 | 100 | |

#### *4.1.1 The functions of the n-grams*

Table 2.4 shows the distribution of 3- and 4-grams according to function in texts produced by linguists whose native language is English (KIAP-EN) and Norwegian (KIAP-NO), respectively. To enable a direct comparison with the previous study, a test of equal proportions was again carried out pairwise for each of the functional classes, with statistically significant results highlighted in grey.

Table 2.4 reveals that n-grams of the informational type are the most salient ones across the board. In particular, informational 3-grams constitute a very high proportion of the total 100 3-gram types. Although the proportion of informational 4-grams is lower, they are still the single-most frequent functional category among the 4-grams in both languages. Thus, not unexpectedly, linguistics as a research register is primarily informational. There is, however, a difference between English and Norwegian in the proportion of informational 4-gram types, which are significantly more frequent in the English data. One potential reason for this will be discussed below (Section 4.1.2).

Regarding the other functions, English 4-gram types show a varied distribution across organisational, evaluative, and to some extent modalising, while the only frequent functional 3-gram type, in addition to informational, is organisational. The Norwegian 'non-informational' 3-grams, on the other hand, are typically either evaluative or organisational, while the 4-grams show the same tendency as the English 4-grams. Situational n-grams are virtually non-existent among the top 100 in both English and Norwegian. This lack of situational n-gram types in the material may be due to the extraction method, which requires recurrence and dispersion of identical sequences. Although such sequences may be frequent in individual texts (e.g. the 4-gram *in hopper and traugott*), they do not often meet the recurrence/dispersion thresholds set. Moreover, Moon (1998: 225) notes that instances of the situational category 'are typically found in spoken discourse as they are responses to or occasioned by the extralinguistic context'.

Perhaps the most striking observation to be made on the basis of Table 2.4 is the Norwegian partiality to evaluative sequences: the numbers of evaluative 3- and 4-gram types are significantly higher in the Norwegian linguistics articles.

It can be concluded that 3- and 4-grams in English and Norwegian linguistics articles are similarly distributed across the functional classes, suggesting that there is some consensus among professionals, regardless of language, on the writing style of a research article at the functional level of n-grams within this discipline. The exceptions are the prominent use of evaluative 3- and 4-gram types in Norwegian and of informational 4-gram types in English.

#### *4.1.2 The form of the n-grams*

A direct comparison of the form of n-grams across languages is challenging, bordering on the impossible, for several reasons.[6] First, there is the general challenge in contrastive analysis of how to make sure to compare like with like. Although our n-grams have been classified within the same functional categories, it may not be fair to juxtapose seemingly similar n-grams, e.g. the evaluative 3-grams *the fact that* and *det faktum at* 'that fact that' or the modalising 4-grams *to be able to* and *er i stand til* 'is in condition to'. In both cases, the English and Norwegian n-grams are intuitively good correspondences of each other; however, their equivalence has not been established on the basis of any objective *tertium comparationis*. In fact, the researchers' own bilingual knowledge is arguably given too much weight, together with the formal similarity attested for the 3-grams in particular. We do not know, for instance, whether the formally similar n-grams have the same semantic and syntactic preferences. Moreover, when carving up languages into recurrent strings of words, systematic morphosyntactic differences between the languages show themselves to have a bearing on the length and internal structure of a recurrent sequence (see, for example, Ebeling & Ebeling, 2017; Granger, 2014; Hasselgård, 2017). Nevertheless, some insight may be gained by examining the actual realisation of the n-grams in English and Norwegian.

For example, we notice a marked difference in the syntactic structure/realisation of English and Norwegian informational 4-grams. While the Norwegian 4-grams are mainly VP- (i.e. clausal) or PP-based, the English 4-grams are mainly NP- (i.e. nominal) or PP-based, to use Chen and Baker's (2010) terms. Typical Norwegian examples are the VP-based *at det ikke er* 'that it/there is not' and å ta utgangspunkt i 'to take startingpoint in' and the PP-based *i form av en* 'in form of a', and *i den forstand at* 'in the sense that'. Further, it can be noted that the VP-based Norwegian 4-grams often include the versatile pronoun *det*, which may correspond to either *it* or *there* in English, both of which are in evidence in the English VP-based 4-grams, albeit not as prominently as in Norwegian.[7] Typical examples of the more nominal English informational 4-grams include *the referent of the* and *the extent to which* and PP-based ones: *on the basis of* and *in a number of*. Both types often include (fragments of) complex noun phrases with a determiner and the preposition *of*. In sum, the two languages clearly differ in their recurrent 4-word sequences, to the extent that English informational 4-grams (typically nominal) significantly outnumber the Norwegian informational 4-grams (typically clausal). The observations regarding English reflect a general tendency, noted by Biber *et al.* (1999: 992), for 'bundles' in academic prose to be nominal rather than clausal.

The number of evaluative n-grams also differs significantly between English and Norwegian (Table 2.4). The evaluative 3- and 4-grams are, with the exception of the two English 3-grams, mainly VP-based in both languages. The 4-grams also have in common the fact that many of them form part of non-personal (self) projection expressions, i.e. anticipatory-*it* stance constructions, such as *it is important to*, *it is clear that* and *det er interessant å* 'it is interesting to'. In addition, Norwegian has a productive and variable sequence that contributes to boosting the frequency of 3- and 4-grams, namely *ut til å|at* 'out to to|that', with or without the verb *se* 'look', nesting within the longer sequence *det ser ut til å|at* 'it looks out to to|that' ≈ 'it seems to|that'. These n-grams are borderline cases between evaluative and modalising. Two closely related n-grams in our English material – *seems to be* and *appears to be* – have rather been classified as modalising, in line with Quirk *et al.* (1985: 146), who suggest that *seem to* and *appear to* are catenatives with 'meanings related to aspect and modality'. We consider the (*det ser*) *ut til å|at* sequences to have a stronger evaluative than modalising content. Similar sequences, such as *kan se ut til* 'can look out to' ≈ 'can/may seem to', are classified as modalising due to the presence of the modal auxiliary *kan*.

To speculate further as to why Norwegian has significantly more evaluative 3- and 4-grams, we refer to the morphosyntactic differences between the languages, discussed above (Section 2.3). Could it be that 3- and 4-word sequences in Norwegian typically correspond to, for example, one or two words in English and would therefore not figure on our lists? While this may apply to some of the n-grams (e.g. *i det hele tatt* 'at all'/'overall'), it does not seem to be a major contributing factor in the material at hand. It also begs the question of why this should be a factor for the evaluative n-grams only.

## 5 Novice vs. Expert Use of N-grams

We have now established similarities and differences in the functions of 3- and 4-grams used by novice learners vs. native speakers of English and by academic professionals in English vs. Norwegian. The final part

**Table 2.5** English n-gram types according to function in native novice (BAWE) vs. native professional writing (KIAP-EN)

| | 3-grams | | | 4-grams | | |
|---|---|---|---|---|---|---|
| | **BAWE** | **KIAP-EN** | **p-value** | **BAWE** | **KIAP-EN** | **p-value** |
| Informational | 46 | 75 | 5.119e-05 ($p < 0.001$) | 42 | 57 | 0.0477 ($p < 0.05$) |
| Situational | 1 | 0 | | 4 | 2 | |
| Evaluative | 24 | 2 | 1.008e-05 ($p < 0.001$) | 29 | 15 | 0.02648 ($p < 0.05$) |
| Modalising | 16 | 2 | 0.001318 ($p < 0.01$) | 11 | 8 | 0.6296 ($p > 0.05$) |
| Organisational | 13 | 21 | 0.1876 ($p > 0.05$) | 14 | 18 | 0.5628 ($p > 0.05$) |
| | 100 | 100 | | 100 | 100 | |

of the puzzle, addressing our third research question, is a comparison between novice and expert writing in English. First, Table 2.5 compares the functional distribution of 3- and 4-gram types in the English native-speaker data: novices in BAWE and professionals in KIAP-EN.

It is clear from Table 2.5 that the British linguistics students do not match the usage of the professionals, as statistically significant differences are found in three of the functional categories of 3-grams and in two categories of 4-grams. Informational 3- and 4-grams are underrepresented in BAWE compared to KIAP-EN (e.g. *account of the*, *denoted by the*, *on the basis of*), whereas evaluative 4-grams (e.g. *is important to note*, *it is clear that*) and modalising 3-grams are overrepresented (e.g. *more likely to*, *the ability to*).

Second, Table 2.6 shows how the learners in VESPA compare with the native-speaker professionals in KIAP-EN. Surprisingly, the learners differ much less from the native expert writers than their native student peers

**Table 2.6** English n-gram types according to function in non-native novice (VESPA) vs. native professional writing (KIAP-EN)

| | 3-grams | | | 4-grams | | |
|---|---|---|---|---|---|---|
| | **VESPA** | **KIAP-EN** | **p-value** | **VESPA** | **KIAP-EN** | **p-value** |
| Informational | 57 | 75 | 0.01116 ($p < 0.05$) | 49 | 57 | 0.3213 ($p > 0.05$) |
| Situational | 0 | 0 | | 0 | 2 | |
| Evaluative | 8 | 2 | 0.1048 ($p > 0.05$) | 15 | 15 | 1 ($p > 0.05$) |
| Modalising | 9 | 2 | 0.06275 ($p > 0.05$) | 14 | 8 | 0.2585 ($p > 0.05$) |
| Organisational | 26 | 21 | 0.5047 ($p > 0.05$) | 22 | 18 | 0.5959 ($p > 0.05$) |
| | 100 | 100 | | 100 | 100 | |

(Table 2.5) in terms of n-gram functions. The only significant difference concerns the use of informational 3-grams. It is hard to interpret Tables 2.5 and 2.6 in a meaningful way as it is somewhat counter-intuitive that the learners should have a better grasp of the functional conventions of the discipline than the native-speaker students. We will supplement this analysis with more qualitative considerations in Section 6.

## 6 Discussion: Linking Up the Contrastive Interlanguage Analysis and the Contrastive Analysis

### 6.1 Comparing functional types of n-grams across the corpora

The CIA and CA analyses presented above show that informational n-grams are the most salient ones across the board. However, while evaluative n-grams are more frequent in Norwegian than in English published articles, the novices show the opposite trend, with evaluative n-grams being more frequent with L1 English students than with Norwegian learners (although the difference in 4-grams is not statistically significant). While the Norwegian learners appear to use evaluative n-grams in a similar fashion to expert English writers (see Table 2.6) there are unexpected similarities between the L1 English novices and L1 Norwegian experts. The L1 English students in BAWE and the L1 Norwegian experts in KIAP-NO have greater proportions of evaluative n-grams than the other two corpora, apparently at the expense of (especially) informational n-grams, and thereby seem to foreground interpretations and evaluations more than the other corpora. Figures 2.2 and 2.3 visualise the distribution of functional types of n-grams across all four sub-corpora. Situational n-grams have been omitted due to their low frequencies.

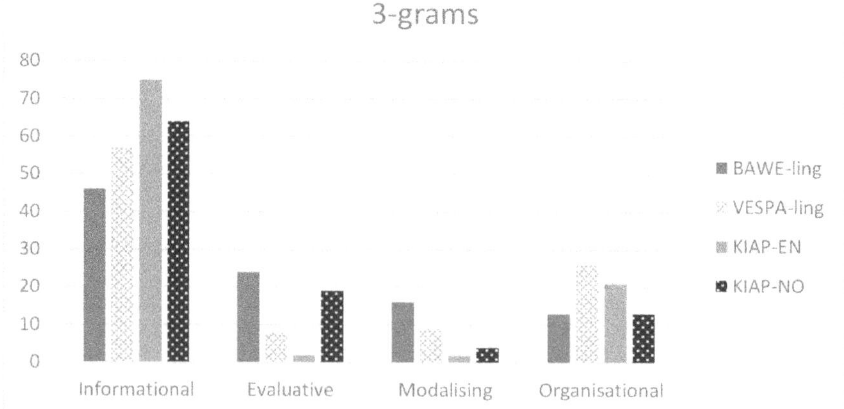


**Figure 2.2** Functional types of 3-grams across the corpora

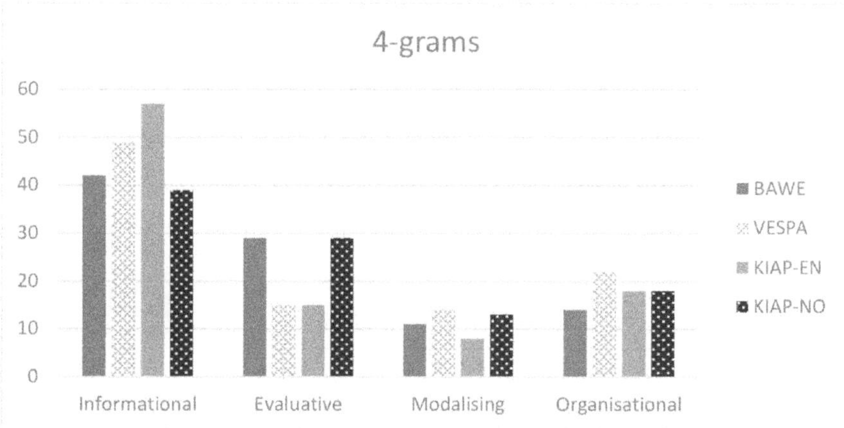


**Figure 2.3** Functional types of 4-grams across the corpora

As noted above, it is difficult to see why Norwegian learners should be more similar to English than to Norwegian expert writers (particularly in their use of 3-grams). However, as the learners represented in the VESPA corpus are students of English, they are probably more used to reading about linguistics in English than in Norwegian and may thus have picked up wordings from their course reading. It is even more remarkable that the L1 English novices should resemble the Norwegian experts more than they do the L1 English experts (see also Table 2.5) in their distribution of functional types of n-grams. It is likely that our focus on *types* rather than *tokens* could be part of the explanation. For example, there are more evaluative tokens among the 20 most frequent 4-gram types in VESPA than in KIAP-EN, even if they have a similar number of types (see Figure 2.3). Furthermore, the broad classification into functional types masks both similarities and differences in the realisation and form of n-grams, to which we now turn.

## 6.2 The realisation and form of the n-grams

A modest number of n-gram types are shared across the corpora. Table 2.7 shows the 4-grams that occur in more than one of the English-language corpora, i.e. BAWE, VESPA and KIAP-EN. It is striking that the majority of the shared 4-grams are general in meaning and give away little about the discipline of the texts. The informational 4-grams in Table 2.7 are almost all either PP-based or NP-based, and most include the preposition *of* (see also Biber *et al.*, 1999: 1014 ff; Chen & Baker, 2010: 35). However, many of the informational n-grams that are *not* shared across the corpora seem to reflect topics that are simply not present (with sufficient distribution and frequencies) in the other corpora. Examples are *the semantics of the*, *the argument structure*

**Table 2.7** Shared 4-gram types across the corpora

| | Informational | Evaluative | Modalising | Organisational |
|---|---|---|---|---|
| BAWE + VESPA + KIAP-EN | at the end of<br>in the case of<br>in the use of<br>on the basis of<br>that there is a<br>the meaning of the<br>the use of the | in the same way<br>it is important to<br>the fact that the | it is possible to<br>to be able to | as well as the<br>in this case the<br>on the other hand |
| BAWE + VESPA | and the use of<br>of the use of | to the fact that | can be found in<br>can be seen in | an example of this<br>example of this is<br>in this essay i<br>is an example of |
| BAWE + KIAP-EN | in terms of the<br>in the context of<br>that there is no<br>the nature of the<br>the way in which<br>the ways in which | by the fact that<br>it is clear that | can be used to | with respect to the |
| VESPA + KIAP-EN | the end of the | | | at the same time |

*of, the semantic bootstrapping, a lexical teddy bear, in the Norwegian translations*. Notably, the novice British writers in BAWE share more identical 4-grams with L1 English experts in KIAP-EN than the learners in VESPA do, which suggests that in terms of actual lexicalisation, the L1 novice writers are closer to the phrasicon of research publications within their discipline.

The shared 3-grams reveal a relatively similar pattern to the 4-grams except that only two interpersonal 3-grams occur in all three corpora (*in the same* and *the fact that*). On the other hand, the two novice corpora share five evaluative and six modalising 3-grams (e.g. *due to the, meaning of the; can also be, can be seen*). In the case of 3-grams, too, there is a greater similarity between the native speakers of English in BAWE and KIAP-EN than between the learners in VESPA and KIAP-EN, especially as regards informational n-grams, while VESPA shares a few more organisational n-grams with the English L1 experts (e.g. *in other words, in the following, in this paper*).

Examining the intuitively similar 3- and 4-grams in Norwegian professional writing (KIAP-NO) and English learner writing (VESPA), with the reservations against direct cross-linguistic comparison of Norwegian and English n-grams expressed above, we find that the highest degree of overlap occurs in the organisational category. In fact, about half of the recurrent organisational n-grams in KIAP-NO have a counterpart in VESPA. Some examples are *i denne artikkelen* ('in this article') – *in this paper/essay, i dette tilfellet – in this case, i tillegg til – in addition to, når det gjelder* ('when it concerns') – *when it comes to, på den annen side* ('on the other side') – *on the other hand, et eksempel på en – an example of a*.[8] In addition, two of the three analogous modalising n-grams are metadiscursive, and thus also have a text-organising function, namely the pairs *jeg vil hevde at* ('I will claim that') – *I would say that* and *i denne artikkelen skal + jeg|vi* ('in this article shall + I|we') – *[in] this essay I will.* This is interesting because it suggests that Norwegian learners of English organise their texts along the lines of academic Norwegian.

The other functional types of n-grams have less 'overlap' between Norwegian and L2 English, although we may note that some evaluative n-grams are similar, e.g. *det er vanskelig å – it is hard/difficult to*. The low degree of formal similarity is presumably due to systemic differences between the languages (Ebeling & Ebeling, 2017; Hasselgård, 2017) as well as differences in topics, particularly in the case of informational n-grams. Interestingly, KIAP-NO, like VESPA, has a good number of n-grams that involve self-reference (cf. Section 3 above and Paquot *et al.*, 2013). These include, in addition to the organisational ones listed above, *det vi kan kalle* ('what we can call'), *kan vi si at* ('can we say that'), and *etter mitt syn* ('in my view'). This agrees with Fløttum *et al.*'s (2006: 70) finding that first-person pronouns are more frequent in Norwegian than in English linguistics articles. The frequent use of self-reference in the English of Norwegian learners can thus potentially be linked to their L1 writing culture. However, this tendency has also been noted by, for example, Granger (2017) for learners of English more generally, as such self-referencing was shown to be typical of quite a few L1 populations, including French, Spanish, Italian, Norwegian, Swedish and German.

As noted above, there are more VP-based (clausal) n-grams in the Norwegian learner corpus than in the English L1 novice corpus, which in return contains more NP-based n-grams, suggesting a more nominal style of writing. Since a similar difference was found between English and Norwegian expert texts, it is possible that the learners' more verbal style comes from their L1, although the developmental factor cannot be ruled out. However, a nominal style has been identified as a hallmark of English academic writing. For example, Biber and Gray (2016: 110) show that academic registers 'have developed a distinctive grammatical style, employing a dense use of nouns and phrasal modifiers rather than verbs and clauses'. This may be illustrated by example (3), which comprises a 4-gram, *the way in which*, which is typical of English academic discourse (Groom, 2019: 303) but not shared by the Norwegian learners.

(3) Duality of language highlights *the way in which* elements and segments of language are combined to form words, expressions and phrases. (BAWE)

It was noted in Section 3 that the Norwegian learners in VESPA underuse extraposition for evaluation, as in example (4) from BAWE. The n-gram lists for KIAP-NO show, however, that evaluative extraposition is as frequent in Norwegian as in English linguistics articles; see

Section 4.1.2 and example (5). The shortage of such n-grams in VESPA is thus not attributable to the learners' L1.

(4) ... and *it is clear that* these different methods of communication are learnt in different ways. (BAWE)
(5) ... og *det er rimelig å* tru at det samme gjelder for norsk. (KIAP-NO)
Lit: "...and *it is reasonable to* think that the same applies to Norwegian."

However, our finding that Norwegian learners use fewer n-grams that reflect passives and nominalisations than their peers in BAWE might be L1-related: there are no 'passive' n-gram types among the top 100 in KIAP-NO and very little evidence of nominalisation. VESPA, on the other hand, does contain passive n-grams, e.g. *be found in the, can be seen as*, which indicates that the learners have adopted wordings from their academic reading in English, albeit in smaller proportions than the novice native writers.

As noted above, Figures 2.2 and 2.3 show an unexpected similarity between BAWE (novice L1 English) and KIAP-NO (expert Norwegian) in the proportions of evaluative n-grams. Further scrutiny of the 4-grams, where the pattern is most pronounced, shows that the proportional similarity is not reflected in the content of the n-grams, as there is little overlap in actual realisations of the 4-grams. The exception is the use of the evaluative frame *it is* ADJ *to/that* and its Norwegian counterpart *det er* ADJ *å/at*, as illustrated in examples (4) and (5) above. Many of the Norwegian evaluative 4-grams comprise a disjunct adverbial, e.g. *er først og fremst* ('is first and foremost'), *i det hele tatt* ('at all'), *til en viss grad* ('to a certain degree'). In comparison, a large proportion of the KIAP-EN list of evaluative 4-grams consists of extraposition and sequences involving the word *fact*. The BAWE list contains more expressions denoting causes and effects, e.g. *a result of the, due to the fact, for the purposes of, this is due to*. The VESPA list is relatively similar to the BAWE one, but shorter and slightly more concerned with (non-causal) relations, e.g. *have to do with, the same meaning as*.

## 7 Concluding Remarks

The present study has used a contrastive analysis of English and Norwegian published academic texts to look for explanations for differences in the use of functional types of n-grams in novice writing between Norwegian learners and native speakers of English, as uncovered in Ebeling and Hasselgård (2015a).

The contrastive analysis proper revealed that the field of linguistics adopts similar writing styles in English and Norwegian in terms of functional classes of frequently occurring 3- and 4-gram types. The main difference between the languages is the markedly more frequent use of evaluative n-grams in the Norwegian research articles. At a more detailed level, regarding the form of the n-grams, it was noted that L1 English linguists prefer a nominal (NP-based) style compared to the more clausal (VP-based) style of L1 Norwegian linguists.

In compliance with the Integrated Contrastive Model (Granger, 1996), the contrastive analysis enabled us to reassess and compare the results from the previous CIA that was similarly concerned with the functions of n-grams. The quantitative analysis gave inconclusive and to some extent contradictory results, in particular the apparent similarities in the proportions of functional types of n-grams between Norwegian learners and English experts, on the one hand, and L1 English students and Norwegian experts, on the other. Moreover, the hypothesis put forward in Section 1 – that the novice writers would resort to more organisational n-grams than the experts – was not substantiated (see Tables 2.5 and 2.6).

The analysis of n-grams gives an indication of how similar texts are in terms of function. However, a deeper understanding is gained if we look 'behind the scenes' at the actual realisations of the n-grams, where we can see how the functions are lexicalised across languages and interlanguages. Comparing the lexicalisations of the n-grams more qualitatively, we found that the writing of Norwegian learners may indeed be coloured by the style of academic articles in their L1. Hence, the Norwegian learners share some lexical and discursive features with L1 expert Norwegian which distinguish their academic writing from L1 English academic writing. In particular, this concerns more clausal n-grams and fewer nominal ones and a more frequent use of self-reference. There were also important similarities in the organisational n-grams between Norwegian learners and Norwegian L1 experts, suggesting that the Norwegian learners of English bear traces of a Norwegian writing culture. However, the scarce use of the evaluative frame *it is* ADJ *that/to* among the learners cannot be attributed to L1 influence, since a formally similar pattern is frequent in KIAP-NO.

The survey of shared n-grams across the corpora showed that the L1 English novices seem closer to the L1 English experts than the learners are. However, at the same time, the Norwegian learners of English also show similarities with L1 writing in English, such as the somewhat more frequent use of passive n-grams than L1 Norwegian and the simple fact, not commented on above, that none of the recurrent n-grams seems unidiomatic. Hence, the present investigation confirms the impression formed in our 2015a study, that 'the Norwegian learners [...] are in fact advanced users of English who are to a great extent able to adapt to disciplinary conventions' (Ebeling & Hasselgård, 2015a: 102) although we can trace a slight Norwegian accent in their writing.

This study has some obvious limitations that need to be reiterated. Not unexpectedly, some of these concern comparability, both in terms of corpus size (see Table 2.1) and the challenges of comparing n-grams across languages (see Section 4.1.2). These are not trivial matters but we have tried to reduce the effect of these variables by pointing them out and, in the latter case, to mainly compare functional classes, thereby keeping the direct cross-linguistic comparison of individual n-grams to a minimum. Nevertheless, the contrastive analysis may not have given a true picture of similarities and differences between English and Norwegian academic phraseology because of the generally greater variability of Norwegian in terms of, for example, spelling and syntax. For example, while the English 3-gram *we have seen* may meet the frequency requirements, the two Norwegian variants *vi har sett|har vi sett* may not, simply because neither of them will meet the frequency threshold (cf. Section 2.3 and previous studies of n-grams in English and Norwegian: Ebeling & Ebeling, 2017; Hasselgård, 2017).

Another limitation concerns the problems related to cross-linguistic comparisons based on comparable corpora, and the absence of a completely unbiased common ground against which comparisons across languages can be made (see Section 4.1.2). However, functional classes are arguably better suited for contrastive analysis based on comparable data of this kind than, for example, lexical studies, as they are abstracted from established grammatical categories and lexicalisations.

In spite of these limitations, the study has contributed further insight into the use of phraseological sequences across several writer groups and we would strongly encourage further research to be conducted in this field. It would be of great interest to apply the same integrated contrastive approach to more disciplines, more L1 learner groups as well as more languages, in order to gain even more knowledge in this area, not least to further differentiate L1 influence from the interlanguage factor (cf. Jarvis, 2000; Paquot, 2013).

## Appendix A

**Table A.1** Top 10 3-gram types according to frequency in the four corpora

| | VESPA | BAWE | KIAP-EN | KIAP-NO |
|---|---|---|---|---|
| 1 | THE USE OF | THE USE OF | THE FACT THAT | AT DET ER 'that it/there is' |
| 2 | IN THE TEXT | IN ORDER TO | THERE IS NO | I FORHOLD TIL 'in relation to' |
| 3 | OF THE TEXT | THE FACT THAT | IN TERMS OF | UT TIL Å 'out to to' (≈ as if) |
| 4 | AN EXAMPLE OF | AS WELL AS | THERE IS A | NÅR DET GJELDER 'when it concerns' (≈ when it comes to) |
| 5 | THERE IS A | DUE TO THE | IN WHICH THE | VED HJELP AV 'with help of' (≈ by means of) |
| 6 | THE TEXT IS | IN TERMS OF | THAT THERE IS | MEN DET ER 'but it/there is' |
| 7 | USE OF THE | BE ABLE TO | THE USE OF | OG DET ER 'and it/there is' |
| 8 | SEEMS TO BE | ONE OF THE | IT IS NOT | MED ANDRE ORD 'with other words' (≈ in other words) |
| 9 | PART OF THE | THERE IS A | THE CASE OF | DET ER IKKE 'it/there is not' |
| 10 | IN ORDER TO | MEN AND WOMEN | AS WELL AS | I DENNE ARTIKKELEN 'in this article' |

**Table A.2** Top 10 4-gram types according to frequency in the four corpora

| | BAWE | VESPA | KIAP-EN | KIAP-NO |
|---|---|---|---|---|
| 1 | IT IS IMPORTANT TO | ON THE OTHER HAND | IN THE CASE OF | SER UT TIL Å 'look out to to' (≈ looks as if) |
| 2 | IN THE CASE OF | THE USE OF THE | ON THE BASIS OF | UT TIL Å VÆRE 'out to to be' (≈ (seems) to be) |
| 3 | AS A RESULT OF | WHEN IT COMES TO | ON THE OTHER HAND | I OG MED AT 'in and with that' (≈ because of) |
| 4 | THE USE OF THE | THE MEANING OF THE | THAT THERE IS A | AT DET IKKE ER 'that it/there is not' |
| 5 | TO BE ABLE TO | THE REST OF THE | WITH RESPECT TO THE | I DET HELE TATT 'in the whole taken' (≈on the whole) |
| 6 | THE WAY IN WHICH | IS AN EXAMPLE OF | HOPPER AND TRAUGOTT 1993 | I DEN FORSTAND AT 'in the sense that' |
| 7 | THE FACT THAT THE | AN EXAMPLE OF THIS | AT THE SAME TIME | PÅ DEN ANNEN SIDE 'on the other side' (≈ on the other hand) |
| 8 | THE WAY WE SPEAK | THE FACT THAT THE | THE END OF THE | DET VIL SI AT 'it will say that' (≈ i.e.) |
| 9 | CAN BE FOUND IN | IS THE USE OF | IN TERMS OF THE | PÅ SAMME MÅTE SOM 'on same way as' (≈ in the same way as) |
| 10 | ON THE OTHER HAND | AS WE CAN SEE | THE FACT THAT THE | SER DET UT TIL 'looks it out to' (≈ it looks as if) |

## Notes

(1) The acronym stems from the Norwegian name of the (corpus) project: Kulturell Identitet i Akademisk Prosa.

(2) The word counts exclude text in footnotes, block quotes and headlines. See Ebeling and Heuboeck (2007) and the corpus manuals for VESPA and BAWE (Heuboeck *et al.*, 2008; Paquot *et al.*, 2010) for information on the annotation that facilitates the automatic exclusion of text not produced by the students, and Fløttum *et al.* (2006: 7) on the word counts in KIAP.

(3) Halliday's definition of mode does not mention different languages but uses the phrase 'symbolic organisation of the text' (Halliday, 1985: 12), which explicitly includes the speech/writing contrast, and has been extended here to also include language code.

(4) Where the number of occurrences of n-gram number 100 was identical for several n-grams, we included the (alphabetically) first n-gram to reach the top 100, in order to get an equal number from each (sub-)corpus.

(5) It is also possible that course assignments in relatively large student groups will have prompted the use of certain expressions across corpus texts in VESPA. See, for example, Ädel (2015: 409), who notes: 'even small differences in prompts or assigned topics affect the written production'.

(6) However, measures have been proposed to counter these challenges (see, for example, Chlumská & Lukeš, 2018; Cortes, 2008; Granger, 2014; Milička *et al.*, 2019).

(7) This is in line with what previous studies have reported regarding the use of dummy subject *det* vs. *it*/*there* constructions in Norwegian and English (Ebeling, 2000; Ebeling & Ebeling, 2020; Gundel, 2002).

(8) Those Norwegian n-grams that are not followed by glosses correspond word for word to their English counterparts.

## References

Ädel, A. (2015) Variability in learner corpora. In S. Granger, G. Gilquin and F. Meunier (eds) *The Cambridge Handbook of Learner Corpus Research* (pp. 401–421). Cambridge: Cambridge University Press.

Alsop, S. and Nesi, H. (2009) Issues in the development of the British Academic Written English (BAWE) corpus. *Corpora* 4 (1), 71–83.

Biber, D. and Conrad, S. (1999) Lexical bundles in conversation and academic prose. In H. Hasselgård and S. Oksefjell (eds) *Out of Corpora: Studies in Honour of Stig Johansson* (pp. 181–190). Amsterdam: Rodopi.

Biber, D. and Gray, B. (2016) *Grammatical Complexity in Academic English: Linguistic Change in Writing*. Cambridge: Cambridge University Press.

Biber, D., Conrad, S. and Cortes, V. (2004) 'If you look at...': Lexical bundles in university teaching and textbooks. *Applied Linguistics* 25 (3), 371–405.

Biber, D., Johansson, S., Leech, G., Conrad, S. and Finegan, E. (1999) *Longman Grammar of Spoken and Written English*. London: Longman.

Chen, Y.-H. and Baker, P. (2010) Lexical bundles in L1 and L2 academic writing. *Language Learning and Technology* 14 (2), 30–49.

Chlumská, L. and Lukeš, D. (2018) Comparing the incomparable? Rethinking n-grams for free word-order languages. In S. Granger, M.-A. Lefer and L. Aguiar de Souza Penha Marion (eds) *Book of Abstracts. Using Corpora in Contrastive and Translation Studies Conference (5th edition)*. CECL Papers 1. Louvain-la-Neuve: Centre for English Corpus Linguistics, Université catholique de Louvain, 40–41. Available at: https://alfresco.uclouvain.be/alfresco/service/guest/streamDownload/workspace/SpacesStore/c850523d-1953-4204-964d-c6d1ee174bfe/UCCTS2018_book_of_abstracts_with%20correction.pdf?guest=true.

Conrad, S. and Biber, D. (2005) The frequency and use of lexical bundles in conversation and academic prose. *Lexicographica* vol. 20, 56–71.

Cortes, V. (2008) A comparative analysis of lexical bundles in academic history writing in English and Spanish. *Corpora* 3 (1), 43–57.

Ebeling, J. (2000) *Presentative Constructions in English and Norwegian: A Corpus-based Contrastive Study*. Oslo: Acta Humaniora.

Ebeling, S.O. (2011) Recurrent word-combinations in English student essays. *Nordic Journal of English Studies* 10 (1), 49–76.

Ebeling, S.O. and Hasselgård, H. (2015a) Learners' and native speakers' use of recurrent word-combinations across disciplines. *Bergen Language and Linguistics Studies (BeLLS)* 6, 87–106.

Ebeling, S.O. and Hasselgård, H. (2015b) Learner corpora and phraseology. In S. Granger, G. Gilquin and F. Meunier (eds) *The Cambridge Handbook of Learner Corpus Research* (pp. 207–229). Cambridge: Cambridge University Press.

Ebeling, S.O. and Heuboeck, A. (2007) Encoding document information in a corpus of student writing: The British Academic Written English corpus. *Corpora* 2 (2), 241–256.

Ebeling, S.O. and Ebeling, J. (2017) A cross-linguistic comparison of recurrent word-combinations in a comparable corpus of English and Norwegian fiction. In M. Janebová, E. Lapshinova-Koltunski and M. Martinková (eds) *Contrasting English and other Languages through Corpora* (pp. 2–31). Newcastle: Cambridge Scholars Publishing.

Ebeling, S.O. and Ebeling, J. (2020) Dialogue vs. narrative in fiction: A cross-linguistic comparison. In S. Granger and M-A. Lefer (eds) *The Complementary Contribution of Comparable and Parallel Corpora to Crosslinguistic Studies*, special issue of *Languages in Contrast* 20 (2), 389–314.

Fløttum, K., Dahl, T. and Kinn, T. (2006) *Academic Voices*. Amsterdam: Benjamins.

Gilquin, G. (2000/2001) The Integrated Contrastive Model: Spicing up your data. *Languages in Contrast* 3 (1), 95–124.

Granger, S. (1996) From CA to CIA and back: An integrated approach to computerized bilingual and learner corpora. In K. Aijmer, B. Altenberg and M. Johansson (eds) *Languages in Contrast. Papers from a Symposium on Text-based Cross-linguistic Studies* (pp. 37–51). Lund Studies in English 88. Lund: Lund University Press.

Granger, S. (2014) A lexical bundle approach to comparing languages: Stems in English and French. In M.-A. Lefer and S. Vogeleer (eds) *Genre- and Register-related Discourse Features in Contrast*, special issue of *Languages in Contrast* 14 (1), 58–72.

Granger, S. (2015) Contrastive interlanguage analysis: A reappraisal. *International Journal of Learner Corpus Research* 1 (1), 7–24.

Granger, S. (2017) Academic phraseology: A key ingredient in successful L2 academic literacy. In R.V. Fjeld, K. Hagen, B. Henriksen, S. Johansson, S. Olsen and J. Prentice (eds) *Academic Language in a Nordic Setting – Linguistic and Educational Perspectives, Oslo Studies in Language* 9 (3), 9–27.

Granger, S. (2018) Tracking the third code. A cross-linguistic corpus-driven approach to metadiscursive markers. In A. Čermáková and M. Mahlberg (eds) *The Corpus Linguistics Discourse. In Honour of Wolfgang Teubert* (pp. 185–204). Amsterdam: Benjamins.

Groom, N. (2019) Construction grammar and the corpus-based analysis of discourses. The case of the WAY IN WHICH construction. *International Journal of Corpus Linguistics* 24 (3), 291–323.

Gundel, J. (2002) Information structure and the use of cleft sentences in English and Norwegian. In H. Hasselgård, S. Johansson, B. Behrens and C. Fabricius-Hansen (eds) *Information Structure in a Cross-linguistic Perspective* (pp. 113–128). Amsterdam: Rodopi.

Halliday, M.A.K. (1985) Context of situation. In M.A.K. Halliday and R. Hasan (eds) *Language, Context and Text: Aspects of Language in a Social-semiotic Perspective* (pp. 3–14). Sydney: University of New South Wales Press.

Halliday, M.A.K. (1994) *An Introduction to Functional Grammar*. London: Arnold.

Hasselgård, H. (2009) Temporal and spatial structuring in English and Norwegian student essays. In R. Bowen, M. Mobärg and S. Ohlander (eds) *Corpora and Discourse – and Stuff. Papers in Honour of Karin Aijmer* (pp. 93–104). Göteborg: Acta Universitatis Gothoburgensis.

Hasselgård, H. (2017) Temporal expressions in English and Norwegian. In M. Janebová, E. Lapshinova-Koltunski and M. Martinková (eds) *Contrasting English and Other Languages through Corpora* (pp. 75–101). Newcastle-upon-Tyne: Cambridge Scholars Publishing.

Hasselgård, H. (2019) Phraseological teddy bears: Frequent lexical bundles in academic writing by Norwegian learners and native speakers of English. In V. Wiegand and M. Mahlberg (eds) *Corpus Linguistics, Context and Culture* (pp. 339–362). Berlin: Mouton de Gruyter.

Hasselgren, A. (1994) Lexical teddy bears and advanced learners: A study into the ways Norwegian students cope with English vocabulary. *International Journal of Applied Linguistics* 4, 237–259.

Heuboeck, A., Holmes, J. and Nesi, H. (2008) The BAWE Corpus Manual. UK: University of Warwick, University of Reading, Oxford Brookes University. http://www.reading.ac.uk/internal/appling/bawe/BAWE.documentation.pdf

Jarvis, S. (2000) Methodological rigor in the study of transfer: Identifying L1 influence in them interlanguage lexicon. *Language Learning* 50 (2), 245–309.

Johansson, S. (2007) *Seeing Through Multilingual Corpora: On the Use of Corpora in Contrastive Studies*. Amsterdam: Benjamins.

Leedham, M. (2015) *Chinese Students Writing in English: Implications from a Corpus-driven Study*. London & New York: Routledge.

Milička, J., Cvrček, V. and Lukešová, L. (2019) N-gram length correspondence in typologically different languages based on a parallel corpus. Conference presentation at CL2019, Cardiff, Wales, UK, 22–26 July 2019, http://www.cl2019.org/.

Moon, R. (1998) *Fixed Expressions and Idioms in English: A Corpus-based Approach*. Oxford: Clarendon Press.

Paquot, M., Hasselgård, H. and Ebeling, S.O. (2013) Writer/reader visibility in learner writing across genres: A comparison of the French and Norwegian components of the ICLE and VESPA learner corpora. In S. Granger, G. Gilquin and F. Meunier (eds) *Twenty Years of Learner Corpus Research: Looking Back, Moving Ahead* (pp. 377–387). Corpora and Language in Use Series. Proceedings of the First Learner Corpus Research Conference. Louvain-la-Neuve: Presses universitaires de Louvain.

Paquot, M., Ebeling, S.O., Heuboeck, A. and Valentin, L. (2010) The VESPA Tagging Manual. Centre for English Corpus Linguistics (CECL), Université catholique de Louvain.

Petch-Tyson, S. (1998) Writer/reader visibility in EFL written discourse. In S. Granger (ed.) *Learner English on Computer* (pp. 107–118). London: Longman.

Quirk, R., Greenbaum, S., Leech, G. and Svartvik, J. (1985) *A Comprehensive Grammar of the English Language*. London: Longman.

R Core Team. (2019) R: A language and environment for statistical computing. R Foundation for Statistical Computing, Vienna, Austria. URL https://www.R-project.org/.

Ringbom, H. (1998) Vocabulary frequencies in advanced learner English: A cross-linguistic approach. In S. Granger (ed.) *Learner English on Computer* (pp. 41–52). London: Longman.

Scott, M. (2016) *WordSmith Tools*. Version 7. Stroud: Lexical Analysis Software.

## Corpora

BAWE – British Academic Written English corpus: http://www.coventry.ac.uk/research/research-directories/current-projects/2015/british-academic-written-english-corpus-bawe/

KIAP – Cultural Identity in Academic Prose: http://www.uib.no/fremmedsprak/23107/kiap-korpuset

VESPA – Varieties of English for Specific Purposes dAtabase, Norwegian component: http://www.hf.uio.no/ilos/english/services/vespa/

# 3 Exploring Learner Corpus Data for Language Testing and Assessment Purposes: The Case of Verb + Noun Collocations

Henrik Gyllstad and Per Snoder

## 1 Introduction

There are many practical uses of testing and assessing the linguistic competence of second language (L2) learners. In second language acquisition (SLA) research, measures of participants' proficiency are central to study design. Furthermore, admission to higher education in many contexts requires non-native speaker students to pass a proficiency test, and language educators may benefit from testing their learners' proficiency for placement purposes. Given the high stakes involved in some of those uses, developing valid and reliable proficiency tests is consequential. One resource to draw on in this regard is a corpus. According to Taylor and Barker (2008), in the 1990s corpus linguistic tools were used to a limited extent in pedagogy and assessment. The last two decades, however, have witnessed an increase of research activity in the convergence of the fields of language testing and assessment (LTA) and corpus linguistics. Corpus data offer several benefits for the test developer: for example, by demonstrating empirically how language is used to balance the subjective intuition of test developers themselves (Barker *et al.*, 2015). However, the potential for learner corpus (LC) data to inform the design of language tests remains an area ripe for investigation. This chapter provides examples of the use of corpora for language testing purposes by exploring the written English phraseological repertoire of L1 Swedish and L1 Italian learners based on data from the *International Corpus of Learner English* (ICLE; Granger *et al.*, 2020) and how it may be used to this end.

## 2 Background

### 2.1 Setting the scene

According to Taylor and Barker (2008), corpora were beginning to be used as reference tools for test developers around the millennium shift. A pioneering and seminal contribution to the budding interest was Alderson's 1996 article entitled 'Do corpora have a role in language assessment?' More recent surveys of uses of corpora in LTA include Barker *et al.* (2015), Callies (2015), Egbert (2017) and Park (2014), some of which appeared in a special issue of the journal *Language Testing* in 2017. Central themes brought up in these surveys include distinguishing between different corpora for different purposes; the importance of rich meta-data in LC; and using LC to show what learners of a language actually *can do* at a specific proficiency level. It is clear from these surveys that corpus data can be used for various LTA purposes: for example, automated linguistic analysis of vast quantities of authentic language produced by native speakers (NS) and non-native speakers (NNS). Target linguistic features at the word, phrase or sentence level are extracted from corpora using software tools and are subjected to comparative analysis across settings and language users, informing test development and test validation (Weigle & Goodwin, 2016).

In the following, rather than aiming for yet another survey, we will highlight examples of the ways in which LTA instruments have been informed by LC data, and how factors such as proficiency, L1 background, and age, have been taken into account. In particular, we will gradually home in on LC use for culling information about learners' phraseological repertoires.

### 2.2 Learner corpora and language testing and assessment

As a first example of learner corpora used for testing purposes, consider the *Cambridge International Corpus* (CIC) of around 320 million words, consisting of a number of sub-corpora, such as the 5-million-word *Cambridge and Nottingham Corpus of Discourse in English* and the 30-million-word *Cambridge Corpus of Academic English*. Importantly, the CIC also contains the 35-million-word *Cambridge Learner Corpus* (CLC). The CLC is based on 135,000 exam scripts from individuals having taken one of the Cambridge ESOL exams, and the data come from 190 countries and from test-takers representing 130 mother tongues. A key component of test development is identifying reliable and valid items that discriminate between test-takers of different proficiency levels. Hargreaves (2000) used word frequency information from the CLC to inform the choice of test items based on learners' proficiency level and to develop a new test format of collocation knowledge although, to our knowledge, it has not yet been used in empirical research.

An example of how specific L1 groups are targeted in test construction can be seen in Usami (2013), who compiled and analysed a corpus of learner English produced by L1 Japanese learners. In this small-scale study, Usami compared two versions (X and Y) for the test item *in spite of* in a multiple-choice format. In both versions, the gapped sentence *He failed his exams* ____________ *really hard* was presented to test-takers, who were asked to choose the correct option out of four with various non-standard spellings and grammatical constructions in the three distractors. The old X version had unsatisfactory measurement properties. The new Y version, whose distractors were errors taken from the learner corpus in question, outperformed the old one on both measures. For example, distractor B in the X version, *in spite working*, only attracted a total of 2% of test-taker responses, whereas the Y version equivalent, *in spite of he worked*, yielded 15%.

LC data are also used to validate the proficiency levels of the Common European Framework of Reference (CEFR; Council of Europe, 2001). The CEFR operationalizes language ability in functional terms as what the L2 learner can do with the language on a 6-level scale from 'basic' to 'proficient' user, A1-C2. These 'can do' statements are language-independent and do not detail which specific grammatical forms or vocabulary a learner at a given level can deploy. This fact has spurred LC research to investigate specific linguistic features in learner texts and relate them to their overall CEFR level as allocated by trained raters (e.g. Gyllstad *et al.*, 2014). Thewissen (2013) analysed accuracy development in a cross-sectional study of ICLE essays and found evidence of progress in terms of gradually fewer errors from the B1-C2 levels, but only two error types showed a steady increase in accuracy across the levels. A vast majority of error types (94%) belonged to either of two stabilization patterns, indicating that L2 development is far from linear in nature. Díez-Bedmar (2018) analysed grammatical accuracy of L1 Spanish learners of English at the B1 level, which allowed her to customize the descriptor to that target L1, specifying that 'grammatical errors related to the use of pronouns and articles ... are likely to appear at least once per composition' (2018: 207).

As for vocabulary use, Lenko-Szymanska (2015) found strong correlations between the CEFR levels A1-B2 assigned to her learner essays and the English Vocabulary Profile (EVP; Capel, 2012), a resource based on the CLC that specifies which vocabulary learners at different CEFR levels know. The most recent EVP version goes beyond single words and includes phrases, phrasal verbs and idioms known by learners at the C1–2 levels on the basis of dictionaries, frequency in L1 use and corpus-based vocabulary lists. The number of idioms in EVP is considerably lower at 247 than the 2,192 phrases and 726 phrasal verbs, which Capel (2012: 11) suggests may result from lack of learner confidence in their correct use. Paquot (2018) analysed three measures of linguistic complexity – syntactic, lexical and phraseological – in learner texts at the B2-C2 levels and found that only the phraseological one (of collocation use) explained a significant proportion of variance in rater assessment.

## 2.3 Learner corpus research on phraseology

Learner corpus research (LCR) applied to phraseology investigates L2 learners' use of recurring word combinations in the target language, by default against a baseline of comparable texts written by native or expert speakers. As argued by Taylor and Barker (2008: 246), collocation (as one type of word combination) is widely seen as 'a distinguishing feature of advanced learner knowledge', and native and learner corpora alike present themselves as tools for querying collocational information on words and phrases for use in test items and tasks on phraseology. This kind of LCR has targeted various categories of phraseological units and has often reconciled a statistical approach to collocations with a phraseological one (see Barfield & Gyllstad, 2009 and Granger & Paquot, 2008 for the distinction between these approaches). The statistical approach is driven by strength of association measures, which by default are *t*-scores and mutual information (MI) scores. Word pairs with high *t*-scores are made up of high-frequency words, for example *black coffee*, while those with high MI scores are made up of low-frequency words, for example *tectonic plates*. Conventionally, a threshold of ≥3 is used for MI score and ≥2 for *t*-score (Schmitt, 2010: 126–131). The phraseological approach focuses on semantic and syntactic categorizations in the analysis of target items, often using a collocational continuum (Howarth, 1998) to describe, for example, the degree of substitutability of word components. A recurring finding is that learner use of phraseology differs quantitatively and qualitatively from that of their NS peers and as a function of their proficiency level and L1 background. While the extraction of target items is generally fully automatic in the frequency-based approach targeting statistical collocations and lexical bundles, target item analysis is not automatized in phraseological approaches as they involve human judgment.

Many LC studies have examined the use of verb + noun (V+N) collocations in L2 English for several reasons: they are the most frequent type of collocations, they form the core meaning of messages, and their correct use is challenging for learners, often due to L1 interference relating to verb choice. Howarth (1998) extracted V+N collocations from a small-scale corpus based on high-frequency verbs and analysed them qualitatively. He found that non-standard forms could be explained by other strategies than L1 interference: for example, blending as in **pay care*, in which *pay attention* and *take care* were fused. Nesselhauf

(2005) analysed V+N collocations extracted manually from the German sub-corpus of the second version of ICLE (Granger *et al.*, 2002). The analysis revealed that 1/3 deviated from the NS norm, notably the choice of delexical verb as in the case of **make homework* rather than the norm *do homework*, which she attributes to interlingual interference based on the German verb *machen*. Laufer and Waldman (2011) analysed an LC of texts produced by L1 Hebrew students of English from three proficiency levels and used NS comparison data from the Louvain Corpus of Native English Essays (LOCNESS) (Granger, 1998). The authors selected the most frequent nouns in the latter corpus and produced concordances from which they identified V+N collocations based on occurrence in collocation dictionaries. The same procedure was repeated for the learner data. Results showed that learners used significantly fewer V+N collocations than NS across proficiency levels with an increase only at the advanced level, and that errors were found at all proficiency levels, 89% of which were potentially induced by L1 interference.

Several LC studies have investigated adjective + noun (A+N) collocations in designs similar to those for V+N collocations reviewed above and some of which produced similar results. Siyanova and Schmitt (2008) compared the use of A+N collocations in the L1 Russian sub-corpus of the ICLE to native data from LOCNESS. Surprisingly, there was no significant difference between the numbers of strong A+N collocations with high MI scores in the two corpora. Durrant and Schmitt (2009) calculated *t*-scores and MI scores of manually extracted premodifier-noun word pairs in NS and NNS texts from various corpora, including the Bulgarian sub-corpus of ICLE. The NNS writers used more high *t*-score collocations than did the NS writers, though the difference was only significant for tokens, not types. Conversely, the NS writers used more high MI score collocations than did the NNS writers, though the difference was significant only for types (2009: 172–174). In a longitudinal study targeting L2 Italian, Siyanova-Chanturia (2015) tracked the development of collocation use among beginner learners over a five-month period (see also Omidian *et al.*, this volume, Chapter 8, for a related study on verb + noun collocations). Her L1 Chinese participants produced significantly more A+N collocations with high MI scores in essays written at the end compared to those written at the beginning of the period.

With the above account as a backdrop, the next sections report on a study aimed at exploring the phraseological repertoire of L1 Swedish and L1 Italian learners' written English based on data from ICLE. Evidence of cross-linguistic influence will be discussed. We will highlight how a learner corpus like ICLE can be drawn on for test development purposes and discuss the outcome in terms of its merits and challenges.

## 3 Data and Methodology

### 3.1 Data

Four corpora and two corpus-based resources were used in the study. The primary data were essays from the most recent version of ICLE (ICLEv3; Granger *et al.*, 2020), containing some 5.7 million words of English written by adult university learners with 25 L1 backgrounds. The learners completed a learner profile with rich metadata. The essays are either argumentative essays or literature examinations and include relevant information on conditions for writing the essays: for example, whether the learners had dictionary access. The ICLE search interface comes with a concordancer and allows for lemmatized searches. We opted to analyse the L1 Italian and L1 Swedish sub-corpora of ICLE (hereafter ICLE-IT and ICLE-SW, respectively), because they differ in how closely related they are to English. ICLE-IT contains 227,170 words and ICLE-SW contains 192,995 words. We also used the 1-billion-word Corpus of Contemporary American English (COCA; Davies, 2008) as a reference corpus for general L1 English, and the 324,304-word Louvain Corpus of Native English Essays (LOCNESS) as a comparative L1 English essay corpus. For the latter we used AntConc (Anthony, 2014), and, to establish collocation status for Italian verb-noun combinations, we used the 26.5-million-word Perugia Corpus (PEC) of written and spoken L1 Italian. A central resource for the study was the New General Service List (NGSL; Browne, 2014). The NGSL is an updated version of West's (1953) General Service List and is a corpus-based frequency list of 2,801 English lemmas that provides 92% coverage for most general English texts.

We focused on the 1,000 most frequent words in the NGSL, from which we selected 128 abstract English nouns, two examples of which are *PROBLEM* and *SYSTEM*. We arrived at the number of nouns for analysis by looking at a comparable study by Laufer and Waldman (2011), who analysed 220 frequent nouns in a LC of 291,000 words. Our ratio of nouns over LC size was comparable to theirs (128 over 193,000). The category of abstract nouns was selected as it was deemed to generate rich data for analysis. The second corpus-based resource was the *Oxford Collocations Dictionary for Students of English* (*OCDE*) (Deuter *et al.*, 2002) for identifying English collocations. Note that the *OCDE*, based on the British National Corpus (BNC), is intended for teachers and learners, not researchers, and more precise information on variables such as frequency is not included (Gyllstad & Schmitt, 2019).

### 3.2 Methodology

We analysed the two sub-corpora ICLE-IT and ICLE-SW using automatic and manual procedures as follows. First, concordances were created for each of the 128 noun lemmas using the ICLE interface.

Second, each concordance was analysed manually and verb collocates for the noun under study within a +/- 4 span were documented and the collocational status of each V+N combination was subject to scrutiny using the secondary corpora presented in Section 3.1. Third, five abstract nouns from each sub-corpus were selected for detailed presentation (see Section 4) as they contained rich material for LTA purposes. We opted to use MI scores and not *t*-scores as our association measure for collocations. This was because we targeted high intermediate to advanced learners of English who, for reasons specified in Section 2.3, were likely to already know high *t*-score collocations, which made the latter less useful for our intended purposes.

## 4 Results

### 4.1 Preliminaries

A summary of the analyses is provided in Table 3.1. We selected eight nouns that yielded rich material for our purposes. *MIND* and *OPPORTUNITY* were analysed in both sub-corpora, whereas *ACTION*, *CAUSE* and *POSSIBILITY* were analysed in ICLE-IT, and *PROBLEM*, *KNOWLEDGE* and *INFORMATION* in ICLE-SW. Frequencies of the investigated noun lemmas in the ICLE sub-corpus and the top five most frequent collocate lexical verb lemmas are reported. We also list the top five most frequent collocate lexical verb lemmas in COCA, as well as the top five verbs in terms of MI score (with a minimum frequency of 10). Finally, the table reports which verbs appear in the OCDE and in the LOCNESS corpus for comparison. We focused on lexical verbs rather than all verbs, as the latter would contain a large number of hits with verbs like *BE*, *HAVE*, and *DO* used as auxiliary verbs, which are less relevant for the study. The analysis for the two shared nouns will be presented in some detail based on the L1 Italian and L1 Swedish data. Then, noteworthy findings pertaining to the remaining six nouns will be highlighted.

### 4.2 Analyses of *MIND* and *OPPORTUNITY* in ICLE-IT

The L1 Italian students combined these two nouns with a range of verb collocates in their essays, which generated ample material for LTA purposes. When a V+N combination in Italian is categorized as a collocation below, it is motivated on the basis of an MI score ≥3 in the L1 Italian reference corpus, or being listed as a phraseological unit in a monolingual Italian Dictionary (Sabatini & Coletti, 2008).

#### *MIND*

There were 172 instances of the noun *MIND* in ICLE-IT and it was combined with 22 different verb collocates. The most frequent collocates

**Table 3.1** Corpus and dictionary data for the eight investigated abstract nouns in this study

| Noun lemma in ICLE sub-corpus and its collocates | | | | Top 5 lexical verb lemma collocates in COCA based on frequency | | Top 5 verb lemma collocates in COCA based on MI score | | | Verb collocates listed in OCDE* | Verbs in LOCNESS (freq.) |
|---|---|---|---|---|---|---|---|---|---|---|
| **Noun lemma (language)** | **Freq.** | **Top 5 lexical verb lemmas in ICLE based on freq.** | **Other lexical verb lemmas in ICLE** | **Verb** | **Freq.** | **Verb** | **MI** | **Freq. (≥10)** | | |
| MIND<br>(IT) | 172 | bear (10)<br>keep (9)<br>open (4)<br>change (2)<br>have (1) | make (1)<br>educate (1)<br>control (1) | keep<br>change<br>make<br>go<br>get | 16203<br>14636<br>9552<br>7449<br>6080 | boggle<br>decolonize<br>enquire<br>wander<br>ingrain<br>+<br>bear<br>keep | 8.30<br>5.78<br>5.21<br>4.39<br>4.08<br>+<br>3.59<br>3.54 | 804<br>17<br>36<br>932<br>48<br>+<br>2513<br>16203 | come into, come to, cross, flash across, go through, spring to \| bear in, keep in \| slip \| be imprinted on, stick in \| prey on \| occupy | change (5)<br>keep (3)<br>open (3)<br>tamper (1)<br>bear (0)<br>spring (0) |
| MIND<br>(SW) | 99 | change (9)<br>keep (6)<br>bear (4)<br>have (4)<br>achieve (2) | spring (2)<br>come (2) | | | | | | | |
| OPPORTUNITY<br>(IT) | 90 | have (27)<br>give (21)<br>offer (3)<br>exploit (2)<br>create (1) | change (1)<br>embrace (1)<br>get (1)<br>provide (0)<br>seize (0) | give<br>provide<br>take<br>get<br>offer | 11329<br>9002<br>5761<br>5169<br>4773 | squander<br>seize<br>cross-examine<br>equalize<br>capitalize<br>+<br>avail<br>provide<br>afford | 5.88<br>5.58<br>5.35<br>4.92<br>4.90<br>+<br>4.35<br>4.07<br>3.89 | 219<br>1385<br>27<br>49<br>231<br>+<br>91<br>9002<br>1114 | have \| find, get \| afford, create, give sb, offer (sb), open up, provide (sb with) \| grasp, seize, take (up), take advantage of \| lose, miss \| pass up | have (7)<br>give (8)<br>provide (7)<br>sieze [sic] (1)<br>offer (0) |
| OPPORTUNITY<br>(SW) | 71 | have (19)<br>give (10)<br>get (8)<br>provide (3)<br>offer (2) | take (1)<br>seize (0)<br>afford (0) | | | | | | | |
| ACTION<br>(IT) | 135 | do (7)<br>pay (5)<br>take (4)<br>control (2)<br>internalize (1) | perform (1)<br>copy (1)<br>imitate (1)<br>make (0) | take<br>see<br>say<br>make<br>get | 22668<br>4173<br>4161<br>3267<br>3118 | condone<br>galvanize<br>forestall<br>justify<br>undertake<br>+<br>commence<br>condemn | 4.45<br>4.33<br>4.10<br>3.98<br>3.81<br>+<br>3.59<br>3.24 | 135<br>62<br>32<br>945<br>393<br>+<br>112<br>299 | take \| call for \| agree on \| leap/ spring/ swing into \| carry out, perform, take \| galvanize/prod/ spur sb into \| bring/ put sth into \| keep/put sb/sth out of | take (16)<br>justify (4)<br>show (3) |

(*Continued on next page*)

**Table 3.1** Corpus and dictionary data for the eight investigated abstract nouns in this study (Continued)

<table>
<tr><th colspan="4">Noun lemma in ICLE sub-corpus and its collocates</th><th colspan="2">Top 5 lexical verb lemma collocates in COCA based on frequency</th><th colspan="3">Top 5 verb lemma collocates in COCA based on MI score</th><th rowspan="2">Verb collocates listed in OCDE*</th><th rowspan="2">Verbs in LOCNESS (freq.)</th></tr>
<tr><th>Noun lemma (language)</th><th>Freq.</th><th>Top 5 lexical verb lemmas in ICLE based on freq.</th><th>Other lexical verb lemmas in ICLE</th><th>Verb</th><th>Freq.</th><th>Verb</th><th>MI</th><th>Freq. (≥10)</th></tr>
<tr><td>CAUSE<br>(IT)</td><td>140</td><td>find (2)<br>have (2)<br>tackle (2)<br>support (2)<br>discover (2)</td><td>understand (1)<br>know (1)<br>further (0)</td><td>know<br>get<br>go<br>say<br>think</td><td>5762<br>5553<br>4747<br>3269<br>2899</td><td>impel<br>further<br>pinpoint<br>espouse<br>donate<br>+<br>rejoice<br>champion</td><td>4.80<br>4.30<br>4.26<br>4.18<br>3.52<br>+<br>3.05<br>2.88</td><td>35<br>81<br>130<br>84<br>302<br>+<br>45<br>323</td><td>1. discover, find, identify 2. have | find | give (sb) | show 3. be committed to, champion, fight for, further, help, promote, serve, support | take up | plead</td><td>further (5)<br>find (3)<br>support (1)<br>fight (1)<br>champion (0)</td></tr>
<tr><td>POSSIBILITY<br>(IT)</td><td>130</td><td>have (29)<br>give (15)<br>reduce (2)<br>preclude (2)<br>offer (2)</td><td>realize (1)<br>consider (1)<br>explore (0)</td><td>consider<br>think<br>open<br>raise<br>see</td><td>1786<br>1623<br>1389<br>1280<br>1266</td><td>foreclose<br>preclude<br>tantalize<br>explore<br>obviate<br>+<br>broach<br>entertain<br>exhaust</td><td>6.07<br>5.79<br>5.25<br>4.78<br>4.63<br>+<br>4.61<br>4.53<br>3.89</td><td>85<br>175<br>27<br>1084<br>11<br>+<br>23<br>180<br>151</td><td>allow/offer sb, open up, raise | see | consider, discuss, examine, explore | accept, admit, acknowledge, entertain, recognize | ignore | deny, eliminate, exclude, preclude, rule out | face | cover | avert | lessen reduce</td><td>consider (1)<br>give (0)<br>have (0)</td></tr>
<tr><td>INFORMATION<br>(SW)</td><td>67</td><td>receive (4)<br>get (3)<br>give (3)<br>obtain (1)<br>digest (1)</td><td>need (1)<br>provide (0)<br>use (0)</td><td>provide<br>get<br>give<br>use<br>need</td><td>20276<br>12112<br>9239<br>8309<br>6666</td><td>disseminate<br>redacting<br>glean<br>divulge<br>disclose<br>+<br>need-to-know<br>declassify<br>withhold<br>collate<br>gather</td><td>6.45<br>6.18<br>5.75<br>5.52<br>5.29<br>+<br>5.17<br>5.09<br>5.02<br>4.59<br>4.41</td><td>1036<br>11<br>501<br>274<br>1846<br>+<br>24<br>67<br>741<br>41<br>3899</td><td>contain | have | retain, store | need, require | ask for, request | look for, seek | find, gain, get, obtain | collect, gather | receive | retrieve | access | disclose, give, impart, provide, supply | leak | pass on | disseminate | exchange | withhold | collate | present</td><td>present (7)<br>receive (7)<br>process (6)<br>need (5)<br>use (5)<br>obtain (2)<br>provide (0)</td></tr>
</table>

(*Continued on next page*)

**Table 3.1** Corpus and dictionary data for the eight investigated abstract nouns in this study (Continued)

<table>
<tr><th colspan="4">Noun lemma in ICLE sub-corpus and its collocates</th><th colspan="2">Top 5 lexical verb lemma collocates in COCA based on frequency</th><th colspan="3">Top 5 verb lemma collocates in COCA based on MI score</th><th rowspan="2">Verb collocates listed in OCDE*</th><th rowspan="2">Verbs in LOCNESS (freq.)</th></tr>
<tr><th>Noun lemma (language)</th><th>Freq.</th><th>Top 5 lexical verb lemmas in ICLE based on freq.</th><th>Other lexical verb lemmas in ICLE</th><th>Verb</th><th>Freq.</th><th>Verb</th><th>MI</th><th>Freq. (≥10)</th></tr>
<tr><td>KNOWLEDGE<br>(SW)</td><td>137</td><td>use (5)<br>get (5)<br>acquire (2)<br>gain (2)<br>take (2)</td><td>lack (1)<br>share (1)</td><td>use<br>make<br>gain<br>share<br>acquire</td><td>2550<br>1733<br>1669<br>1584<br>1406</td><td>impart<br>systematize<br>disclaim<br>acquire<br>disseminate<br>+<br>disavow<br>glean<br>possess<br>broaden<br>gain</td><td>6.06<br>5.25<br>5.08<br>5.07<br>4.84<br>+<br>4.76<br>4.58<br>4.51<br>3.89<br>3.79</td><td>260<br>11<br>16<br>1406<br>124<br>+<br>45<br>82<br>709<br>99<br>1669</td><td>acquire, gain | have | demonstrate, flaunt, parade, show off | test | apply | share | spread | broaden, extend, improve, increase | deny</td><td>have (8)<br>use (3)<br>apply (1)<br>acquire (1)<br>gain (1)<br>grasp (1)</td></tr>
<tr><td>PROBLEM<br>(SW)</td><td>367</td><td>have (39)<br>solve (36)<br>deal (14)<br>face (9)<br>create (7)</td><td>cause (6)<br>approach (2)</td><td>solve<br>get<br>say<br>think<br>go</td><td>27378<br>16815<br>14943<br>11462<br>10105</td><td>solve<br>externalize<br>troubleshoot<br>exacerbate<br>beset<br>+<br>ameliorate<br>rectify<br>alleviate</td><td>6.74<br>5.62<br>5.03<br>5.02<br>4.79<br>+<br>4.41<br>4.17<br>4.14</td><td>27378<br>234<br>126<br>904<br>218<br>+<br>116<br>172<br>452</td><td>be, pose, present | have | bring, cause, create | be beset with | encounter, face | raise | identify | consider, discuss | address, combat, tackle, grapple with | avoid | deal with, solve | alleviate, ease, exacerbate | explore</td><td>solve (32)<br>cause (18)<br>have (11)<br>face (10)<br>deal (8)<br>create (5)<br>exacerbate (2)</td></tr>
</table>

Note: Some verbs are shown having zero (0) occurrences. They appear here since these verbs are referred to in comparisons across sources in the running text.
*The vertical lines are those used in the dictionary to denote different meanings; due to lack of space, not all verbs listed in OCDE are presented here.

were: *BEAR* (in), *KEEP* (in) and *OPEN*. The first two are listed in *OCDE* and so are three other ones found in ICLE-IT: *CONTROL, HAVE* (in) and *COME* (into). The L2 learners can therefore be said to have a large store of phraseological units for *MIND*. However, the Italian collocation *TENERE* (a) *MENTE* corresponds to both *KEEP* (in) and *BEAR* (in) *'MIND'* and it is a moot point whether cross-linguistic influence (CLI) is involved. CLI seems to account for several single occurrence verb collocates forming non-conventionalized verb-noun combinations in English. One example is *EDUCATE 'MIND'*, which is a likely case of transfer from the Italian collocation *EDUCARE LA MENTE* as used in sentence (1).

(1) All we can do is **educate minds** of people to be responsible and aware of their actions. (IT02030)

A check in LOCNESS generated 61 occurrences of *MIND*, and it most commonly collocated with *CHANGE*. The top three MI scores in COCA were found for the verbs *BOGGLE, DECOLONIZE,* and *ENQUIRE*, none of which was used by the L2 learners in this study. It should be noted that the learners used three verb collocates found among the top 11 MI scores in COCA: *KEEP*, *BEAR* and *CHANGE*, which indicates that the writers also have these types of collocations in their repertoire.

### *OPPORTUNITY*

The noun *OPPORTUNITY* occurred 90 times in ICLE-IT in combination with 15 different verbs, most frequently with *HAVE, GIVE* and *OFFER*. These three collocates are listed in *OCDE* and so is *CREATE*, which occurred once. Except for *EXPLOIT*, which occurred twice, the other verb collocates were used only once and several of them may be due to CLI as their literal translations are Italian collocations, two cases in point being *IMPROVE 'OPPORTUNITY'* (based on *MIGLIORARE OPPORTUNITÀ*) and *EXPLOIT 'OPPORTUNITY'* (based on *SFRUTTARE OPPORTUNITÀ*) as in example (2).

(2) ... or has **exploited** this **opportunity** (ITB08002)

A search in LOCNESS yielded 69 occurrences of *OPPORTUNITY*, and its most frequent verb collocates were GIVE, HAVE and PROVIDE. The top three MI scores in COCA were with the following verb collocates: *SQUANDER*, *SEIZE* and *CROSS-EXAMINE*, none of which was used by our L2 learners. They thus displayed a limited store of phraseological units with the noun *OPPORTUNITY*, which may inform the design of tests.

## 4.3 Analyses of *MIND* and *OPPORTUNITY* in ICLE-SW

### *MIND*

Ninety-nine hits were found for the lemma noun *MIND*, with its most frequent verb collocates being *CHANGE*, *KEEP*, *HAVE* and *BEAR*. The last one merits a closer look. An example of the use of *BEAR* is given in example (3).

(3) ...when we talk about longer prison terms we must **bear in mind** that in Sweden the hardest punishment is twelve years... (SWUG2021)

This is an interesting instance of a more idiomatic usage. *BEAR* and *KEEP* appear here in a figurative sense. A LOCNESS comparison shows that these are in fact not very common, with only three instances of *KEEP* and no instances of *BEAR*. Can this be taken as evidence of infrequent NS use? As shown in Table 3.1, a search in COCA shows that they are frequently used. The absence of hits in LOCNESS may therefore be a result of its limited size. *KEEP* is the most frequent lexical verb, whereas *BEAR* is listed as the 15th most frequent verb lemma. *KEEP* is clearly much more frequent than *BEAR*, close to eight times as common, but the MI scores are relatively similar. The verbs with the highest MI scores in COCA are, again, *BOGGLE* and *DECOLONIZE*. Neither is present in the ICLE-SW texts, but this could be due to the topics of the written texts. Using the phrase *the mind boggles* may be felt to contain a style or register feature which Swedish writers are not comfortable with. Alternatively, it could be that it is an example of very proficient vocabulary (phraseological) usage. A search in LOCNESS yields only two hits, however, and they are both subject predicative constructions, as illustrated in example (4). Thus, based on a comparison with NS data of comparable age and study level, we should not expect *BOGGLE* to appear frequently.

(4) The money involved in such a corporation is **mind boggling** and hard for the common person to comprehend. (ICLE-US-IND-0001.1)

### *OPPORTUNITY*

A search for the lemma *OPPORTUNITY* in the ICLE-SW rendered 71 hits. The most frequently used verbs were *HAVE*, GIVE and *GET*. All three are listed in both *OCDE* and in COCA, but perhaps a more interesting comparison here are more conventionalized and formal uses in English, like *SEIZE* and *AFFORD*. As to the latter, the use of this lemma in the sense 'to provide something or allow something to happen' (*Longman Dictionary of Contemporary English*, LDOCE) is arguably a sign of lexical sophistication, as its more well-known monetary or temporal meaning of 'to have enough money to buy or pay for something' and 'to have enough time to do something', respectively, would be expected to be acquired prior to its extended use. *SEIZE* and *AFFORD* are both listed in the *OCDE*, and in COCA *SEIZE* has the second highest MI score, whereas *AFFORD* appears at rank 11. In LOCNESS, however, where the noun *OPPORTUNITY* is used 69 times, no hits for *AFFORD* are found and only one for *SEIZE*, though with the spelling *sieze* [*sic*]. The ICLE-SW texts feature one more formal usage: *FURNISH*, as seen in example (5). This use, with the meaning 'to supply or provide something' (*LDOCE*), is clearly more formal and figurative.

(5) ... to other parts of the world by tele – and datacommunications **furnish** even more **opportunities** and give an edge to the challenge. (SWUG2014)

No hits for this combination were found in LOCNESS, but there were 22 hits in COCA, though with an MI score of only 1.54, which is below the conventionalized threshold of 3 (Schmitt, 2010). This is arguably due to the much more common use of *FURNISH* with its literal meaning of 'to put furniture and other things into a house or room', often in the construction 'furnish something with something' as in example (6), a COCA concordance taken from a travel section in the *Washington Post*.

(6) You didn't exactly want to kick your shoes off in **the salon**, which was **furnished with velvet sofas, a piano, lavish flower arrangements and oil paintings of distinguished-looking people**.

### 4.4 Findings from analysing the remaining six nouns from ICLE-IT and ICLE-SW

Here we comment on some of the findings from our analyses of the remaining nouns in Table 3.1. We focus on observations relevant from a CLI perspective and the question of the use of high-frequency vs lower-frequency combinations.

A number of observations related to CLI is possible. One example can be found in the noun *POSSIBILITY* from ICLE-IT. With 130 instances and 20 different verb collocates, the most common are *HAVE* and *GIVE*. Interestingly, neither *HAVE* nor *GIVE* is listed in *OCDE*, and there are no occurrences in LOCNESS. CLI is a plausible explanation for the large number of occurrences for the verb collocates *HAVE* and *GIVE* as their literal translations in Italian *AVERE* and *DARE* form collocations with *POSSIBILITÀ*. It is also possible that our L2 learners overgeneralized the collocability of verb collocates with *POSSIBILITY* based on its semantic proximity with *OPPORTUNITY* which, as we saw above, forms collocations with these two verbs.

CLI is also interesting to discuss in the case of *ACTION* and *CAUSE* in ICLE-IT. *ACTION* appeared with 14 different verb collocates, and, as can be seen in Table 3.1, the three most frequent ones were *DO*, *PAY* (for) and *TAKE*. One use of DO is shown in example (7):

(7) ... one often yields to the temptation of **doing actions** which require less effort (ITRS2035)

The non-conventionalized and relatively frequent use of *DO ACTION* is unlikely to be due to influence from Italian as the literal translation **FARE AZIONE* is not an Italian collocation, while *COMPIERE AZIONE* ('perform action') is. Instead, it may be hypothesized that *DO* was chosen as it is a multipurpose delexical or 'light' verb that forms collocations with many actions (see Liu, 2010 for a corpus-based discussion on how 'light' verbs such as *DO* and *MAKE* combine with nouns in English). As to *ACTION*, we observe that our Italian writers displayed a limited phraseological repertoire, an observation that may be exploited for LTA purposes. As to *CAUSE*, several of the single occurrence verb collocates have direct translational equivalents in Italian. An example of its usage is given in (8), which illustrates the use of *REMOVE 'CAUSE'* as in *RIMUOVERE CAUSA*, a collocation in Italian but not in English.

(8) ... people who live in a honest way and **remove** any **causes** that could worsen a problem (ITT02031)

One observation pertains to cases where possible CLI interacts with the trend that learners prefer high-frequency collocations over collocations consisting of lower frequency words, with high MI scores. For the noun lemma *PROBLEM* in ICLE-SW, there were 367 instances, and the most common verb collocates of this noun were *HAVE*, *SOLVE*, *DEAL* (with), and *FACE*. In terms of potential CLI, the main Swedish translation equivalent of *SOLVE* is *LÖSA*, and *LÖSA* is featured in the Swedish collocation *LÖSA ETT PROBLEM*. Thus, the similarities here are a help to the Swedish learners, and they clearly seem to prefer *SOLVE* as a staple verb. An example is shown in (9).

(9) There is a pervading assumption that human ingenuity will **solve all problems** as they appear or that we somehow can do without nature. (SWUL1008)

A COCA search shows that the collocate *SOLVE* is among the most frequent lexical ones. However, this verb also has the highest MI score in COCA. Other verbs with high MI scores include *EXACERBATE*, *AMELIORATE*, *RECTIFY* and *ALLEVIATE*. Except for *SOLVE*, none of these was found in the Swedish texts. If used, they may convey a high level of lexical proficiency, and for this reason this observation can inform test creation.

Two more examples of potential overuse of high-frequency verb collocates can be found in the data for the nouns *KNOWLEDGE* and *INFORMATION*. For both these nouns the verb *GET* is commonly used. In the case of *INFORMATION*, one of the most frequently used verbs by the ICLE-SW writers, *GET*, is not at all attested in LOCNESS, nor in *OCDE*, and features relatively low as the 20th most common lexical verb in COCA. In the case of *KNOWLEDGE*, the verb *GET* is also frequent, whereas lower frequency options are used to a lesser extent. Consequently, *GET* may be another usage which appears as a safe bet to learners, but which is not so frequent in the native corpora.

## 5 Discussion

This study is innovative in drawing on multiple corpus-based sources for L2 proficiency test development. The advantage of our approach is that it provides an informed and more complete perspective that is missing in single-source approaches.

As a point of departure, what are the more obvious affordances of using learner corpora to inform language testing and assessment, in this case with an emphasis on phraseology? Straightforward cases are infelicitous uses found in a particular learner corpus, which can be used as distractors for specific L1 groups, in receptive, multiple-choice test formats. Ideally, as far as possible, the distractors should reflect typical L2 learners' errors, and it is therefore important to focus on uses based on texts from several writers, and not just idiosyncrasies from one or two individuals. Furthermore, through access to L1 speakers, or speakers having an advanced command of the L1 itself (or both), it is possible to identify potential L1-induced cross-linguistic influence. Still, a caveat is called for here. We know that differences between two languages – an L1 and an L2 – do not necessarily lead to negative transfer, and that similarities do not always lead to positive transfer. What is needed is a comparison of different L1 writer groups (see Jarvis, 2000 for a call for methodological rigour in this area). This is one of the advantages of multi-L1 learner corpora such as ICLE.

That learners in general find light verbs difficult is well known (Gyllstad, 2007; Wang, 2016). A number of examples of this was found in ICLE-IT. The writers used the questionable verb *DO* with the noun *ACTION*, whereas *TAKE* would have been a more conventionalized choice. This could be used in the design of tests of receptive English collocation knowledge using Gyllstad's (2007) COLLEX format with decontextualized options as in example (10), asking the test-taker to mark which one out of three options is a word combination commonly used by NS of English (for more on test formats for phraseology, see Gyllstad, 2020; Gyllstad & Schmitt, 2019).

| | | | a | b | c |
|---|---|---|---|---|---|
| (10) a. do action | b. take action | c. make action | ☐ | ☐ | ☐ |

Another observation based on the noun *ACTION* from the ICLE-IT is shown in (11), which was used several times in the plural form together with *TAKE* and also *DO* as in this example:

(11) ... to **take** legal **actions** to prevent and detect crimes I think it is the only way to face this problem (ITT02008)

A check in COCA reveals that the singular form of *ACTION* in the verb-adjective-noun collocation *TAKE LEGAL ACTION* by far outnumbers the plural form, with 93 vs. 3 instances. This observation could inform the design of another test of receptive English collocation knowledge, as displayed in example (12).

(12)

| | | | |
|---|---|---|---|
| The situation had become so serious that the only solution for the company was to ____________ and they had contacted two law firms to this end. | take | legally | action |
| | do | legal | actions |
| | make | juridical | – |

In this case, information from the ICLE-IT texts can be used to create a format where each item features a context and several choices to be made in terms of a V+N combination. This format, used in Revier's CONTRIX format (2009), capitalizes on the fact that collocational knowledge often entails knowing not only the main lexical components but also additional grammatical components like determiners or prepositions and, as in example (12), grammatical number (singular vs. plural). The test-taker's task is to make a choice in all three columns to the right.

In general, for the nouns we investigated, there were more examples of infelicitous V+N combinations in the ICLE-IT than in the ICLE-SW texts. This could be an artifact of the small number of nouns investigated, and an effect of those particular verbs. Alternatively, it may be an indication of a higher level of proficiency amongst the Swedish learners of English. In any case, ICLE lacks proficiency information. As Nesselhauf (2006: 146) notes: the writers 'are considered advanced learners on the basis of their status and not on the basis of their actual language proficiency'. Thus, rather than being accompanied by some sort of well-established proficiency measure, the learners whose texts make up the corpus are assumed to be advanced on the basis of level of study (see Barker *et al.*, 2015: 527–528). Even though it makes sense to expect level of study to correlate with level of proficiency in the target language (see, for example, Gyllstad, 2007), without an independent objective measure, we are left with an assumption that may or may not hold true. This could be remedied by researchers having the texts assessed by trained raters, as in Thewissen (2013). Also, to be fair, it should be noted that years of English teaching at school and university and length of stay in an English-speaking country are given for each text. Furthermore, the ICLE handbook (Granger *et al.*, 2020: 11) says that 'the proficiency level ranges from higher inter-mediate to advanced', as shown by a table (2020: 12) displaying the range of CEFR levels for 20 randomly selected essays per sub-corpus.

Another issue highlighted in our analysis is the tendency amongst many learners to use high-frequency word combinations like *solve a problem* and *get an opportunity* rather than, for example, *address a problem* and *seize an opportunity*. In a study of Norwegian learners of English and their vocabulary and collocation use, Hasselgren (1994) accounts for a phenomenon called 'lexical teddy bears', viz. the way in which learners rely on words they feel safe with. This, Hasselgren argues, sometimes leads to the use of infelicitous word combinations, or at least an overuse of certain constructions. More recently, Granger has referred to these as 'pet phrases' (2019: 240). In a similar vein, Durrant and Schmitt (2009) found that learners over-use word combinations characterized by high *t*-scores, whereas their employment of combinations consisting of lower-frequency words, characterized by high MI-scores, reflects under-use. The same trends were observed by Granger and Bestgen (2014), Paquot (2018) and Wang (2016). Paquot (2018) looked at phraseological use across CEFR levels and found that there was a difference between types of word combinations – in the sense that A+N combination use could not be used to predict CEFR level, but that V+N could – for the higher proficiency end of the CEFR scale. At the same time, studies have indicated that A+N combinations may be easier to learn than V+N combinations (e.g. Peters, 2016; Szudarski & Conklin, 2014).

Irrespective of such differences, the question here is how this type of information can be used for LTA purposes. For receptive multiple-choice item formats, the most obvious high-frequency collocate(s) of a frequent noun could be avoided, and instead feature lower-frequency but still conventionalized verbs which come with higher MI scores (see example 13).

(13) ☐ seize an opportunity ☐ cease an opportunity ☐ afford an opportunity

Example (13) shows an item format called DISCO (Eyckmans, 2009) in which the task for the test-taker is to choose those two collocations that are idiomatic in English (idiomatic here meaning conventionalized), thus ruling one of the three out. In this item, the high-frequency collocates of

*OPPORTUNITY*, for example *HAVE* and *GET*, are not used, but rather the less frequent SEIZE and *AFFORD* are used. In the distractor, the verb *CEASE* has been used, potentially tempting for learners who are not sure about orthography, and who may not know the difference in voicing between this verb and *SEIZE*.

What about the use of LC data for productive assessment formats? Are there such uses and, if so, what are they? One way to draw on the observed difference for word combinations between NS and learners is by scoring written composition. In a nutshell, more extended use of combinations associated with higher MI values could, for example, be given higher scores. This could be done in automatic scoring approaches – what Park (2014) refers to as Automated Essay Scoring (AES) (see also Shermis & Burstein, 2013). AES systems evaluate texts through measuring multiple features: for example, mechanics, coherence, errors, lexical and syntactic complexity, organization, and development. It is not known if any existing AES systems measure collocational quality (though see approaches in Kyle and Eguchi, Chapter 6 in this volume), but it is not far-fetched to envision algorithms for calculating scores for each identified collocation in a text. The use of information like MI scores for traditional human scoring, however, is less obvious. Potentially, for a set topic, where a number of specific constructions can be expected with a high level of probability, a scoring key could list a number of alternative wordings, and suggest different scores, as in example (14) featuring the noun *PROBLEM*:

(14)

| LOWER MI SCORE ITEMS | HIGHER MI SCORE ITEMS |
|---|---|
| *solve a problem* | *ameliorate a problem* |
| *fix a problem* | *alleviate a problem* |
| *deal with a problem* | *rectify a problem* |

However, this approach is fraught with challenges. First, the process of anticipating particular constructions based on essay topics is far from straightforward. For example, which V+N constructions can we expect in a text written on the topic 'Environmental challenges in the 21st century'? One way is to look at NS texts on the topic, and conduct a lexical and phraseological analysis. Still, it may not provide rich enough information. Second, a procedure for compiling constructions for lower and higher score bins must be established. This could be based on measures like *t*-scores and MI scores, where constructions with high *t*-scores would receive lower scores than those with high MI scores. Even so, this comes across as a very crude measure, and additional factors need to be taken into account. One step to add could be to ask native speakers to evaluate the level of sophistication as well as appropriacy of a selection of constructions, and to factor that into the analysis. Third, the question of lexical diversity and sophistication (see, for example,

Kyle & Crossley, 2015) no doubt becomes relevant. One could argue that the use of several synonymous constructions makes for a better text. For example, in a paragraph on how to deal with a problem, the initial use of, say, *How can we solve existing environmental problems* can be followed up later in the paragraph by the use of *Thus, X presents itself as one way to alleviate one of these problems*.

A further point for discussion is how to deal with questions like representativeness of LC. Even if available LC are relatively large (~200,000 words for each ICLE sub-corpus (L1); 1 million words in the Japanese English as a Foreign Language Learner Corpus), we may still find very few instances of a particular construction we are interested in. If an assumed infelicitous combination is attested in only 1–3 cases, how can we be sure that constitutes good data to draw on for test construction and assessment formats? It appears to be important to use additional, larger (non-LC) corpora for reference, as we have done in our analysis reported in this chapter. These also provide robust information on measures like MI and *t*-scores. In reference to the use of association measures, however, future studies may rely on alternatives to the conventional *t*-score and MI score used in this study. Brezina and Fox and Omidian *et al.* (Chapters 7 and 8 in this volume) use a measure called Log Dice (Gablasova *et al.*, 2017), which shows promise, having several advantages over the MI measure. In particular, the MI measure relies on random co-occurrence, which is problematic as language structure is not random. Also, it tends to favour lower frequency word pairs. The Log Dice equation overcomes this as it does not include the expected frequency. It is also not affected by corpus size, as is the case with MI.

On reflection, our study represents a different perspective than many of the chapters in the volume (cf. Brezina & Fox; Kyle & Eguchi; Omidian *et al*; Rubin *et al.*). Commonly, the approach is to identify and rank collocations in learners' writing or speech with a view to rating their productions. Our approach illustrates an alternative, namely to use learner corpus data to create tailor-made test items. Although there are examples of researchers highlighting the benefit of LC data for LTA purposes, to the best of our knowledge this is rarely implemented in standard tests. We hope that our study will spark a heightened interest in pursuing this avenue.

Finally, even though our approach described in this chapter has a preponderance towards identifying erroneous or infelicitous uses by learners, or at least comes across as having such tilt, we want to emphasize that the use of learner corpora also provides valuable information on what L2 learners do know and what they can do. In our analysis of the verb collocates of the frequent nouns used in the Swedish and Italian sections of the LC, we came across many instances that were testament to native-like usage. Thus, there are clear benefits of also using learners' correct phraseological uses for LTA purposes. Also, although the focus of the study was on L2 testing and not on pedagogy, it is worth pointing out that the results could be used to design exercises and other instructional materials aimed at weaning learners off high-frequency verbs: for example, those that were discussed above in relation to the nouns *OPPORTUNITY* and *PROBLEM*. Such exercises could be used in English for academic purposes courses to complement other relevant learning resources such as the Academic Collocation List by Ackerman and Chen (2013), the added value of our results being that they are L1-specific. Testing and pedagogy are two sides of the same coin and it is essential that they be closely linked.

## 6 Conclusion

This study investigated how LC data can be used to inform the development of language tests and assessments. Against a backdrop of published surveys and previous work on the use of LC data for testing purposes, and specifically tests of phraseological skills, the chapter analyses V+N collocation data taken from the Italian and Swedish sub-corpora of ICLEv3. The results show that careful analyses of LC data can provide useful information for test item construction using L1-specific learner corpus data that introduce the L1 variable indirectly, without having to include words in the learners' L1.

Examples include the selection of distractors in multiple-choice tests of receptive phraseological knowledge in English, and the scoring of learner production such as written essays based on association strength measures such as MI. The study shows that a mix of automated and manual analyses provides rich data sets to draw on, and that it is necessary also to consult data from larger general-purpose corpora as well as dedicated NS corpora like LOCNESS for comparison. In some cases, however, it might be better to use a register-specific corpus (e.g. the academic part of the BNC or COCA for a comparison with learner essays), as this allows a more relevant comparison than general-purpose corpora like the BNC or COCA. Our findings corroborate previous observations that learners rely disproportionally on collocations based on high-frequency words, to the detriment of those featuring lower-frequency words. An additional conclusion is that it is important to compare collocational use by writers of different L1s to get a better grasp of potential cross-linguistic influence. We hope that our contribution stimulates further research into the usefulness of LC data for language testing and assessment purposes.

## References

Ackerman, K. and Chen, Y.-H. (2013) Developing the Academic Collocation List (ACL) – A corpus-driven and expert-judged approach. *Journal of English for Academic Purposes* 12, 235–247.

Alderson, J.C. (1996) Do corpora have a role in language assessment? In J.A. Thomas and M.H. Short (eds) *Using Corpora for Language Research* (pp. 248–259). London: Longman.

Anthony, L. (2014) *AntConc* (Version 3.4.4) [computer software]. Tokyo: Waseda University.

Barfield, A. and Gyllstad, H. (2009) Introduction: Researching L2 collocation knowledge and development. In A. Barfield and H. Gyllstad (eds) *Researching Collocations in Another Language: Multiple Interpretations* (pp. 1–18). Basingstoke & New York: Palgrave Macmillan.

Barker, F., Salamoura, A. and Saville, N. (2015) Learner corpora and language testing. In S. Granger, G. Gilquin and F. Meunier (eds) *The Cambridge Handbook of Learner Corpus Research* (pp. 511–534). Cambridge: Cambridge University Press.

Browne, C. (2014) A new general service list: The better mousetrap we've been looking for? *Vocabulary Learning and Instruction* 3 (2), 1–10.

Callies, M. (2015) Using learner corpora in language testing and assessment: Current practice and future challenges. In E. Castello, K. Ackerley and F. Coccetta (eds) *Studies in Learner Corpus Linguistics: Research and Applications for Foreign Language Teaching and Assessment* (pp. 21–35). Frankfurt: Peter Lang.

Callies, M. and Götz, S. (eds) (2015) *Learner Corpora in Language Testing and Assessment.* Amsterdam: Benjamins.

Capel, A. (2012) Completing the *English Vocabulary Profile*: C1 and C2 vocabulary. *English Profile Journal* 3, 1–14.

Council of Europe (2001) *Common European Framework of Reference for Languages: Learning, Teaching, Assessment.* Cambridge: Cambridge University Press.

Davies, M. (2008) The Corpus of Contemporary American English (COCA): 1.1 billion words, 1990-present. Available online at https://www.english-corpora.org/coca/.

Deuter, M., Greenan, J., Noble, J. and Phillips, J. (eds) (2002) *Oxford Collocations Dictionary for Students of English.* Oxford: Oxford University Press.

Díez-Bedmar, M.B. (2018) Fine-tuning descriptors for CEFR B1 level: Insights from learner corpora. *ELT Journal* 72 (2), 199–209.

Durrant, P. and Schmitt, N. (2009) To what extent do native and non-native writers make use of collocations? *International Review of Applied Linguistics in Language Teaching* 47 (2), 157–177.

Egbert, J. (2017) Corpus linguistics and language testing: Navigating uncharted waters. *Language Testing*, Special Issue on Corpus Linguistics and Language Testing, Guest Editor Sara T. Cushing, 34 (4), 555–564.

Eyckmans, J. (2009) Toward an assessment of learners' receptive and productive syntagmatic knowledge. In A. Barfield and H. Gyllstad (eds) *Researching Collocations in Another Language: Multiple Interpretations* (pp. 139–152). Basingstoke & New York: Palgrave Macmillan.

Gablasova, D., Brezina, V. and McEnery, T. (2017) Collocations in corpus based language learning research: Identifying, comparing and interpreting the evidence. *Language Learning* 67 (S1), 155–179.

Granger, S. (1998) The computer learner corpus: A versatile new source of data for SLA research. In S. Granger (ed.) *Learner English on Computer* (pp. 3–18). London & New York: Addison Wesley Longman.

Granger, S. (2019) Formulaic sequences in learner corpora: Collocations and lexical bundles. In A. Siyanova-Chanturia and A. Pellicer-Sánchez (eds) *Understanding Formulaic Language: A Second Language Acquisition Perspective* (pp. 228–247). New York: Routledge.

Granger, S. and Paquot, M. (2008) Disentangling the phraseological web. In S. Granger and M. Paquot (eds) *Phraseology: An Interdisciplinary Perspective* (pp. 27–49). Amsterdam: Benjamins.

Granger, S. and Bestgen, Y. (2014) The use of collocations by intermediate vs. advanced non-native writers: A bigram-based study. *International Review of Applied Linguistics in Language Teaching* 52 (3), 229–252.

Granger, S., Dagneaux, E. and Meunier, F. (eds) (2002) *International Corpus of Learner English*. Louvain-la-Neuve: Presses universitaires de Louvain.

Granger, S., Dupont, M., Meunier, F., Naets, H. and Paquot, M. (2020) *The International Corpus of Learner English*. Version 3. Louvain-la-Neuve: Presses universitaires de Louvain.

Gyllstad, H. (2007) Testing English collocations: Developing receptive tests for use with advanced Swedish learners. PhD thesis, Lund University.

Gyllstad, H. (2020) Measuring knowledge of multiword items. In S. Webb (ed.) *The Routledge Handbook of Vocabulary Studies* (pp. 387–405). Abingdon & New York: Routledge.

Gyllstad, H. and Schmitt, N. (2019) Testing formulaic language. In A. Siyanova-Chanturia and A. Pellicer-Sánchez (eds) *Understanding Formulaic Language: A Second Language Acquisition Perspective* (pp. 174–191). New York: Routledge.

Gyllstad, H., Granfeldt, J., Bernardini, P. and Källkvist, M. (2014) Linguistic correlates to communicative proficiency levels of the CEFR: The case of syntactic complexity in written L2 English, L3 French and L4 Italian. In L. Roberts, I. Vedder and J.H. Hulstijn (eds) *EUROSLA Yearbook*. vol. 14 (pp. 1–30). Amsterdam: Benjamins.

Hargreaves, P. (2000) How important is collocation in testing the learner's language proficiency? In M. Lewis (ed.) *Teaching Collocation: Further Developments in the Lexical Approach* (pp. pp. 205–23). Hove: Language Teaching Publications.

Hasselgren, A. (1994) Lexical teddy bears and advanced learners: A study into the ways Norwegian students cope with English vocabulary. *International Journal of Applied Linguistics* 4 (2), 237–258.

Howarth, P. (1998) Phraseology and second language proficiency. *Applied Linguistics* 19 (1), 24–44.

Jarvis, S. (2000) Methodological rigor in the study of transfer: Identifying L1 influence in the interlanguage lexicon. *Language Learning* 50 (2), 245–309.

Kyle, K. and Crossley, S.A. (2015) Automatically assessing lexical sophistication: Indices, tools, findings, and application. *TESOL Quarterly* 49 (4), 757–786.

Laufer, B. and Waldman, T. (2011) Verb-noun collocations in second language writing: A corpus-analysis of learners' English. *Language Learning* 61 (2), 647–672.

*LDOCE* (2003) *Longman Dictionary of Contemporary English* (4th edn). Harlow: Pearson Education.

Leńko-Szymańska, A. (2015) The English Vocabulary Profile as a benchmark for assigning levels to learner corpus data. In M. Callies and S. Götz (eds) *Learner Corpora in Language Testing and Assessment* (pp. 115–140). Amsterdam: Benjamins.

Liu, D. (2010) Going beyond patterns: Involving cognitive analysis in the learning of collocations. *TESOL Quarterly* 44 (1), 4–30.

Nesselhauf, N. (2005) *Collocations in a Learner Corpus*. Amsterdam: Benjamins.

Nesselhauf, N. (2006) Researching L2 production with ICLE. In S. Braun, K. Kohn and J. Mukherjee (eds) *Corpus Technology and Language Pedagogy: New Resources, New Tools, New Methods* (pp. 141–156). Frankfurt: Peter Lang.

Paquot, M. (2018) Phraseological competence: A missing component in university entrance language tests? Insights from a study of EFL learners' use of statistical collocations. *Language Assessment Quarterly* 15 (1), 29–43.

Park, K. (2014) Corpora and language assessment: The state of the art. *Language Assessment Quarterly* 11 (1), 27–44.

Peters, E. (2016) The learning burden of collocations: The role of interlexical and intralexical factors. *Language Teaching Research* 20 (1), 113–138.

Revier, R.L. (2009) Evaluating a new test of whole English collocations. In A. Barfield and H. Gyllstad (eds) *Researching Collocations in Another Language* (pp. 49–59). London: Palgrave Macmillan.

Sabatini, F. and Coletti, V. (2008) *Dizionario Della Lingua Italiana*. Milano: Rizzoli Larousse.

Schmitt, N. (2010) *Researching Vocabulary: A Vocabulary Research Manual*. Basingstoke & New York: Palgrave Macmillan.
Shermis, M.D. and Burstein, J. (eds) (2013) *Handbook of Automated Essay Evaluation: Current Applications and New Directions*. London: Routledge.
Siyanova-Chanturia, A. (2015) Collocation in beginner learner writing: A longitudinal study. *System* 53, 148–160.
Siyanova, A. and Schmitt, N. (2008) L2 learner production and processing of collocations: A multi-study perspective. *The Canadian Modern Language Review* 64 (3), 429–458.
Szudarski, P. and Conklin, K. (2014) Short-and long-term effects of rote rehearsal on ESL learners' processing of L2 collocations. *TESOL Quarterly* 48 (4), 833–842.
Taylor, L. and Barker, F. (2008) Using corpora for language assessment. In E. Shohamy and N.H. Hornberger (eds) *Encyclopedia of Language and Education* (pp. 241–254, 2nd edn). New York: Springer.
Thewissen, J. (2013) Capturing L2 accuracy developmental patterns: Insights from an error-tagged EFL learner corpus. *The Modern Language Journal* 97 (S1), 77–101.
Usami, H. (2013) Using a learner corpus to improve distractors multiple choice grammar questions. In S. Granger, G. Gilquin and F. Meunier (eds) *Twenty Years of Learner Corpus Research: Looking Back, Moving Ahead. Proceedings of the First Learner Corpus Research Conference (LCR 2011)* (pp. 455–462). Louvain-la-Neuve: Presses universitaires de Louvain.
Wang, Y. (2016) *The Idiom Principle and L1 influence: A Contrastive Learner-Corpus Study of Delexical Verb + Noun Collocations*. Amsterdam: Benjamins.
Weigle, S.C. and Goodwin, S. (2016) Applications of corpus linguistics in language assessment. In D. Tsagari and J. Banerjee (eds) *Contemporary Second Language Assessment* (pp. 209–224). London: Bloomsbury.

# 4 The Passive and the Lexis-Grammar Interface: An Inter-varietal Perspective

Gaëtanelle Gilquin and Sylviane Granger

## 1 Introduction

The passive has traditionally been seen as a purely grammatical phenomenon, resulting from the transformation of an active sentence. From a foreign/second language (L2) perspective, it is a complex grammatical structure involving morphology and syntax as well as aspects related to text organization and register. For L2 learners, the difficulty is compounded by the fact that the forms, meanings and contexts of use of the passive differ greatly across languages. As a result, the passive has been shown to pose great difficulties to L2 learners, both in comprehension and production.

Unlike traditional approaches, corpus-based studies of the passive have shown that the passive is not a purely grammatical phenomenon. First, the distinction between the active and the passive is not a strict dichotomy but a gradient ranging from fully verbal to fully adjectival. Second, the passive displays lexical effects, with some verbs being more attracted to the passive voice than others and/or typically used in a limited set of phraseological units. Yet, this view is still largely absent from the field of second language acquisition. In this chapter, we adopt the view of the passive as a lexico-grammatical phenomenon to study different varieties of L2 English as produced by learners from eight mother tongue (L1) backgrounds, representing both English as a foreign language (EFL) and English as a second language (ESL). The focus is on BE-passives only.

The chapter is structured as follows. Section 2 describes the passive as a multifaceted construction and shows what aspects of the passive are dealt with in reference and instructional materials. Section 3 provides an overview of L2 studies of the passive, with a focus on errors, underuse, and lexical and phraseological patterning. In Section 4 we consider the continuum between EFL and ESL underlying our choice of L2 varieties, while in Section 5 we describe our data and methodology. The results are presented in Section 6, which examines the frequency of the passive, and in Section 7, which looks at the lexis-grammar interface, and, more precisely, the passive ratio and phraseological sequences. Section 8 concludes the chapter.

## 2 The Passive: A Multifaceted Construction

Whilst essentially considered as a grammatical structure, the passive is the result of the interplay between a range of other factors. In this section we first present the aspects that have traditionally been described – albeit to varying degrees – in reference and ELT (English language teaching) grammars, i.e. grammar, discourse and register. We then turn to the more recently uncovered lexical and phraseological aspects, which have yet to make their way into reference and instructional materials. In the third subsection we address the passive gradient, i.e. the categorization of passive constructions along a continuum ranging from the most central representatives to the most peripheral.

### 2.1 Grammar, discourse and register

The passive has pride of place in all reference grammars of English. It is usually presented as a structural counterpart of the more basic active construction. For Huddleston and Pullum (2002: 46), the passive construction can be described derivatively, i.e. in terms of how it differs from the basic, canonical construction. As illustrated in (1), the active-passive transformation involves the addition of the BE auxiliary (or less frequently GET) and the past participle morpheme of the main verb, and re-ordering of the object and subject. The object becomes the subject of the passive sentence. The subject is shifted to post-verbal position and becomes a prepositional phrase introduced by the preposition *by* (or occasionally some other preposition); in many cases, it is simply omitted (agentless passive).

(1) a. Pat solved the problem.
    b. The problem was solved by Pat. (Huddleston & Pullum, 2002: 46)

The active and passive constructions are syntactically different but their propositional meanings are essentially the same. The main problem is therefore to know when to use either structure, i.e. to be aware of their respective discourse functions. One of the essential factors to consider in this connection is that the passive construction is an 'information-packaging construction' (Huddleston & Pullum, 2005: 242), which can make it possible to re-establish the normal given-new order in the sentence, as illustrated by (2), where the active (2a) has a new-information subject and the passive (2b) a more typical old-information subject.

(2) a. A dog attacked me in the park.
b. I was attacked by a dog in the park. (Huddleston & Pullum, 2005: 242)

Other factors involve thematic coherence, the principle of end weight and, for the agentless passive, omission of the agent because it is unknown, redundant or general (Biber *et al.*, 1999: 938–942; Huddleston & Pullum, 2002: 1443–1447).

Another factor which tips the balance to the use of the active or passive voice is the register of the text: some registers favour the passive, others disfavour it. This aspect is alluded to in most grammars but is especially in evidence in corpus-based grammars, most notably Biber *et al.* (1999), which compares the frequency of the passive in four genres – conversation, fiction, news and academic prose. The analysis shows that the passive is most frequent in academic prose, where it accounts for 25% of all finite verbs, and least frequent in conversation, where it accounts for only 2%; it is also common in news (15%). Several studies of academic texts written by both L1 and L2 writers have demonstrated that the passive is a linguistic feature that is positively associated with success in quantitative writing assessment (Wilson, 2006).

Arguably 'one of the thorniest problems in L2 grammar instruction' (Hinkel, 2002: 233), the passive is also a key focus in ELT grammars and textbooks. However, as shown by a survey of ELT grammars (Granger, 2013), the sections on the passive are biased towards the structural aspects, to the detriment of aspects pertaining to functions and contexts of use. Larsen-Freeman and Celce-Murcia's (2016: 352) grammar is a notable exception, though, as the authors explicitly state that, while most EFL/ESL grammars seem to assume that the greatest challenge for learners is the form of the passive, their perspective is different: 'Our experience has shown us that it is learning when to use the English passive that presents the greatest long-term challenge to ESL/EFL students'. On the whole, however, the bulk of the sections in ELT grammars is devoted to passive morphology (addition of BE and past participle morpheme), the different passive clause types (monotransitive, ditransitive, impersonal, etc.) and issues related to aspect, tense and modality. The main focus is on the active-passive transformation of decontextualized sentences, regularly resulting in highly unidiomatic sentences (such as *That John couldn't possibly win was recognized by everyone* in Cowan, 2008: 394). A great deal of attention is also directed to constraints on the passive, in particular the issue of unpassivizable verbs. Not all transitive verbs can be passivized: verbs like *have*, *cost*, *equal*, *last* or *resemble* do not normally have corresponding passive forms (**Two houses are had by John*). This observation is often mistakenly extended to the whole category of stative verbs (Cowan, 2008: 400; Larsen-Freeman & Celce-Murcia, 2016: 356). This marked focus on passive constraints may lead learners to avoid the passive and is certainly not conducive to encouraging them to use it, which should be a major objective (Parrott, 2000: 287, 295). It is all the more detrimental as it reinforces the generally negative view of the passive found in many style guides and writing instruction manuals. For Garner (2016: 676), for example, one ought to have 'a presumption against the passive', the active having 'palpable advantages in most contexts' (see Pullum, 2014, for a rebuttal of stylistic charges against the passive).

## 2.2 Lexis and phraseology

The passive is not only a grammatical structure that makes it possible to reorganize discourse elements and that varies according to register: it is also a construction that has been shown to display strong lexical and phraseological preferences, although such aspects tend to be neglected in reference and instructional materials.

The main lexical aspects that are included in grammars are lists of verbs that cannot passivize. Verbs are presented as either passivizable or unpassivizable. However, corpus studies have shown that verbs display different degrees of passivizability. Biber *et al.* (1999: 478) provide lists of lexical verbs that have a very high passive frequency, including verbs that mostly occur in the passive in academic prose (e.g. BE *based* (*on*), BE *situated*). Granger (2013) computed the passive ratio (i.e. the number of passive forms of a verb over the total number of occurrences of that verb) of the verbs used in the BNC Baby, a subset of the British National Corpus.[1] The results highlight considerable differences, with the verb OBLIGE, for example, displaying a ratio of 68.2% and the verb WANT a ratio as low as 0.8%. Using the method of collostructional analysis, Gries and Stefanowitsch (2004) also underline the strong association of certain verbs with the passive and show that verbs attracted to the passive tend to belong to distinctive semantic classes. These results lead the authors to claim that the active-passive pair is not 'a purely syntactic alternation' (Gries & Stefanowitsch, 2004: 108) and that the 'passive voice is a construction in its own right with its own specific semantics' (2004: 110). ELT grammars have not yet taken into account this interdependence between grammar and lexis, which is one of the hallmarks of corpus linguistics. Some grammars provide general comments such as 'Use of the passive is partly a matter of choice, though some verbs may be used more often in passive than active' (Vince, 2008: 34), which are too vague to be helpful. It should be noted, however, that corpus-based resources have begun to integrate lexical aspects into their section on passives.

Going beyond the verbs that are preferred in the active vs passive voice, Lehmann and Schneider (2009) investigate the interaction between the voice of verbs and their subjects/objects. They highlight, among other things, typical subject-passive verb combinations in their corpus data (e.g. *shot* as a subject of *fired* or *breakfast* as a subject of *served*), as well as subject-verb combinations that are exclusively found in the passive (e.g. *hotel* and *situated* or *little* and *known*). Studies of lexical bundles have also frequently brought to light phraseological sequences that include a passive verb, especially in academic writing. Biber *et al.* (1999: 1019–1020), for example, describe patterns such as 'anticipatory *it* + verb phrase' where the verb is usually in the passive, as illustrated by *it can be seen* or *it should be noted*, and 'passive verb + prepositional phrase fragment', as in *are shown in table* or *is referred to as* (see also Hyland, 2008; Rowley-Jolivet, 2001). Such insights have not really made their way into ELT grammars yet, although rare references can be found in some corpus-based ELT grammars: Conrad and Biber (2009: 46, 50) give examples of clusters made up of a verb in the passive and a preposition (*be associated with*, *can be interpreted as*, *be accompanied by*, etc.); Swales and Feak (2004: 120–121) mention the use of passive verbs in references to a visual (*illustrated in*, *seen from*, etc.); Bunting and Diniz (2013: 237) list verbs that frequently occur in the structure '*it* + passive form of the present perfect' (e.g. *suggested*, *reported*) and modals that frequently occur with passive *it* constructions (*can*, *should*, *could* and *must*), as in *it can be argued that*.

## 2.3 The passive gradient

While it is customary to refer to 'the passive' as if it were a unitary structure, many grammarians and linguists point to the ambiguity of the BE + past participle (BE *Ved*) construction. As early as 1966, in the first fully corpus-based study of the passive in a range of mostly written registers, Svartvik identified no fewer than eight categories distributed along a continuum ranging from the most central passives which 'have close systemic transformational relation with the active voice' (Svartvik, 1966: 156) to less central ones which have 'mixed verbal and adjectival properties' (1966: 147) and/or for which 'agent extension is unlikely or impossible' (1966: 148). Examples (3) to (10) are examples given by Svartvik to illustrate the eight categories, ordered from the most central to the most peripheral, and specify the terms used to refer to each of them.

(3) He *was given* this puppy by a farmer in the Welsh hills [animate agent passive]

(4) The removal of large quantities of water (...) *is facilitated* by a high pressure in the kidneys [inanimate agent passive]
(5) These sex differences (...) *can* also *be initiated* by injection of anterior pituitary extracts [Janus-agent passive]
(6) The invitation *hadn't been* very felicitously *phrased* [agentless passive]
(7) I*'ve* always *been* far too *inclined* to treat important objects as part of my own petty existence [attitudinal passive]
(8) Gerald *was* suddenly very *annoyed* [emotive passive]
(9) *Is* the thesis *finished*? [nonagentive passive/statal passive]
(10) Cavill *was unimpressed* by this sally [compound passive]

This categorization relies on a large number of criteria. For example, adjectival characteristics include the possible modification of the *Ved* form by the intensifying adverb *very* (cf. sentence (8)) and the replacement of BE by copulas such as BECOME, GET or FEEL. Granger (1983) uses similar criteria in her corpus-based investigation of the passive in spoken registers. She also breaks down BE *Ved* constructions into several categories, but unlike Svartvik she reserves the term 'passive' to central passives 'which stand in direct alternation to a semantically equivalent active verbal group' (Granger, 1983: 108). In addition to this category, she distinguishes two categories of pseudo-passives (adjectival and verbal), peripheral and mixed combinations, and assigns a special status to BE *Ved* constructions that 'share all characteristics of passives but whose active counterpart is far less common', the 'usually passive' category (Granger, 1983: 112). Her aim in distinguishing this category was to encourage researchers not to limit themselves to lists of verbs that cannot passivize but to also highlight verbs 'that never or rarely activize' (Granger, 1983: 236).

The borders between these categories are characterized by a high degree of fuzziness and overlap, represented by Granger in the form of three interlocking circles (1983: 107). As pointed out by Palmer (1987: 85), the criteria used are 'matters of degree rather than absolute criteria'. There are 'degrees of "adjectiveness"' (Palmer, 1987: 89) and 'numerous dubious cases where a corresponding active form might be thought possible' (Palmer, 1987: 87). As rightly observed by Rowley-Jolivet (2001: 46), '[t]he boundary between adjectival and verbal passives has been the subject of much linguistic discussion, but with little consensus'.

The idea of a passive gradient is generally absent from ELT grammars. When the ambiguity of the BE *Ved* structure is mentioned at all, it is usually presented as a binary distinction between passives and adjectives which can easily be disambiguated in context (see, for example, Cowan, 2008: 403; Parrott, 2000: 292). Reference grammars do recognize the existence of a passive gradient but differ in the way they subcategorize the passive categories and the terms used to refer to them. Quirk *et al.* (1985: 167) put forward a 'passive gradient' made up of three categories, i.e. central passives, semi-passives and pseudo-passives, but only consider the first one as passive. Biber *et al.* (1999: 475) acknowledge that '[p]assive constructions form a fuzzy category' which includes adjectival and stative (i.e. statal) passives, but decide to adopt 'a relatively broad definition of passive, excluding only forms that are clearly adjectival in function'. This still leaves room for a great deal of uncertainty as there are no clear-cut criteria to establish adjectival status and, in the words of the authors themselves, the passive 'forms a cline with the copular verb + participial adjective clause pattern' (Biber *et al.*, 1999: 936). In another section of the grammar the authors note that they also exclude idioms such as *be bound to* and *be supposed to*, 'which do not admit of any active-passive variation' but include stative passives for which 'it is difficult to draw a clear borderline' (Biber *et al.*, 1999: 937). It is clear from this brief survey that the term 'passive' is highly ambiguous. In its strict, most usual sense, it refers to verbal constructions that stand in direct alternation with an active construction. However, it can also be used as an all-embracing term to refer to all BE *Ved* constructions including those that display adjectival characteristics and have an indirect relation to the active or no active counterpart at all, or it can cover only specific subsets of these constructions. There is also great indeterminacy in the terminology used to refer to the structural categories, which adds to the confusion.

## 3 The Passive in L2 Studies

The passive has been the subject of many L2 studies. In these studies, the notion of passive is often taken for granted and examples show that the targeted forms are usually central passives. In corpus-based studies, very little information, if any, is given on the criteria used to select the BE *Ved* forms. Some of the studies, primarily those relying on experimental data, have focused on the grammaticality (or rather ungrammaticality) of passives with a view to understanding how the passive is processed by learners (Section 3.1). Studies based on learner corpus data, on the other hand, have investigated aspects of use: the frequency of the passive (Section 3.2) and its lexical and phraseological patterning (Section 3.3).

### 3.1 Misuse

A large number of L2 studies of the passive (e.g. Chung, 2014; Ju, 2000; Kondo, 2005; Oshita, 2000) focus on overpassivization of intransitive verbs like *happen*, *disappear* or *die*, resulting in erroneous sentences such as **John was died in 1968*. Most of these studies rely on experimental data, in particular controlled elicitation tasks and grammaticality judgments tests, and try to identify the factors that play a part in these errors, factors such as animacy, the presence or not of a transitive counterpart, L1 influence and proficiency level. While some factors prove to have a strong impact on the number and types of errors, several findings are inconclusive and even contradictory. This is the case, for example, of L1 effects, with Kondo (2005: 160) concluding that overpassivization is universal to second language learners and Chung (2014) finding strong L1 effects. It is important to bear in mind, however, that most overpassivization studies are based on limited data from a small number of – usually Asian – learner populations. In a corpus study of overpassivization based on a much more diversified database, Granger (2013) found significant differences between learner populations, with some populations, particularly non-Asian ones, producing very few overpassivization errors or none at all.

### 3.2 Underuse

One aspect that cannot be investigated on the basis of experimental data is frequency of use. As pointed out by Hinkel (2004: 6) in her investigation of tense, aspect and voice, 'when learners participate in controlled experiments that focus on forms of verbs, the requisite tasks are completed and verb forms are produced regardless of whether NNSs (non-native speakers) of English would actually venture to use these particular tenses, aspects and/or voice in real-life L2 text production'. Corpus data, however, give direct access to actual use and non-use. Hinkel (2004) compared academic texts written by native speakers of English and learners from six L1 backgrounds (Arabic, Chinese, Indonesian, Japanese, Korean and Vietnamese) and found a significant underuse of the passive in NNS essays compared to native speaker texts. She added that this underuse is all the more significant as the native writers were novice writers who had not yet fully mastered the conventions of written academic discourse. Xiao (2007) noted a highly significant underuse in a study focused on Chinese learners. The same result was obtained for a wide range of learner populations (cf., for example, Granger, 1997, 2013). Although several authors attribute the underuse of the passive (at least partly) to a lower frequency of the passive in the learners' mother tongue, more research is necessary to tease out developmental and L1-induced factors.

### 3.3 Lexical and phraseological patterning

The impact of lexical choices on the use (or not) of the passive is hardly ever taken into account in L2 studies. Yet, Möller (2017: 288), focusing on CLIL (Content and Language Integrated Learning) and non-CLIL learners of English, underlines the importance of such choices when noting that non-CLIL learners may give the impression that they 'master the passive better than they actually do' (Möller, 2017: 290) because of the particularly high frequency of the verb ALLOW in the passive, which, she argues, is the result of the acquisition of the chunk *be allowed* rather than the acquisition of the passive as such.

The comparison of lexical bundles in native and non-native English has been the topic of several studies (see Ebeling & Hasselgård, Chapter 2 in this volume). Some of these phraseological patterns rely on the use of the passive. Allen (2010), for example, points out that lexical bundles made up of a passive verb and a prepositional phrase represent 6% of all lexical bundles in a corpus of research papers written in English by Japanese science students, as against 30% in native academic writing (Hyland, 2008). Interestingly, Allen (2010) also notes an overuse of certain passive lexical bundles, and in particular *it is* (*widely*/*well*) *known that* and (*it*) *can be said* (*that*). The latter, he suggests, could have been transferred from the learners' L1. Granger (1998) compares passive frames of the type '*it* + (modal) + passive verb (of saying/thinking) + *that*-clause' (e.g. *it is said that*...; *it can be claimed that*...) with their active counterpart '*I* or *we*/*one*/*you* + (modal) + active verb (of saying/thinking) + *that*-clause' (e.g. *I maintain that*...; *one could say that*...) in native and French-speaking learner corpus data. She shows that, while there is no significant difference in the use of the passive structure, the learners heavily overuse the active structure, with about four times as many occurrences in the learner corpus as in the native corpus. Shaw and Liu (1998), adopting a longitudinal perspective, reveal an increase in passive metadiscoursal phrases over time (e.g. *it can be concluded that*) and a corresponding decrease in active metadiscoursal phrases (e.g. *as a conclusion I can say*). As appears from Salazar (2014: 118ff.), this tendency can even continue to the point where passive structures become overused and active structures underused.

## 4 The EFL-ESL Continuum

Our study of the passive will be carried out from an inter-varietal perspective, comparing native English with non-native English, but also comparing several non-native varieties with each other. Within non-native varieties of English, a distinction is traditionally drawn between EFL and ESL (see Quirk *et al.*, 1985: 4–5). The former describes a situation in which English is learned through instruction, with little or no exposure to the target language in everyday life, except for international purposes. The latter refers to a situation in which English is acquired through exposure in everyday life (e.g. via the national media), possibly combined with more formal instruction. The main criterion that is used to distinguish between EFL and ESL is the status of English in a country: if English is an official or semi-official language in the country, it is considered a second variety; otherwise, it is regarded as a foreign variety.

The traditional dichotomy between EFL and ESL has, however, given way to a continuum, recognizing the existence of a grey zone between typical EFL and typical ESL situations. Both sociolinguistic and linguistic considerations have led to this recognition. From a sociolinguistic point of view, it has become clear that some countries present a mixed EFL-ESL situation. Scandinavian countries, for example, are EFL countries in the sense that English does not have any official status, but they have come to resemble ESL countries because of the increasingly widespread use of English for intranational purposes (see Simensen, 2010). The continuum between EFL and ESL has also emerged linguistically, with some varieties presenting both EFL and ESL linguistic features. Edwards (2014), for example, demonstrates that the use of the progressive in Dutch English displays characteristics of EFL (e.g. in terms of overall frequency) as well as characteristics of ESL (cf. extension to stative verbs). Multifactorial analyses have also shown that EFL and ESL varieties do not necessarily cluster in two separate groups. Rautionaho *et al.*'s (2018) analysis of the progressive, for instance, reveals the existence of clusters of EFL varieties (French and Polish English) and of ESL varieties (Nigerian and Singaporean English), but also one cluster bringing together Finnish English, an EFL variety, and Indian English, an ESL variety.

In this study, we compare typical EFL varieties (English produced by speakers of French, German, Korean and Serbian) with varieties that are claimed to display both EFL and ESL features: English produced by speakers of Chinese from Hong Kong, speakers of Dutch from the Netherlands, speakers of Norwegian and speakers of Tswana. Hong Kong English can be described as an ESL variety because of the colonial past of Hong Kong but is often claimed to have transitioned from ESL to EFL (Görlach, 2002: 109–110). English in the Netherlands is traditionally seen as an EFL variety 'moving towards ESL status' (Edwards, 2014: 175). Norway, as a Scandinavian country, has arguably experienced the same shift (see above). As for Tswana English, it appears to have a hybrid status, in between EFL and ESL (Gilquin & Granger, 2011: 75). For the sake of simplicity and despite their hybrid status, in what follows we refer to these varieties as ESL (or ESL-like) varieties.[2]

We are interested in comparing EFL and ESL learners to native speakers of English, with respect to the frequency of the passive, as well as its lexical preferences and phraseological sequences. In addition, we want to compare EFL and ESL learners with each other. Following a usage-based view of language acquisition (see Diessel, 2014), we expect the passive to be used in a more native-like manner in ESL than in EFL. This is because the passive construction is assumed to gradually emerge, with all its (grammatical, discursive, stylistic, lexical and phraseological) features, as a result of exposure to many instances of the construction. ESL learners, with their enhanced exposure to the target language in different domains of everyday life, are therefore expected to have a better command of the passive construction than EFL learners, who receive limited input in the target language in more restricted contexts (mainly instructional ones). Given the marked, non-canonical nature of the passive construction (Huddleston & Pullum, 2002: 46), the degree of exposure should play a particularly important role in the production of the passive, as suggested by Ellis *et al.* (2015: 364): 'Learning the usages that are normal or unmarked from those that are unnatural or marked requires a huge amount of immersion in the speech community'. Finally, since all learner populations are presumably situated differently along the EFL-ESL continuum, we can assume that there will also be some variation between the eight populations under study with respect to how native-like their use of the passive is. Our research questions can be summarized as follows:

RQ1 Do learners of English use the passive in a native-like manner in terms of frequency?
RQ2 Do learners of English use the passive in a native-like manner in terms of lexical preferences?
RQ3 Do learners of English use the passive in a native-like manner in terms of phraseological sequences?
RQ4 Do ESL learners use the passive differently from EFL learners (in terms of frequency, lexical preferences and phraseological sequences)?

RQ1 will involve the comparison of relative frequencies, while RQ2 will examine the passive ratio of individual verbs. RQ3 will rely on the qualitative analysis of some selected phraseological patterns in the passive. Finally, RQ4 will focus more precisely on the comparison between EFL and ESL with respect to all these aspects.

## 5 Data and Methodology

### 5.1 Data

The L2 data were taken from the third version of the International Corpus of Learner English (ICLE; Granger *et al.*, 2020), a corpus made up of (mainly) argumentative texts written by university students from different mother tongue backgrounds. Although ICLE is officially a corpus of EFL, some of its data were collected in more ESL-like contexts (see also Gilquin & Granger, 2011). The choice of ICLE samples for the present study relied on this specificity. Using the ICLE online interface,

**Table 4.1** Breakdown of the corpora, by number of texts and word count

| | Number of texts | Number of words |
|---|---|---|
| **ICLE** | **3,174** | **1,793,680** |
| **EFL** | **1,467** | **860,314** |
| FR | 311 | 203,326 |
| GE | 431 | 229,712 |
| KR | 400 | 224,655 |
| SE | 325 | 202,621 |
| **ESL** | **1,707** | **933,366** |
| DU | 92 | 134,391 |
| HK | 780 | 386,041 |
| NO | 316 | 212,324 |
| TS | 519 | 200,610 |
| **LOCNESS** | **298** | **264,886** |

eight subcorpora were compiled: four representing EFL populations (French-speaking Belgian students [FR], German students [GE], Korean students [KR] and Serbian students [SE]) and four representing ESL-like populations (Dutch-speaking students from the Netherlands [DU], Chinese-speaking Hong Kong students [HK], Norwegian students [NO] and Tswana students [TS]). Two main criteria were applied to select the relevant data, namely students' native language and the institution where the data were collected. For the French subcorpus, for example, we kept only the texts written by students with French as a native language, and among those we excluded three texts that had been collected in institutions outside the French-speaking part of Belgium (one in Spain, one in Sweden and one in the Dutch-speaking part of Belgium). In total, 3,174 texts corresponding to 1,793,680 words were selected for analysis. As a native baseline, we used data from the Louvain Corpus of Native English Essays (LOCNESS), and more precisely the essays written by British and American university students. Taken together, they constitute a corpus of 298 texts and 264,886 words. Table 4.1 shows the breakdown per corpus and, for ICLE, per variety and population. It should be noted that, because of the criteria that were applied, the subcorpora vary in size, from 386,041 words for the ICLE-HK subcorpus to only 134,391 words for the ICLE-DU subcorpus.

## 5.2 Methodology

Our search for passive forms centred around 20 verbs that are often used in the passive voice in expert academic writing. In order to choose these verbs, we searched a part-of-speech (POS) tagged version of the academic component of the BNC Baby, made up of c. 1 million words. All lexical verbs tagged as past participles and immediately following the lemma BE were extracted, together with their frequency in this passive pattern. The 15 most frequent forms were selected for analysis: *considered*, *described*, *found*, *given*, *known*, *made*, *needed*, *provided*, *said*, *seen*, *shown*, *suggested*, *taken*, *used* and *written*. In line with the concept of passive gradient (Section 2.3), we also aimed to investigate passive forms that are usually not taken into consideration in studies of the passive. With this aim in view, we looked for forms ending in *–ed* and tagged as adjectives, immediately preceded by the lemma BE. We selected the 5 most frequent forms in the corpus, namely *concerned*, *interested*, *involved*, *satisfied* and *supposed*. It is interesting to note that the same forms used in similar contexts were sometimes tagged as past participles and sometimes as adjectives. Compare (11), where *given* is tagged as a past participle (VVN), with (12), where it is tagged as an adjective (JJ), despite its clearly verbal nature. This shows that the tagging of forms as either past participles or adjectives in *–ed* is arbitrary at times, which further justifies our decision to also count as passives forms that are tagged as adjectives.

(11) While reading a piece of literature, the audience *is given_VVN* more time to accept the knowledge with which it has been confronted. (LOCNESS)

(12) Because the knowledge is conveyed in a familiar language, through a familiar medium of text, the reader *is given_JJ* time in which to accept his own misconceptions (…) (LOCNESS)

On the basis of a POS tagged version of LOCNESS and ICLE, we extracted all the occurrences of the 20 selected forms preceded by the lemma BE, allowing for the possibility of one word between these two elements.[3] All the concordance lines were examined manually to exclude cases that were clearly not passive constructions, e.g. *It* ***is*** *a* ***given*** *that school uniform will turn into the mainstream medium for connecting to the old memories*. Phrasal verbs (e.g. *Recycling will* ***be given*** *up*) were also discarded on the grounds that they represent different verbs and tend to occur in different phraseological patterns. All the other concordances (765 in LOCNESS and 3,968 in ICLE) were kept for analysis, even cases where the form was more adjectival (e.g. *However, only few managers* ***are concerned*** *about the harmful effects of their business policies*), with the exception of compound adjectives spelled with a hyphen (e.g. *well-known*). This was done to avoid any arbitrary distinction along the passive gradient – one that, moreover, would most probably not correspond to any actual distinction in the learner's mind. All these forms will be referred to in the analysis as passives, with no distinction between central and more peripheral cases.[4]

For each verb in each (sub)corpus, we calculated the relative frequency of the passive (number of occurrences of the passive out of the total number of words in the (sub)corpus). We also computed the passive ratio, which represents the proportion of passive uses out of all the occurrences of the lemma. The passive ratio is normally computed by looking at verbal forms only (see Section 2.2). However, since we also included some forms tagged as adjectives in our analysis, we computed the passive ratio by adding up the verbal and adjectival forms. For *involved* in LOCNESS, for example, we extracted 29 passive forms, of which 10 were tagged as past participles and 19 as adjectives. When searching for the frequency of the lemma INVOLVE, we took account of both INVOLVE as a verb (93 occurrences) and INVOLVED as an adjective (41 occurrences), for a total of 134 occurrences. The passive ratio for INVOLVE in LOCNESS was thus calculated by dividing the sum of the passive forms (29) by the sum of the (verbal and adjectival) lemmas (134), which resulted in a passive ratio of 21.6%. For both frequencies and passive ratios, statistical significance was measured through a chi-square test with Bonferroni correction.

## 6 Passive Frequency

Overall, grouping together the 20 verbs under study, the passive appears to be underused by the learners, with a relative frequency of 221.2 per 100,000 words in our ICLE sample, to be compared with 288.8 in LOCNESS. This underuse is found to characterize both EFL and ESL populations, despite a slightly higher (but not significantly different) frequency in the ESL data (226.2 per 100,000 words) than in the EFL data (215.9 per 100,000 words).

Table 4.2 shows the absolute and relative frequency of the passive in LOCNESS and the different ICLE subcorpora, with the asterisk indicating a statistically significant difference between the ICLE subcorpus and LOCNESS. The highest frequency is found in ICLE-DU and ICLE-FR, which include proportionally more passive verbs than LOCNESS, although the difference is not statistically significant. All the other ICLE subcorpora include proportionally fewer passive verbs than LOCNESS, and all of them, except ICLE-TS, present a significant underuse of the passive in comparison with the native baseline (as signalled by the minus sign).

These results confirm earlier studies that have brought to light a tendency, among learners, to underuse the passive voice (Section 3.2), but they also show that not all learner populations are (equally) affected by this underuse. Interestingly, no clear distinction emerges between the EFL and ESL-like populations: not only is there no statistically significant difference in frequency between the EFL and ESL data (see above), but if we look at the populations with the highest and lowest frequency of

**Table 4.2** Absolute and relative frequency (per 100,000 words) of the passive in LOCNESS and ICLE subcorpora

| Corpus | Absolute frequency | Relative frequency |
|---|---|---|
| ICLE-DU | 417 | 310.3 |
| ICLE-FR | 616 | 303.0 |
| LOCNESS | 765 | 288.8 |
| ICLE-TS | 555 | 276.7 |
| ICLE-SE*- | 472 | 232.9 |
| ICLE-NO*- | 483 | 227.5 |
| ICLE-GE*- | 393 | 171.1 |
| ICLE-HK*- | 656 | 169.9 |
| ICLE-KR*- | 376 | 167.4 |

Note: the asterisk indicates a statistically significant difference between the ICLE subcorpus and LOCNESS; the minus sign indicates a significant underuse.

passives (top and bottom of Table 4.2), we find both types of learners represented (ICLE-DU/ICLE-FR and ICLE-KR/ICLE-HK). This suggests that, contrary to what a usage-based view of language acquisition would predict, differences in the degree of exposure to the target language do not necessarily lead to differences in the frequency of the passive.

While most studies of the passive merely consider its overall frequency, we were particularly interested in possible variation between the different verbs, as a way of measuring the impact of lexis on the use of the passive. The results for the relative frequency revealed striking disparities between certain verbs. In ICLE-TS, for example, which shows no overall difference with LOCNESS, four verbs turn out to be significantly underused in the passive (MAKE, SEE, SHOW, WRITE), whereas three verbs are significantly overused (TAKE, GIVE, PROVIDE). In ICLE-FR, another subcorpus with no overall significant difference in comparison with LOCNESS, three verbs are significantly underused in the passive (USE, SEE, SHOW) and four are significantly overused (FIND, SAY, CONCERN, INTEREST). While two of the overused passive forms in ICLE-FR – CONCERN and INTEREST – are mostly tagged as adjectives in the corpora, it should be emphasized that some of their uses are clearly verbal (e.g. *as far as x* BE *concerned*). Thus, the overuse of these forms does not simply reflect an overuse of adjectives. These differences in the relative frequency of certain passive verbs demonstrate that the passive is not necessarily a grammatical rule that applies across the board, affecting all transitive verbs in the same way. In order to further investigate the lexical aspects of the passive, in the next section we rely on the measure of passive ratio.

## 7 The Lexis-Grammar Interface

### 7.1 The passive ratio

The relative frequency of a verb in the passive could be influenced by the overall frequency of this verb. A passive verb could thus be underused in a learner corpus simply because the verb itself is less often used by the learners (e.g. due to the learners' unfamiliarity with this verb or as a consequence of the topic on which the learners had to write). The passive ratio provides a more reliable measure by taking the overall frequency of the verb into account and by calculating the proportion of passive uses out of all the occurrences (active and passive) of the verb.

The first column of Table 4.3 shows the passive ratio, in descending order, of the 20 verbs under study in LOCNESS. The passive ratios differ widely, from 73.9% for INTEREST to 6.1% for SAY. Interestingly, the verbs with a high passive ratio do not only include forms that were selected via a search for past participles (e.g. CONSIDER, SEE, USE), but also, and even more prominently, forms that were selected via a search for adjectives in *–ed*. This is the case of the top three passives, INTEREST, SUPPOSE and CONCERN; the other two forms chosen among adjectives, namely SATISFY and INVOLVE, are well ranked too, with a passive ratio higher than 20%. Among these forms tagged as adjectives, some have clear adjectival features in most of their occurrences (cf. INTEREST, SATISFY), while others are actually mostly used as verbal forms (cf. SUPPOSE, CONCERN), and yet others combine adjectival and verbal features. This justifies our inclusive

**Table 4.3** Passive ratio of the 20 verbs in LOCNESS and ICLE (in descending order)

| LOCNESS passive ratio (%) | | ICLE passive ratio (%) | |
|---|---|---|---|
| INTEREST | 73.9 | SUPPOSE | 67.9 |
| SUPPOSE | 58.1 | INTEREST | 65.7 |
| CONCERN | 52.9 | CONCERN | 53.3 |
| CONSIDER | 46.2 | DESCRIBE | 33.7*+ |
| SATISFY | 37.5 | SATISFY | 33.3 |
| SEE | 24.1 | CONSIDER | 30.9*- |
| USE | 22.3 | INVOLVE | 19.6 |
| INVOLVE | 21.6 | GIVE | 12.9 |
| GIVE | 16.5 | WRITE | 12.5 |
| NEED | 15.7 | FIND | 12.1 |
| SHOW | 14.8 | USE | 11.4*- |
| DESCRIBE | 13.7 | SEE | 10.4*- |
| WRITE | 12.4 | SAY | 8.5 |
| MAKE | 10.2 | NEED | 7.9*- |
| FIND | 10.0 | SUGGEST | 7.6 |
| SUGGEST | 9.5 | TAKE | 7.5 |
| TAKE | 8.2 | MAKE | 7.1*- |
| PROVIDE | 7.1 | PROVIDE | 7.1 |
| KNOW | 6.9 | SHOW | 6.2*- |
| SAY | 6.1 | KNOW | 5.0 |

Note: the asterisks indicate statistically significant differences and are accompanied by a plus sign for a ratio significantly higher in ICLE than in LOCNESS and a minus sign for a significantly lower ratio.

approach, which consisted in taking both past participles and adjectives in *–ed* into account. This also suggests that the so-called peripheral representatives of the passive may in fact be more central than usually assumed, at least quantitatively speaking.

The comparison of these results with those in the second column of Table 4.3 makes it possible to highlight differences in passive ratio between native and non-native English (the asterisks indicate statistically significant differences and are accompanied by a plus sign for a ratio significantly higher in ICLE than in LOCNESS and a minus sign for a significantly lower ratio). Despite a difference in ranking, the top three forms are the same in LOCNESS and ICLE, and their passive ratios do not differ significantly. Further down the list, the rankings present many more differences, and several verbs in ICLE have a passive ratio that is significantly different from that in LOCNESS. In most cases, this difference corresponds to a lower passive ratio in ICLE (CONSIDER, USE, SEE, NEED, MAKE, SHOW); in only one case does it correspond to a higher passive ratio in ICLE (DESCRIBE). The difference in passive ratio between LOCNESS and ICLE is sometimes quite considerable, with some passive ratios being at least twice as high in one corpus as in the other (cf. DESCRIBE, USE, SEE, NEED, SHOW).

After considering ICLE as a whole, we made a distinction between the ICLE subcorpora corresponding to EFL varieties and those corresponding to ESL-like varieties. Figure 4.1 represents the passive ratio of the different verbs in EFL and ESL, with the line showing the passive ratio in LOCNESS. Few bars in the graph extend far beyond

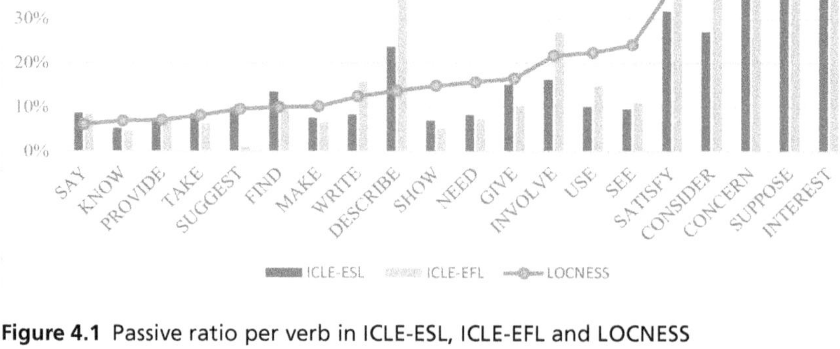


**Figure 4.1** Passive ratio per verb in ICLE-ESL, ICLE-EFL and LOCNESS

the native line. Overall (i.e. all verbs taken together), the passive ratios in both ICLE-EFL (12%) and ICLE-ESL (11.2%) are significantly lower than the passive ratio in LOCNESS (15.6%). DESCRIBE is the only verb whose passive ratio is significantly higher in non-native writing (EFL) than in native writing. While EFL and ESL follow generally similar tendencies, certain verbs display significant differences between EFL and ESL: WRITE, INVOLVE, USE, CONSIDER and CONCERN have significantly higher passive ratios in EFL than in ESL, whereas TAKE, SUGGEST and GIVE have significantly higher passive ratios in ESL than in EFL. It is sometimes EFL that is closer to the native baseline (cf., e.g. FIND), and sometimes it is ESL (cf., e.g. GIVE). It is thus not exactly the case that ESL learners, with their higher exposure to English, display a more native-like behaviour than EFL learners. The picture turns out to be much more nuanced.

Turning now to the specific learner populations, it appears that, besides variation between verbs, there is also inter-varietal variation. Table 4.4 summarizes the results of statistical significance tests comparing, for each verb, the passive ratios in LOCNESS and the individual ICLE subcorpora. A majority of the cells (121 out of 160, i.e. three-quarters) are empty, indicating that there is no statistically significant difference between LOCNESS and the ICLE subcorpus. In 30 cases, a minus sign reveals a significantly lower passive ratio in the ICLE subcorpus, while in 9 cases, a plus sign reveals a significantly higher passive ratio in the ICLE subcorpus. Of the 20 verbs, 5 display no significant differences at all with native English across the ICLE subcorpora, namely INTEREST, PROVIDE, SATISFY, SUGGEST and WRITE. Five other verbs present a significant difference for one subcorpus only: CONCERN in ICLE-FR (+), DESCRIBE in ICLE-SE (+), FIND in ICLE-HK (+), INVOLVE in ICLE-HK (–) and KNOW in ICLE-NO (–). In one case, for the verb SEE, all the ICLE subcorpora present a significantly lower passive ratio in comparison with the native baseline. In the other cases, we see a mixture of non-significant, significantly lower and/or significantly higher results.

On the basis of a list of the exact passive ratios for each verb in LOCNESS (see Table 4.3) and in the different ICLE subcorpora (see Appendix A, Table A.1), a hierarchical cluster analysis was carried out, which made it possible to produce the dendrogram shown in Figure 4.2.[5] The dendrogram provides a general overview of the overall degree of similarity between the different populations. Three significantly distinct clusters emerge from the analysis: one with ICLE-KR and ICLE-HK, another one with ICLE-TS and ICLE-SE, and a third one with the remaining ICLE subcorpora – FR, DU, NO, GE – and the native corpus. Interestingly, all three clusters include at least one EFL variety and one ESL-like variety. This seems to challenge the usage-based prediction that different types and amounts of exposure to the target language

**Table 4.4** Comparison of the passive ratios in the ICLE subcorpora with the native baseline

| Verb | ICLE-EFL | | | | ICLE-ESL | | | |
|---|---|---|---|---|---|---|---|---|
| | FR | GE | KR | SE | DU | HK | NO | TS |
| CONCERN | + | | | | | | | |
| CONSIDER | | – | – | | | – | | |
| DESCRIBE | | | | + | | | | |
| FIND | | | | | | + | | |
| GIVE | | | – | | | – | | + |
| INTEREST | | | | | | | | |
| INVOLVE | | | | | | – | | |
| KNOW | | | | | | | – | |
| MAKE | | | – | – | | – | | |
| NEED | | – | | – | | | – | – |
| PROVIDE | | | | | | | | |
| SATISFY | | | | | | | | |
| SAY | + | | | | + | | | |
| SEE | – | – | – | – | – | – | – | – |
| SHOW | – | – | | | | – | | |
| SUGGEST | | | | | | | | |
| SUPPOSE | | | – | + | | | | |
| TAKE | | | – | | | – | | + |
| USE | | | | – | + | – | | |
| WRITE | | | | | | | | |

should lead to different linguistic behaviours in the L2, but it confirms the results of other multifactorial analyses showing that EFL and ESL do not necessarily cluster in two separate groups (see Section 4). As for closeness to native English, in addition to ICLE-DU and ICLE-NO – two ESL-like varieties –, ICLE-GE and ICLE-FR – two EFL varieties – turn out to cluster with LOCNESS and hence to resemble the native variety most closely. It will also be noticed that this cluster includes three Germanic L1s (Dutch, Norwegian and German). This could be due to the typological closeness of these languages to English, to the language proficiency of these learner populations,[6] or to other factors which cannot be further investigated here but which could outweigh the distinction between EFL and ESL.

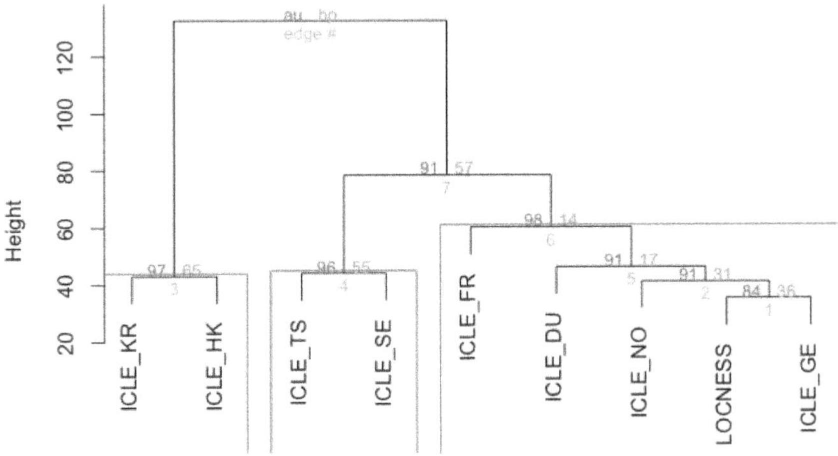


**Figure 4.2** Dendrogram of the hierarchical cluster analysis of passive ratios

Note: AU stands for 'approximately unbiased'; it corresponds to the values on the left. BP stands for 'bootstrap probability'; it corresponds to the values on the right.

## 7.2 Phraseological sequences

Passive verbs have their own phraseologies. For example, they have their preferred collocates (e.g. *an action/a position/a step is taken*) and form (semi-)idiomatic expressions (e.g. *is taken into account/into consideration/for granted*). However, these types of phrasemes are not specific to passive use and do not feature in sufficient numbers with the selected verbs in our corpora. They will therefore not be investigated here. Instead, we investigate two types of patterns that form typical chunk-like passive sequences and are sufficiently frequent to allow for comparisons between the subcorpora. We first focus on passive patterns with the verb CONCERN, one of the verbs that stood out as being significantly overused in only one subcorpus, i.e. ICLE-FR. Our objective is to assess to what extent the overuse of the verb might be explained by its phraseological patterning. We then investigate impersonal *it*-patterns that occur with several of the selected verbs. The analysis centres on the verbs KNOW and SAY, which display sufficient instances of the pattern to allow for meaningful analysis, although in view of the size of the subcorpora, the figures remain quite low. The approach adopted in this section involves a close examination of concordance lines and is therefore essentially qualitative.

### *7.2.1* BE concerned *patterns*

The two main phraseological patterns of BE *concerned* in LOCNESS are BE *concerned with* and *as far as x* BE *concerned*. Together they account for 78% of the occurrences of BE *concerned* in the corpus. The ICLE learners are familiar with these patterns and display relatively similar proportions of use (between 52% and 73%, depending on the subcorpus), except for two populations that clearly stand out. ICLE-HK displays a very low proportion of 11%. This is mainly due to the fact that the Hong Kong learners tend to use BE *concerned* on its own, as illustrated by examples (13) and (14). This finding shows that passive ratio is not all: the Hong Kong learners' passive ratio for CONCERN does not differ quantitatively from the native baseline, but the qualitative analysis reveals that many of the forms are unidiomatic. ICLE-FR, on the other hand, displays a very high proportion of phraseological uses (91%), mainly due to the frequent use of the *as far as x* BE *concerned* pattern, which alone accounts for 80% of the passive uses (vs only 30% in LOCNESS). In the majority of cases (56 out of 90 occurrences) the French-speaking learners use the pattern at the beginning of the sentence as a topic introducer (examples (15) and (16)). Two factors could account for this overuse: form-function mapping from the frequent – albeit active – formula *en ce qui concerne x* in the learners' L1, reinforced by a general tendency among learners to cling on to a limited number of formulae that they feel comfortable with, the so-called 'teddy bear' effect (Hasselgård, 2019; Hasselgren, 1994). It is the overuse of this pattern that accounts for the significantly higher passive ratio of CONCERN in ICLE-FR. If the pattern is excluded, the passive ratio decreases from 82% to 47% and it becomes non-significantly different from LOCNESS. This example therefore highlights the importance of taking both lexical and phraseological factors into account in analyses of the passive.

(13) However, the cost of the railway is one of the matter *being* most *concerned*. (ICLE-HK)
(14) At the same time, the production of importation of cigarette should also *be concerned*. (ICLE-HK)
(15) *As far as* Europe *is concerned*, what we can observe is a marked tendency to specialization (ICLE-FR)
(16) *As far as* the garden *is concerned*, it is divided into two parts (ICLE-FR)

#### *7.2.2 Impersonal* it*-patterns*

The *it*-patterns with KNOW and SAY are instantiated in all the ICLE subcorpora.[7] The proportion of passive uses they represent varies greatly but does not reveal a distinct EFL-ESL divide. The patterns with KNOW are especially common in ICLE-HK and ICLE-SE, where they account for more than half of the passive verb forms (54% and 75% respectively, compared to 8% in LOCNESS). ICLE-HK displays a similar overuse for the pattern with SAY (77%) and also displays more impersonal patterns with SEE and SUGGEST than the other groups. This overuse may be due to teaching. Milton and Freeman (1996: 130) observe that Hong Kong learners are 'taught indiscriminately to mark their discourse with a subset of lexical expressions which are used sparingly, if at all, by native speakers', a practice that can reinforce learners' general tendency to overuse a small set of 'phraseological teddy bears' (Hasselgård, 2019). A similar tendency to overuse the *it can be said* pattern was noted by Allen (2010) for Japanese learners and attributed to L1 transfer (see Section 3.3). Although L1 transfer does not account for the use of this passive pattern by French-speaking learners (French does not have a direct equivalent of *it can be said*), it is clearly a strong potential factor in the use of the corresponding active structure. While ICLE-FR only contains 12 occurrences of the passive pattern with SAY, it contains 125 occurrences of the active *we/you/one* (aux.) *say that* pattern, the most frequently used sequence being *we can/could say that*, a literal translation of the French discourse formula *on peut/pourrait dire que*. This tendency is not shared by the Hong Kong learners, who rarely use the active pattern. This example illustrates the competition that can exist between an active and a passive phraseological pattern, the winner in the case of the French-speaking learners being the active pattern, presumably because of the influence of the corresponding French pattern.

Over and above the number of *it*-patterns, it is interesting to look at their different lexicalizations. Each pattern allows for a great deal of variation but this variation is not infinite: the patterns are not fully prefabricated but keep a degree of prefabrication. Some of the patterns used by the ICLE learners are fully idiomatic (see examples (17) and (18)), while others are much less idiomatic, as illustrated by examples (19) to (22). Such instances tend to show that learners are not yet fully aware of the phraseological nature of these patterns. Their use can thus be described as midway between Sinclair's (1991) 'open-choice principle' and 'idiom principle'.

(17) *it is said* that recycling is an expensive method (ICLE-HK)
(18) *It can be said* that reading is more suitable for people who prefer spending time alone than socializing with others (ICLE-SE)
(19) *It is not said without reason* that once you have a television you got the whole world (...) (ICLE-NO)
(20) *It can be well known* that the target of study is to gain knowledge in the school (ICLE-HK)
(21) *It is wide known* that university degree is the first and basic step in the life of the future (ICLE-SE)
(22) *It has also been clearly seen and studied* that poverty can also cause HIV/AIDS epidemic in Africa (ICLE-TS)

## 8 Conclusion

This chapter has adopted a lexico-grammatical perspective to study the use of the passive (including its less central representatives) by EFL and ESL-like learners. It has revealed an overall underuse of the passive in EFL and ESL, visible among Serbian, Norwegian, German, Hong Kong and Korean learners (RQ1). It has also demonstrated that different verbs display different degrees of attraction towards the passive and that learners do not necessarily have the same lexical preferences as native writers (RQ2). Some verbs (e.g. PROVIDE) are closer to the native baseline than others (e.g. SEE) and some populations (e.g. ICLE-DU) display more native-like lexical preferences than others (e.g. ICLE-HK). In terms of phraseological sequences (RQ3), certain distinctive patterns emerge from the learner corpus data (e.g. *as far as x* BE *concerned* in ICLE-FR), among which some unidiomatic phrases that seem to be the result of both the 'open-choice principle' and the 'idiom principle'. As regards the comparison between EFL and ESL (RQ4), overall they appear to display similar tendencies, most notably the general underuse of the passive. While a few differences have been highlighted (e.g. in the passive ratio of certain individual verbs), these do not necessarily go in the direction predicted by a usage-based perspective, i.e. with the ESL learners using the passive in a more native-like manner than the EFL learners. Several explanations could be put forward to explain these unexpected results. First, they could be explained by the usage-based view itself: ESL learners receive more input, but this input may not be native-like in the first place; it is also likely to be mostly spoken or spoken-like, with relatively few instances of the passive, which is more typical of writing. This underlines the importance of considering the nature of the input in a usage-based perspective. Our results could also be explained by the impact of other factors such as L1 influence, proficiency level, teaching and developmental effects, or date of compilation of the (sub)corpora, which may outweigh the impact of the EFL-ESL continuum. Another possible explanation might be that the ESL-like populations that we have selected display too many traces of EFL and therefore do not differ fundamentally, or in a systematic way, from the EFL populations examined. Our study, however, does not make it possible to test the validity of these explanations. Replication studies are needed to assess the generalizability of our findings, based on different L2 corpora and/or relying on expert rather than novice baseline data, and taking more factors into account.

The study has also brought to light the very important role that lexico-grammar plays in passive constructions, both through the widespread use of forms tagged as adjectives (some of which are actually fully verbal or combine adjectival and verbal features) and through the attraction of certain verbs to the passive voice. The BE passive has traditionally been seen as a purely grammatical phenomenon, unlike the GET passive, whose lexical aspects are often recognized in the literature. Rühlemann (2007: 121), for example, writes the following about the GET passive: 'To be sure, it *is* a grammatical structure, but it is at least equally, if not more so, a lexical structure' (emphasis original). The same, it could be argued, applies to the BE passive. In terms of pedagogical implications, this means that learners should not only (or not mainly) be taught how to construct a passive structure but, as Salazar (2014: 127) puts it, they 'should learn which structures should be used with which words and in which contexts'. More effort should therefore be channelled into the teaching of phraseological aspects of the passive, and the development of tools and methods that can facilitate the acquisition of such aspects. The passive is clearly not the only linguistic structure that could benefit from a lexico-grammatical approach to grammar, but it is undoubtedly a strong candidate to start the ball rolling.

## Appendix A

**Table A.1** Passive ratio of the 20 verbs in ICLE subcorpora (in descending order)

| ICLE-EFL | | | | | | | |
|---|---|---|---|---|---|---|---|
| ICLE-FR | | ICLE-GE | | ICLE-KR | | ICLE-SE | |
| CONCERN | 81.75 | INTEREST | 69.44 | INTEREST | 64.29 | SUPPOSE | 86.84 |
| SUPPOSE | 78.13 | SUPPOSE | 64.10 | CONCERN | 40.54 | DESCRIBE | 59.57 |
| INTEREST | 71.74 | CONCERN | 49.18 | SATISFY | 33.33 | INTEREST | 54.84 |
| CONSIDER | 39.11 | SATISFY | 40.00 | CONSIDER | 28.31 | CONSIDER | 46.85 |
| DESCRIBE | 35.90 | INVOLVE | 29.73 | INVOLVE | 27.03 | CONCERN | 41.67 |
| WRITE | 21.82 | CONSIDER | 25.00 | WRITE | 18.06 | SATISFY | 39.29 |
| SATISFY | 21.43 | USE | 21.82 | SUPPOSE | 15.79 | INVOLVE | 37.93 |
| INVOLVE | 19.30 | PROVIDE | 13.95 | USE | 14.72 | WRITE | 20.00 |
| USE | 18.68 | SEE | 11.15 | DESCRIBE | 14.29 | GIVE | 13.15 |
| FIND | 17.03 | DESCRIBE | 11.11 | NEED | 9.12 | SEE | 9.75 |
| SEE | 14.63 | GIVE | 9.59 | FIND | 8.97 | USE | 9.62 |
| NEED | 13.48 | SAY | 7.74 | GIVE | 8.91 | SAY | 9.22 |
| SAY | 12.68 | FIND | 7.26 | SEE | 6.88 | FIND | 8.91 |
| MAKE | 11.25 | NEED | 6.70 | SHOW | 6.45 | TAKE | 7.96 |
| PROVIDE | 10.34 | KNOW | 6.67 | MAKE | 4.75 | SHOW | 7.20 |
| GIVE | 10.26 | MAKE | 6.40 | SAY | 4.67 | MAKE | 6.32 |
| TAKE | 9.28 | SHOW | 5.52 | PROVIDE | 4.60 | PROVIDE | 4.76 |
| KNOW | 3.90 | TAKE | 4.84 | KNOW | 4.09 | KNOW | 3.59 |
| SUGGEST | 3.85 | WRITE | 2.78 | TAKE | 3.39 | NEED | 2.33 |
| SHOW | 2.58 | SUGGEST | 0.00 | SUGGEST | 0.00 | SUGGEST | 0.00 |

| ICLE-ESL | | | | | | | |
|---|---|---|---|---|---|---|---|
| ICLE-DU | | ICLE-HK | | ICLE-NO | | ICLE-TS | |
| SUPPOSE | 75.00 | INTEREST | 64.00 | SUPPOSE | 72.73 | SUPPOSE | 68.18 |
| INTEREST | 73.91 | CONCERN | 32.41 | INTEREST | 55.00 | INTEREST | 66.67 |
| CONSIDER | 47.78 | SUPPOSE | 27.27 | SATISFY | 53.57 | DESCRIBE | 50.00 |
| CONCERN | 47.37 | FIND | 19.59 | CONCERN | 50.00 | CONCERN | 39.13 |
| SATISFY | 42.86 | CONSIDER | 17.08 | CONSIDER | 34.41 | CONSIDER | 36.00 |
| DESCRIBE | 39.13 | SATISFY | 16.67 | DESCRIBE | 23.08 | INVOLVE | 33.78 |
| USE | 34.72 | SEE | 10.00 | SUGGEST | 17.65 | GIVE | 30.50 |
| INVOLVE | 20.63 | SUGGEST | 10.00 | USE | 17.40 | SATISFY | 24.44 |
| WRITE | 17.14 | NEED | 9.87 | INVOLVE | 13.89 | PROVIDE | 19.23 |
| FIND | 16.67 | KNOW | 9.09 | GIVE | 12.19 | USE | 16.67 |
| SAY | 15.43 | INVOLVE | 7.23 | SHOW | 10.66 | TAKE | 15.58 |
| SEE | 13.46 | GIVE | 6.38 | SAY | 10.24 | SUGGEST | 7.69 |
| NEED | 13.40 | USE | 6.13 | SEE | 10.00 | NEED | 7.42 |
| SHOW | 13.28 | MAKE | 6.00 | FIND | 8.26 | SEE | 6.91 |
| GIVE | 12.50 | PROVIDE | 4.87 | MAKE | 8.20 | FIND | 6.91 |
| PROVIDE | 11.84 | SAY | 4.80 | WRITE | 5.83 | SHOW | 6.25 |
| MAKE | 11.74 | SHOW | 4.26 | NEED | 5.06 | MAKE | 6.14 |
| KNOW | 11.05 | TAKE | 3.95 | TAKE | 4.63 | SAY | 6.08 |
| TAKE | 10.40 | DESCRIBE | 0.00 | PROVIDE | 3.70 | KNOW | 4.63 |
| SUGGEST | 4.35 | WRITE | 0.00 | KNOW | 0.82 | WRITE | 3.23 |

## Notes

(1) http://www.natcorp.ox.ac.uk/corpus/babyinfo.html
(2) It should be noted that we approach the EFL-ESL continuum from the starting point of an EFL corpus (see Gilquin, 2016: 228–235), rather than relying on the comparison of an EFL corpus and an ESL corpus (see Gilquin, 2016: 235–241), which means that we will not cover the full spectrum of the EFL-ESL continuum.
(3) The optimal distance between BE and the *Ved* form was determined by means of a pilot study which compared the number of passive forms retrieved and the amount of noise (i.e. irrelevant hits) in ICLE-FR and ICLE-DU when varying the number of intervening words, from 0 to 3. The results were very similar in both subcorpora, with three-quarters of the data having no intervening words. By allowing for one word between BE and the *Ved* form, it was possible to retrieve 15% more of the data, with very little noise. While allowing for 2–3 intervening words would retrieve 10% more of the data, it would also result in a great number of irrelevant hits, which would have to be discarded manually. Taking one intervening word into account thus seemed to be a good compromise in terms of precision and recall.
(4) It must be emphasized that some passive constructions will not have been retrieved by our procedure: constructions with the GET passive auxiliary, constructions with more than one word between the passive auxiliary and the *Ved* form, passive constructions with no passive auxiliary (e.g. *As argued by...*), with mistagged elements (e.g. a past participle tagged as a past tense) or with non-standard forms (e.g. BE *know*, BE *gaven*).
(5) The hierarchical cluster analysis used the Euclidean distance and the Ward agglomerative method. In the dendrogram, AU stands for 'approximately unbiased' and BP for 'bootstrap probability'. The identification of the significant clusters relied on the AU values. We thank Samantha Laporte for her help with this analysis.
(6) The rating of a random sample of twenty essays per subcorpus according to the Common European Framework of Reference for Languages (see Granger *et al.*, 2020: 12) shows that a majority of the essays in ICLE-DU, ICLE-GE and ICLE-NO are rated as either C1 or C2; the same is true of ICLE-FR. This is to be contrasted with ICLE-KR, ICLE-TS and ICLE-HK, which all have a majority of B2 or lower essays. ICLE-SE is an exception in this respect, since it includes a majority of C1/C2 essays but does not cluster with LOCNESS in the dendrogram.
(7) With one exception: there is no occurrence of the *it*-pattern with KNOW in ICLE-NO.

## References

Allen, D. (2010) Lexical bundles in learner writing: An analysis of formulaic language in the ALESS learner corpus. *Komaba Journal of English Education* 1, 105–127.

Biber, D., Johansson, S., Leech, G., Conrad, S. and Finegan, E. (1999) *Longman Grammar of Spoken and Written English*. Harlow: Pearson.

Bunting, J.D. and Diniz, L. (with Reppen, R.) (2013) *Grammar and Beyond 4*. Cambridge: Cambridge University Press.

Chung, T. (2014) Multiple factors in the L2 acquisition of English unaccusative verbs. *IRAL* 52 (1), 59–87.

Conrad, S. and Biber, D. (2009) *Real Grammar. A Corpus-Based Approach to English*. New York: Pearson.

Cowan, R. (2008) *The Teacher's Grammar of English*. Cambridge: Cambridge University Press.

Diessel, H. (2014) Usage-based linguistics. In M. Aronoff (ed.) *Oxford Bibliographies in 'Linguistics'*. New York: Oxford University Press.

Edwards, A. (2014) The progressive aspect in the Netherlands and the ESL/EFL continuum. *World Englishes* 33 (2), 173–194.

Ellis, N.C., Simpson-Vlach, R., Römer, U., Brook O'Donnell, M. and Wulff, S. (2015) Learner corpora and formulaic language in second language acquisition research. In S. Granger, G. Gilquin and F. Meunier (eds) *The Cambridge Handbook of Learner Corpus Research* (pp. 357–378). Cambridge: Cambridge University Press.
Garner, B.A. (2016) *Garner's Modern English Usage* (4th edn). Oxford: Oxford University Press.
Gilquin, G. (2016) Discourse markers in L2 English: From classroom to naturalistic input. In O. Timofeeva, A.-C. Gardner, A. Honkapohja and S. Chevalier (eds) *New Approaches to English Linguistics: Building Bridges* (pp. 213–249). Amsterdam: Benjamins.
Gilquin, G. and Granger, S. (2011) From EFL to ESL: Evidence from the International Corpus of Learner English. In J. Mukherjee and M. Hundt (eds) *Exploring Second-Language Varieties of English and Learner Englishes: Bridging a Paradigm Gap* (pp. 55–78). Amsterdam: Benjamins.
Görlach, M. (2002) English in Singapore, Malaysia, Hong Kong, Indonesia, the Philippines ... a second or a foreign language? In M. Görlach (ed.) *Still More Englishes* (pp. 99–117). Amsterdam: Benjamins.
Granger, S. (1983) *The Be + Past Participle Construction in Spoken English with Special Emphasis on the Passive*. Amsterdam: Elsevier Science Publishers.
Granger, S. (1997) Automated retrieval of passives from native and learner corpora: Precision and recall. *Journal of English Linguistics* 25 (4), 365–374.
Granger, S. (1998) Prefabricated patterns in advanced EFL writing: Collocations and formulae. In A.P. Cowie (ed.) *Phraseology: Theory, Analysis, and Applications* (pp. 145–160). Oxford: Oxford University Press.
Granger, S. (2013) The passive in learner English: Corpus insights and implications for pedagogical grammar. In S. Ishikawa (ed.) *Learner Corpus Studies in Asia and the World* (pp. 5–15). Kobe: Kobe University, School of Languages and Communication.
Granger, S., Dupont, M., Meunier, F., Naets, H. and Paquot, M. (2020) *The International Corpus of Learner English, Version 3*. Louvain-la-Neuve: Presses universitaires de Louvain.
Gries, S.Th. and Stefanowitsch, A. (2004) Extending collostructional analysis: A corpus-based perspective on 'alternations'. *International Journal of Corpus Linguistics* 9 (1), 97–129.
Hasselgård, H. (2019) Phraseological teddy bears: Frequent lexical bundles in academic writing by Norwegian learners and native speakers of English. In M. Mahlberg and V. Wiegand (eds) *Corpus Linguistics, Context and Culture* (pp. 339–362). Berlin: De Gruyter.
Hasselgren, A. (1994) Lexical teddy-bears and advanced learners: A study into the ways Norwegian students cope with English vocabulary. *International Journal of Applied Linguistics* 4 (2), 237–260.
Hinkel, E. (2002) Why English passive is difficult to teach (and learn). In E. Hinkel and S. Fotos (eds) *New Perspectives on Grammar Teaching in Second Language Classrooms* (pp. 233–260). Mahwah, NJ: Lawrence Erlbaum.
Hinkel, E. (2004) Tense, aspect and the passive voice in L1 and L2 academic texts. *Language Teaching Research* 8 (1), 5–29.
Huddleston, R. and Pullum, G.K. (2002) *The Cambridge Grammar of the English Language*. Cambridge: Cambridge University Press.
Huddleston, R. and Pullum, G.K. (2005) *A Student's Introduction to English Grammar*. Cambridge: Cambridge University Press.
Hyland, K. (2008) As can be seen: Lexical bundles and disciplinary variation. *English for Specific Purposes* 27 (1), 4–21.
Ju, M.K. (2000) Overpassivization errors by second language learners: The effect of conceptualizable agents in discourse. *Studies in Second Language Acquisition* 22 (1), 85–111.
Kondo, T. (2005) Overpassivization in second language acquisition. *IRAL* 43 (2), 129–161.

Larsen-Freeman, D. and Celce-Murcia, M. (with Frodesen, J., White, B. and Williams, H.) (2016) *The Grammar Book: Form, Meaning, and Use for English Language Teachers* (3rd edn). Boston, MA: National Geographic Learning.
Lehmann, H.M. and Schneider, G. (2009) Parser-based analysis of syntax-lexis interactions. In A.H. Jucker, D. Schreier and M. Hundt (eds) *Corpora: Pragmatics and Discourse* (pp. 477–502). Amsterdam: Rodopi.
Milton, J. and Freeman, R. (1996) Lexical variation in the writing of Chinese learners of English. In C. Percy, C. Meyer and I. Lancashire (eds) *Synchronic Corpus Linguistics* (pp. 121–131). Amsterdam: Rodopi.
Möller, V. (2017) *Language Acquisition in CLIL and non-CLIL Settings: Learner Corpus and Experimental Evidence on Passive Constructions*. Amsterdam: Benjamins.
Oshita, H. (2000) *What is happened* may not be what appears to be happening: A corpus study of 'passive' unaccusatives in L2 English. *Second Language Research* 16 (4), 293–324.
Palmer, F.R. (1987) *The English Verb*. Longman Linguistics Library. Harlow: Addison Wesley Longman.
Parrott, M. (2000) *Grammar for English Language Teachers*. Cambridge: Cambridge University Press.
Pullum, G. (2014) Fear and loathing of the English passive. *Language and Communication* 37, 60–74.
Quirk, R., Greenbaum, S., Leech, G. and Svartvik, J. (1985) *A Comprehensive Grammar of the English Language*. London: Longman.
Rautionaho, P., Deshors, S.C. and Meriläinen, L. (2018) Revisiting the ENL-ESL-EFL continuum: A multifactorial approach to grammatical aspect in spoken Englishes. *ICAME Journal* 42, 41–78.
Rowley-Jolivet, E. (2001) Activating the passive: A comparative study of the passive in scientific conference presentations and research articles. *Recherche et pratiques pédagogiques en langues de spécialité. Les Cahiers de l'Apliut* 20 (4), 38–52. http://journals.openedition.org/apliut/4750
Rühlemann, C. (2007) Lexical grammar: The GET-passive as a case in point. *ICAME Journal* 31, 111–127.
Salazar, D. (2014) *Lexical Bundles in Native and Non-native Scientific Writing: Applying a Corpus-based Study to Language Teaching*. Amsterdam: Benjamins.
Shaw, P. and Liu, E.T.K. (1998) What develops in the development of second-language writing? *Applied Linguistics* 19 (2), 225–254.
Simensen, A.M. (2010) English in Scandinavia: A success story. In D. Wyse, R. Andrews and J. Hoffman (eds) *The Routledge International Handbook of English, Language and Literacy Teaching* (pp. 472–483). New York, NY: Routledge.
Sinclair, J. (1991) *Corpus, Concordance, Collocation*. Oxford: Oxford University Press.
Svartvik, J. (1966) *On Voice in the English Verb*. The Hague: Mouton.
Swales, J.M. and Feak, C.B. (2004) *Academic Writing for Graduate Students: Essential Tasks and Skills* (2nd edn). Ann Arbor, MI: University of Michigan Press.
Vince, M. (2008) *Macmillan English Grammar in Context. Advanced*. Oxford: Macmillan Education.
Wang, Y. (2010) Classification and SLA studies of passive voice. *Journal of Language Teaching and Research* 1 (6), 945–949.
Wilson, C.B. (2006) Passing scores and passive voice: A case for quantitative analysis in writing assessment. *Exchanges: The Online Journal of Teaching and Learning in the CSU*.
Xiao, R. (2007) What can SLA learn from contrastive corpus linguistics? The case of passive constructions in Chinese learner English. *Indonesian Journal of English Language Teaching* 3 (1), 1–19.

# Part 3: The Learner Phrasicon: Developmental Approaches

# 5 Phraseological Complexity as an Index of L2 Dutch Writing Proficiency: A Partial Replication Study

Rachel Rubin, Alex Housen and Magali Paquot

## 1 Introduction

Language teaching and assessment in Europe are heavily informed by the Common European Framework of Reference for Languages (CEFR; Council of Europe, 2001), which has been lauded for its potential to increase standardisation and transparency in language education and testing across Europe. The Common Reference Levels (A1-C2) of the CEFR are widely implemented in language certification exams across Europe and are often adopted as entrance requirements, such as in university entrance policies and national residency policies (Deygers *et al.*, 2018). At the same time, the CEFR has also been criticised for the lack of empirical foundations of its proficiency levels and corresponding linguistic competence scales (Alderson, 2007; Hulstijn, 2007), which often fail to address linguistic features that play a demonstrable role in L2 performance and proficiency (Hulstijn *et al.*, 2010).

Linguistic competence is specified within the CEFR as one of the core components of communicative language competence (alongside sociolinguistic competence and pragmatic competence), and is further divided among lexical, grammatical, semantic, phonological, orthographic, and orthoepic competences (Council of Europe, 2001). The accompanying descriptor scales describe linguistic competence in terms of range (general linguistic range and vocabulary range) and control (grammatical accuracy and vocabulary, phonological, and orthographical control), mapping these onto the six common reference levels. The distinction between these two dimensions is intended to reflect 'the need to take account of the complexity of the language used rather than just registering mistakes' (Council of Europe, 2018: 131). Still, complexity as specified in both the lexical and grammatical descriptor scales is vague and does not reflect the extensive findings in second language acquisition (SLA) research linking L2 proficiency and linguistic complexity across various domains of language (e.g. lexis, syntax, morphology) (Housen *et al.*, 2019).

The CEFR description of lexical competence is divided between single word forms and 'fixed expressions', which include sentential formulae (e.g. *How do you do?*), phrasal idioms (e.g. *He kicked the bucket*, *as white as snow*), fixed frames (e.g. *Please may I have…*), phrasal verbs (e.g. *to check out*), and fixed collocations (e.g. *to make a speech/a mistake*). Phraseological units are additionally accounted for, to a limited extent, within the scales for vocabulary range and control. The C2 band of the vocabulary range scale mentions, for example, command of 'idiomatic expressions and colloquialisms' (Council of Europe, 2001: 132). There is some indication that the CEFR has begun to acknowledge the role of lexical co-occurrence phenomena, as the updated description of the lexical competence (vocabulary range and control) mentions the notions of association, collocation, and lexical chunks (Council of Europe, 2018: 134). However, these have not been well incorporated into the descriptor scales. According to the structure of linguistic competence outlined within the CEFR, which adheres to a grammar/lexis divide, phraseological units are situated firmly within the range of the lexicon, where they are treated largely as fixed units. As there is no phraseological competence independently accounted for among the CEFR descriptor scales, linguistic complexity is underrepresented in this domain.

In an investigation of phraseological complexity in L2 English across the B2-C2 CEFR levels, Paquot (2018, 2019) highlights the need for a phraseological competence among the linguistic competences described within the CEFR. Investigations into the use of phraseological units across proficiency levels have demonstrated the importance of phraseological development for L2 proficiency, particularly at the upper-intermediate to advanced levels of proficiency (e.g. Durrant & Schmitt, 2009; Granger & Bestgen, 2014). These findings stem from both the traditional approach to phraseology, characterised by linguistically defined phraseological units often said to be stored as a whole in the mental lexicon, as well as the frequency-based approach, which stresses the importance of patterns of (continuous and discontinuous) co-occurrence for L2 performance and proficiency (cf. Paquot & Granger, 2012). Language assessment rubrics, however, do not yet reflect the role that frequency-based phraseological units (e.g. statistical collocations and lexical bundles) play in L2 acquisition and proficiency, and generally underrepresent the role of phraseology altogether.

From a CEFR-based assessment perspective, the linguistic competences according to which language productions are evaluated are intended to be suitable for cross-linguistic applications. It follows that arguments for the inclusion of linguistic competences and measures thereof need be accompanied by empirical evidence of the cross-linguistic nature of the proposed construct. The study presented in this chapter therefore considers the role of phraseological competence, indicated by means of phraseological complexity measures, in the assessment of L2 Dutch proficiency according to a CEFR-based assessment scheme.

## 2 Phraseological Complexity

The past 20 years have seen an exploration of the use of phraseological units in learner language (Paquot & Granger, 2012). Paquot's (2018, 2019) research agenda draws from quantitative approaches to both phraseology and L2 complexity in order to evaluate the phraseological competence as a central component of linguistic competence alongside the lexical and grammatical competences. Building on Ortega's (2003: 492) definition of linguistic complexity, Paquot defines phraseological complexity as 'the range of phraseological units that surface in language production and the degree of sophistication of such phraseological units' (Paquot, 2019: 124). Paquot's research focuses on the diversity (range) and sophistication of relational co-occurrences (i.e. two lexical units representing an underlying grammatical relation), extracted on the basis of grammatical dependency annotations. To operationalise these two dimensions, Paquot's phraseological measures build on measures of lexical diversity and sophistication. Specifically, the root type-token ratio (RTTR, a variation on the type-token ratio accounting for text length) is used as a measure of phraseological diversity, calculating the number of unique relational co-occurrences (e.g. direct object relations) over the square root of the total number of that type of relational co-occurrence ($T/\sqrt{N}$). Measures of lexical sophistication are typically frequency-based, often measured for example in proportions of words occurring within certain frequency bands derived from compiled word frequency lists. The frequency-based approach to phraseology, operating under similar assumptions regarding frequency of (co-)occurrence patterns in L2 acquisition, offers a phraseological alternative to the lexical frequency measures, namely statistical association measures. As pointwise mutual information (MI) has been shown to bring out word combinations made up of closely associated medium-to-low-frequency words, Paquot (2018, 2019) proposes to use measures derived from MI to gauge phraseological sophistication (see Table 5.1). An alternative approach implemented by Paquot to measure phraseological sophistication relies on an academic collocation list to determine the ratio of academic to non-academic relational co-occurrences.

In a partial replication of Paquot's (2018, 2019) investigation of L2 English writing, the study reported on in this chapter investigates whether phraseological competence also plays a role in the assessment

**Table 5.1** Overview of phraseological diversity and sophistication measures put forth by Paquot (2018, 2019)

| Phraseological Diversity | Phraseological Sophistication |
|---|---|
| Root type-token ratios of grammatical dependencies [T/√N] | Pointwise mutual information (MI) means for three grammatical dependencies:<br>-dobj (verb + direct object)<br>-amod (adjectival modifier + noun)<br>-advmod (adverbial modifier + adjective/verb/adverb) |
| | Proportion of grammatical dependencies in collocational bands (MI-based) |
| | Ratio of academic to total dependencies |

of L2 Dutch writing at the B1 and B2 CEFR levels, which often serve as threshold levels for various language requirements. The present study is guided by the following research questions:

RQ1 To what extent do phraseological complexity measures contribute to the prediction of L2 Dutch writing assessment across the B1 and B2 CEFR levels?
RQ2 How do measures of phraseological complexity compare to traditional measures of grammatical and lexical complexity in the assessment of L2 Dutch written productions?
RQ3 How does phraseological complexity in L2 Dutch assessment compare to the results observed for L2 English in Paquot (2018, 2019)?

## 3 Data

The Dutch learner data analysed here are collected from the written portion of the Certificaat Nederlands als Vreemde Taal (CNaVT; Certificate of Dutch as a Foreign Language), an L2 Dutch certification exam administered by the Centrum voor Taal en Onderwijs (CTO; Center for Language and Education) at the KU Leuven. The CNaVT exams are offered at four levels of the CEFR, ranging from A2 to C1, and cover five domains of language use (i.e. society–informal, society–formal, professional, educational, and educational–professional). The exams are administered at host institutions throughout the world and are evaluated centrally in Belgium according to an evaluation model divided among formal and communicative criteria. For each CNaVT exam, productions are assessed according to rubrics developed for each task, and learners receive an overall pass or fail outcome for the exam based on a combination of their scores for the individual tasks. Table 5.2 provides a concise overview of the distribution of learners across exam level (the present study is restricted to the B1 and B2 levels) and of the size of the corpus components.

**Table 5.2** Distribution of L2 Dutch learners across exam levels

| Exam level | Result | Learners | Tokens | Mean length(SD) |
|---|---|---|---|---|
| **B1** | Pass | 139 (62%) | 31,090 (68%) | 223.67 (47.88) |
| | Fail | 87 (38%) | 14,886 (32%) | 171.10 (54.7) |
| | **Total** | **226** | **45,976** | |
| **B2** | Pass | 698 (69%) | 210,598 (72%) | 301.72 (58.92) |
| | Fail | 318 (31%) | 83,250 (28%) | 261.79 (58.08) |
| | **Total** | **1,016** | **293,848** | |

The majority of the learners (57%) are L1 French speakers from Belgium. The only other L1 groups of notable size are L1 German (17%) and L1 Dutch (9%; heritage speakers). The remaining 17% of learners come from various multilingual language backgrounds. The format of the exam is task-based, and the tasks at each exam level are intended to correspond to communicative settings associated with the domain of language use targeted by each particular exam (the five domains are listed above). For each writing task, the learners were provided with a combined oral and written prompt. The texts analysed here were written in response to three different tasks, one at the B1 exam level (from 2016) and two at B2 (from 2016 and 2017). All three tasks require learners to write a report on the contents of an audio recording and a corresponding text. The topics of the three prompts include: (i) an interview with an author (B1), (ii) a globalisation lecture (B2), and (iii) a lecture about algae (B2). The present study does not take into consideration these task-related variables.

## 4 Methods

### 4.1 Partial replication

In line with the cross-linguistic aims of the CEFR, the present study explores whether phraseological competence is also central in L2 Dutch CEFR-based assessment, in a partial replication of Paquot's (2018, 2019) investigation of phraseological complexity in L2 English. A partial replication design allows for the evaluation of the generalisability of our research findings through the manipulation of (one or more) elements of the original research design (Porte, 2012). Preserving the original research questions and methodology, the present study targets learners of a different target language (i.e. Dutch), at a lower cross-section of the proficiency spectrum (B2-C2 for L2 English and B1-B2 for L2 Dutch here). The extraction of phraseological units and the computation of phraseological complexity measures in the present study follow the procedures outlined by Paquot (2018, 2019). The selection of complexity measures is limited by the availability of Dutch-language natural language processing (NLP) tools, but the core dimensions of complexity measured by Paquot have been represented here (i.e. syntactic: length and elaboration; lexical: diversity and sophistication; and phraseological: diversity and sophistication). More detailed information about the choice of complexity measures in the present study is presented in Sections 4.3 and 4.4.

## 4.2 Corpus pre-processing

All text files were automatically lemmatised, part-of-speech (POS) tagged, and annotated with grammatical dependencies using the Alpino dependency parser for Dutch (van Noord, 2006). The texts were not corrected for orthographic or grammatical errors, but recent research using the same Dutch-language NLP tools as the present study to process L2 Dutch data found that 'correcting the texts did not significantly alter the complexity measures' (Bulon *et al.*, 2017: 11).

The statistical association measure, MI, implemented in the measures of phraseological sophistication, is computed on the basis of the LASSY Groot corpus (van Noord *et al.*, 2006), a Dutch reference corpus of over 500 million tokens covering a range of text genres. The LASSY Groot corpus is available pre-annotated with POS-tags and dependency relations, following the same NLP pipeline as the learner data. The linguistic annotations in the reference corpus are stored in XML structure, and the dependency triples were therefore extracted using XQuery scripts following the procedure outlined in Bouma and Kloosterman (2007). The same transformation from the dependency triples (see Table 5.3) to the desired format for the dependency relations was carried out on the dependencies extracted from LASSY Groot and the learner texts. This procedure included some further annotation to distinguish between various modifier relations. Adverbial modifier relations include adverb + verb (*snel* + *loop*; 'fast' + 'walk'), adverb + adjective (*erg* + *snel*; 'very' + 'fast'), and adverb + adverb (*heel* + *erg*; 'very' + 'very') combinations; due to low frequencies of adverbial modifiers per text, it was not possible to consider these relations individually. Frequency counts were then calculated for three target dependency relations extracted from the reference corpus, i.e. direct object, adjectival modifier, and adverbial modifier relations (following Paquot, 2018, 2019). Lastly, these dependencies were formatted according to the specified input format for the Ngram Statistics Package (NSP;

**Table 5.3** Stages of formatting dependency relations. Example: direct object dependency *krijg* + *boete* ('get' + 'fine')

| Alpino output – dependency triples | Dependency relation | NSP input |
|---|---|---|
| krijg/[0,1]\|verb\|hd/obj1\|boete/ [2,3]\|noun\|p.1.s.1 | dobj(krijg+verb, boete+noun) | krijg<>boete<>3804 433234 10513 |

Banerjee & Pedersen, 2003), which was used to compute MI scores for the dependencies extracted from LASSY Groot. MI scores were assigned to dependencies extracted from the learner corpus on the basis of the LASSY Groot dependencies. A comparison of the three stages of formatting is presented in Table 5.3 for the direct object dependency *krijg* + *boete*, which translates to 'get' + 'fine' (as in, *He parked his car illegally and got a fine*).

### 4.3 Grammatical and lexical complexity measures

Traditional measures of grammatical and lexical complexity were computed using the T-Scan tool for Dutch text analysis (Pander Maat *et al.*, 2014). The tool takes as input raw text files and outputs a CSV file with values for more than 400 measures of text quality, many of which are commonly implemented as complexity metrics. The grammatical and lexical measures included in this analysis were chosen with consideration for: (i) comparability with the measures investigated in Paquot (2018, 2019), and (ii) the underlying constructs that the measures are intended to tap into. Recent L2 complexity research has placed emphasis on expanding the traditionally 'reductionist' approach to measuring L2 complexity, which focuses primarily on syntactic elaboration and lexical diversity (Housen *et al.*, 2019). Without a large body of L2 Dutch complexity research to inform the present study, the measures included here are intended to tap into various proposed dimensions of complexity (see Table 5.4 for a list of grammatical and lexical complexity measures).

The set of syntactic complexity measures chosen here includes global measures (such as length of production), common measures of sentential elaboration (i.e. subordination and coordination), developmental indices based on patterns of first language acquisition (D-level[1]), fine-grained measures targeting specific grammatical constructions (e.g. nominalisations and passive forms), and measures operationalising dependency distance (i.e. the distance between a head and a dependent within a dependency grammar framework, which is linked to the presence of various modifying structures and the structural complexity thereof) (see Table 5.4). Morphological complexity has been demonstrated to correlate with L2 proficiency in morphologically richer languages (e.g. De Clercq & Housen, 2019), and one measure of morphological complexity computed by T-Scan has therefore been included in the analysis (morphemes per word). This combination of grammatical measures is felt to be sufficiently varied, not overly redundant, and incorporates both large- and fine-grained measures, situating this analysis well within contemporary L2 complexity research (Housen *et al.*, 2019).

While the measures proposed to gauge syntactic complexity are quite varied, most measures of lexical complexity center around two of its most widely researched subcomponents, namely lexical

**Table 5.4** Grammatical and lexical complexity measures computed in the present analysis

| Grammatical measures | | Lexical measures | |
|---|---|---|---|
| Morphological measures | | *Sophistication (frequency-based)* | Lemma frequency logarithm (excluding names) |
| | Morphemes per word | | Proportion of content words among the 1,000 most frequent words |
| Syntactic measures | | | |
| *Length* | Words per sentence<br>Words per clause | | Proportion of content words among the 5,000 most frequent words |
| *Elaboration* | Number of finite clauses per sentence<br>Number of clauses per sentence<br>Multiple finite embeddings<br>Multiple embeddings | *Diversity* | TTR lemmas<br>MTLD lemmas<br>TTR content words<br>MTLD content words |
| | Coordinated main clauses<br>Coordinated subordinate clauses | *Density* | Density of content words<br>Density of compositional nominal compounds |
| *Developmental* | D-level (developmental level)<br>Proportion of sentences with D-level above 4 | *Length* | Corrected word length in letters for nouns |
| *Specific structures* | Density of nominalisations<br>Density of passive forms<br>Density of adverbial modifiers<br>Density of adjectival modifiers | | |
| *Dependency distance (in words)* | Verb and subject<br>Verb and direct object<br>Noun and article<br>Verb and head of verbal complement<br>Verb and separable particle<br>Average dependency distance | | |

diversity and sophistication. Diversity measures computed by T-Scan include TTR (type-token ratio) and MTLD (measure of textual lexical diversity), computed on the basis of words, lemmas, names, and content words (lemmas and content words were chosen over words and names). Frequency-based measures are one of the most traditional operationalisations of lexical sophistication (Kyle & Crossley, 2016). Three frequency-based measures are included in the present analysis: the lemma frequency logarithm (base 10), the proportion of content words among the 1,000 most frequent words, and the proportion of content words among the 5,000 most frequent words. Additional lexical complexity measures computed for this data set include density measures (of content words and of compositional nominal compounds) and one measure of length: corrected word length for nouns.

## 4.4 Phraseological complexity measures

Phraseological diversity and sophistication are investigated using measures outlined in Paquot (2018, 2019), and a complete list can be

**Table 5.5** Phraseological complexity measures computed in the present analysis

**Phraseological measures**

| **Diversity** | **Sophistication (MI-based)** | |
|---|---|---|
| Root type-token ratio [T/√N] for direct object dependencies | **Mean:** | MI mean direct object dependencies<br>MI mean adjectival modifier dependencies<br>MI mean adverbial modifier dependencies |
| Root type-token ratio [T/√N] for adjectival modifier dependencies | **IQR:** | MI IQR direct object dependencies<br>MI IQR adjectival modifier dependencies<br>MI IQR adverbial modifier dependencies |
| Root type-token ratio [T/√N] for adverbial modifier dependencies | **Collocational bands:** | Proportion of target dependencies in each of the following collocational bands:<br>Below threshold (< 5 occurrences in reference corpus)<br>Non-collocational (MI < 3)<br>Collocational: low (3 ≤ MI < 5)<br>Collocational: medium (5 ≤ MI < 7)<br>Collocational: high (7 ≤ MI) |

consulted in Table 5.5. For phraseological diversity, the root type-token ratio (RTTR) is computed for each of the three target dependency relations (direct object, adjectival modifier, adverbial modifier) as the distinct types of each target dependency over the square root of the total number of occurrences of the target dependency. The MI scores computed in the corpus pre-processing procedure serve as the basis for the various phraseological sophistication measures. The mean MI score and the MI IQR (interquartile range) are calculated for each learner text using in-house R scripts (R Core Team, 2017), respectively measuring the average MI score of each target dependency per text and the spread of MI scores for each target dependency per text. Mean MI and MI IQR measures were computed on the basis of all dependencies extracted from a text (for each of the three target dependencies), and also excluding dependencies occurring fewer than five times in the reference corpus (i.e. 'below threshold' dependencies). The remaining measures of phraseological sophistication operationalise the proportion of target dependencies that fall within a certain range of MI scores. The collocational bands start from the 'below threshold' dependencies, which occur less than five times in the reference corpus, increasing incrementally across in total five bands of collocation strength. These measures were all adopted directly from Paquot (2018, 2019) with the exception of the MI IQR measures, which have been included here to account for the variation in the sophistication of the phraseological units used by learners.

## 4.5 Statistical analysis

The research questions outlined in Section 2 are investigated by means of multifactorial regression modelling, where the assessment of

L2 proficiency (represented by the binary pass/fail outcome variable) is modelled as a linear combination of the linguistic complexity measures computed. With this approach, we gain an understanding of the components of complexity that were prominent in the assessment of proficiency at both CEFR levels. RQ1 and RQ2 are directly addressed in the output of the binary logistic regression model: the extent to which phraseological complexity measures can contribute to the prediction of the pass/fail outcome of the B1 and B2 CNaVT exams is inferred from the significance and effects of these predictors in the model. The significance and effects of these measures are compared with that of the grammatical and lexical complexity measures to address RQ2. The results of this analysis are then compared with the results reported by Paquot (2018, 2019) in order to determine the cross-linguistic effectiveness of phraseological complexity measures, corresponding to RQ3.

The measures of lexical, syntactic, morphological, and phraseological complexity presented in Sections 4.3 and 4.4 were explored for normality. Variables exhibiting a non-normal distribution were transformed to approximate the normal distribution (by means of the log2, logit, or square-root transformations, see Table 5.6). Complexity measures were explored in a correlation matrix for potential multicollinearity issues. Variables exhibiting moderate to high degrees of collinearity (Pearson's $r \geq .7$) were removed from the analysis, on a case-by-case basis (preference was given to variables demonstrating a clear relationship with the pass/fail outcome, and that were not collinear with additional variables). From the collocational-band measures of phraseological sophistication, one measure per target dependency (direct object, adjectival modifier, adverbial modifier) was selected as these variables are compositional (i.e. they represent proportions of a whole) and should not be (directly) included together in the model (Hron *et al.*, 2012).[2] In order to avoid overfitting, TTR of lemmas was excluded, as MTLD of lemmas is a variation on the TTR and demonstrated a stronger relationship with the outcome variable. At this stage, 25 of the original 54 measures remained. Interaction terms between the numeric predictors (complexity measures) and the binary CEFR level of the exam (B1 and B2) were also entered into the model in order to identify complexity measures with a different effect across the two CNaVT exams. Predictors in the model were further selected in a stepwise selection procedure using the likelihood-ratio test (LRT) as a model comparison criterion. The statistical analysis was carried out in R (R Core Team, 2017).

## 5 Results

Here we present the results of a binary multiple logistic regression that models the pass/fail outcome of B1 and B2 CNaVT exams as a

**Table 5.6** Description of variables included in final regression model

| Variable name | Description |
|---|---|
| Pass/fail | Pass/fail outcome variable |
| CEFR | CEFR level (B1 or B2) |
| Morphemes_word | Morphemes per word (excluding names) |
| Proportion_freq5000 | Proportion of content words among the 5,000 most frequent words |
| MTLD_lemma | MTLD of lemmas |
| MI_mean_dobj | Mean MI for dobj dependencies (excluding 'below threshold') |
| MI_mean_amod | Mean MI for amod dependencies (excluding 'below threshold') |
| MI_mean_advmod | Mean MI for advmod dependencies (excluding 'below threshold') |
| RTTR dobj | RTTR of dobj dependencies |
| RTTR advmod | RTTR of advmod dependencies |
| Dobj_high_MI | Proportion of dobj with high MI (square root) |
| Amod_high_MI | Proportion of amod with high MI (logit) |
| Words_sentence | Words per sentence (log2) |
| Coord_subclause | Coordinated subclauses (square root) |
| D-level_4 | Proportion of sentences with D-level ≥ 4 (logit) |
| Nominalisations | Density of nominalisations (square root) |
| Passives | Density of passives (square root) |
| DD_SV | Dependency distance (DD) between subject and verb (log2) |
| DD_AN | DD between article and noun (log2) |
| DD_VVC | DD between verb and head of verbal complement (square root) |
| **Interactions** | |
| CEFR:Morphemes_word | CEFR and Morphemes per word |
| CEFR:Proportion freq5000 | CEFR and Proportion of content words among the 5,000 most frequent words |
| CEFR:MTLD_lemma | CEFR and MTLD of lemmas |
| CEFR:RTTR_advmod | CEFR and TTR of advmods |
| CEFR:Amod_high_mi | CEFR and Proportion of amods with high MI (logit) |
| CEFR:Words_sentence | CEFR and Words per sentence (log2) |
| CEFR:D-level_4 | CEFR and Proportion of sentences with D-level ≥ 4 (logit) |
| CEFR:Nominalisations | CEFR and Density of nominalisations (square root) |

linear function of the complexity measures remaining after the variable selection procedure. The formula of the final model is the following:

formula = Pass/fail ~ CEFR + Morphemes_word + Proportion_freq5000 + MTLD_lemma + MI_mean_dobj + MI_mean_amod + MI_mean_advmod + RTTR_dobj + RTTR_advmod + Dobj_high_MI + Amod_high_MI + Words_sentence + Coord_subclause + D-level_4 + Nominalisations + Passives + DD_SV + DD_AN + DD_VVC + CEFR:Morphemes_word + CEFR:Proportion_freq5000 + CEFR:MTLD_lemma + CEFR:RTTR_advmod + CEFR:Amod_high_MI + CEFR:Words_per_sentence + CEFR:D-level_4 + CEFR:Nominalisations

As can be seen in the formula above, the final regression model consists of 19 predictor variables and eight interaction terms (a list of these measures can be found in Table 5.6). Reducing the predictors any further did not improve the fit of the model to the dataset (based on the Akaike Information Criterion, AIC). The output of the model is presented in Table 5.7. The pseudo-$R^2$ measure presented here (Nagelkerke's $R^2 = .38$) indicates a moderate improvement over the null model. As binary logistic regression approaches aim to accurately classify levels of a binary variable while accounting for a range of explanatory variables, we can also consider the classification/prediction accuracy of our model by comparing predicted outcomes to observed outcomes. Overall classification accuracy for the model presented here is 76%, while precision and recall are 79% and 87% respectively (F1 score = 84%). This model significantly ($p < .01$) outperforms both the random baseline (57%) as well as a more conservative baseline (68%), which corresponds to the proportion of observations associated with the more frequent level of the dependent variable. With a closer look, it is clear that the model predicts more accurately for the pass level of the dependent variable than for the fail level (i.e. the reference level); this is most probably related to the fact that the pass level of the dependent variable is more frequent in this data set and is therefore more likely to be predicted accurately (as these cases have had a greater influence on the model).

The standardised intercept (standardised coefficients are represented by $\beta$ in Table 5.7) indicates this greater baseline chance of passing the exam ($\beta = 1.45$, on the log odds scale where 0 = equal likelihood of both levels of the dependent variable) as opposed to failing. Predictors with a positive regression coefficient ($\beta$ = standardised; B = unstandardised) contribute to the likelihood of predicting the pass level of the dependent variable, while predictors with a negative regression coefficient detract from this likelihood. Here we will stick to the standardised coefficients to present the results of the analysis, as these are measured in standard deviation units which can be compared across the varying scales of the predictors.[3] Odds ratios (O.R. in Table 5.7) for each coefficient are presented for ease of interpretation: a 0 on the log odds scale (ranging from $-\infty$ to $+\infty$) corresponds to a 1 on the odds scale (ranging from 0 to $+\infty$). Negative coefficients on the log odds scale and values from 0 to 1 on the odds scale detract from the likelihood of predicting the pass level of the dependent variable while positive coefficients on the log odds scale and values > 1 on the odds scale increase the likelihood of predicting the pass level (see Gries, 2013: 300 for more on the log odds and odds scales).

In what follows, we present the effects of the various complexity measures in the model in terms of the predicted effect on the likelihood of passing the exam. We begin first with the interaction effects, because these will determine how we interpret the main effects. When

**Table 5.7** Binary multiple logistic regression model summary

**Model fit:**

| Model $\chi^2(27) = 378.88$, p < .01 | | | | Nagelkerke's $R^2$:.38 | | |
|---|---|---|---|---|---|---|
| **Predictors** | **B** | **S.E.** | $\beta$ | **O.R.** | **z** | **Pr(>\|z\|)** |
| Intercept** | −15.98 | 5.46 | 1.45 | 4.24 | −2.93 | <.01 |
| CEFR_B2 | 0.34 | 6.33 | −0.38 | 0.69 | 0.05 | .96 |
| Morphemes_word | −1.56 | 2.9 | −0.1 | 0.91 | −0.54 | 0.59 |
| Proportion_freq5000 | −0.23 | 2.65 | −0.02 | 0.98 | −0.09 | 0.93 |
| MTLD_lemma | −0.03 | 0.02 | −0.37 | 0.69 | −1.57 | 0.12 |
| MI_mean_dobj** | 0.34 | 0.08 | 0.09 | 1.45 | 4.13 | <.01 |
| MI_mean_amod* | 0.15 | 0.08 | 0.19 | 1.21 | 2 | 0.05 |
| MI_mean_advmod** | 0.71 | 0.16 | 0.38 | 1.46 | 4.35 | <.01 |
| RTTR_dobj** | 0.56 | 0.13 | 0.44 | 1.55 | 4.26 | <.01 |
| RTTR_advmod** | 1.44 | 0.36 | 1.24 | 3.45 | 4 | <.01 |
| Dobj_high_MI* | 1.29 | 0.52 | 0.19 | 1.21 | 2.48 | <.05 |
| Amod_high_MI | −0.55 | 0.34 | −0.53 | 0.59 | −1.61 | 0.11 |
| Words_sentence* | 1.85 | 0.72 | 0.60 | 1.83 | 2.56 | <.05 |
| Coord_subclause* | 1.06 | 0.42 | 0.23 | 1.26 | 2.53 | <.05 |
| D-level_4 | −0.57 | 0.31 | −0.43 | 0.65 | −1.85 | 0.06 |
| Nominalisations | 0.13 | 0.16 | 0.27 | 1.31 | 0.82 | 0.41 |
| Passives** | 0.22 | 0.06 | 0.3 | 1.35 | 3.76 | <.01 |
| DD_SV** | 1 | 0.28 | 0.32 | 1.38 | 3.63 | <.01 |
| DD_AN | 0.83 | 0.51 | 0.15 | 1.17 | 1.64 | 0.1 |
| DD_VVC | −0.42 | 0.22 | −0.14 | 0.87 | −1.88 | 0.06 |
| CEFR_B2:Morphemes_word | 5.75 | 3.47 | 0.35 | 1.28* | 1.66 | 0.1 |
| CEFR_B2:Proportion_freq5000 | 6 | 3.13 | 0.47 | 1.57 | 1.91 | 0.06 |
| CEFR_B2:MTLD_lemma** | 0.05 | 0.02 | 0.68 | 1.36 | 2.69 | <.01 |
| CEFR_B2:RTTR_advmod* | −0.95 | 0.37 | −0.81 | 1.54 | −2.53 | <.05 |
| CEFR_B2:Amod_high_MI | 0.62 | 0.35 | 0.6 | 1.07 | 1.77 | 0.08 |
| CEFR_B2:Words_sentence* | −1.98 | 0.79 | −0.65 | 0.95 | −2.51 | <.05 |
| CEFR_B2:D-level_4 | 0.53 | 0.34 | 0.4 | 0.97 | 1.55 | 0.12 |
| CEFR_B2:Nominalisations* | −0.37 | 0.18 | −0.76 | 0.61 | −2.1 | <.05 |

Note: B = coefficient; S.E. = standard error (for unstandardised coefficients); $\beta$ = standardised coefficient; O.R. = odds ratio (odds ratios of interaction terms are calculated as follows: $e^{(\beta_1 + \beta_2)}$); z = z-statistic; Pr(>|z|) = p-value.
* = significant at p < .05
** = significant at p < .01

a significant interaction is identified between a predictor and the CEFR level, the effect of the variable will differ between the two CEFR levels. Four interaction effects emerge as significant (indicated with asterisks in Table 5.7) in the final model in addition to eight main effects.

Section 5.1 presents the effects of the phraseological measures in the model and Section 5.2 presents the effects of the lexical and syntactic measures.

## 5.1 Phraseological complexity measures

There is one significant interaction effect among the phraseological complexity measures, namely CEFR:RTTR of advmod dependencies. When the CEFR level of the exam is B1, each standardised unit increase in the RTTR of advmod dependencies is associated with a factor 3.45 increase (245%) in the odds of predicting the pass level of the dependent variable. However, when the CEFR level of the exam is B2, each unit increase in the RTTR of advmods is only associated with a factor 1.54 increase (54%) in the odds of predicting the pass level. Put differently, an increase in the RTTR of advmod dependencies results in a nearly five times larger increase in the likelihood of predicting the pass level of the outcome variable for the B1 exam compared with the B2 exam. The different effect of RTTR of advmods on the prediction of the pass/fail outcome variable across the B1 and B2 CNaVT exams is presented graphically in Figure 5.1. An additional five measures of phraseological complexity emerged as significant main effects in the final model: mean MI of dobj dependencies, mean MI of amod dependencies, mean MI of advmod dependencies, RTTR of dobj dependencies, and Proportion of dobj dependencies with high MI.

The measure of phraseological complexity with the largest effect is the interaction effect of RTTR of advmods described above. A unit

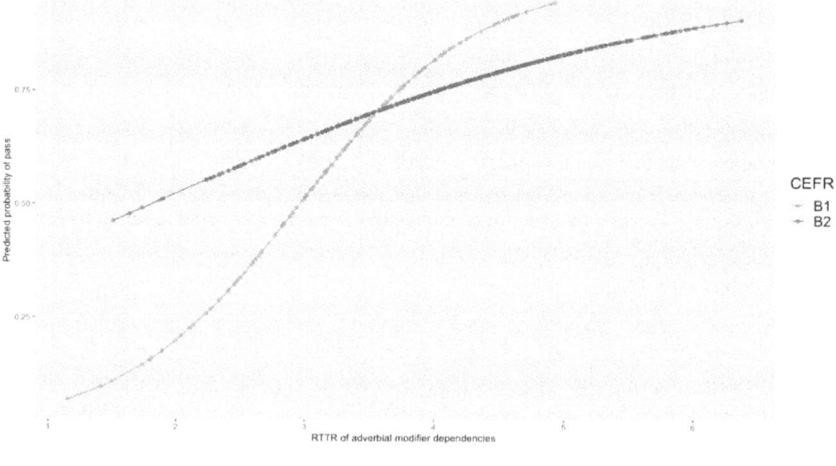


**Figure 5.1** Effect plot for RTTR of adverbial modifier dependencies

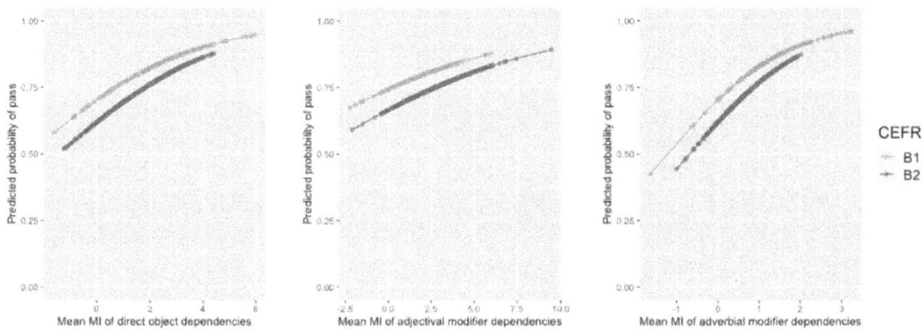


**Figure 5.2** Effect plots for mean MI of all target dependencies

increase in the remaining phraseological complexity indices is associated with an increase by a factor of between 1.21 (21%) and 1.55 (55%) in the odds of predicting the pass level. The effects of the mean MI score (phraseological sophistication) for the three target dependencies on the predicted probability of the pass level of the outcome variable are presented graphically in the effect plots in Figure 5.2. The mean MI score of each target dependency has a similar effect across both CEFR levels, although the slope is steepest for the adverbial modifier relations, representing a stronger effect on the outcome variable.

## 5.2 Lexical and syntactic complexity measures

Significant interaction effects can be identified between the CEFR level of the exam and one lexical measure (MTLD of lemmas), as well as two syntactic measures (Words per sentence and Density of nominalisations). At the B1 CEFR level, a unit increase in the MTLD of lemmas leads to a decrease in the odds of predicting the pass level (though this effect is not significant), while at the B2 level, this leads to an increase in the odds. A unit increase in Words per sentence is associated with a factor 1.83 (83%) increase in the odds of predicting the pass level at the B1 CEFR level, and a factor .95 (5%) decrease in the odds of predicting the pass level at the B2 level (Figure 5.3). The final significant interaction is between CEFR level and Density of nominalisations, which is associated with an increase in the odds of predicting the pass level at B1 (not significant) and a decrease at B2, per unit increase in the predictor scale.

An additional three measures of syntactic complexity exhibited significant main effects: Coordinated subclauses, Density of passives, and Dependency distance between a subject and verb. The effects of these three predictors (measured in change in odds of predicting pass

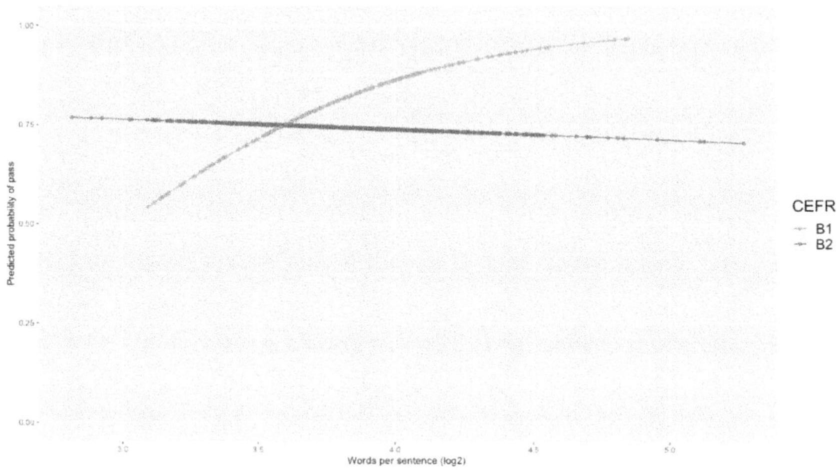


**Figure 5.3** Effect plot for Words per sentence

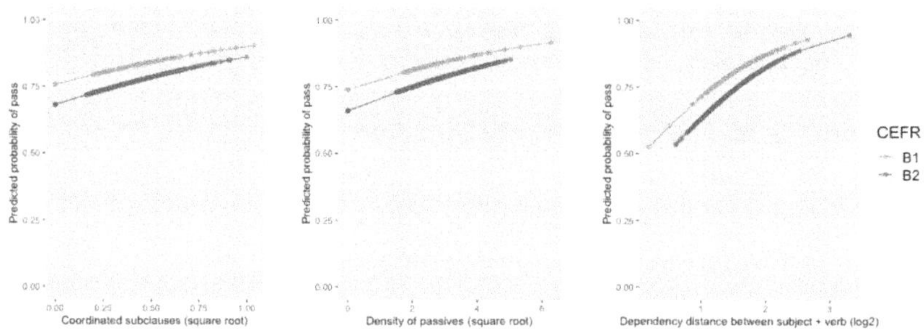


**Figure 5.4** Effect plots for main effects of syntactic complexity measures

level per unit increase of predictor) range from an increase by a factor of 1.26 (26%) to 1.38 (38%) (see Figure 5.4). Similar to the trends observed in Figure 5.2 for the phraseological measures, the effects of the three syntactic measures presented in Figure 5.4 are stable across CEFR level. The measure of dependency distance between subject and verb demonstrates a steeper slope, reflecting a larger effect on the outcome.

## 6 Discussion

In this section, the research questions presented in Section 2 are revisited and discussed in light of the results presented in Section 5. In order to address RQ3, which deals with the cross-linguistic performance of phraseological complexity measures, the results obtained in the present analysis are compared with results from Paquot's (2018, 2019) investigations into phraseological complexity in L2 English.

## 6.1 RQ1: Phraseological complexity and L2 Dutch assessment

The output of the regression model, presented in Section 5, indicates the prominent role of measures of both phraseological diversity and sophistication in the prediction of the pass/fail outcome variable. Specifically, we have identified five significant main effects, and one significant interaction effect, of these measures in the final model. Among these measures, the largest observed effects are for the measures of phraseological diversity (RTTR of advmod and dobj dependencies), although the effect of RTTR of advmods is significantly larger for the B1 exam than for the B2 exam (see Figure 5.1). More tangibly, this result highlights a relationship between the range of adverbial modifiers (e.g. *vrijwel* + *onmogelijk*; 'nearly' + 'impossible') and verb + direct object dependencies (e.g. *publiceer* + *onderzoeksresultaat*; 'publish' + 'research_results') used by the learners and the assessment of learner proficiency. Measures of mean MI score for each of the three target dependencies exhibit significant main effects, associated with increases by a factor of 1.21 (21%) to 1.46 (46%) in the odds of predicting the pass level of the dependent variable, for each unit increase in the standardised predictor scales. Thus, not only does the diversity of phraseological units contribute to a greater likelihood of a positive proficiency evaluation, but also the sophistication of these units (i.e. the association strength between the constituent parts of the unit, measured in MI). Examples of each of the three target dependencies can be consulted in Table 5.8 (MI > 6 upper half; MI < 1 lower half). As expected, dependencies with a lower MI score tend to consist of more high-frequency individual lexical items than dependencies with a higher MI score. For example, as verbal heads of low-MI adverbial modifier relations, we encounter the high-frequency verbs *maken* (in *nieuw* + *maak*; 'new' + 'make') and *doen* (in *kwalitatief* + *doe*; 'qualitatively' + 'do').

To contextualise the results further, Table 5.9 presents all verb + direct object dependencies extracted from both a passing and a failing B2 CNaVT text. Overall, the Pass text exhibits more verb + direct object dependencies that are on average more sophisticated than the units extracted from the Fail text. In terms of diversity, the two texts are similar in that they do not contain any recurring verb + direct object dependencies. However, they are also very different in the range of dependency types used by the two learners (30 for the pass text and 7 for the fail text), a characteristic that is reflected in their respective RTTR values.[4] In terms of sophistication, the Pass text exhibits a higher average MI value (for dependencies occurring at least five times in the reference corpus) than the Fail text, which has a negative MI mean. The Pass

**Table 5.8** Examples of target dependencies extracted from CNaVT texts with low and high MI scores

**MI > 6**

| dobj | amod | advmod |
|---|---|---|
| *Stoot_uit + CO2* ('emit' + 'CO2'); | *alternatief + brandstof* ('alternative'+ 'fuel'); | *jammer + genoeg* ('unfortunate'+ 'enough'); |
| *activeer + hersengebieden* ('activate' + 'brain areas'); | *tropisch + regenwoud* ('tropical' + 'rainforest'); | *'normaal' + 'gezien'* ('normally' + 'seen'); |
| *vaar + bootje* ('sail' + 'boat_diminutive'); | *communicatief + vaardigheid* ('communicative' + 'skill'); | *vrijwel + onmogelijk* ('nearly' + 'impossible'); |
| *laat_door + zonnestraal* ('let_through' + 'sunshine'); | *hernieuwbaar + energie* ('renewable' + 'energy'); | *ernstig + ziek* ('severely' + 'ill'); |
| *scan + hersenen* ('scan' + 'brain'); | *onderscheidend + kenmerk* ('distinguishing' + 'feature'); | *absoluut + noodzakelijk* ('absolutely' + 'necessary'); |
| *ga_tegen + opwarming* ('prevent' + 'warming'); | *hellenistisch + periode* ('Hellenistic' + 'period'); | *deels + aangeleerd* ('partly' + 'learned'); |
| *los_op + probleem* ('solve' + 'problem'); | *industrieel + revolutie* ('industrial' + 'revolution'); | *bijna + allemaal* ('nearly' + 'all') |
| *publiceer + onderzoeksresultaat* ('publish' + 'research_results'); | *kort + termijn* ('short' + 'term') | |
| *stuur + email* ('send' + 'email') | | |

**MI < 1**

| dobj | amod | advmod |
|---|---|---|
| *geef + interesse* ('give' + 'interest'); | *licht + meer* ('light' + 'lake'); | *nieuw + maak* ('new'+ 'make'); |
| *maak + antwoord* ('make' + 'answer'); | *nieuw + gebruik* ('new' + 'use'); | *niet + nu* ('not' + 'now'); |
| *zeg + oplossing* ('say' + 'solution'); | *snel + mens* ('fast' + 'person'); | *ook + vroeg* ('also' + 'early'); |
| *heb + gebruik* ('have' + 'use'); | *nodig + omstandigheid* ('necessary' + 'circumstance'); | *helemaal + nodig* ('completely' + 'necessary'); |
| *spreek + probleem* ('speak' + 'problem'); | *goed + markt* ('good' + 'market'); | *gewoon + snel* ('just' + 'quick'); |
| *vraag + verhaal* ('ask' + 'story'); | *goed + straat* ('good' + 'street'); | *kwalitatief + doe* ('qualitatively' + 'do'); |
| *beïnvloed + het* ('influence' + 'it'); | *slecht + stad* ('bad' + 'city'); | *helemaal + groei_uit* ('totally' + 'outgrow') |
| *neem + invloed* ('take' + 'influence'); | *gezond + wereld* ('healthy' + 'world') | |
| *onderzoek + verschil* ('research' + 'difference') | | |

text also includes one high-MI verb + direct object dependency (*smelt* + *ijs*; 'melt' + 'ice'), while the Fail text contains no dependencies above the 'non-collocational' band. Furthermore, 6 of the 7 verb + direct object dependencies extracted from the failing learner text include the three high-frequency verbs *hebben* ('have'), *krijgen* ('get'), and *maken* ('make'). For the Pass text, only 10 out of the 30 verbs occurring in the extracted verb + direct object dependencies can be accounted for by the high-frequency verbs *hebben* ('have'), *zetten* ('place'), *nemen* ('take'), and *houden* ('hold'). The remaining two-thirds of the dependencies extracted from the Pass text consist of less frequent verbs and/or nouns and idiomatic verb + direct object combinations (e.g. *houd* + *rekening*; 'take into consideration'). These observations align with the output of

**Table 5.9** Direct object dependencies from passing and failing examples of B2 texts

| | | Dependency | MI | Collocational band | Mean MI (excl. below threshold) | RTTR |
|---|---|---|---|---|---|---|
| B2 | Pass | leg_uit + overeenkomst (explain + agreement) | −1.88 | below threshold | 2.56 | 5.57 |
| | | leg_uit + verschil (explain + difference) | 3.74 | low | | |
| | | gebruik + fotosynthese (use + photosynthesis) | 2.65 | below threshold | | |
| | | produceer + energie (produce + energy) | 3.58 | low | | |
| | | verander + *Koolstofdioxide (change + *Carbon_dioxide) | NA | NA | | |
| | | verander + voeding_stof (change + nutrient) | NA | NA | | |
| | | verander + water (change + water) | 1.19 | non-collocational | | |
| | | heb + blad (have + leaf) | −0.02 | non-collocational | | |
| | | heb + plant_structuur (have + plant_structure) | NA | NA | | |
| | | heb + wortel (have + root) | 1.98 | non-collocational | | |
| | | breng_mee + ze (bring_along + them) | −0.93 | non-collocational | | |
| | | produceer + kleurstof (produce + pigment) | 5.65 | medium | | |
| | | produceer + zulk (produce + such) | NA | NA | | |
| | | bied + alternatief (offer + alternative) | 5.45 | medium | | |
| | | bied + voordeel (offer + advantage) | 4.49 | low | | |
| | | win + diesel (extract + diesel) | 0.95 | below threshold | | |
| | | kweek + ze (cultivate + them) | 0.72 | non-collocational | | |
| | | lever + olie (deliver + oil) | 2.47 | non-collocational | | |
| | | heb + water (have + water) | −0.58 | non-collocational | | |
| | | verbruik + water (consume + water) | 4.57 | low | | |
| | | heb + record (have + record) | −1.12 | non-collocational | | |
| | | zet + *dimentilsulfide (put + *dimenthyl_sulfide) | NA | NA | | |
| | | zet + vorming (put + formation) | −2.87 | below threshold | | |
| | | zet + vrij (set + free) | 0.18 | below threshold | | |
| | | smelt + ijs (melt + ice) | 7.42 | high | | |
| | | houd_tegen + zon_licht (hold_back + sun_light) | NA | NA | | |
| | | houd + rekening ('take_into_consideration') | 5.93 | medium | | |
| | | houd + *wereld_climaat (keep + *world_climate) | NA | NA | | |
| | | neem + koolstofdioxide (take + carbon_dioxide) | NA | NA | | |
| | | houd_bij + dit (keep_up + this) | −1.01 | non-collocational | | |
| | Fail | presenteer + school (present + school) | −2.04 | below threshold | −1.17 | 2.65 |
| | | heb + eeuw (have + century) | −0.93 | non-collocational | | |
| | | heb + zich (have + him/herself) | −3.76 | non-collocational | | |
| | | krijg + geld (get + money) | 0.71 | non-collocational | | |
| | | krijg + invloed (get + influence) | −0.58 | non-collocational | | |
| | | heb + mens (have + person) | −0.71 | non-collocational | | |
| | | maak + wat (make + something) | −1.72 | non-collocational | | |

*indicates an orthographic error in the phraseological unit, and in one case improper capitalisation; NA indicates a dependency that was not found at all in the reference corpus.

the regression model, where three verb + direct object measures emerged as significant main effects (i.e. with the same effect across the two CEFR levels): mean MI score, RTTR, and the proportion of high-MI verb + direct object dependencies. The model accurately predicts the outcome of the texts presented in Table 5.9, although these predictions are also made on the basis of the other measures included in the final model (both the significant and non-significant predictors).

At this stage, and without proper insight into the decisions of the evaluators, it is not possible to determine how the phraseological competence factored into these assessment decisions. The present analysis has relied on a global evaluation of learner proficiency that includes the assessment of additional tasks (e.g. short answers and argumentative texts), and therefore cannot be accounted for solely on the basis of the texts analysed here. On the other hand, the phraseological competence does not feature prominently among the CNaVT assessment models, leaving some open questions surrounding this observed relationship between phraseological complexity and the outcome of the exam.

Of the eight significant main effects and the four significant interaction effects, the phraseological measures comprise five of the main effects and one interaction effect. Furthermore, measures of phraseological complexity demonstrate the largest effect sizes in the model, with the exception of the interaction effect between CEFR level and Words per sentence. Put more directly, in response to RQ1, the measures of phraseological complexity investigated here contribute substantially to the prediction of the pass/fail outcome variable in the regression model. These results confirm that complexity measures tapping into phraseological phenomena (or co-occurrence phenomena) will help to better model the full range of learner proficiency (Paquot, 2019).

## 6.2 RQ2: A comparison with grammatical and lexical complexity measures

Measures of syntactic and lexical complexity are well-established indicators of L2 proficiency in SLA (for an overview, see Bulté & Housen, 2012). Still, the narrow focus of these measures on syntax and lexis, the large-grained nature of many of the measures, and the lack of operationalisations at several domains of language central to L2 development continue to draw criticism (e.g. Housen *et al.*, 2019: 9).

The comparison between phraseological and lexical measures is of particular interest, as phraseological units are often categorised with the lexicon (Bulté & Housen, 2012; Kim *et al.*, 2018) in complexity research, or are evaluated as part of the lexical competence in language assessment frameworks (e.g. in the CEFR). The measures of lexical diversity (MTLD of lemmas) and sophistication (Proportion of words among the 5,000 most frequent words) considered here do not emerge as significant in the model (except for the interaction term CEFR:MTLD lemma, which is associated with an increase in the odds of passing at the B2 level). The regression coefficients for these two predictors exhibit a large standard error (see S.E. column in Table 5.7), indicating a high degree of variation among the learners in the sample (i.e. these measures are not stable across this sample). There are several potential explanations for the fact that the phraseological measures contribute more to the model, and this analysis does not conclusively support any one in particular. On the one hand, phraseological and lexical complexity measures may capture the same information, the phraseological measures being more informative than lexical measures for the prediction of the pass/fail outcome variable of the B1 and B2 CNaVT exams. On the other hand, these measures may also tap into two distinct constructs, where lexical complexity is not as informative as phraseological complexity in the prediction of the pass/fail outcome. Lastly, the measures of lexical complexity here approach the lexis as a system, whereas the phraseological measures target specific grammatical dependencies; these results may therefore reflect an overall advantage of more fine-grained measures.

Significant main effects are observed for three syntactic complexity measures (Coordinated subclauses, Density of passives, and Dependency distance between a subject and verb), along with two significant interaction effects (Words per sentence and Density of nominalisations). The trend observed for Words per sentence, i.e. a positive relationship with the likelihood of passing the B1 exam and a negative relationship (with a small effect) with the likelihood of passing at B2, corresponds to previous findings of the non-linear relationship between global syntactic complexity measures and L2 proficiency (Norris & Ortega, 2009). Linguistic development across proficiency levels therefore does not appear to remain constant across all domains of language, or across domains of linguistic complexity more specifically. The syntactic measures that feature prominently in the model presented here at both B1 and B2 CEFR levels are also notably more fine-grained (the three main effects listed above), corresponding to: the degree of coordination at the level of the subclause, the frequency of passive constructions, and the degree of subject postmodification, respectively.

### 6.3 RQ3: Cross-linguistic comparison

On a more general level, the patterns observed for the role of phraseological complexity in the assessment of L2 Dutch proficiency (in the context of the B1 and B2 CNaVT exams) are in line with the results of the analyses conducted for L2 English by Paquot (2018, 2019), where measures of phraseological sophistication were found to outperform measures of syntactic and lexical complexity in distinguishing between upper-intermediate and advanced learners of English. However, whereas measures of phraseological diversity did not influence the CEFR levels assigned to the L2 English texts, these measures (for the adverbial modifier and direct object dependencies) contribute significantly to the prediction of the outcome variable in the present study. In fact, phraseological diversity measures exhibit larger effects in the model than phraseological sophistication measures. Also common across the two languages is the relative importance of phraseological measures targeting adverbial modifier and direct object dependencies, as opposed to adjectival modifier dependencies.

While measures of syntactic and lexical complexity did not contribute to the assessment of L2 English proficiency across the B2-C2 learners in Paquot's (2018, 2019) analyses, these measures do play a role in the modelling of the pass/fail outcome of the L2 Dutch CNaVT productions, particularly the syntactic complexity measures. It should also be noted that most of the syntactic measures that emerge as significant in the present study were not considered in Paquot's (2018, 2019) investigations of L2 English (i.e. Density of nominalisations, Coordinated subclauses, Density of passives, and Dependency distance between a subject and verb). Any comparisons drawn between the results obtained by Paquot for L2 English and the results presented here for L2 Dutch should be undertaken with caution, as differences in the research designs extend beyond target language and proficiency (e.g. available tools for computing complexity measures, available learner corpus data, type of proficiency indicator, etc.). Still, this analysis has demonstrated that the relevance of phraseological complexity is not unique to L2 English, but also holds for the assessment of L2 Dutch proficiency. As 'the CEFR is intended to be relevant to all languages, and is therefore not language specific' (Hulstijn *et al.*, 2010: 16), measures of phraseological complexity are therefore promising cross-linguistic indicators of language proficiency in standardised assessment frameworks. At the very least, these aspects of learner language should not be overlooked.

## 7 Conclusion

The present study has investigated the role of phraseological complexity measures in the assessment of L2 Dutch proficiency through a partial replication design. This approach is motivated by the observed importance of co-occurrence phenomena for L2 development and proficiency on the one hand (Durrant & Schmitt, 2009; Granger & Bestgen, 2014), and the need for more cross-linguistic evidence thereof on the other hand. Both Paquot's investigations into L2 English and the present study are grounded in the CEFR approach to language proficiency, which has been widely implemented in language assessment throughout Europe. While both linguistic complexity and phraseology have been identified as key dimensions of L2 development and proficiency, these dimensions are neither central nor well-defined in the CEFR descriptor scales (for linguistic competences), which are arguably the most impactful component of the CEFR (Hulstijn *et al.*, 2010: 13). Whereas syntactic and lexical complexity are accounted for within the grammatical and lexical competences (respectively) to some degree, albeit in vague terms, phraseological competence is reduced to the mention of 'idiomatic expressions and colloquialisms' (Council of Europe, 2001: 112) in the lexical competence descriptor scale, restricted to the C1-C2 proficiency bands. Paquot's (2018, 2019) investigation of phraseological complexity across the B2-C2 CEFR levels in L2 English therefore marks a preliminary exploration of the role that phraseological competence, indicated by phraseological complexity, might also play in the assessment of L2 proficiency, despite being underrepresented in assessment grids.

A similar approach to the exploration of the role of phraseological competence in CEFR-based assessment has been adopted here, while shifting focus to L2 Dutch. The present study is also complementary to previous research establishing the development of linguistic competences across the (B1 and B2) CEFR levels (Hulstijn *et al.*, 2012) in L2 Dutch, where complexity has not featured prominently. The results and the discussion presented in this chapter lead to the conclusion that phraseological competence, explored here through phraseological complexity, is a significant contributing factor to the assessment of proficiency at the B1 and B2 levels of the CNaVT exam. The effect of text topic and L1 background, which have both been shown to influence the assessment of writing performance (Paquot *et al.*, 2021), are not taken into consideration in the present study. Future research will need to account for these effects in order to accurately model the relationship between dimensions of linguistic complexity (including phraseological complexity) and L2 proficiency.

Furthermore, we have approached the assessment of L2 Dutch proficiency from a binary pass/fail perspective, and the findings must therefore be interpreted in terms of the assessment of learner productions, as opposed to the description of linguistic performances across CEFR levels. To address the latter, productions need to be assessed for proficiency level, after which a description of the manifestation of complexity across CEFR levels can be attempted. As mentioned in Section 6.1, our understanding of the observed relationship between phraseological complexity and the exam outcome would further benefit from direct insight into the decisions made by the evaluators. Further research should also seek to investigate additional L2s, as well as a wider range of phraseological units. Specifically, while the present study has focused on grammatical dependencies, there is a range of phraseological units worthy of investigation under this framework. Kyle and Eguchi (Chapter 6 of this volume) report that grammatical dependencies may be better indicators of phraseological competence than bigrams in L2 English. This remains to be explored for L2 Dutch, as well as the effect of larger n-grams or lexical bundles. Nonetheless, the findings presented here strengthen the argument for the cross-linguistic nature of phraseological competence, the cross-linguistic validity of phraseological complexity measures, and, consequently, for the inclusion of a phraseological dimension among CEFR-based assessment grids.

## Notes

(1) D-level (Developmental level) is a syntactic measure based on a scale (1–8) of stages of first language acquisition, where level 1 syntactic structures are acquired earliest and level 8 syntactic structures are acquired latest (Pander Maat *et al.*, 2014).
(2) The highest collocational band measure for which there was enough evidence was selected for each target dependency: proportion of dobj dependencies with high MI, proportion of amod dependencies with high MI, and proportion of advmod dependencies with low MI.
(3) This is important, as we naturally observe more variation in scores for measures such as TTR of advmods (which ranges from 1.16 to 6.38) as opposed to proportion measures such as Proportion of words among the 5,000 most frequent words (which range from 0 to 1).
(4) This property of the RTTR is a result of the formula for the calculation of the measure ($T/\sqrt{N}$), which takes the square root of the token count as a denominator.

## References

Alderson, J.C. (2007) The CEFR and the need for more research. *The Modern Language Journal* 91 (4), 659–663.
Banerjee, S. and Pedersen, T. (2003) The design, implementation, and use of the Ngram Statistics Package. In A. Gelbukh (ed.) *Computational Linguistics and Intelligent Text Processing: 4th International Conference, CICLing 2003, Mexico City, Mexico, February 16–22, 2003* (pp. 370–381). Berlin & Heidelberg: Springer.
Bouma, G. and Kloosterman, G. (2007) Mining syntactically annotated corpora with XQuery. In *Proceedings of the Linguistic Annotation Workshop* (pp. 17–24). Prague: Association for Computational Linguistics.
Bulon, A., Hendrikx, I., Meunier, F. and Van Goethem, K. (2017) Using global complexity measures to assess second language proficiency: Comparing CLIL and non-CLIL learners of English and Dutch in French-speaking Belgium. *Papers of the Linguistic Society of Belgium* 11 (1), 1–25.
Bulté, B. and Housen, A. (2012) Defining and operationalising L2 complexity. In A. Housen, F. Kuiken and I. Vedder (eds) *Dimensions of L2 Performance and Proficiency* (pp. 21–46). Amsterdam & Philadelphia: Benjamins.
Council of Europe (2001) *Common European Framework of Reference for Languages: Learning, Teaching, Assessment*. Cambridge: Cambridge University Press.
Council of Europe (2018) *Common European Framework of Reference for Languages: Language, Teaching, Assessment. Companion Volume with New Descriptors.* Cambridge: Cambridge University Press.
De Clercq, B. and Housen, A. (2019) The development of morphological complexity: A cross-linguistic study of L2 French and English. *Second Language Research* 35 (1), 71–97.
Deygers, B., Hamnes Carlsen, C., Saville, N. and Van Gorp, K. (2018) The use of the CEFR in higher education: A brief introduction to this special issue. *Language Assessment Quarterly* 15 (1), 1–2.
Durrant, P. and Schmitt, N. (2009) To what extent do native and non-native writers make use of collocations? *International Review of Applied Linguistics in Language Teaching* 47 (2), 157–177.

Granger, S. and Bestgen, Y. (2014) The use of collocations by intermediate vs. advanced non-native writers: A bigram-based study. *International Review of Applied Linguistics in Language Teaching* 52 (3), 229–252.

Gries, S.T. (2013) *Statistics for Linguistics with R: A Practical Introduction*. Berlin: De Gruyter.

Housen, A., De Clercq, B., Kuiken, F. and Vedder, I. (2019) Multiple approaches to complexity in second language research. *Second Language Research* 35 (1), 3–21.

Hron, K., Filzmoser, P. and Thompson, K. (2012) Linear regression with compositional explanatory variables. *Journal of Applied Statistics* 39 (5), 1115–1128.

Hulstijn, J.H. (2007) The shaky ground beneath the CEFR: Quantitative and qualitative dimensions of language proficiency. *The Modern Language Journal* 91 (4), 663–667.

Hulstijn, J.H., Alderson, J.C. and Schoonen, R. (2010) Developmental stages in second-language acquisition and levels of second-language proficiency: Are there links between them? In I. Bartning, M. Martin and I. Vedder (eds) *Communicative Proficiency and Linguistic Development: Intersections between SLA and Language Testing Research* (pp. 11–20). European Second Language Association.

Hulstijn, J.H., Schoonen, R., de Jong, N.H., Steinel, M.P. and Florijn, A. (2012) Linguistic competences of learners of Dutch as a second language at the B1 and B2 levels of speaking proficiency of the Common European Framework of Reference for Languages (CEFR). *Language Testing* 29 (2), 203–221.

Kim, M., Crossley, S.A. and Kyle, K. (2018) Lexical sophistication as a multidimensional phenomenon: Relations to second language lexical proficiency, development, and writing quality. *The Modern Language Journal* 102 (1), 120–141.

Kyle, K. and Crossley, S.A. (2016) The relationship between lexical sophistication and independent and source-based writing. *Journal of Second Language Writing* 34, 12–24.

van Noord, G. (2006) At last parsing is now operational. In *Proceedings of TALN 2006* (pp. 20–42). Leuven: Association pour le Traitement Automatique des Langues.

van Noord, G., Schuurman, I. and Vandeghinste, V. (2006) Syntactic annotation of large corpora in STEVIN. In *Proceedings of the Fifth International Conference on Language Resources and Evaluation (LREC'06)*. Genoa, Italy: European Language Resources Association (ELRA). http://www.lrec-conf.org/proceedings/lrec2006/pdf/329_pdf.pdf.

Norris, J.M. and Ortega, L. (2009) Towards an organic approach to investigating CAF in instructed SLA: The case of complexity. *Applied Linguistics* 30 (4), 555–578.

Ortega, L. (2003) Syntactic complexity measures and their relationship to L2 proficiency: A research synthesis of college-level L2 writing. *Applied Linguistics* 24 (4), 492–518.

Pander Maat, H., Kraf, R., van den Bosch, A., Dekker, N., van Gompel, M., Kleijn, S., Sanders, T. and van der Sloot, K. (2014) T-Scan: A new tool for analyzing Dutch text. *Computational Linguistics in the Netherlands Journal* 4, 53–74.

Paquot, M. (2018) Phraseological competence: A missing component in university entrance language tests? Insights from a study of EFL learners' use of statistical collocations. *Language Assessment Quarterly* 15 (1), 29–43.

Paquot, M. (2019) The phraseological dimension in interlanguage complexity research. *Second Language Research* 35 (1), 121–145.

Paquot, M. and Granger, S. (2012) Formulaic language in learner corpora. *Annual Review of Applied Linguistics* 32, 130–149.

Paquot, M., Naets, H. and S. Th. Gries (2021) Using syntactic co-occurrences to trace phraseological complexity development in learner writing: Verb + object structures in LONGDALE. In B. Le Bruyn and M. Paquot (eds) *Second Language Acquisition and Learner Corpora*. Cambridge: Cambridge University Press.

Porte, G. (2012) *Replication Research in Applied Linguistics*. Cambridge: Cambridge University Press.

R Core Team. (2017) *R: A Language and Environment for Statistical Computing* [Computer software manual]. Vienna, Austria: R Foundation for Statistical Computing.

# 6 Automatically Assessing Lexical Sophistication Using Word, Bigram, and Dependency Indices

Kristopher Kyle and Masaki Eguchi

## 1 Introduction

Productive lexical proficiency is an important indicator of judgments of speaking and writing quality (Kyle & Crossley, 2015; Laufer & Nation, 1995). Productive lexical proficiency is often measured using indices related to lexical sophistication, which has most often been conceptualized as the number of infrequent words in a text (Read, 2000). A number of studies have demonstrated that more proficient second language users tend to produce less frequent words than those who are less proficient (Crossley *et al.*, 2013; Laufer & Nation, 1995). Recent investigations have also found meaningful relationships between other word features (such as concreteness and contextual distinctiveness[1]) and judgments of production quality (e.g. Berger *et al.*, 2017; Kyle *et al.*, 2018). It is well known, however, that proficient word use requires more than the ability to produce advanced words in isolation (Nation, 2001; Römer, 2009; Sinclair, 1991), and that an important aspect of lexical proficiency is the ability to use words in appropriate lexico-grammatical contexts. For example, a number of recent studies have found that more proficient second language users tend to use more frequent and more strongly associated adjacent word combinations such as *aware of*, *rather than* and *agree with* (Bestgen & Granger, 2014; Garner *et al.*, 2019; Kyle & Crossley, 2015). Very recently, researchers have also found a positive relationship between the strength of association between dependency bigrams (e.g. verbs and their direct objects such as *pursue* + *career*, *place* + *emphasis* and *conduct* + *study*) and writing proficiency (Paquot, 2018, 2019; Rubin *et al.*, Chapter 5 of this volume). While research has indicated the importance of each of the aforementioned units of analysis in isolation, what is not clear is the relative contribution of each in judgments of proficiency. This study represents an attempt to address this issue by investigating the relative importance of indices related to single words, bigrams, and dependency bigrams in predicting holistic scores of writing proficiency.

## 2 Indicators of Lexical Proficiency

Lexical sophistication has most often been conceptualized as a feature of single words (Laufer & Nation, 1995; Read, 2000). Recently, however, a number of studies have investigated the relationship between production quality (broadly construed) and word use features that go beyond single words, such as the association strength of adjacent words and dependency bigrams (Bestgen & Granger, 2014; Garner *et al.*, 2019; Paquot, 2019). In this section, a brief review of literature related to indicators of lexical proficiency at the word, *n*-gram, and dependency bigram levels is given. We also report on a small number of studies that have investigated features both at and above the level of the word.

### 2.1 Words as indicators of lexical proficiency

Lexical sophistication has often been referred to as the 'number of low frequency words that are appropriate to the topic and style of writing' (Read, 2000: 200). This oft-cited definition highlights the importance that reference-corpus frequency has played in measuring lexical sophistication within the field. It is generally accepted across theoretical perspectives that frequency of exposure/use is an important factor in word learning (e.g. O'Grady, 2008): words that are encountered more frequently are more likely to be learned (and learned more quickly) than those that are encountered less frequently. Word frequencies derived from reference corpora (large collections of electronic texts designed to be representative of language use in a particular domain) provide a useful indication of how frequently a language user will encounter a word. Accordingly, frequency information provides an estimation of how likely it is that a person will know a particular word. High frequency words (such as *make* and *do*) are expected to be known by most language users, while lower frequency words (such as *proletarian* and *angulation*) are only expected to be known by older/more educated L1 users and more proficient L2 users. Accordingly, given a particular task, more proficient L2 users will tend to use a higher proportion of low frequency words than their less proficient counterparts.

The relationship between word frequency and production quality has been demonstrated (with small to moderate effects) in a number of cross-sectional studies (e.g. Guo *et al.*, 2013; Kyle & Crossley, 2015; Laufer & Nation, 1995). Laufer and Nation (1995), for example, examined the relationship between second language (L2) proficiency level and the reference-corpus frequency of words used in argumentative essays. They found that higher proficiency learners used significantly fewer high frequency words and more low frequency words than lower proficiency learners. In a related study, Kyle and Crossley (2015) found a small, negative relationship between the mean reference-corpus frequency of content words and lexical proficiency scores for L2 free writes. This indicated that essays with higher lexical proficiency scores tended to include more infrequent content words. Similarly, Kyle and Crossley (2016) found that higher scoring argumentative essays written as part of the Test of English as a Foreign Language (TOEFL) tended to include a higher proportion of lower frequency content words (though the effect size was small).

Although the studies outlined above indicate that reference-corpus frequency is clearly a helpful indicator of word difficulty, it has at least two notable limitations when used in isolation. First, features beyond frequency of exposure (such as saliency) can affect the ease with which a word is learned. For example, words that are more concrete, such as *apple* or *cobra*, may be easier to learn than words of similar frequency that are less concrete, such as *justice* or *inevitable* (Brysbaert *et al.*, 2014; Paivio, 1971; Schwanenflugel *et al.*, 1988). Second, although reference corpora provide a reasonable approximation of word exposure (particularly for high frequency words), they do not fully or accurately represent the language exposure of a particular learner (this issue is likely magnified for L2 learners). Accordingly, although a fairly consistent relationship has been found between L2 lexical proficiency and word frequency, these relationships have been relatively weak (small to moderate effects). However, studies that have used both frequency norms and other indices of word difficulty (such as concreteness and contextual diversity) have explained a substantial amount of the variance in L2 production quality scores. Kyle and Crossley (2015), for example, explored the relationship between productive lexical proficiency scores for timed free write essays and a range of lexical indices. They found that indices related to contextual distinctiveness (e.g. range) and saliency (e.g. meaningfulness) contributed meaningfully to the final predictor model (and frequency was not included). In a subsequent study that expanded on the variety of features investigated, Kyle *et al.* (2018) found that a wide variety of lexical indices (such as contextual distinctiveness and hypernymy) added to the variance in lexical proficiency scores explained by frequency. In fact, frequency explained a relatively small amount of the variance in lexical proficiency scores (3.6%) compared to other lexical indices (such as contextual distinctiveness, which alone explained 13.9% of the variance).

## 2.2 *N*-grams as indicators of lexical proficiency

An important aspect of productive language proficiency is phraseological competence (i.e. knowing which words fit together in a

**Table 6.1** Examples of bigrams at various frequency and strength of association ranks in COCA

| Rank | Bigram | Frequency (per million) | Rank | Bigram | MI Score |
|---|---|---|---|---|---|
| 1 | of_the | 855534 | 1 | iwo_jima | 13.680 |
| 2 | in_the | 708247 | 2 | corina_lecca | 13.630 |
| 3 | it_be | 485525 | 3 | cystic_fibrosis | 13.430 |
| 4 | be_a | 395073 | 4 | walkie_talkie | 13.338 |
| 5 | to_the | 344242 | 5 | honky_tonk | 13.314 |
| 2001 | and_can | 5374 | 2001 | ford_motor | 7.140 |
| 2002 | with_two | 5374 | 2002 | metropolitan_museum | 7.139 |
| 2003 | help_to | 5373 | 2003 | bay_packers | 7.139 |
| 2004 | love_to | 5370 | 2004 | presidential_nomination | 7.138 |
| 2005 | that_come | 5364 | 2005 | cruise_missile | 7.137 |
| 5001 | do_thing | 2592 | 5001 | %_dietary | 5.394 |
| 5002 | a_heavy | 2592 | 5002 | entirely_different | 5.394 |
| 5003 | to_explore | 2592 | 5003 | football_league | 5.394 |
| 5004 | a_mother | 2592 | 5004 | mail_message | 5.394 |
| 5005 | you_that | 2591 | 5005 | faster_than | 5.393 |

particular context; Nation, 2001; Römer, 2009; Sinclair, 1991). One way to estimate phraseological competence is to measure the characteristics of word combinations used by learners. One of the most common units of analysis is the *n*-gram, which is a contiguous sequence of *n* words. Two-word sequences (bigrams) and three-word sequences (trigrams) are most commonly used, although sequences of four words (e.g. lexical bundles; Biber *et al.*, 2004) or larger are also used. See Table 6.1 for examples of frequent and strongly associated bigrams in the newspaper and magazine sections of the Corpus of Contemporary American English (COCA; Davies, 2009). Research has indicated that more proficient language users tend to use *n*-grams that are more frequent and more strongly associated in the target language domain. Bestgen and Granger (2014), for example, found a positive relationship between bigram strength of association (measured by mutual information scores) and narrative writing quality scores. Similar results have also been found between *n*-gram strength of association scores and argumentative essay scores (e.g. Bestgen, 2017; Garner *et al.*, 2019; Granger & Bestgen, 2014), written lexical proficiency scores (Kyle *et al.*, 2018), and a variety of L2 examination scripts (Bestgen, 2016).

*N*-gram strength of association indices have demonstrated a reasonably consistent, positive relationship with productive proficiency scores, suggesting that they are a useful indicator of lexical and phraseological proficiency. Effect sizes for these indices have ranged from small to moderate (from $r = .22$ to $r = .43$), and multivariate studies have indicated a complementary relationship between *n*-gram strength of association and word-level indices such as frequency (e.g. Kyle *et al.*, 2018). Furthermore, *n*-grams are straightforward to analyse and can be extracted reliably with very little technical expertise. Nonetheless, *n*-gram indices have at least two weaknesses. First, *n*-grams capture a number of relationships, including (but not limited to) grammatical relationships (e.g. articles + nouns, auxiliary verb sequences such as *have been* + *V-ing*, etc.) and fixed/semi-fixed phraseological units (e.g. *on the other hand*). Without constraining *n*-gram sequences to particular parts of speech (see Bestgen & Granger, 2014) and/or conducting thorough post-hoc analyses (see Biber *et al.*, 2004), it is difficult to determine the lexico-grammatical relationship(s) reflected by an *n*-gram's strength of association. Second, not all phraseological units are completely fixed or feature contiguous word sequences (e.g. O'Donnell *et al.*, 2013). For example, a direct object may be quite removed from its verb, and even adjectives are not always immediately adjacent to the nouns they modify.

## 2.3 Dependency bigrams as indicators of lexical proficiency

A recent, alternative method to the use of *n*-grams for estimating phraseological competence is to measure the characteristics of lexical items that are linked via a particular grammatical function (but may be separated by intervening words; Paquot, 2018, 2019). For example, using this method one could examine the reference-corpus frequency and/or strength of association of grammatical relations such as verb-direct object, verb-adverb, and adjective-noun (among others). See Table 6.2 for examples of dependency bigrams of various association strengths in COCA.

Recent research by Paquot (2018, 2019) has demonstrated that dependency bigrams are useful indicators of writing proficiency. Paquot (2019) investigated differences in mean strength of association (in this case, mutual information scores) across writing samples produced by intermediate to advanced learners of English (Common European Framework of Reference for Languages levels B2-C2). Paquot found meaningful differences in adjective-noun strength of association between B2 and C2 (but not between adjacent levels). Meaningful differences in verb-adverb strength of association were found between B2 and both C1 and C2 levels, but not between C1 and C2 levels. Finally, meaningful differences in verb-direct object strength of association were found between all levels except between B2 and C1. Similarly, Paquot (2018) found that the mean strength of association between verb-direct object and noun-adjective dependency relationships accounted for 25% of the variance in CEFR writing scores. Rubin *et al.*

**Table 6.2** Examples of three dependency bigram types at various strengths of association in COCA

| Verb–Direct Object | Adjectival Modifier–Noun | Verb–Adverbial Modifier |
|---|---|---|
| | High MI (7 < MI) | |
| chew–gum | tooth–decay | impair–neurologically |
| vote–democratic | pearl–necklace | low–moderately |
| bridge–gap | upset–stomach | sob–uncontrollably |
| | Middle MI (3 < MI ≤ 7) | |
| overcome–obstacle | certified–educator | adjust–seasonally |
| invade–privacy | exponential–increase | summarize–succinctly |
| extend–reach | pressing–issue | illustrate–colorfully |
| stand–chance | gradual–accumulation | dress–casually |
| catch–bus | steady–increase | enlarge–slightly |
| | Low MI (1 < MI ≤ 3) | |
| feel–relief | accurate–account | believe–wrongly |
| offer–protection | lasting–change | oppose–initially |
| seek–solution | enormous–increase | ask–insistently |
| visit–city | influential–people | affect–particularly |
| make–improvement | ongoing–issue | summarize–well |

(Chapter 5 of this volume) found similar results for L2 Dutch. Together, these studies demonstrate that dependency bigrams are useful indicators of writing proficiency.

## 2.4 Complementary models

Primarily, features of lexical and phraseological proficiency have been investigated in isolation or in small sets of related indices (e.g. Bestgen & Granger, 2014; Laufer & Nation, 1995; Paquot, 2019). However, a few recent studies have found that word level and *n*-gram level indices of lexical proficiency work in a largely complementary manner. Kyle *et al.* (2018), for example, found that bigram strength of association, trigram proportion scores, and a collection of word-level indices accounted for approximately 58% of the variance in written lexical proficiency scores. As found in previous studies, more lexically proficient writers tended to use more strongly associated bigrams, a higher proportion of frequent trigrams, and more sophisticated words (e.g. words with lower contextual diversity). Almost equal proportions of the variance were explained by *n*-gram indices (28%) and by word-level indices (30%). This and related findings (e.g. Bestgen, 2017; Kim *et al.*, 2018) highlight the important roles that both word knowledge and phraseological competence play in judgments of productive lexical proficiency. At least one study (Paquot, 2018), however, found significant relationships between written proficiency levels for dependency bigram strength of association, but not for word frequency. This suggests that dependency bigram strength of association and frequency indices may not be complementary, although this bears further investigation. The degree to which dependency bigrams add complementary information about lexical proficiency and/or supersede the information provided by *n*-grams is unknown. This study attempts to address these issues by investigating the relative importance of word level, bigram level, and dependency bigram level indices in predicting writing quality scores. Accordingly, this study is guided by the following research questions:

RQ1 What is the relationship between writing proficiency scores and indices of word frequency, contextual distinctiveness, concreteness, bigram strength of association, and dependency bigram strength of association?

RQ2 What is the relative contribution of indices of word frequency, contextual distinctiveness, concreteness, bigram strength of association, and dependency bigram strength of association?

## 3 Data and Methodology

### 3.1 Learner corpus

The learner corpus for this project includes 480 argumentative essays from the Test of English as a Foreign Language (TOEFL) public use dataset.[2] The public use dataset consists of responses to two forms of the TOEFL ($n$ = 240 for each form) collected from actual administrations of the TOEFL. The test-takers represent the population that takes the TOEFL, and therefore includes a wide variety of L1s and learning environments (see Table 6.3 for the writing prompts). The writing tasks were timed (30 minutes) and were scored by at least two trained raters using a rubric with a 5-point scale.[3] If the two raters disagreed on the score by more than a full point, a third rater was also used. See Table 6.4 for descriptive statistics for the learner corpus.

**Table 6.3** Writing prompts for independent essays in the TOEFL public use dataset

| Test Form | Prompt Instructions |
|---|---|
| 1 | Do you agree or disagree with the following statement? It is more important to choose to study subjects you are interested in than to choose subjects to prepare for a job or career. Use specific reasons and examples to support your answer. |
| 2 | Do you agree or disagree with the following statement? In today's world, the ability to cooperate well with others is far more important than it was in the past. Use specific reasons and examples to support your answer. |

**Table 6.4** Overview of the learner corpus

| Prompt | N | Number of Words | Mean Score | Standard Deviation |
|---|---|---|---|---|
| 1 | 240 | 77,238 | 3.83 | 0.86 |
| 2 | 240 | 74,252 | 3.47 | 0.91 |

## 3.2 Linguistic analyses

The linguistic analyses were conducted with a Python script. Indices from four categories were selected, including word frequency, concreteness, word contextual distinctiveness, bigram strength of association, and dependency bigram strength of association. The indices that were considered from each category are outlined below.

### *3.2.1 Word frequency*

Word frequency norms were derived from the magazine and newspaper subsections of the Corpus of Contemporary American English (COCA; Davies, 2009) and were based on lemmas. Prior to calculating frequency norms, the corpus was part-of-speech (POS) tagged using the SpaCy POS tagger (Explosion AI, 2018). Only content words, which were defined as nouns, adjectives, lexical main verbs (excluding *to be* and auxiliary uses of verbs) and adverbs of manner, were considered in the analysis. The SpaCy dependency parse output was used to differentiate between use of verbs such as *to have* and *to do* as auxiliary verbs and as main verbs. All frequency values were logarithmically transformed in order to account for the Zipfian (Zipf, 1935) distribution of language data. Frequency indices were calculated for each of the parts of speech associated with content words (nouns, verbs, adjectives, and adverbs) and for the combination of all content words in a text. Frequency indices represent the mean frequency score for the words in a learner text. Any words occurring in a learner text that were not extant in the reference corpus were ignored (including misspellings, which were rare).

### *3.2.2 Concreteness*

Concreteness indices are based on Brysbaert *et al.*'s (2014) norms, which cover 40,000 English words. To obtain concreteness scores, participants were asked to rate each word on a 5-point scale for concreteness. Each word was given a score by approximately 20 participants, and the scores were averaged across individuals. Words that are more concrete (e.g. *baby*, *bellybutton* and *unicycle*) are theorized to be easier to learn (Paivio, 1971; Schwanenflugel *et al.*, 1988) than words that are less concrete (e.g. *unpopularity*, *doubt*, *regain*). Additionally, more concrete words are likely more salient than their less concrete counterparts (Crossley *et al.*, 2016). Concreteness indices were calculated for content words and represent the mean concreteness score for content words in a learner text. Any content words in the learner text that were not represented in the concreteness database were ignored.

### *3.2.3 Contextual distinctiveness*

Contextual distinctiveness can be measured in relation to corpus co-occurrence patterns or through behavioral norms. For this study, one corpus-based index and one behavioral index were selected. The corpus-based index, McD (McDonald & Shillcock, 2001), represents the predictability of a word's lexical context (operationalized as a 5-word window) based on relative entropy.[4] Words that have constrained lexical contexts (e.g. *allegedly, lone* and *glory*) are more contextually distinct than words that can occur in a variety of contexts (e.g. *over*, *close* and *today*). The behavioral norm-based index relies on the University of South Florida (USF) association norms (Nelson *et al.*, 2004). The USF association norms are derived from the results of a word associates test in which participants are asked to write the first word that comes to mind when provided with a stimulus word. The USF index represents the number of stimuli words that elicited a particular word. Words that were elicited by fewer stimuli (e.g. *adversary*, *cupboard* and *flirt*) are considered to be more contextually distinct, while words that were elicited by many stimuli (e.g. *car*, *good* and *people*) are considered to be less contextually distinct. Note that for McD, higher scores indicate greater distinctiveness (greater entropy) while for USF, lower scores indicate greater distinctiveness (elicited by fewer words).

### *3.2.4 Bigram strength of association*

Bigram strength of association norms were derived from the magazine and newspaper subsections of the COCA (Davies, 2009). There are a number of methods for calculating strength of association. In this study, we tested the use of three different calculation methods, including T, Mutual Information (MI), and delta-p. See Table 6.5 for a summary of each calculation method (and examples). T and MI represent the joint probability that two items will co-occur (Evert, 2005). T scores tend to highlight frequent words, while MI scores tend to highlight lower frequency words. In some cases, the strength of association between words is relatively even. However, in many cases this is not true. For example, in the bigram *plethora of*, the word *plethora* occurs quite frequently (and rather exclusively) with the word *of*. In other words, if we see the word *plethora*, there is a good chance that the next word will be *of*. However, the word *of* is not a particularly good predictor of the word *plethora*. If we see the word *of*, we know that any number of words could precede it. The strength of association measure delta-p accounts for the directional nature of the strength of association between two items (see, for example, Gries & Ellis, 2015). Specifically, delta-p represents the

**Table 6.5** Bigram strength of association measures

| Index | Formula | Strongly associated | Weakly associated |
|---|---|---|---|
| T | $\frac{observed - expected}{\sqrt{observed}}$ | *of the* | *of when* |
| | | *there be* | *that of* |
| | | *more than* | *get and* |
| Mutual information (MI) | $\log\left(\frac{observed}{expected}\right)$ | *walkie talkie* | *the not* |
| | | *pinot noir* | *from in* |
| | | *nobel laureate* | *these the* |
| Delta-p (left to right) | *P*(*Word*2\|*Word*1) – *P*(*Word*2\|–*Word*1) | *insofar as* | *next the* |
| | | *plethora of* | *far fetched* |
| | | *roomful of* | *no brainer* |
| Delta-p (right to left) | *P*(*Word*1\|*Word*2) – *P*(*Word*1\|–*Word*2) | *full fledged* | *the have* |
| | | *no brainer* | *plethora of* |
| | | *far fetched* | *insofar as* |
| Delta-p (max) | *maximum_score*(*deltap_LR* \| *deltap_RL*) | *insofar as* | *the have* |
| | | *full fledged* | *next the* |
| | | *roomful of* | *other life* |

probability of an outcome (i.e. a word) given a cue (i.e. another word) minus the probability of the outcome without the cue. In this study, three versions of delta-p were calculated. In the first version, (delta-p left to right), the first word in the bigram was the cue and the second word was the outcome. In the second version (delta-p right to left), the second word was the cue and the first word was the outcome. In the final version (delta-p max) the highest score between delta-p (left to right) and delta-p (right to left) was used for each item. As with all other indices in this study, index scores for a text represent the mean value for all items in that text. Any items that do not occur in the database are ignored.

### *3.2.5 Dependency bigram strength of association*

Dependency bigram strength of association indices were derived from the magazine and newspaper subsections of the COCA (Davies, 2009). SpaCy (Explosion AI, 2018) was used to identify all grammatical dependency relationships in the reference corpus and in the learner texts. Four dependency relationships, including noun-adjective, verb-adverb, verb-direct object, and verb-subject were considered. In all cases, lemmas were used. As with the bigram indices above, three types of strength of association indices were calculated, including T, MI, and delta-p. Examples of each index for verb-direct object relations are included in Table 6.6.

In order to ensure that the dependency parser was accurate with the L2 data in the study, 100 sentences were randomly sampled from

**Table 6.6** Dependency bigram strength of association examples (verb-direct object relations)

| Index | Formula | Strongly associated | Weakly associated |
|---|---|---|---|
| T | $\frac{observed - expected}{\sqrt{observed}}$ | *do what* | *do idea* |
| | | *do job* | *provide it* |
| | | *make decision* | *do choice* |
| Mutual information (MI) | $\log\left(\frac{observed}{expected}\right)$ | *suborn perjury* | *make benefit* |
| | | *slake thirst* | *do choice* |
| | | *hath fury* | *make question* |
| Delta-p (head as cue) | *P*(*dobj*\|*verb*) – *P*(*dobj*\|–*verb*) | *bide time* | *determine it* |
| | | *toe line* | *put kabosh* |
| | | *wreak havoc* | *see hardcopy* |
| Delta-p (dependent as cue) | *P*(*verb*\|*dobj*) – *P*(*verb*\|–*dobj*) | *put kabosh* | *toe line* |
| | | *see hardcopy* | *crane neck* |
| | | *wreak havoc* | *have protest* |
| Delta-p (max) | *maximum_score*(*deltap_HC* \| *deltap_DC*) | *bide time* | *determine it* |
| | | *toe line* | *have protest* |
| | | *see hardcopy* | *see ball* |

the learner corpus and manually analysed. The results of this analysis indicated that the dependency parser accurately tagged the four dependency relationships considered in this study. Table 6.7 includes the precision, recall, and F1 scores for each dependency relationship. Precision refers to the proportion of items (e.g. verb-direct object bigrams) that the system identified as verb-direct bigrams that were correctly identified. In the Table 6.7, we see that 98% of the identified verb-direct object bigrams identified by the system were actually verb-direct object pairs. Recall refers to the proportion of items (e.g. verb-direct object pairs) in the total sample that were identified by the system. In the Table 6.7, we see that 94.2% of the total number of verb-direct object bigrams in the corpus were identified by the system. The F1 score represents the harmonic mean of the precision and recall scores. In this case, the F1 score is 96%, which represents high overall parser accuracy in identifying verb-direct object bigrams (state of the art dependency

**Table 6.7** Dependency parsing performance for four relations

| Dependency relation | Precision | Recall | F1 |
|---|---|---|---|
| noun – adjective | .951 | .987 | .969 |
| verb – adverb | .986 | .986 | .986 |
| verb – direct object | .980 | .942 | .960 |
| verb – subject | .949 | .960 | .954 |

average parser accuracy for all dependency relationships is around 90%; Chen & Manning, 2014; Explosion AI, 2018).

## 3.3 Statistical analyses

In order to address the research questions, a linear regression was conducted to predict the TOEFL holistic essay scores using the word, bigram, and dependency indices. All statistical analyses were conducted using R (R Core Team, 2016).

### *3.3.1 Preliminary index selection*

All indices were first checked visually for normality. Any indices that clearly violated a normal distribution were excluded from further analysis. Next, indices were checked to ensure that the indices had a linear relationship with the dependent variable (using scatterplots) and that the relationship was meaningful ($|r| >= .100$). Additionally, only one strength of association index for each bigram/dependency bigram relationship was used (whichever had the strongest relationship with the dependent variable). Finally, all remaining indices were checked for multicollinearity ($|r| >= .700$). In any multicollinear groups, only the index with the strongest relationship with the dependent variable was retained.

### *3.3.2 Statistical model*

A linear regression model was constructed in the following steps.

First, indices that met the preliminary selection criteria were considered in the analyses.

Second, a best-subset regression was conducted using the dredge() function, which is a component of the MuMIn package (Bartón, 2019) in R. The best-subset regression approach constructs all possible models given the set of predictors entered in the analysis. This is conceptually preferred over the stepwise method, where the final result may be affected by the order in which the predictors are considered (Field *et al.*, 2012). Once a series of models had been constructed, these were compared to select the best-fitting model. This was done using a commonly used model fit index, the Bayesian Information Criterion (BIC). The BIC was used in the current study because it prefers a simple, parsimonious model by balancing out the model fit and the number of predictors (Field *et al.*, 2012).

Third, the final model based on the best-subset regression was checked for the assumption of linear models, including the independence of error, normality of error, and multicollinearity of the predictors (e.g. tolerance values and flipped sign effects[5]). Any predictors that showed the opposite polarity in the regression parameter to that of bivariate correlation with the dependent variable were removed from the model, and the model was re-run.

Fourth, to identify the relative contributions of each predictor, the calc.relimpo() function, which is a component of the relimpo package (Grömping, 2006), was used. The advantage of using this approach over examining the conventional $R^2$ change in this study was that we were interested in determining the unique contributions of each predictor in a bottom-up manner. In the regression analysis, all the predictors were centered around their means, so that the intercept of the model can be meaningfully interpreted. In this chapter, we report the final model with the relative importance index for the predictors. R script and data files are available at https://github.com/kristopherkyle/dependency_bigrams_Kyle_Eguchi_2021.

## 4 Results

The descriptive statistics for eleven indices that remained after the preliminary index selection (see Section 3.3.1) are presented in Table 6.8. These included two contextual distinctiveness indices, four dependency bigram indices, four word-frequency indices, and one lemma bigram index. Next, a set of Pearson correlation analyses was conducted to see the extent to which the eleven indices are associated with the holistic TOEFL writing scores. Table 6.9 gives a summary of the correlations (see Appendix A, Table A.1, for the correlation matrix). Overall, individual indices demonstrated small relationships with writing score. Among

**Table 6.8** Descriptive statistics for the eleven lexical and phraseological indices

| | | | | | *95%CI* | |
|---|---|---|---|---|---|---|
| **Index** | **Level** | ***M*** | ***SD*** | ***SE*** | ***LL*** | ***UL*** |
| McD | Word (contextual distinctiveness) | 0.771 | 0.117 | 0.005 | 0.760 | 0.781 |
| USF | Word (contextual distinctiveness) | 35.341 | 8.194 | 0.374 | 34.608 | 36.074 |
| Adjective frequency (log) | Word (frequency) | 9.959 | 0.843 | 0.038 | 9.884 | 10.035 |
| Adverb frequency (log) | Word (frequency) | 8.650 | 2.782 | 0.127 | 8.402 | 8.899 |
| Content word frequency (log) | Word (frequency) | 10.387 | 0.335 | 0.015 | 10.357 | 10.417 |
| Main verb frequency (log) | Word (frequency) | 10.648 | 0.478 | 0.022 | 10.605 | 10.690 |
| Lemma bigram SOA (deltap_strongest) | Bigram | 0.095 | 0.016 | 0.001 | 0.094 | 0.097 |
| Noun–adjective (MI) | Dependency bigram | 1.594 | 0.663 | 0.030 | 1.535 | 1.653 |
| Verb–adverb SOA (deltap_strongest) | Dependency bigram | 0.034 | 0.022 | 0.001 | 0.032 | 0.036 |
| Verb–dobj SOA (MI) | Dependency bigram | 1.382 | 0.517 | 0.024 | 1.336 | 1.428 |
| Verb–subject SOA (deltap_depcue) | Dependency bigram | 0.056 | 0.037 | 0.002 | 0.053 | 0.060 |

Note: M = mean; SD = standard deviation; SE = standard error; CI = confidence interval; LL = lower limit; UL = upper limit.

**Table 6.9** Correlations between variables of interest and holistic writing quality scores

| Index | Description | *r* | *p* |
|---|---|---|---|
| McD | contextual diversity based on corpus data | 0.363 | <.001 |
| USF | contextual diversity based on word associates test data | –0.332 | <.001 |
| Verb–adverb SOA (deltap_strongest) | SOA between verbs and adverb modifiers (via deltap_strongest) | 0.261 | <.001 |
| Noun–adjective (MI) | SOA between nouns and adjectives (via MI) | 0.254 | <.001 |
| Verb–dobj SOA (MI) | SOA between verbs and direct objects (via MI) | 0.224 | <.001 |
| Adjective frequency (log) | Adjective frequency (log transformed) | –0.208 | <.001 |
| Content word frequency (log) | Content word frequency (log transformed) | –0.193 | <.001 |
| Lemma bigram SOA (deltap_strongest) | SOA between adjacent words (via deltap_strongest) | 0.174 | <.001 |
| Adverb frequency (log) | Adverb of manner frequency (log transformed) | 0.134 | 0.003 |
| Verb–subject SOA (deltap_depcue) | SOA between verbs and subjects (via deltap_depcue) | 0.133 | 0.003 |
| Main verb frequency (log) | Main verb frequency (log transformed) | –0.129 | 0.004 |

them, two indices of contextual distinctiveness (McD and USF) showed the strongest correlations.

To determine which indices uniquely contributed to the essay quality, we conducted a best-subset linear regression using the eleven indices. The BIC indicated that the best model included two contextual distinctiveness indices (i.e. McD and USF), one POS specific word frequency (main verb frequency) and three dependency bigrams (noun–adjective, verb–adverb, and verb–direct object). This model was checked for the assumption of linear models. During this process, main verb frequency demonstrated a flipped-sign effect. Accordingly, main verb frequency was removed from the final model, and the model was re-run. Table 6.10 presents the final model, which contains five predictors.

In total, the five predictors explained 23.4% of the variance in the TOEFL independent writing holistic score. The intercept indicates that an average individual with respect to all the lexical and phraseological indices included in this model would score 3.427 on the TOEFL holistic score. According to the relative importance index ($R^2$), the two categories of indices – contextual distinctiveness and dependency bigrams – explained a similar proportion of the total explained variance in the dataset: 12.4% by two contextual distinctiveness indices together, and 11.4% by three dependency bigram indices altogether.

**Table 6.10** The final predictor model

| Predictors | *B* | *SE* | *p* | *β* | 95% CI for *β* LL - UL | $R^2$ |
|---|---|---|---|---|---|---|
| (Intercept) | 3.427 | .035 | <.001 | | | |
| McD | 1.338 | .373 | <.001 | .177 | .080 – .274 | .067 |
| Noun–Amod (MI) | .206 | .055 | <.001 | .154 | .073 – .234 | .038 |
| USF | –.018 | .005 | .001 | -.165 | –.259 – –.070 | .057 |
| Verb–Advmod Delta P Strongest | 7.681 | 1.686 | <.001 | .187 | .106 – .267 | .046 |
| Verb–Dobj (MI) | .273 | .070 | <.001 | .159 | .079 – .239 | .034 |
| Observations | 480 | | | | | |
| $R^2/R^2$ adjusted | 0.242 / 0.234 | | | | | |
| BIC | 1156.138 | | | | | |

Note: *B* = beta weight; β = standardized beta weight; CI = confidence interval; *LL* = lower limit; *UL* = upper limit; SE = standard error.

## 5 Discussion

The results indicated small to medium effects between the indices investigated and TOEFL writing proficiency scores. The best model (using the BIC criteria) included two word-level indices of contextual diversity and dependency bigram strength of association indices and explained approximately 23% of the variance in holistic scores. The findings suggest that more proficient second language writers tend to use words that are less contextually diverse (i.e. are more context specific) and noun-adjective, verb-direct object and verb-adverb combinations that are more strongly associated. The findings with regard to each research question are discussed in the following subsections.

### 5.1 Research Question 1

Research Question 1 was concerned with the relationship between individual indices and holistic writing quality scores. The findings related to Research Question 1 are organized by index type and are discussed in turn.

#### *5.1.1 Word-level indices*

Six word-level indices of lexical sophistication were initially entered into the model. Two indices of contextual diversity (McD and USF) demonstrated moderate ($|r| > .300$) correlations with holistic writing proficiency scores and were included in the final predictor model. These results generally align with previous research (Berger *et al.*, 2017), which found similar trends between USF and McD and judgments of spoken lexical proficiency. Tables 6.11 and 6.12 illustrate this point: i.e. the higher-scoring excerpt (Table 6.12) contains more words with high contextual

**Table 6.11** McD contextual diversity scores for a low scoring essay

| Excerpt | Content words | McD contextual diversity |
|---|---|---|
| [...] For living properly and **highly status** there is necessary to have a good job. To find a good job there must essencial to reada good **subject**. To reading a good subject every people can get a good job to lead their life and to make their **career**. [...] | live | 0.534 |
| | properly | 0.497 |
| | highly | 1.035 |
| | status | 3.173 |
| | necessary | 0.615 |
| | have | 0.077 |
| | good | 0.292 |
| | job | 0.292 |
| | find | 0.324 |
| | good | 0.292 |
| | job | 0.292 |
| | must | 0.089 |
| | essencial | n/a |
| | reada | n/a |
| | good | 0.292 |
| | subject | 1.63 |
| | read | 0.494 |
| | good | 0.292 |
| | subject | 1.63 |
| | people | 0.199 |
| | can | 0.098 |
| | get | 0.128 |
| | good | 0.292 |
| | job | 0.292 |
| | lead | 0.496 |
| | life | 0.438 |
| | make | 0.301 |
| | career | 1.266 |
| | *M* | 0.591 |

Note: Excerpt from essay Form1-20073007-Item2, which earned a score of 2

distinctiveness (e.g. *motivate*, *selfish*, *satisfaction*). This contrasts sharply with the lower-scoring example (Table 6.11), which contains very few contextually distinctive words except for ones directly borrowed from the prompt (i.e. *subject*, *career*; see Table 6.3 for the prompt).

Four indices of frequency demonstrated weak correlations ($|r| < .300$ and $>.100$) with holistic scores but were not included in the final predictor model. More proficient writers tended to use less frequent content words overall, and, in particular, tended to use less frequent adjectives

**Table 6.12** McD contextual diversity scores for a high scoring essay

| Excerpt | Content words | McD contextual diversity |
|---|---|---|
| [...] True **happiness** lies in our heart. This one statement aptly **summarizes** my point of view. As children we always do things that drive us or **motivate** us. As **selfish** as it sounds, this is an innate quality in all human beings. We definitely carry this on **even** through our adulthood. Hence, going against this only **hampers** our success and sense of self **satisfaction** as **well**. [...] | true | 0.624 |
| | happiness | 2.217 |
| | lie | 0.602 |
| | heart | 0.513 |
| | statement | 0.777 |
| | aptly | n/a |
| | summarize | 1.878 |
| | point | 0.622 |
| | view | 0.897 |
| | child | 0.439 |
| | always | 0.211 |
| | do | 0.118 |
| | thing | 0.244 |
| | drive | 0.575 |
| | motivate | 1.631 |
| | selfish | 1.833 |
| | sound | 0.59 |
| | innate | n/a |
| | quality | 0.949 |
| | human | 0.755 |
| | being | 0.744 |
| | definitely | 0.344 |
| | carry | 0.51 |
| | even | 1.365 |
| | adulthood | n/a |
| | go | 0.131 |
| | only | 0.16 |
| | hamper | 2.387 |
| | success | 0.862 |
| | sense | 0.582 |
| | self | 0.751 |
| | satisfaction | 1.791 |
| | as | 2.973 |
| | well | 2.161 |
| | *M* | 0.975 |

Note: Excerpt from essay, Form1-20073278-Item2, which earned a score of 4.5.

and main verbs. This finding aligns with a number of previous studies (Kyle & Crossley, 2015; Kyle *et al.*, 2018; Laufer & Nation, 1995) and demonstrates the relatively consistent relationship between frequency and perceptions of productive proficiency. In contrast, adverb frequency was positively correlated with writing proficiency scores, indicating that more proficient writers tended to use more common adverbs of manner. In this study, noun frequency was not meaningfully related to writing quality scores, which may be due to the fact that writers responded to the same two prompts (and recycled the relevant nouns). Additionally, although concreteness has been a meaningful predictor of lexical proficiency in a number of studies (Kim *et al.*, 2018; Kyle *et al.*, 2018), it demonstrated a negligible relationship with writing quality scores.

#### *5.1.2 N-gram strength of association*

A number of previous studies have demonstrated small to moderate relationships between *n*-gram strength of association and production quality (Bestgen & Granger, 2014; Garner *et al.*, 2019; Kyle *et al.*, 2018). The results of this study generally supported previous findings. A small ($r$ = .174), positive relationship was found between bigram strength of association and writing quality scores. This finding indicates that, on average, more proficient writers used more conventional two-word sequences than less proficient writers. Additionally, this study is the first to use the delta-p (max) index, which performed better than MI, T, or either direction of delta-p. However, the variance in essay scores explained by bigram association strength was subsumed by other indices and it was not included in the final model.

#### *5.1.3 Dependency bigram indices*

Two previous studies (Paquot, 2018, 2019) indicated that more proficient writers tended to use more strongly associated dependency bigrams, but that this relationship may vary across dependency types and proficiency levels. In general, the current study aligns with previous studies. Four dependency strength of association indices (noun-adjective, verb-adverb, and verb-direct object, verb-subject) demonstrated small positive relationships with writing quality scores. This indicates that, on average, higher proficiency learners tend to use dependency bigrams that are more conventional. Three of the four indices were included in the final predictor model, suggesting that they explain complementary portions of the variance in quality scores. For the noun-adjective and verb-direct object bigrams, MI (which was also used in Paquot's studies) was the most predictive strength of association index. For verb-adverb combinations, the most predictive strength of association index was delta-p (strongest). More research is needed to explore the qualitative differences in the types of relationships that are highlighted by MI scores and delta-p.

Table 6.13 provides examples of dependency bigram use in lower scoring and higher scoring essays. In the lower scoring example, dependency bigrams tended to be absent from the reference corpus (e.g. *exchange product*), have weak association scores (e.g. *work together*), or even be in negative (repelling) relationships (e.g. *extra thing*) (Paquot, 2019). By contrast, dependency bigrams in the higher scoring sample are likely to be in stronger relationships on average (e.g. *avoid conflict, simple gesture*). This largely mirrors the previous findings by Bestgen and Granger (2014) and Paquot (2019), who reported a larger number of negatively associated *n*-grams and dependency bigrams in their lower proficiency learner writings, respectively.

While this convergence would suggest generalizable relationships between the writing quality and the statistical associations of different phraseological units, it is important to reiterate that dependency bigram and *n*-gram measures differ in an important way. Dependency bigram association strengths highlight lexical co-occurrences within particular grammatical relationships (e.g. verbs and direct objects) in a precise manner. *N*-gram association strengths, on the other hand, may highlight a variety of relationships (grammatical and otherwise). Although this issue can be somewhat mitigated by constraining *n*-grams to specific POS sequences (e.g. adjective-noun), such a tactic will miss many instances of the desired construction.

Furthermore, it was found that the learners' production on the four dependency bigram measures was either not meaningfully correlated or demonstrated weak correlations ($-.01 \leq r \leq .143$; see Appendix A, Table A.1). This is rather surprising since one might conceptualize collocation knowledge as an umbrella notion. However, the current result suggests that learners' collocation production may be specific to certain dependency types, and collocations from different dependency types may constitute distinct constructs in learners' phrasicon (see also Brezina & Fox, Chapter 7 of this volume). This issue is deserving of future research.

## 5.2 Research Question 2

Research Question 2 was concerned with the relative importance of each index in the predictor model. Eleven indices were entered into a best-subsets multiple regression. The most parsimonious model included five predictors and explained approximately 23% of the variance in essay scores. This variance was explained by word level and dependency bigram level indices in a rather balanced fashion. The two indices of contextual diversity accounted for approximately 12% of the variance, while the three dependency bigram indices accounted for approximately 11% of the variance. Indices related to word frequency and bigram strength of association were subsumed by contextual diversity and dependency bigram indices. The correlation matrix for indices entered into the final model (see Appendix A, Table A.1) suggests that the indices of contextual diversity likely subsumed the variance explained by the indices of frequency (e.g. lemma frequency demonstrated moderate to strong correlations with

**Table 6.13** Dependency bigrams for mid- and high scoring essays

| | | Verb–Direct Object | | *Verb–Adverbial Modifier* | | Noun–Adjectival Modifier | |
|---|---|---|---|---|---|---|---|
| Proficiency | Excerpt | gov_dep | MI | gov_dep | DeltaP strongest | gov_dep | MI |
| Middle (Score = 3) | From the first day people start to **exchange** their own **products**, cooperation has been presented. It was the cooperation between each members in a family. They *worked together* to **supply** their **own** *then* ***collect*** extra **things** to sell. | **exchange_product** | na | *work_together* | 0.050 | day_first | 1.474 |
| | | **supply_own** | na | *collect_then* | –0.004 | product_own | 0.007 |
| | | **collect_thing** | –0.160 | | n/a | thing_extra | –1.515 |
| High (Score = 5) | Quite simply, if there are more and more of us living in a limited amount of space we must learn to cooperate in order to **avoid conflict** and **live** a **life** in harmony with our sorroundings. From a simple gesture like **providing** a fellow **citizen** with directions, to assiting a work colleague with an upcoming deadline, it just has to be done. | **avoid_conflict** | 3.492 | | n/a | amount_limited | 2.617 |
| | | **live_life** | 4.793 | | n/a | gesture_simple | 2.490 |
| | | **provide_citizen** | 0.172 | | n/a | citizen_fellow | 4.170 |

Note: NA indicates that a bigram of this type did not occur in the excerpt.
Verb–Direct Objects are presented in **bold**; Verb–Adverbial Modifiers are shown in *Italics*; Noun–Adjectival Modifiers are underlined.

McD and USF). Bigram strength of association only demonstrated small correlations with the dependency bigram strength of association indices but demonstrated a moderate correlation with McD. This suggests that contiguous bigrams do indeed measure word use characteristics that are distinct from dependency bigrams. Given the strength of bigram and trigram strength of association in other studies (e.g. Bestgen & Granger, 2014; Garner *et al.*, 2019; Kyle *et al.*, 2018), it is not suggested that these indices be abandoned without further investigation, and there is reason to believe that they may in fact work in concert with indices of dependency bigram strength of association. However, more research with different learner corpora is needed to investigate this.

It should be noted that the amount of variance in production quality scores explained by the model in this study (23%) is lower than some other studies that have used more index types (e.g. Guo *et al.*, 2013) and/or used different indices of lexical sophistication and phraseological competence (e.g. Kyle & Crossley, 2016). Guo *et al.* (2013), for example, used a wide variety of indices related to lexical characteristics, lexical diversity, syntactic complexity, and the number of words per essay to predict TOEFL essay scores. Their model explained 65% of the variance in essay scores, which is clearly much higher than in the current study. However, number of words per essay accounted for the lion's share of the explained variance (47.8% of the total variance explained), and features related to lexical sophistication accounted for only slightly more of the variance, as in this study (13.8%). Kyle and Crossley (2016) used all the indices related to lexical sophistication that are available in the Tool for the Automatic Analysis of Lexical Sophistication (TAALES). Their predictor model explained approximately 36% of the variance in TOEFL scores using indices related to contextual distinctiveness (range for all words based on the British National Corpus [BNC]), bigram frequency (based on the BNC), hypernymy, and imageability. Contextual distinctiveness and bigram frequency explained the largest portions of variance in the model (16.7 % and 17.8%, respectively). It is important to note, however, that the variance explained by bigram frequency is dependent on the contextual distinctiveness index (the bivariate correlation between bigram frequency and score was quite low, $r = .107$). In this study, frequency and strength of association norms were drawn from the newspaper and magazine subsections of COCA. This was deemed appropriate because the length and nature of argumentative essays aligned more closely with newspaper and magazine articles than other sections of COCA (e.g. academic journal articles). Nonetheless, future research should investigate the degree to which this choice was appropriate. COCA was chosen over other large corpora (such as the BNC) as it more closely aligns with the language domain of the TOEFL (which is used widely as a language proficiency standard at universities in the United States). Additionally, more sophisticated indices of contextual distinctiveness (McD and USF instead of range) and bigram strength of association (MI, T, and delta-p instead of frequency) were used in this study. A priori, these were more sophisticated measures deemed more appropriate, but in the end were somewhat less predictive. More research is needed to investigate which reference corpora (e.g. Granger & Bestgen, 2017) and/or calculation methods are most strongly related to judgments of production quality (and why).

## 6 Conclusion

This study has indicated that word level indices (contextual distinctiveness) and dependency bigram strength of association explain a moderate amount of the variance in holistic scores of writing quality in a complementary manner. Additionally, the study has reported that dependency bigrams can be automatically extracted from L2 writing samples with a high degree of accuracy.

The results of the study also have several implications for L2 writing instruction and assessment. First, the findings add to a growing body of literature that suggests that lexical and phraseological indices contribute roughly equally to human judgments of proficiency (e.g. Pawley & Syder, 1983). Additionally, building on Paquot (2018), this study suggests that the assessment of phraseological proficiency should encompass a range of collocation types (e.g. verb–direct objects, verb-adverbial modifiers, and noun–adjectival modifiers). For teaching and learning contexts, this suggests that vocabulary instruction should include a focus on phraseological competence. One starting point may be to focus on commonly occurring dependency collocations highlighted above. For assessment contexts, there are at least two important implications. First, it may be important for scoring rubrics to mention explicitly features related to phraseological proficiency. Second, in large-scale assessments that use automatic essay scoring, adding dependency bigram indices to scoring models may strengthen the assessment's validity argument.

There are a few limitations that should be addressed in future research. First, our findings are restricted to a single type of learner production, namely argumentative essays. Future research should investigate whether these relationships are similar across a variety of modes and task types. Second, this study used average association scores for collocations. Although this is a widely used method (e.g. Bestgen & Granger, 2014; Paquot, 2019), it may obscure the overall profiles of collocation distributions within individual essays. Finally, in this study the dependent variable was holistic scores of writing quality. While investigating the linguistic predictors of these scores is worthwhile, it should be noted that the rubric used to assign scores included features beyond lexical proficiency (such as organization, argumentation, and syntactic features). In order to more clearly identify the correlates of judgments of lexical proficiency and sophistication in particular, more focused rubrics are needed. This is a worthwhile area for future research.

## Appendix A

**Table A.1** Correlation matrix for final variables

| | Index | Score | 1 | 2 | 3 | 4 | 5 | 6 | 7 | 8 | 9 | 10 |
|---|---|---|---|---|---|---|---|---|---|---|---|---|
| 1 | McD | 0.363 | | | | | | | | | | |
| 2 | USF | –0.332 | –0.557 | | | | | | | | | |
| 3 | Verb–adverb SOA (deltap_strongest) | 0.261 | 0.191 | –0.143 | | | | | | | | |
| 4 | Noun–adjective (MI) | 0.254 | 0.194 | –0.157 | 0.121 | | | | | | | |
| 5 | Verb–dobj SOA (MI) | 0.224 | 0.179 | –0.115 | –0.011 | 0.106 | | | | | | |
| 6 | Adjective frequency (log) | –0.208 | –0.259 | 0.293 | –0.001 | –0.277 | –0.093 | | | | | |
| 7 | Content word frequency (log) | –0.193 | –0.643 | 0.494 | –0.106 | –0.156 | –0.169 | 0.476 | | | | |
| 8 | Lemma bigram SOA (deltap_strongest) | 0.174 | 0.325 | –0.184 | 0.183 | 0.043 | 0.112 | –0.013 | –0.098 | | | |
| 9 | Adverb frequency (log) | 0.134 | 0.126 | –0.004 | 0.070 | 0.011 | 0.031 | 0.083 | 0.071 | 0.135 | | |
| 10 | Verb–subject SOA (deltap_depcue) | 0.133 | 0.326 | –0.240 | 0.143 | –0.023 | 0.050 | 0.014 | –0.149 | 0.256 | 0.083 | |
| 11 | Main verb frequency (log) | –0.129 | –0.603 | 0.338 | –0.061 | –0.157 | –0.232 | 0.223 | 0.686 | –0.201 | 0.004 | –0.143 |

## Notes

(1) Contextual distinctiveness refers to a family of word-level indices that measures the range of semantic and/or lexical contexts where a word occurs. There are two broad approaches to operationalizing context; using psychological word association data or analysing a large-reference corpus. The current study uses indices that reflect both approaches to contextual distinctiveness (see Section 3.2.3).

(2) Researchers may request access to the TOEFL public use dataset by submitting a research proposal and a request form to ETS. Please see https://www.ets.org/research/contact/data_requests/ for more information.

(3) The rubric can be found at https://www.ets.org/s/toefl/pdf/toefl_writing_rubrics.pdf

(4) Relative entropy is an information-theoretic measure that computes the dissimilarity between two probability distributions (McDonald & Shillcock, 2001). In McD, this is used to estimate the degree to which the occurrence of a target word predicts the occurrence of the words surrounding it. The more dissimilar the distributions of the surrounding lexical contexts with and without the target word are in a large reference corpus, the more lexically constrained (i.e. contextually distinct) a word is.

(5) Occasionally in multivariate models, predictor variables will change signs. For example, a variable that has a positive relationship with holistic essay score might end up having a negative predictor weight in the model. This can happen for at least two related reasons. One reason is model overfitting (e.g. too many related variables are being used), and the other is interactions between variables. In this study, we take a conservative approach and treat any flipped signs as an indicator of overfitting.

## References


Bartoń, K. (2019) *MuMIn: Multi-Model Inference* (Version 1.43.6) [Computer software]. https://cran.r-project.org/web/packages/MuMIn/index.html.

Berger, C.M., Crossley, S.A. and Kyle, K. (2017) Using novel word context measures to predict human ratings of lexical proficiency. *Journal of Educational Technology & Society* 20 (2), 201–212.

Bestgen, Y. (2016) Using collocational features to improve automated scoring of EFL texts. In V. Kordoni, K. Cholakov, M. Egg, S. Markantonatou and P. Nakov (eds) *Proceedings of the 12th Workshop on Multiword Expressions* (pp. 84–90). Berlin: Association for Computational Linguistics.

Bestgen, Y. (2017) Beyond single-word measures: L2 writing assessment, lexical richness and formulaic competence. *System* 69, 65–78.

Bestgen, Y. and Granger, S. (2014) Quantifying the development of phraseological competence in L2 English writing: An automated approach. *Journal of Second Language Writing* 26, 28–41. https://doi.org/10.1016/j.jslw.2014.09.004.

Biber, D., Conrad, S. amd Cortes, V. (2004) If you look at ...: Lexical bundles in university teaching and textbooks. *Applied Linguistics* 25 (3), 371–405. https://doi.org/10.1093/applin/25.3.371

Brysbaert, M., Warriner, A.B. and Kuperman, V. (2014) Concreteness ratings for 40 thousand generally known English word lemmas. *Behavior Research Methods* 46 (3), 904–911.

Chen, D. and Manning, C.D. (2014) A fast and accurate dependency parser using neural networks. In A. Moschitti, B. Pang and W. Daelemans (eds) *Proceedings of the 2014 Conference on Empirical Methods in Natural Language Processing* (pp. 740–750). Doha, Qatar: Association for Computational Linguistics. https://cs.stanford.edu/~danqi/papers/emnlp2014.pdf.

Crossley, S.A., Cobb, T. and McNamara, D.S. (2013) Comparing count-based and band-based indices of word frequency: Implications for active vocabulary research and pedagogical applications. *System* 41 (4), 965–981. https://doi.org/10.1016/j.system.2013.08.002.

Crossley, S.A., Kyle, K. and Salsbury, T. (2016) A usage-based investigation of L2 lexical acquisition: The role of input and output. *The Modern Language Journal* 100 (3), 702–715.
Davies, M. (2009) The 385+ million word Corpus of Contemporary American English (1990–2008+): Design, architecture, and linguistic insights. *International Journal of Corpus Linguistics* 14 (2), 159–190. https://doi.org/10.1075/ijcl.14.2.02dav.
Evert, S. (2005) The statistics of word co-occurrences: Words pairs and collocations. Unpublished PhD thesis, University of Stuttgart.
Explosion AI (2018) SpaCy language models. [Open source library for natural language processing.] https://spacy.io/models/en#en_core_web_sm.
Field, A., Miles, J. and Field, Z. (2012) *Discovering Statistics Using R*. London & Thousand Oaks, CA: Sage.
Garner, J., Crossley, S. and Kyle, K. (2019) N-gram measures and L2 writing proficiency. *System* 80, 176–187. https://doi.org/10.1016/j.system.2018.12.001.
Granger, S. and Bestgen, Y. (2014) The use of collocations by intermediate vs. advanced non-native writers: A bigram-based study. *International Review of Applied Linguistics in Language Teaching* 52 (3), 229–252.
Granger, S. and Bestgen, Y. (2017) Using collgrams to assess L2 phraseological development: A replication study. In P. Haan, R. de Vries and S. van Vuuren (eds) *Language, Learners and Levels: Progression and Variation* (pp. 385–408). Louvain-la-Neuve, Belgium: Presses universitaires de Louvain.
Gries, S.T. and Ellis, N.C. (2015) Statistical measures for usage-based linguistics. *Language Learning* 65 (S1), 228–255. https://doi.org/10.1111/lang.12119.
Grömping, U. (2006) Relative importance for linear regression in R: The package relaimpo. *Journal of Statistical Software* 17 (1), 1-27. https://doi.org/10.18637/jss.v017.i01.
Guo, L., Crossley, S.A. and McNamara, D.S. (2013) Predicting human judgments of essay quality in both integrated and independent second language writing samples: A comparison study. *Assessing Writing* 18 (3), 218–238.
Kim, M., Crossley, S.A. and Kyle, K. (2018) Lexical sophistication as a multidimensional phenomenon: Relations to second language lexical proficiency, development, and writing quality. *The Modern Language Journal* 102 (1), 120–141.
Kyle, K. and Crossley, S.A. (2015) Automatically assessing lexical sophistication: Indices, tools, findings, and application. *TESOL Quarterly* 49 (4), 757–786. https://doi.org/10.1002/tesq.194.
Kyle, K. and Crossley, S.A. (2016) The relationship between lexical sophistication and independent and source-based writing. *Journal of Second Language Writing* 34, 12–24. https://doi.org/10.1016/j.jslw.2016.10.003.
Kyle, K., Crossley, S.A. and Berger, C.M. (2018) The tool for the automatic analysis of lexical sophistication (TAALES): Version 2.0. *Behavior Research Methods* 50 (3), 1030–1046. https://doi.org/10.3758/s13428-017-0924-4.
Laufer, B. and Nation, I.S.P. (1995) Vocabulary size and use: Lexical richness in L2 written production. *Applied Linguistics* 16 (3), 307–322. https://doi.org/10.1093/applin/16.3.307.
McDonald, S.A. and Shillcock, R.C. (2001) Rethinking the word frequency effect: The neglected role of distributional information in lexical processing. *Language and Speech* 44 (3), 295–322.
Nation, I.S.P. (2001) *Learning Vocabulary in Another Language*. Cambridge: Cambridge University Press.
Nelson, D.L., McEvoy, C.L. and Schreiber, T.A. (2004) The University of South Florida free association, rhyme, and word fragment norms. *Behavior Research Methods, Instruments, & Computers* 36 (3), 402–407.
O'Donnell, M.B., Römer, U. and Ellis, N.C. (2013) The development of formulaic sequences in first and second language writing: Investigating effects of frequency, association, and native norm. *International Journal of Corpus Linguistics* 18 (1), 83–108. https://doi.org/10.1075/ijcl.18.1.07odo.

O'Grady, W. (2008) Innateness, universal grammar, and emergentism. *Lingua* 118 (4), 620–631.

Paivio, A. (1971) *Imagery and Verbal Processes*. New York, NY: Holt, Rinehart & Winston.

Paquot, M. (2018) Phraseological competence: A missing component in university entrance language tests? Insights from a study of EFL learners' use of statistical collocations. *Language Assessment Quarterly* 15 (1), 29–43.

Paquot, M. (2019) The phraseological dimension in interlanguage complexity research. *Second Language Research* 35 (1), 121–145.

Pawley, A. and Syder, F.H. (1983) Two puzzles for linguistic theory: Nativelike selection and nativelike fluency. In J.C. Richards and R.W. Schmidt (eds) *Language and Communication* (pp. 191–226). New York, NY: Longman.

R Core Team (2016) A language and environment for statistical computing. Computing 1. R Foundation for Statistical Computing. https://www.R-project.org/.

Read, J. (2000) *Assessing Vocabulary*. Cambridge: Cambridge University Press.

Römer, U. (2009) The inseparability of lexis and grammar: Corpus linguistic perspectives. *Annual Review of Cognitive Linguistics* 7 (1), 140–162. https://doi.org/10.1075/arcl.7.06rom.

Schwanenflugel, P.J., Harnishfeger, K.K. and Stowe, R.W. (1988) Context availability and lexical decisions for abstract and concrete words. *Journal of Memory and Language* 27 (5), 499–520.

Sinclair, J.M. (1991) *Corpus, Concordance, Collocation*. Oxford: Oxford University Press.

Zipf, G.K. (1935) *The Psycho-biology of Language. An Introduction to Dynamic Philology*. Boston, MA: Houghton Mifflin.

# 7 Adjective + Noun Collocations in L2 and L1 Speech: Evidence from the Trinity Lancaster Corpus and the Spoken BNC2014

Vaclav Brezina and Lorrae Fox

## 1 Introduction

Phraseological knowledge represents an important component of linguistic competence (e.g. Bestgen & Granger, 2014; Gablasova *et al.*, 2017; Howarth, 1998). It is an essential part of naturally sounding language production and successful communication. A simple look at the short excerpt below (1) from the Trinity Lancaster Corpus (Gablasova *et al.*, 2019) reveals the omnipresence of collocations, chunks, idiomatic sequences, phrases, etc. in L2 speech. These are underlined in example (1).

(1) before the starting I er like to er outline the principle er or main points in my er topic er in the first place traditional classrooms talking about traditional classrooms if are they the best places or the <only> places to learn and to teach in? er in the second place traditional methodologies are they certainly or best tools and at the end of this presentation I'd like to er to talk you about effective teachers how to recognise them and how to be one of them [TLC, 2_SP_30].

Let us focus on the last underlined expression: *effective teachers*. This is an adjective + noun combination; these are one of the most frequent syntactic structures in English. The appropriate use of the adjective *effective* in combination with *teacher* demonstrates phraseological knowledge on the part of the L2 speaker, which is suitable for a semi-formal spoken presentation on an educational topic. Arguably, using this combination points to a higher level of phraseological sophistication than simply saying a *good* or *excellent teacher*. Phraseology is thus often a matter of preference (in a given context), choice and co-selection of words.

The aim of this chapter is to investigate adjective + noun collocations in the Trinity Lancaster Corpus Sample (2.7 million words) and compare these with adjective + noun collocations in L1 speech sampled in the Spoken British National Corpus 2014 (10 million words). The study compares the use of adjective + noun collocations across three proficiency levels, B1 – B2 – C1/C2, of the Common European Framework of Reference (CEFR) and also pays attention to the L1 background of L2 speakers. The chapter discusses different aspects of the collocational relationship and implications of these aspects for second language acquisition (SLA). We formulated the following overarching research question to guide this study: What is the nature of adjective + noun collocations in L2 speech?

## 2 Adjective + Noun Collocations in Context

Although researchers differ in their approaches to and terminology on phraseology (Paquot & Granger, 2012), there is general agreement about the importance of formulaic structures. They contribute to idiomatic language use, processing and acquisition as well as to overall language fluency, in both L1 and L2 (e.g. Martinez & Schmitt, 2012; Paquot, 2018; Wray, 2013). Phraseology is also important from the pedagogical perspective. Research has found that the use of phraseology can increase perceived proficiency of language learners. Boers *et al.* (2006) established that L2 speakers who used formulaic sequences in speech were thought to be more fluent in their language production by blind judges. Similar findings have been reported for writing (Ohlrogge, 2009). Collocations are one form of formulaic structure and there are two broad approaches to investigating them: frequency-based (statistical collocations) and traditional (restricted collocations; Granger, 2018). As suggested by Granger (2018: 231), this chapter takes a combined approach to the study, looking for a specific syntactic structure, namely the adjective + noun combination and measuring the statistical association; this helps maintain the focus of the study and the consistency of the target features identified.

Phraseology poses challenges for L2 learners. Hasselgren (1994) noted overuse of 'lexical teddy bears', phrasal units learned early and then heavily relied upon as L2 speakers advance through the learning process. L2 speakers' use of phraseology has also been compared with L1 speakers. When investigating intensifier + adjective collocations, Granger (1998) discovered both overuse and underuse of specific collocations, which may be linked to various degrees of salience of word combinations and L2 speaker's L1 background. In a longitudinal case study on L2 phraseological development, Li and Schmitt (2009: 85) noted heavy reliance on 'a limited range of phrases, sometimes to the point where judges considered the usage non-nativelike'. Investigating verb-noun collocations in written English of native Hebrew speakers, Laufer and Waldman (2011) found fewer collocations at all proficiency levels than in native speaker data. Although the number of collocations increased at an advanced level, errors were still present despite the learners engaging in communicative teaching techniques. Overuse of adjectival collocates with certain types of nouns can also be seen in a corpus of L1 Taiwanese written English when compared with the British National Corpus (Shih, 2000). Learners tended to overuse the adjective 'big', especially in combination with abstract nouns (45% of cases), a feature which appeared only in 30% of L1 uses. Finally, Choi (2019) found evidence of both underuse of delexical collocations and overuse of high-frequency verbs in L1 Korean written English when compared to an L1 corpus and noted possible influences from overgeneralisation and L1 transfer.

L1 background has been reported to play a role in L2 phraseological use, with cross- linguistic differences occurring in various types of construction, including verb + noun collocations (Gyllstad & Snoder, Chapter 3 of this volume). Looking specifically at adjective + noun collocations, Wolter and Gyllstad (2013) found that when the L1 and L2 are typologically and lexically similar, there is evidence that L1 influences L2 collocational processing. Taking a contrastive phraseological approach, Maurer-Stroh (2005) found that errors such as collocational mismatches and false friends in German and English equivalent adjective + noun collocations could be explained by the hypothesis of transferability (Bahns, 1993). Similarly, Taka and Luka (2013) suggested that indications of collocation usage in Croatian students' essays could reflect transfer from their L1, particularly considering general adjective overuse and overreliance on phraseological units. Conversely, Bahardoust and Moeini (2012) did not find written collocations being influenced by EFL learners' L1.

Considering L2 proficiency, Li and Schmitt (2010) investigated the development of adjective + noun collocations used in academic texts by four advanced English learners using case studies. They employed a statistical approach to longitudinally track collocational proficiency development and found little change in the usage of adjective + noun collocations over one academic year. This finding is also supported by a recent longitudinal learner corpus study of adjective + noun combinations in L2 Italian (Siyanova-Chanturia & Spina, 2019), which did not find a straightforward effect of L2 proficiency. Instead, as the authors argue: 'following extended exposure to the L2, as learners become more able language users and as they acquire more extensive (single word) vocabularies, they also tend to experiment more with word combinatorial mechanisms and, as a result, produce less idiomatic, less nativelike word sequences' (2019: 32). Similarly, Omidian *et al.* (Chapter 8 of this volume) show the complex nature of phraseological development. The authors used linear mixed-effects model analysis to study verb + noun collocations within three dimensions in L2 Italian: exclusivity, phrase frequency and phrasal diversity. In particular, they noted aspects of non-linearity in the phrasal diversity and exclusivity dimensions when considering language proficiency; A1 level (beginner) learners were the only group demonstrating a longitudinal increase in collocation diversity while B1 level (intermediate) learners produced more strongly associated collocations when exploring exclusivity, with random individual variation also being found.

In contrast, other studies have discovered some effect of L2 proficiency on the use of adjective + noun collocations. Granger and Bestgen (2014) identified differences between intermediate and advanced learners' use of collocations (n-grams) in English academic writing, including adjective + noun combinations. The study confirmed the L2 proficiency hypothesis, which predicts 'a smaller proportion of lower-frequency, strongly-associated, collocations [attested by MI] and a larger proportion of high-frequency collocations [attested by t-score] in the intermediate learner texts than in the advanced learner texts' (Granger & Bestgen, 2014: 238). Further, Sonbul (2015) investigated frequency effects on collocational processing in an experimental study, when L1 and L2 speakers were exposed to synonymous adjective + noun collocations. The study found that proficiency affected the off-line sensitivity measure, where participants rated written English sentences based on typicality. Both L1 and L2 speakers were found to show some sensitivity to collocational frequency in the on-line condition measured by eye-tracking, demonstrating possible similarities in language processing shared by the two groups.

The results of previous studies thus offer a complex and often contradictory picture on the development of L2 phraseological competence and the relationship between L1 and L2 phraseological use. It is important to realise that phraseological competence is often evaluated, especially in pedagogical contexts, within the broader framework of native and non-native language use. Although there are many commonalities between L1 and L2 speakers, L1 speaker performance is often perceived as the target or baseline for L2. Llurda (2016) explained that this has been fuelled mostly by Western approaches to teaching and learning languages, as to speak 'native-like' has historically been the goal. Previously, researchers found that even highly proficient language learners may never achieve this (Long, 1990), while others established that some learners can attain language norms typical for native speakers (Birdsong, 1992). The term 'native speaker' is also not without controversy: the concept proposes a dichotomy of native speaker and non-native speaker rather than considering a continuum of learning. Others have argued that 'native speaker' is, in fact, a social construct (Seargeant, 2013), which leads to an issue of how a native speaker should be defined (Davies, 2003). Is this to based on actual language use or learners' linguistic background? Instead, Cook (2007) argued that the proficient L2 speaker should be the target in L2 language teaching. With this in mind, care must be taken when undertaking research to learn more about both the L1 and L2 speakers' language use. Corpus methods provide the advantage of using real-life data to describe linguistic patterns and to compare similarities and differences. The comparison itself should be evaluatively neutral to avoid inferring the 'native speaker' as ideal or the learner as deficient.

Current research into L2 use of collocations often employs corpus techniques to compare language across variables that mirror SLA interests such as proficiency levels and L1 background. Using large amounts of data, as in a corpus, allows researchers to identify patterns of use that would not otherwise be found. Many corpus-based studies have involved investigating written collocations, and this is partly driven by the availability of corpora, with written data being generally much easier to compile. However, written and spoken language differ fundamentally in aspects such as grammar (Leech, 2000). Likewise, collocations are used differently, with Biber *et al.* (1999: 993ff) observing that speech is more phraseological than written language. This is perhaps due to the greater cognitive strain that speaking demands in terms of language processing and memory (Wray, 2000). Essentially, we rely on phrases in speech to make communication easier for the interlocutors and this is why it is of interest to study collocations within this mode. This chapter aims to shed light on the use of adjective + noun collocations within the under-researched register of spoken interactional English.

## 3 Data and Methodology

### 3.1 Data

In the study, two corpora of spoken English were used. The Trinity Lancaster Corpus Sample represents L2 speech in semi-formal settings (during an exam eliciting both academic language and personal interaction), while the Spoken British National Corpus 2014 is a sample of current British informal L1 conversations. It is important to note that the nature of the L2 interactions is somewhat different from the L1 interactions, due to the difference in the settings. The two corpora are thus not exact counterparts and caution needs to be exercised when interpreting the sources of the differences between these two datasets.

**Table 7.1** Number of L2 speakers (and word tokens) across proficiency levels, L1s and cultural backgrounds in the Trinity Lancaster Corpus Sample – conversation and discussion tasks

| **L1/cultural background** | **Proficiency level according to CEFR** | | |
|---|---|---|---|
| | **B1** | **B2** | **C1/C2** |
| China | 80 (63,503) | 70 (65,522) | 30 (35,548) |
| India | 100 (102,668) | 100 (117,019) | 30 (50,074) |
| Italy | 100 (79,781) | 100 (102,390) | 60 (75,415) |
| Mexico | 100 (81,488) | 70 (71,648) | 60 (71,861) |
| Russia | 40 (22,145) | 28 (32,526) | – |
| Spain | 100 (74,256) | 100 (94,702) | 60 (64,672) |
| *Total* | 520 (423,841) | 468 (483,807) | 240 (297,570) |

Let us look at the corpora in more detail. The Trinity Lancaster Corpus Sample (TLC Sample) is a balanced 2.7-million-word sample taken from the Trinity Lancaster Corpus (TLC; Gablasova *et al.*, 2019). It is compiled from transcribed recordings of Trinity College London's Graded Examination in Spoken English (GESE). The corpus has been annotated with the CLAWS tagger[1] (C6 tagset).

The distribution of L2 speakers in the TLC Sample across three proficiency levels of the Common European Framework of Reference (CEFR) (Council of Europe, 2001), and L1 and cultural backgrounds is displayed in Table 7.1. More details about the corpus (nature of tasks included, transcription conventions, etc.) can be found in Gablasova *et al.* (2019).

For this research, only the conversation and discussion tasks were considered in the analysis as these two tasks occur across all proficiency levels; this was important to ensure that the effect of task is kept constant. Both the conversation and the discussion are dialogic tasks between an L2 and an L1 speaker of English. A conversation task elicits a dialogue on a topic of general interest such as 'Society and living standards', 'Personal values and ideals' and 'National environmental concerns', while the discussion task focuses on a topic selected by the L2 speakers according to their interests (for a detailed description of the tasks see Gablasova *et al.*, 2019: 142ff). Both these tasks thus offer a large variety of topics, which are fairly randomly distributed across proficiency levels and L1 backgrounds; the topic is thus not considered as a predictor (independent variable) in this study.

The Spoken BNC2014 (Love *et al.*, 2017) is a 10-million-word sample of spoken conversational British English. It contains 668 speakers and provides additional rich metadata such as age, gender and socioeconomic status for the 1,251 recordings. Further details about the corpus can be seen in Table 7.2.

**Table7.2** Corpus characteristics of the Spoken BNC2014

| | |
|---|---|
| **Speakers** | 668 |
| **Recordings** | 1,251 |
| **Words** | 10,527,369 |
| **L1** | British English |
| **L2s (self-reported bilinguals)**[2] | Arabic, Cantonese, Dutch, French, German, Gujarati, Irish, Italian, Kikuyu, Kutchi, Russian, Spanish, Swedish, Turkish, Urdu and Welsh |
| **Ages** | 2–91 |

## 3.2 Methodology

The data was searched using Sketch Engine (Kilgarriff *et al.*, 2014) to extract adjective + noun combinations with possible multiple adjectives and intervening elements such as hesitation marks (*er*, *erm*). A complex CQL query was formulated to capture this pattern. The query is shown below:

```
[tag="J.*" & word!="[A-Z][a-z]+"] [tag="J.*" & word!="[A-Z][a-z]+"]
{0,1} [tag="UH.*" | word="and"]{0,2} [tag="J.*" & word!="[A-Z]
[a-z]+"]{0,1} [tag="N.*" & tag!="NP.*"]
```

It was established that this query has a high precision and a high recall. The precision was 97% with non-accurate hits involving the use of *like* and *just* as spoken features that had been mistagged as adjectives. Recall was tested on a sample of six texts with three male and three female speakers across four language backgrounds and different proficiency levels. These texts were manually annotated and compared with the results of the automated procedure. The recall was 98.02%. The obtained precision and recall levels were deemed sufficient for the present study.

A series of PHP scripts (PHP is a flexible all-purpose scripting language) using regular expressions were used to further process and compare the L2 and L1 data. In this process, disfluencies such as *n-new year* were normalised to allow a fair comparison of the collocation strength. The comparison of L1 and L2 collocation use follows the method applied in Granger and Bestgen (2014), originally devised by Durrant and Schmitt (2009). Adapting this method, we used the Spoken BNC2014 as the reference corpus for the L2 performance in the TLC Sample. The values of collocational strength of individual adjective + noun combinations in L2 were assigned based on the L1 use in the Spoken BNC2014.

The unit of analysis in the comparisons is a collocation type. This allows more precise measuring of the evidence of collocational knowledge in individual speakers than if tokens were considered. We also decided against using lemmas as the units of analysis, following Shin and Nation (2008) who focused on types over lemmas and word families; they found evidence that different types of the same lemma/ word family attract different collocates. Statistical analyses were carried out using Lancaster Stats Tools online (Brezina, 2018).

## 4 Results

This section deals with the results of the study, focusing on the frequency, types and collocational strength of the target feature (adjective + noun combinations). The results are then discussed in Section 5.

### 4.1 Frequency of adjective + noun combinations

Overall, there were 23,833 instances of adjective + noun combinations in the TLC Sample. On average, this constitutes 19.8 occurrences of this structure per 1,000 words in the dataset. The relative frequency per 1,000 tokens does not show any differences in the distribution of this structure across different proficiency levels. The only difference observable is between the L1 benchmark (with lower relative frequency) and L2 performance. However, as indicated in the data section (Section 3.1), the nature of the L1 interactions is different from the tasks in the L2 corpus, and the relative frequency per 1,000 tokens may simply be an indicator of the overall frequency of nouns in the two corpora. We therefore need to consider the relative frequency of adjective + noun combinations per the number of nouns in the datasets. In this case, a more interesting pattern emerges. The latter normalisation is in fact more precise because it focuses on the adjectival modification of noun phrases (the focus of this study) rather than a competition between (modified) nouns and other word classes in the corpus. The details can be seen in Table 7.3.

In order to estimate statistical significance of the observation, 95% confidence intervals (95% CIs) around group means were calculated and displayed in a form of error bars (for more information about this technique, see Brezina, 2018: 146). This visualisation takes into

**Table 7.3** Adjective + noun combinations per proficiency level

| Proficiency | Absolute frequency of adj + noun | Tokens | Nouns | Relative frequency per 1000 tokens | Relative frequency per 1000 nouns |
|---|---|---|---|---|---|
| B1 | 8,168 | 423,841 | 58,275 | 19.27 | 140.54 |
| B2 | 9,817 | 483,807 | 65,709 | 20.29 | 148.19 |
| C1/C2 | 5,848 | 297,570 | 37,328 | 19.65 | 155.39 |
| L1 – benchmark | 176,258 | 11,035,380 | 1,178,207 | 15.97 | 153.03 |

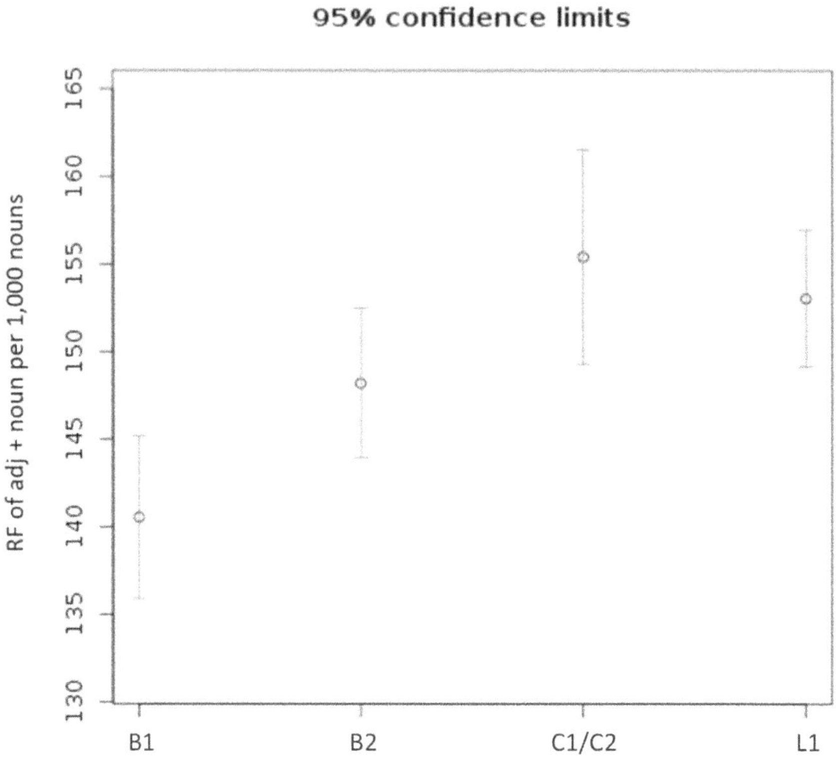


**Figure 7.1** Relative frequency of adjective + noun combinations per 1,000 nouns (group means and 95% CIs)

consideration inter-speaker variation and the amount of evidence present in the individual proficiency-based subcorpora. The circle in the graph indicates the mean value of the relative frequency of adjective + noun combinations per 1,000 nouns, while the error bars show the interval, where the mean is likely to lie in 95 % of samples taken from the same population. Largely overlapping confidence intervals indicate that the result is not statistically significant (taken from the same population); non-overlapping error bars point to statistically significant results. As can be seen from Figure 7.1, the B1 level differs from C1/C2 as well as from the L1 performance in the Spoken BNC2014. There is no statistically significant difference between B1 and B2 or among the B2 – C1/C2 – L1 groups. This tendency has been confirmed by the one-way ANOVA with Bonferroni corrected t-tests as post hoc tests ($F$ (3, 1905) = 7.55; $p < .001$; $\omega = 0.101$; small effect; post-hoc B1 vs. C1&C2 and B1 vs. L1 p< .001). Further statistical testing (ANOVA) did not show an effect of L1 background ($F$ (1, 1242) = 2.48; $p = .115$).

## 4.2 Types of adjective + noun combinations

Regarding the nature of typical adjective + noun collocations in the dataset, Table 7.4 displays the top 5 nouns in terms of their frequency at different proficiency levels and in the L1 data. Their most frequent (as measured by collocation frequency) and most exclusive combinations (as measured by the MI score) are recorded in Table 7.4. While this section explores typical cases of adjective + noun combinations from a

**Table 7.4** Top 5 nouns and their adjectival collocates in TLC Sample and the Spoken BNC2014

| Corpus | Proficiency | Nouns | Absolute frequency | Most frequent adjective modifications (collocate frequency) | Most exclusive adjective modifications (MI score) |
|---|---|---|---|---|---|
| TLC Sample | B1 | people | 1474 | other, young, poor | poor, rich, corrupt |
| | | school | 1094 | primary, high, middle | nursing, elementary, primary |
| | | money | 882 | little, important, extra | extra, lucky, little |
| | | time | 777 | long, free, last | sleeping, spare, free |
| | | years | 654 | next, recent, past | recent, past, last |
| | B2 | people | 2565 | other, young, old | qualified, illiterate, elder |
| | | time | 1170 | long, free, good | spare, rough, olden |
| | | things | 1093 | other, different, new | spooky, meaningful, chemical |
| | | school | 976 | high, primary, middle | primary, elementary, secondary |
| | | years | 844 | last, early, next, | past, recent, early |
| | C1/C2 | people | 2889 | young, other, old | handicapped, Brazilian, elder |
| | | things | 946 | other, good, bad | politic, mean, controversial |
| | | way | 860 | good, different, other | positive, certain, proper |
| | | time | 813 | long, next, ancient | spare, changing, ancient |
| | | children | 697 | little, other, young | little, own, young |
| BNC2014 | L1 – benchmark | thing | | other, good, whole | petrol-driven, withered, strawberry-flavoured |
| | | stuff | | good, other, new | power-based, anti-mosquito, run-of-the-mill |
| | | people | | gay, normal, stupid | heterosexual, like-minded, effeminate |
| | | person | | only, other, good | non-lazy, clean-living, debauched |
| | | way | | other, good, long | joking, uncivilized, convoluted |

more qualitative perspective, the actual statistical scores are analysed in Section 4.3. Rather than categorising collocations into low/medium/high collocational bands (e.g. Bestgen & Granger, 2014), which ultimately begs the question of appropriate cut-off points, we conceptualise the collocational relationship as a continuum best described from the perspective of frequency and exclusivity (cf. also Gablasova *et al.*, 2017).

Overall, there is a large overlap in the nouns frequently appearing in the adjective + noun combinations across the proficiency levels and the L1 baseline, e.g. the noun *people* occurs in every group. Considering frequent collocates of these nouns, there is also a large overlap in the L2 data. For example, the collocation *young/other* + *people* runs across all proficiency levels. The L1 baseline, however, shows less overlap in these frequent collocations with the L2 data. For instance, the top 3 most frequent adjectival collocates of the noun *people* are *gay, normal* and *stupid*. The L1 speakers thus use different frequent adjectival collocates for the same nouns when compared to the L2 speakers, while there is similarity in collocations for the L2 speakers regardless of the proficiency level. Looking at MI score collocates, we can see that exclusive collocates are more specific to a particular proficiency level because these often reflect low-frequency combinations, which are topic-related such as *corrupt people* (B1), *chemical things* (B2) and *anti-mosquito stuff* (L1).

To further investigate the overlap among the different proficiency levels and contrast this with L1 use, we looked at the ranking of specific collocations in different groups of speakers. After extracting a master list consisting of 42 adjective + noun collocations that appeared in all three proficiency levels, we ranked each collocation according to the frequency of occurrence per proficiency level. The same collocations were then found in the Spoken BNC2014 and ranked. Pairwise Spearman's correlations (ρ) are reported in Table 7.5.

Overall, there are strong positive correlations between all proficiency levels; the correlations with L1 use are noticeably lower but still reasonably high (above 0.5). It needs to be noted that the similarities and differences observed are to some extent topic related. Interestingly, the correlations do not show a clear linear development through proficiency levels. The strongest correlation (0.859) was observed between the B1 and the C1/C2 proficiency levels. To illustrate the overlap, Table 7.6

**Table 7.5** Commonalities in adjective + noun collocation frequency ranks

| | B1 | B2 | C1/C2 | L1 |
|---|---|---|---|---|
| **B1** | 1.00** | 0.774** | 0.859** | 0.508** |
| **B2** | | 1.00** | 0.813** | 0.507** |
| **C1/C2** | | | 1.00** | 0.534** |
| **L1** | | | | 1.00** |

Note: Significance codes: ** .01.

**Table 7.6** Top 20 adjective + noun collocations and their overlap

| Frequency rank | B1 | B2 | C1/C2 | L1 baseline |
|---|---|---|---|---|
| 1 | other people | other people | young people | little bit |
| 2 | foreign language | high school | good thing | other day |
| 3 | mobile phone | big problem | other people | long time |
| 4 | other country | young people | mobile phone | other people |
| 5 | healthy food | big city | other country | other thing |
| 6 | little bit | public figure | good way | good thing |
| 7 | good way | global warming | high school | good idea |
| 8 | primary school | good thing | other thing | whole thing |
| 9 | important thing | mobile phone | little bit | only thing |
| 10 | long time | long time | bad thing | other side |
| 11 | high school | other country | important thing | other way |
| 12 | fast food | good idea | good idea | bloody hell |
| 13 | other thing | important thing | social network | good job |
| 14 | young people | little bit | other hand | bad thing |
| 15 | other language | good way | equal opportunity | different thing |
| 16 | good thing | bad thing | big problem | good friend |
| 17 | social network | other thing | long time | big thing |
| 18 | free time | good job | old people | little thing |
| 19 | middle school | good friend | rich people | good time |
| 20 | favourite sport | early memory | primary school | good way |

☐ Shared among B1 & B2 & C1/C2 ☐ Shared among B1 & B2 &C1/2 and L1

displays the actual collocations across proficiency levels and the L1 baseline; only the top 20 collocations are included in this summary.

Despite the overall similarities, some differences can be observed in Table 7.6; these can be attributed to the topic of the conversation, such as *fast food* and *mobile phone*. For example, within the B1 level both *fast food* and *healthy food* occurred within the top 20 collocates and were not present in other proficiency levels.

## 4.3 Frequency, MI score and log Dice collocations

In this section, we look at the effect of L1 and proficiency on collocation frequencies, MI scores and log Dice scores. Three multi-way (factorial) ANOVA models were built to investigate the effect of L1 and proficiency as predictors as well as their interaction. The results of the analyses are reported in Tables 7.7 – 7.9.

As can be seen from Tables 7.7 – 7.9, while all three analyses identified an L1 effect, the effect of proficiency and an interaction between proficiency and L1 was statistically significant only with log Dice scores.

**Table 7.7** Multi-way ANOVA: Collocation frequencies

| | Df | Sum Sq. | Mean Sq. | F value | Pr (>F) | Significant? |
|---|---|---|---|---|---|---|
| L1 | 11 | 352098 | 32009 | 3.206 | 0.000259 | *** |
| Proficiency | 2 | 19899 | 9949 | 0.996 | 0.369510 | |
| L1:Proficiency | 17 | 195734 | 11514 | 1.153 | 0.297060 | |
| Residuals | 1211 | 12092176 | 9985 | | | |

Note: Significance codes: ***.001, *.05.

**Table 7.8** Multi-way ANOVA: MI scores

| | Df | Sum Sq. | Mean Sq. | F value | Pr (>F) | Significant? |
|---|---|---|---|---|---|---|
| L1 | 10 | 73.1 | 7.308 | 3.973 | 2.33e-05 | *** |
| Proficiency | 2 | 1.9 | 0.949 | 0.516 | 0.5972 | |
| L1:Proficiency | 17 | 48.2 | 2.837 | 1.542 | 0.0727 | |
| Residuals | 1205 | 2216.5 | 1.839 | | | |

Note: Significance codes: ***.001, *.05.

**Table 7.9** Multi-way ANOVA: log Dice scores

| | Df | Sum Sq. | Mean Sq. | F value | Pr (>F) | Significant? |
|---|---|---|---|---|---|---|
| L1 | 10 | 16.9 | 1.6922 | 1.852 | 0.0480 | * |
| Proficiency | 2 | 5.6 | 2.7918 | 3.055 | 0.0475 | * |
| L1:Proficiency | 17 | 26.5 | 1.5560 | 1.703 | 0.0366 | * |
| Residuals | 1205 | 1101.2 | 0.9138 | | | |

Note: Significance codes: ***.001, *.05.

Focusing on proficiency, Table 7.10 shows mean values and standard deviations of collocation frequencies, MI scores and log Dice scores for three proficiency groups in the TLC Sample, calculated on the basis of L1 baseline in the Spoken BNC2014. The last column with sparklines displays the tendency of development of a particular collocation index across proficiency levels. In this analysis, we are trying to establish if any of the proficiency levels is closer to the L1 usage in terms of these three indices and what the overall trend is.

**Table 7.10** Comparison of collocation statistics across proficiency levels

| Proficiency | B1 | B2 | C1/C2 | Tendency |
|---|---|---|---|---|
| **Mean collocation frequency (SD)** | 99.88 (112.79) | 103.40 (93.09) | 112.50 (88.43) |  |
| **Mean MI score (SD)** | 5.41 (1.50) | 5.34 (1.33) | 5.36 (1.19) |  |
| **Mean log Dice (SD)** | 7.20 (1.13) | 7.24 (0.83) | 7.39 (0.82) |  |

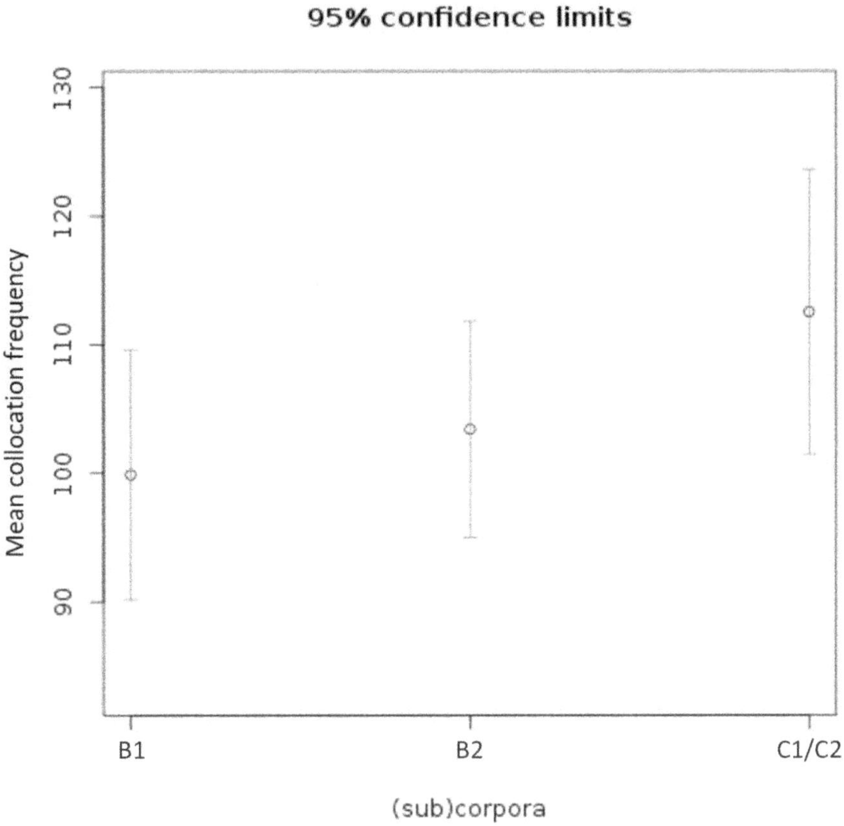


**Figure 7.2** Comparison of the three proficiency levels using the mean collocation frequency (95% CIs)

As can be seen from Table 7.10, two of the indices (mean collocation frequency and log Dice) increase with proficiency; mean MI score, on the other hand, follows an opposite trend. Note that while the MI score is designed to identify exclusive collocates and penalises high frequency combinations, log Dice highlights combinations that are both exclusive and relatively frequent (for more information see Brezina, 2018: 73–74 and Gablasova *et al.*, 2017). We can also observe that standard deviations in each group are fairly high (compared to the mean), indicating large inter-speaker differences. The overall picture is best illustrated with three graphs with 95% confidence intervals around the mean values of the respective statistics. These are displayed in Figures 7.2–7.4. Largely overlapping 95% CIs indicate non-significant results.

In order to test whether L2 speakers tend to repeat the same formulaic sequences multiple times, the type/token ratios of the adjective + noun combinations were also computed per proficiency

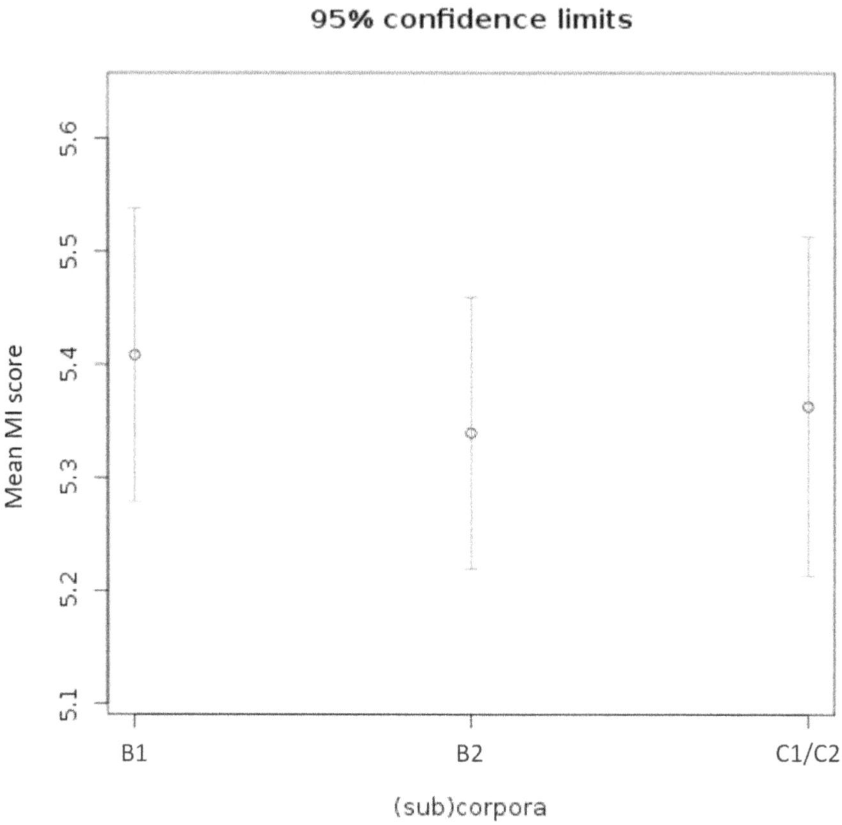


**Figure 7.3** Comparison of the three proficiency levels using the mean MI score (95% CIs)

level. Table 7.11 reports the results. As can be seen, the mean type/token ratios of adjective + noun combinations are comparable across all three proficiency levels; the L1 baseline, however, has considerably higher mean type/token ratios, indicating less repetition in L1 speech than in L2 speech. Note that, for comparability, type/token ratios for the L1 baseline were computed for a subset of scripts with the same range of adjective + noun tokens (1–73) as the L2 data; this is because type/token ratios of any kind are dependent on text length and are negatively correlated with token counts (Brezina, 2018: 57ff).

**Table 7.11** Type/token ratio (TTR) of adjective + noun combinations

| Proficiency | B1 | B2 | C1/C2 | L1 baseline |
|---|---|---|---|---|
| Mean collocation TTR (SD) | 0.86 (0.12) | 0.85 (0.11) | 0.86 (0.09) | 0.93 (0.07) |

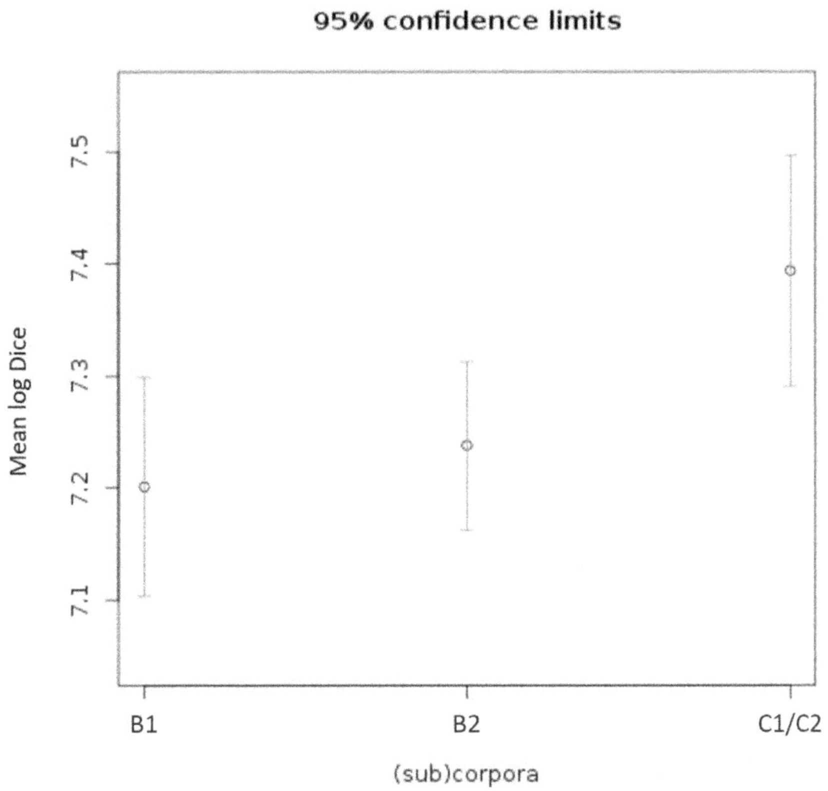


**Figure 7.4** Comparison of the three proficiency levels using the mean log Dice (95% CIs)

## 5 Discussion

The results indicate a complex picture related to the use of adjective + noun combinations in L2 and L1 speech. The focus of the discussion will be on L2 use with L1 serving as a reference point. The frequencies of adjective + noun combinations observed in L2 speech are considerably lower (on average 19.8 occurrences per 1,000 words) than what has been reported in the literature for L2 writing. Granger and Bestgen (2014), for instance, report 45.4 adjective + noun bigrams per 1,000 words in L2 student essays. This effect is likely related to the variation in the frequencies of noun phrases across different registers of speech and writing (e.g. Biber, 1988). Indeed, L1 use in the Spoken BNC2014 showed even fewer adjective + noun combinations (on average 15.97 per 1,000 words) due to the fact that these data include less formal and less informational types of interaction than the TLC Sample data. Less informational and more involved registers, to use Biber's (1988) terminology, typically occur with fewer noun phrases in general. In order to focus on phraseological aspects of adjective + noun combinations, therefore, we looked at three areas of interest, namely (i) frequencies of modified noun phrases (adjective + noun) out of all noun phrases, (ii) types of adjective + noun combinations and (iii) collocational strength of the observed combinations. These three areas are now discussed.

First, the analysis of the frequencies of modified noun phrases revealed an interesting pattern of differences. The B1 spoken performance differed from both the C1/C2 level and the L1 baseline with both C1/C2 and the L1 groups using statistically significantly more modified noun phrases than the B1-level speakers. The B1-level distinction is a critical point within language development. This echoes previous research from Thewissen (2015), who found improvement in lexical phrase accuracy in B1- to B2-level writers but noted a lack of linear progression beyond these adjacent proficiency groups. This seems to point to higher syntactic complexity (cf. Biber *et al.*, 2011) as well as to a higher level of phraseological complexity at higher levels of proficiency. Focusing on the latter, depending on the opportunity for use in a specific context, the ability to co-select an appropriate adjective to modify a noun can be seen as an indicator of the phraseological complexity of the text/spoken discourse and phraseological competence on the part of the L2 speaker. This can be demonstrated most clearly with patterns where the adjective forms an optional element of the noun phrase, thus enhancing it from the perspective of phraseology. This can be exemplified with the following three utterances taken from the TLC Sample.

(2) I don't really get the question sorry (B1 level, 2_8_RU_4)
(3) it's kind of hard question (B1 level, 2_6_IN _65)
(4) this is a a really challenging question (C2 level, IN_13)

In example (2), the noun *question* is not modified by an adjective, while examples (3) and (4) show two possible modifications with approximately the same meaning. It can be argued that while *hard question* is a more frequent combination in the TLC Sample (10 occurrences), *challenging question* (2 occurrences) is a more exclusive combination and hence more phraseologically complex. The relative MI scores in the TLC Sample of *hard question* and *challenging question* are 6.6 and 9.5 respectively, which underscores this fact. In contrast to the non-modified noun phrase in (2), the co-occurrence of *hard* and *challenging* with the noun *question* brings evidence of phraseological knowledge by L2 speakers.

Second, the investigation of the types of collocation in the data revealed a variety of adjective + noun collocations and their occurrence across proficiency levels. Here, we considered two approaches to identifying collocations using (i) the collocation frequency and (ii) the MI score. The collocation frequency is the frequency of co-occurrence of the noun and the adjective. Highly frequent combinations such as *free time, young people*, *other thing*, etc., are fairly general and thus have the ability to occur across different contexts. The combinations identified using the MI score (e.g. *chemical things, handicapped people*), on the other hand, are exclusive and often context specific (Gablasova *et al.*, 2017). In the literature (e.g. Granger & Bestgen, 2014; Li & Schmitt, 2009), the MI score is typically contrasted with the t-score, demonstrating the same type of polarity as in the present study because the t-score is highly correlated with the collocation frequency; more recent studies (e.g. Siyanova-Chanturia & Spina, 2019) abandon the problematic t-score in favour of collocation frequency and other measures. For a more detailed discussion of appropriate collocation measures, see Gablasova *et al.* (2017).

On a more general level, collocation measures operate on two principal scales of frequency and exclusivity (Brezina, 2018: 71). These scales recognise the frequency and the exclusivity of the collocational relationship as two important features of word combinations in language, which are also highlighted in this study. We have seen that L2 speakers in the TLC Sample used a similar range of high frequency collocations in a similar frequency rank order as demonstrated by the large Spearman's correlations (above 0.77). This range, however, differed to some extent from the L1 baseline (Spearman's ρ approximately 0.5). Frequent adjective + noun combinations that were shared across the proficiency levels and the L1 baseline included collocations such as *little bit, long time, other people, other thing* and *good thing.* The frequent L1 combinations not shared in the top 20 frequent collocations in the TLC Sample included examples such as *bloody hell, bad thing, good thing* and *big thing*. However, we have to note that while the L1 interactions were informal and between interlocutors who knew each other well (friends and family, Love *et al.*, 2017), the L2 interactions were semi-formal and between interlocutors with some power hierarchy (Gablasova *et al.*, 2019). The absence of swear-word combinations (*bloody hell*) and vague expressions (*bad thing, good thing, big thing*) from the top 20 frequency lists in the L2 data can thus also be explained by this difference in the nature of the interaction.

A side effect of looking at exclusivity (using the MI score) is the identification of some combinations which demonstrate lexical rather than phraseological knowledge. A prime example of these combinations in this study is the occurrence of compound nouns such as *high school, middle school* and *mobile phone*. Similar combinations (e.g. *nitrous oxide*, *Hippocratic oath* and *pop music*) figure also in the list of collocations (n-grams) identified using the MI score in Granger and Bestgen (2014). Strictly speaking, these combinations point to the use of particular naming strategies and terminology in L2 production rather than to the ability to combine words in a particular way (phraseological competence). From the perspective of vocabulary learning, such combinations demonstrate the breadth rather than the depth of vocabulary (cf. Read, 2004). They are thus likely to be correlated with the topic of the spoken exchange, chosen at a higher level than the sentence/utterance level (choice of topic at the textual level).

Third, when interpreting the collocational strength of the observed adjective + noun combinations (see Table 7.10), we need to bear in mind different properties of collocates identified using different collocation statistics. In this study, we looked at three measures highlighting different aspects of the collocational relationship between adjectives and nouns on the frequency and exclusivity scales (Brezina, 2018; Gablasova *et al.*, 2017). The collocation frequency highlights frequent, non-exclusive combinations, while the MI score focuses on infrequent but highly exclusive combinations. We have also added a third measure, log Dice, which identifies relatively exclusive combinations, which are also reasonably frequent. The log Dice score, therefore, represents a measure, which offers a balance between frequency and exclusivity (Omidian *et al.*, Chapter 8 of this volume; Rychlý, 2008).

In the study, we observed that all three collocation measures show an effect of speakers' L1. L1 has been recognised in the literature (e.g. Wolter & Gyllstad, 2013) as an important factor in phraseological knowledge, with L1 transfer effects being reported (Maurer-Stroh, 2005; Takač & Lukač, 2013). In our study, we contrasted six L1 and cultural backgrounds with typologically different languages (Chinese vs. Italian vs. Hindi, etc.). It is therefore not surprising to find differences in the collocation measures across these backgrounds. However, we need to exercise caution and not automatically assume L1 transfer without proper analysis of phraseological mechanisms in the individual L1 contexts (cf. Granger, 2015). A more in-depth investigation of this variable is, however, beyond the scope of the present study.

The only statistically significant difference related to L2 proficiency was between the B1 and the C1/C2 group when the mean strength of collocations was calculated using the log Dice score. This demonstrates that the higher proficiency level (C1/C2) spoken production included more adjective + noun combinations that are relatively frequent and exclusive than the lower B1 level. Examples of high log Dice score collocations in C1/C2 are the following: *good life, extended family, real time* and *sore throat*. This is in line with Thewissen's (2015) finding related to lexical phrase accuracy showing a clear distinction between the higher proficiency bands and the B1 group, who 'produced a higher number of "wide-of-the-mark" errors' (2015: 187).

From the perspective of second language acquisition, there is a certain tension between the frequency of co-occurrence and the exclusivity of the combination. High frequency of co-occurrence of two words points to a high probability of repeated exposure of the language learner to these combinations and the possibility of statistical (implicit) learning (e.g. Saffran, 2003). On the other hand, very frequent combinations might not get noticed and hence might not be committed to memory. As Divjak (2019: 4) points out: '[t]here is no pure frequency effect: experience cannot be reduced to frequency as experience is filtered through attention before being committed to memory'. There could be a fundamental processing difference of formulaic language between L1 and L2 speakers regarding the frequency and exclusivity of phraseological units. Ellis *et al.* (2008) found L1 English speakers had shorter recognition response times for statistical collocations with higher MI scores, a measure of exclusivity, while L2 speakers' shorter reaction times correlated with the frequency of occurrence of the collocation. Sonbul (2015), in a study of adjective + noun collocations, found frequency to have a similar effect on typicality rating of collocations for both L1 and L2 speakers; L2 proficiency also played a role, with more proficient L2 speakers showing greater sensitivity to collocation frequency.

Given this complex picture, and the importance of both frequency and exclusivity, we can argue that for restricted collocations, such as those in this study, it may be more apt to consider both measures combined. While in corpus-based research we cannot control for psychological variables such as attention, we can hypothesise that a collocation measure that takes into account both frequency and exclusivity of the collocation might be able to provide access to the proficiency effect better than measures that deal either with frequency or exclusivity alone. The results of this study clearly seem to indicate the plausibility of this hypothesis.

Considering the perspective of L2 production, high frequency combinations have been hypothesised to appear with larger proportions in lower proficiency texts (intermediate) than in higher proficiency texts (advanced) (Granger & Bestgen, 2014). This study did not find evidence for this claim in spoken L2 data: no difference was observed in the use of the MI and frequency-based collocations across the proficiency levels. Instead, the evidence points to a more complex picture of non-linear development of phraseological competence, where individual differences between speakers play a major role. The need to consider individual differences and changing contexts has also been highlighted by Larsen-Freeman (2006) in her case study of five L1 Chinese speakers learning English, which shows that language attainment develops dynamically. A similar conclusion has been put forward in Siyanova-Chanturia and Spina (2019), who investigated the development of adjective + noun collocations in L2 Italian in a longitudinal learner corpus. The results demonstrated phraseological development to be complex, with higher proficiency speakers not using more idiomatic language systematically. Another longitudinal study, by Omidian *et al.* (Chapter 8 of this volume), brings further evidence about phraseological development as a multi-faceted and non-linear process, noting that exclusivity and diversity in verb + noun collocations are not only influenced by time and language proficiency but also, importantly, by individual learner differences.

Finally, the effect of repetition of the same adjective + noun combinations needs to be briefly considered. In this study (see Section 3.2), a methodological decision was made to focus on collocation types rather than tokens (cf. Granger & Bestgen, 2014 who considered both bigram types and tokens). This means that the same adjective + noun combination are counted only once in the speech of the same speaker. However, we observed that the type/token ratios of these combinations differed between L2 speech on the one hand and the L1 baseline on the other hand, with L1 speakers using fewer repetitions. This is in line with previous studies of lexical repetition and lexical complexity in L1 and L2 (e.g. Connor, 1984; Crossley & McNamara, 2012; Ferris, 1994) and supports the idea of 'lexical teddy bears' proposed by Hasselgren (1994). Nevertheless, when investigating repetition, we always need to consider its multiple functions (Molenda *et al.*, 2018). One of these is lexical cohesion, as demonstrated in example (5).

(5) L1 okay alright tell me about supersonic cars

L2 **supersonic cars** are are not like just normal **normal cars** they are too fast to stop to stop <unclear=the super car er sonic> cars you don't there are **special brakes** there are two sets of parachutes and much more t-to to to stop **supersonic cars**

L1 parachutes

L2 yes like there are some **supersonic cars** which <are which company> has made er the main **supersonic car** is Thrust SSC wh-which is <unclear> which is more than some two thousand one hundred and ninety eight kilometres per hour (B2 level, 2_8_IN_17).

In example (5), the topic of discussion is 'supersonic cars'; these are contrasted with 'normal cars'. All adjective + noun combinations in L2 speech are highlighted in bold. This example demonstrates the use of a technical term ('supersonic cars'), which cannot be easily paraphrased and whose repetition by both interlocutors forms a natural part of the conversation and a means of lexical cohesion. However, for this script, the type/token ratio of adjective + noun combinations is fairly low (0.42) compared to the B2 group mean of 0.85 and the L1 baseline of 0.93. In this script, there are 23 unique adjective + noun types and 55 occurrences of these structures (tokens). Nevertheless, it would be incorrect to interpret 'supersonic cars' as a lexical teddy bear and a sign of limited phraseological competence.

## 6 Conclusion

This study offers a unique insight into the use of adjective + noun collocations in spoken L2, thus complementing previous research, which largely focused on written language. The picture that emerges is a complex one. Three major trends are observable in the data. First, a proficiency effect on the proportion of modified nouns can be seen, with B1 speakers using statistically significantly fewer collocations of this type than C1/C2 speakers and the L1 baseline group. Second, there is a proficiency effect on the collocation strength measured using the log Dice score: higher proficiency level (C1/C2) speakers used more relatively frequent and exclusive adjective + noun combinations than B1-level speakers. These two points seem to indicate a threshold in phraseological development at the B1 level. Third, an L1 effect on collocation strength regardless of the measure (frequency, MI score, log Dice) is apparent in the data. Speakers with different L1 backgrounds systematically use collocations of varying strength, which could point to L1 transfer effects, although more investigation is needed in this area.

Overall, however, the study revealed more potential similarities than differences in the use of adjective + noun combinations across proficiency levels, and large individual differences between speakers. We paid attention to both statistically significant as well as non-significant (negative) results. While the former are easier to interpret as evidence of a difference likely to occur in the population, the latter invite us to explore further the relationships, with a view to seeking more evidence. This means that a non-significant result is not evidence of no relationship between the variables in question. However, reporting such results is crucial for providing the whole picture and for the ability of the field to build on previous studies in replication and meta-analysis (Lehrer *et al.*, 2007; Brezina, 2018: 267).

While the study offers numerous insights into the use of adjective + noun collocations in L2 speech, it also has its limitations, imposed by the scope and focus of this research. Successful use of collocations does not depend only on the suitable (target-like) co-selection of two words (which we largely discussed in this chapter), but also on the appropriate use of the collocations in a specific context. This area clearly deserves a more detailed exploration. A prime example of this aspect is the frequent use of the adjective + noun combination *bloody hell* in the Spoken BNC2014 and its absence in the TLC Sample. In this case, the absence is entirely justifiable because the use of swear words in the semi-formal context of the interactions in the TLC Sample would not be appropriate. This also raises a more general question of a suitable L1 baseline for L2 production and the role of the native speaker in this comparison (Seargeant, 2013), which needs to be considered in future studies.

The complexity of a phenomenon such as collocations always requires paying attention to different levels of interpretation of the results and possible alternative interpretations. When analysing collocations, we need therefore to consider both the quantitative aspects (collocation frequency and strength) and the qualitative and contextual aspects (types of collocation and the appropriateness of their use). In future studies it might therefore be advisable to separate different types of adjective + noun collocations, such as compounds, from collocations in the strict sense. Also, we should not assume a single trajectory of language acquisition in all L2 speakers because learning experience is multi-faceted, often involving progress, regression and more progress, etc. (De Bot *et al.*, 2007).

## Acknowledgement

The writing of this chapter was supported by ESRC grants no. EP/P001559/1 and ES/R008906/1.

## Notes

(1) http://ucrel.lancs.ac.uk/claws/.
(2) Speakers were asked to report if they were bilingual and, if so, what their L2 was other than British English (Table 7.2). Twenty-eight (4.2%) speakers responded positively and specified the listed languages (see http://corpora.lancs.ac.uk/bnc2014/doc/BNC2014manual.pdf).

## References

Bahardoust, M. and Moeini, M.R. (2012) Lexical and grammatical collocations in writing production of EFL learners. *The Journal of Applied Linguistics* 5 (1), 61–86.
Bahns, J. (1993) Lexical collocations: A contrastive view. *ELT Journal* 47 (1), 56–63.
Bestgen, Y. and Granger, S. (2014) Quantifying the development of phraseological competence in L2 English writing: An automated approach. *Journal of Second Language Writing* 26, 28–41.
Biber, D. (1988) *Variation Across Speech and Writing.* Cambridge: Cambridge University Press.
Biber, D., Gray, B. and Poonpon, K. (2011) Should we use characteristics of conversation to measure grammatical complexity in L2 writing development? *TESOL Quarterly* 45 (1), 5–35.
Biber, D., Johansson, S., Leech, G., Conrad, S. and Finegan, E. (1999) *Longman Grammar of Spoken and Written English*. London: Longman.
Birdsong, D. (1992) Ultimate attainment in second language acquisition. *Language* 68 (4), 706–755.
Boers, F., Eyckmans, J., Kappel, J., Stengers, H. and Demecheleer, M. (2006) Formulaic sequences and perceived oral proficiency: Putting a lexical approach to the test. *Language Teaching Research* 10 (3), 245–261.
Brezina, V. (2018) *Statistics in Corpus Linguistics: A Practical Guide*. Cambridge: Cambridge University Press.
Choi, W. (2019) A corpus-based study on 'delexical verb + noun' collocations made by Korean learners of English. *The Journal of Asia TEFL* 16 (1), 279–293.
Connor, U. (1984) A study of cohesion and coherence in ESL students' writing. *Paper in Linguistics* 17 (3), 301–316.
Cook, V.J. (2007) The goals of ELT: Reproducing native-speakers or promoting multicompetence among second language users? In J. Cummins and C. Davison (eds) *International Handbook of English Language Teaching* (pp. 237–248). New York, NY: Springer.

Council of Europe (2001) *Common European Framework of Reference for Languages: Learning, Teaching, Assessment*. Cambridge: Cambridge University Press.

Crossley, S.A. and McNamara, D.S. (2012) Predicting second language writing proficiency: The roles of cohesion and linguistic sophistication. *Journal of Research in Reading* 35 (2), 115–135.

Davies, A. (2003) *The Native Speaker: Myth and Reality*. Clevedon: Multilingual Matters.

De Bot, K., Lowie, W. and Verspoor, M. (2007) A dynamic systems theory approach to second language acquisition. *Bilingualism: Language and Cognition* 10 (1), 7–21.

Divjak, D. (2019) *Frequency in Language: Memory, Attention and Learning*. Cambridge: Cambridge University Press.

Durrant, P. and Schmitt, N. (2009) To what extent do native and non-native writers make use of collocations? *IRAL-International Review of Applied Linguistics in Language Teaching* 47 (2), 157–177.

Ellis, N., Simpson-Vlach, C. and Maynard, C. (2008) Formulaic language in native and second language speakers: Psycholinguistics, corpus linguistics, and TESOL. *TESOL Quarterly* 42 (3), 375–396.

Ferris, D.R. (1994) Lexical and syntactic features of ESL writing by students at different levels of L2 proficiency. *TESOL Quarterly* 28 (2), 414–420.

Gablasova, D., Brezina, V. and McEnery, T. (2017) Collocations in corpus-based language learning research: Identifying, comparing, and interpreting the evidence. *Language Learning* 67 (S1), 155–179.

Gablasova, D., Brezina, V. and McEnery, A. (2019) The Trinity Lancaster Corpus: Development, description and application. *International Journal of Learner Corpus Research* 5 (2), 126–158.

Granger, S. (1998) Prefabricated patterns in advanced EFL writing: Collocations and formulae. In A.P. Cowie (ed.) *Phraseology: Theory, Analysis, and Applications* (pp. 145–60). Oxford: Oxford University Press.

Granger, S. (2015) Contrastive interlanguage analysis: A reappraisal. *International Journal of Learner Corpus Research* 1 (1), 7–24.

Granger, S. (2018) Formulaic sequences in learner corpora: Collocations and lexical bundles. In A. Siyanova-Chanturia and A. Pellicer-Sánchez (eds) *Understanding Formulaic Language: A Second Language Acquisition Perspective* (pp. 228–247). New York, NY: Routledge.

Granger, S. and Bestgen, Y. (2014) The use of collocations by intermediate vs. advanced non-native writers: A bigram-based study. *International Review of Applied Linguistics in Language Teaching* 52 (3), 229–252.

Hasselgren, A. (1994) Lexical teddy bears and advanced learners: A study into the ways Norwegian students cope with English vocabulary. *International Journal of Applied Linguistics* 4 (2), 237–258.

Howarth, P. (1998) Phraseology and second language proficiency. *Applied Linguistics* 19 (1), 24–44.

Kilgarriff, A., Baisa, V., Bušta, J., Jakubíček, M., Kovář, V., Michelfeit, J., Rychlý, P. and Suchomel, V. (2014) The Sketch Engine: Ten years on. *Lexicography* 1, 7–36.

Larsen-Freeman, D. (2006) The emergence of complexity, fluency, and accuracy in the oral and written production of five Chinese learners of English. *Applied Linguistics* 27 (4), 590–619.

Laufer, B. and Waldman, T. (2011) Verb-noun collocations in second language writing: A corpus analysis of learners' English. *Language Learning* 61 (2), 647–672.

Leech, G. (2000) Grammars of spoken English: New outcomes of corpus-oriented research. *Language Learning* 50 (4), 675–724.

Lehrer, D., Leschke, J., Lhachimi, S., Vasiliu, A. and Weiffen, B. (2007) Negative results in social science. *European Political Science* 6 (1), 51–68.

Li, J. and Schmitt, N. (2009) The acquisition of lexical phrases in academic writing: A longitudinal case study. *Journal of Second Language Writing* 18 (2), 85–102.

Li, J. and Schmitt, N. (2010) The development of collocation use in academic texts by advanced L2 learners: A multiple case study approach. In D. Wood (ed.) *Perspectives on Formulaic Language: Acquisition and Communication* (pp. 2–46). London & New York: Continuum.

Llurda, E. (2016) Native speakers? English and ELT: Changing perspectives. In G. Hall (ed.) *The Routledge Handbook of English Language Teaching* (pp. 51–64). London: Routledge.

Long, M.H. (1990) Maturational constraints on language development. *Studies in Second Language Acquisition* 12 (3), 251–285.

Love, R., Dembry, C., Hardie, A., Brezina, V. and McEnery, T. (2017) The Spoken BNC2014: Designing and building a spoken corpus of everyday conversations. *International Journal of Corpus Linguistics* 22 (3), 319–344.

Martinez, R. and Schmitt, N. (2012) A phrasal expressions list. *Applied Linguistics* 33 (3), 299–320.

Maurer-Stroh, P. (2005) 'House-high favourites?' A contrastive analysis of adjective-noun collocations in German and English. *ELOPE: English Language Overseas Perspectives and Enquires* 2 (1–2), 57–64.

Molenda, M., Pęzik, P. and Osborne, J. (2018) Self-repetitions in learners' spoken language: A corpus-based study. In V. Brezina and L. Flowerdew (eds) *Learner Corpus Research: New Perspectives and Applications* (pp. 90–111). London: Bloomsbury.

Ohlrogge, A. (2009) Formulaic expressions in intermediate EFL writing assessment. In R. Corrigan, A. Moravcsik, H. Ouali and K. M. Wheatley (eds) *Formulaic Language, Volume 2: Acquisition, Loss, Psychological Reality, and Functional Explanations* (pp. 387–404). Amsterdam & Philadelphia: Benjamins.

Paquot, M. (2018) Phraseological competence: A missing component in university entrance language tests? Insights from a study of EFL learners' use of statistical collocations. *Language Assessment Quarterly* 15 (1), 1–15.

Paquot, M. and Granger, S. (2012) Formulaic language in learner corpora. *Annual Review of Applied Linguistics* 32, 130–149.

Read, J. (2004) Research in teaching vocabulary. *Annual Review of Applied Linguistics* 24 (1), 146–161.

Rychlý, P. (2008) A lexicographer-friendly association score. In P. Sojka and A. Horák (eds) *Proceedings of Recent Advances in Slavonic Natural Language Processing, RASLAN* (pp. 6–9). Brno, Czech Republic: Masaryk University.

Saffran, J.R. (2003) Statistical language learning: Mechanisms and constraints. *Current Directions in Psychological Science* 12 (4), 110–114.

Seargeant, P. (2013) Ideologies of nativism and linguistic globalization. In S.A. Houghton and D.J. Rivers (eds) *Native-Speakerism in Japan: Intergroup Dynamics in Foreign Language Education* (pp. 231–242). Bristol: Multilingual Matters.

Shih, H.-H.R. (2000) Collocation deficiency in a learner corpus of English: From an overuse perspective. *Proceedings of the 14th Pacific Asia Conference on Language, Information and Computation* (pp. 281–288). Tokyo: Waseda University International Conference Center.

Shin, D. and Nation, P. (2008) Beyond single words: The most frequent collocations in spoken English. *ELT Journal* 62 (4), 339–348.

Siyanova-Chanturia, A. and Spina, S. (2019) Multi-word expressions in second language writing: A large-scale longitudinal learner corpus study. [Advance online publication.] *Language Learning* 70 (2), 420–463.

Sonbul, S. (2015) Fatal mistake, awful mistake, or extreme mistake? Frequency effects on off-line/on-line collocational processing. *Bilingualism: Language and Cognition* 18 (3), 419–437.

Takač, V.P. and Lukač, M. (2013) How word choice matters: An analysis of adjective-noun collocations in a corpus of learner essays. *Jezikoslovlje* 14 (2–3), 385–402.
Thewissen, J. (2015) *Accuracy Across Proficiency Levels: A Learner Corpus Approach*. Louvain-la-Neuve, Belgium: Presses universitaires de Louvain.
Wolter, B. and Gyllstad, H. (2013) Frequency of input and L2 collocation processing: A comparison of congruent and incongruent collocations. *Studies in Second Language Acquisition* 35 (3), 451–482.
Wray, A. (2000) Formulaic sequences in second language teaching: Principle and practice. *Applied Linguistics* 21 (4), 463–489.
Wray, A. (2013) Formulaic language. *Language Teaching* 46 (3), 316–334.

# 8 Development of Formulaic Knowledge in Learner Writing: A Longitudinal Perspective

Taha Omidian, Anna Siyanova-Chanturia
and Stefania Spina

## 1 Introduction

Phraseology has established itself as an integral part of second language (L2) learning and teaching. It has spawned major investigatory efforts in both research and practice across various fields of inquiry, such as corpus linguistics, psycholinguistics, and language education (see Siyanova-Chanturia & Pellicer-Sanchez, 2019). In the past three decades, a variety of phrasal configurations (collocations, lexical bundles, idioms, etc.) has been identified, examined, and linked to the natural production of both spoken and written discourse. These configurations are often referred to as *multi-word expressions* (MWEs), a terminology that encompasses a wide range of lexical units above the single word level (see Siyanova-Chanturia & Omidian, 2020). Research in this area has demonstrated that MWEs constitute a substantial portion of natural language and that such phraseological units are a key factor in successful language learning. As evidenced by many studies, language users' mental lexicon – an inventory of lexical entries – is not only composed of single words but also comprises a wide range of MWEs, hence the term 'phrasicon' (e.g. Pawley & Syder, 1983).

Research has focused on the identification and analysis of lexical entries forming the L2 learner phrasicon. Evidence from this line of research suggests that L2 learners' knowledge of MWEs is not as extensive as that of L1 speakers, and that learners tend to overuse a limited range of MWEs in their spoken or written production (see Granger, 2019). Much of this research, however, has looked at the L2 phrasicon from a rather fixed perspective: that is, investigating learners' phraseological competence at a single point in time. While valuable, this approach fails to illustrate the dynamic processes underlying the development of phraseological knowledge in an L2 (Li & Schmitt, 2009). Thus far, relatively few studies have explored the development of the L2 phrasicon over a period of time. Fewer still have investigated this development employing a sizeable number of participants.

As a result, despite the strong evidence base that the study of phraseology has established in the past few decades, our understanding of how the learner phrasicon develops over time is still limited. In the present contribution, we sought to shed light on the developmental aspect of the L2 phrasicon, by tracing the trajectory of MWEs used in a longitudinal corpus of learner writing. For this purpose, we collected and analysed longitudinal corpus data from a representative sample of L2 learners, focusing on the production of one kind of MWEs, namely verb-noun sequences.

In the remainder of this section, we first review previous longitudinal research on L2 phraseological competence and discuss the approaches adopted to operationalize this knowledge, so as to allow for comparisons with the study reported in this chapter. We then describe the rationale for the present contribution, focusing on key outstanding issues in the existing literature on longitudinal L2 phraseology.

## 1.1 The development of L2 phraseological competence

### *1.1.1 Evidence from longitudinal case studies*

The notion of phraseological competence rests on the growing recognition that the ability to produce meaning in a language is bound up with understanding associations and interconnections between lexical items (e.g. Sinclair, 2004). From this perspective, words have the natural tendency to make meaning by their combinations, constructing phrasal configurations that span two or more words. This phraseological view of language belies the notion that language learning is the simple memorization of single words and syntactic rules. Instead, it supports the idea that learning a language involves a process of acquiring knowledge about the associations between words.

In one of the earliest longitudinal studies of L2 lexical knowledge, Schmitt (1998) tracked the acquisition of 11 words by three advanced learners of English over the course of a year. He measured various types of word knowledge of the selected items, including the knowledge of their syntactic information and the associations they have with other related words. Schmitt (1998) observed a lack of parallel progression between syntactic and association knowledge of the target words. Schmitt's (1998) finding echoes Bahns and Eldaw's (1993) proposition that learners' knowledge of word associations does not necessarily expand in parallel with their general vocabulary and syntactic knowledge.

In a more recent study, focused primarily on the development of L2 phraseological competence, Li and Schmitt (2009) investigated the acquisition of MWEs produced by an advanced L2 learner of English over a period of approximately 10 months. Unlike recent longitudinal studies that have followed a quantitative approach (i.e. frequency-based approach, more on this below), Li and Schmitt (2009) adopted a qualitative approach (i.e. phraseological approach) to identifying and extracting MWEs. This approach has its roots in the so-called Russian school of phraseology (Cowie, 1994) and it is often characterized by its heavy reliance on impressionistic evidence (e.g. native speaker judgments) for the definition and extraction of phraseological units. The results of Li and Schmitt (2009) showed that the learner acquired new MWEs and achieved mastery of previously learned phrases. However, Li and Schmitt (2009) also observed that the development of the learner's phraseological competence was not consistent. In particular, the diversity of MWEs employed by the learner did not consistently increase over time. Rather, the learner preferred to err on the side of caution by using a small group of already well-known and 'safe' phrases repetitively. This finding is particularly important as it suggests that learners may choose to be conservative in using newly acquired phrases.

In an attempt to extend the findings of Li and Schmitt (2009), Li and Schmitt (2010) followed four advanced-level L2 learners of English over a period of 12 months. Unlike Li and Schmitt (2009), however, this study adopted a frequency-based approach, in which various frequency-based measures of phraseological competence (diversity, *t*-score and MI score, more on these below) were employed to identify patterns of development in learner *collocation* production. In the frequency-based tradition, collocations are referred to as a set of two or more words that co-occur more frequently than would be expected by chance (*make progress*, *break a habit*, see Sinclair, 2004). Focusing on the development of adjective-noun collocations in the learners' academic essays, Li and Schmitt (2010) found that, while the four learners greatly varied in their use of the target collocations, their phraseological competence on average showed modest or no improvement over time. These results led the authors to conclude that one academic year may not be long enough for L2 learners to exhibit substantial improvement in their phraseological knowledge and that researchers should be cautious about the possible variation that might exist among individual learners in the acquisition and production of MWEs.

In another case study, Yuldashev *et al.* (2013) explored patterns of development in the use of a particular kind of MWEs, namely *concgrams*. In the 'neo-Firthian' tradition, concgrams are defined as any meaningful permutations of the collocational patterns generated as a result of the association between two or more words (e.g. *is that* [AB], *that is* [BA], *is possible that* [ACB], where A and B are the target words and C is an intervening word, see Cheng *et al.*, 2008). Yuldashev and colleagues (2013) tracked the use of concgrams generated by the Spanish words *es* ('is') and *que* ('*that*') in blog posts and messaging texts written by three L2 learners of Spanish over the course of one academic year. Akin to Li and Schmitt (2010), a high degree of variability was observed among the three learners, with one learner showing more improvement over time than the other two.

While the above studies tracked L2 phraseological development in written production, Crossley and Salsbury (2011) traced this development in the spoken output of six L2 learners of English over a period of 12 months. In particular, the two authors focused on how the production accuracy of *lexical bundles* develops over time. Lexical bundles can be defined as frequently recurring contiguous word combinations (*the notion of, the aim of this paper is to*; also see Omidian *et al.*, 2018). Focusing on the production of 2-word lexical bundles in learner speech, Crossley and Salsbury (2011) also observed individual variation among the learners in the use of these bigrams. But, unlike Li and Schmitt (2010), Crossley and Salsbury (2011) found an overall significant growth in the learners' production accuracy of native-like bigrams, suggesting that one year of L2 language exposure might be sufficient for initial development of L2 phraseological competence.

Evidence from the above-reviewed studies presents a detailed picture of how the learner phrasicon expands and develops over time. The case-study approach adopted in these studies allows for a fine-grained analysis of learner progress and a detailed exploration of individual differences. However, since this approach focuses on a rather limited number of participants (often just one learner), it can impose limitations on the generalizability of the findings obtained. Given that many diverse factors (e.g. language proficiency, exposure) can have an impact on the L2 acquisition of phraseological knowledge (see Granger, 2019), longitudinal investigations employing a larger participant pool can help us gather more conclusive evidence about the developmental aspect of the learner phrasicon.

#### *1.1.2 Evidence from large-scale longitudinal studies*

The ideal source for a longitudinal study of the learner phrasicon is large-scale corpus data collected from a sizeable group of learners at various points in time (see Granger, 2019). Due to the challenges involved in aggregating this type of data, large-scale longitudinal studies of the learner phrasicon are still rare. Only a few longitudinal studies in this area have utilized data from a relatively large number of L2 learners. An example of such studies is Yoon (2016). Yoon (2016) examined the development of verb-noun collocations (e.g. *gain confidence*) in narrative and argumentative essays produced by 51 learners over the course of one semester. He then compared L2 collocations with those used in native speaker essays. Adopting a frequency-based approach, Yoon measured the association strength of verb-noun combinations using Mutual Information (MI) scores. MI is an association measure that quantifies the degree to which two (or more) words are likely to co-occur (see Gries & Durrant, 2019). MI is known to favour low-frequency but highly 'exclusive' collocations (e.g. *femme fatale,* see Gablasova *et al.*, 2017). The results of Yoon's (2016) study showed no developmental improvements in either narrative or argumentative essays in terms of the association strength of verb-noun collocations. The comparison between L1 and L2 essays, however, showed that L2 argumentative essays contained significantly weaker (verb-noun) collocations than L1 argumentative essays. Since MI tends to assign larger values to low-frequency collocations, this indicates that, compared to native speakers, L2 learners tend to use fewer low-frequency (or exclusive) collocations in argumentative writing.

In another longitudinal study, Bestgen and Granger (2014, also see Bestgen & Granger, 2018; Granger & Bestgen, 2017) employed the CollGram technique to examine L2 collocation use. This technique, originally developed by Durrant and Schmitt (2009), assigns association scores (e.g. MI score) to L2 contiguous MWEs (e.g. adjective-noun word pairs) on the basis of their frequency information in a large reference corpus (e.g. the British National Corpus or Corpus of Contemporary American English). Bestgen and Granger (2014) employed this technique along with two association measures: MI score and *t*-score. *T*-score is another measure of association strength, which, unlike MI, gives prominence to high-frequency collocations. Bestgen and Granger (2014) first extracted all bigrams from the Michigan State University Corpus of English as Second Language writing, which contains 171 essays written by 57 university-age learners of English over the course of one semester. MI- and *t*-scores were then calculated for each extracted bigram based on their frequency information retrieved from an L1 reference corpus (i.e. the COCA). The results showed a significant decrease in the use of collocations comprising frequent grammatical words (e.g. pronouns, prepositions) that are less typical of native speaker writing (as represented by *t*-scores). Additionally, higher quality essays were found to contain more strongly associated bigrams (as represented by MI scores). Adopting a similar research technique, Siyanova-Chanturia (2015) traced the use of adjective-noun collocations in essays written by 36 L2 learners of Italian during a 6-month intensive language course. She calculated frequencies and MI scores of L2 adjective-noun word pairs based on three reference corpora of L1 Italian writing. Classifying learner collocations into different frequency and MI-score bands, Siyanova-Chanturia (2015) found that L2 learners of Italian used more high-frequency and strongly associated collocations (e.g. *città natale* 'birth place', *aria fresca* 'fresh air') over time.

While findings from the above large-scale longitudinal studies have provided important insights into how L2 phraseological competence develops over time, they are limited in that they are based on group results and thus often fail to adequately represent individual-level differences among participants. As was mentioned earlier, case-study research in this area has consistently demonstrated that learners may vary considerably in their acquisition and use of phraseological units. Indeed, by focusing on a small group of learners, case studies are in a unique position to provide the sufficient granularity required for understanding some aspects of individual variability in L2 phraseological knowledge. However, large-scale longitudinal studies can also shed light on learner variability: for example, by using advanced statistical techniques. A case in point is Garner and Crossley (2018). These authors used Latent Curve Modelling (LCM) to examine the development and use of bigrams and trigrams in the oral production of 57 L2 English learners over a period of 4 months. LCM allows for the estimation of a mean growth trajectory for all learners as well as a unique growth curve for each individual learner (see Curran *et al.*, 2010 for further discussion). Using LCM allowed Garner and Crossley (2018) to include learner characteristics (e.g. proficiency level) and contextual factors (e.g. conversation partners) in their analysis and control for the effects of these variables. Garner and Crossley found an increase in the use of the target sequences over the 4-month period. The use of bigrams, but not trigrams, was also predicted by learners' proficiency level, such that beginner-level learners experienced greater growth in spoken bigram frequency compared to advanced-level learners. LC models also revealed that learners whose conversation partners were L2 English speakers produced more frequent bigrams over time than those whose conversation partners were native speakers.

Another example of using advanced statistical methods to investigate L2 phraseological development can be found in a recent study by Siyanova-Chanturia and Spina (2019). Siyanova-Chanturia and Spina (2019) examined the development and use of L2 collocations in learner writing using mixed-effects modelling. Using mixed-effects models allowed Siyanova-Chanturia and Spina (2019) to assess the effect of various predictors (e.g. time, essay topic, proficiency level) on the development of L2 collocations and to examine whether learners varied in their acquisition and use of these items over time. The results of their analysis showed that higher proficiency and greater exposure to an L2 may not necessarily entail more target-like output and may even result in greater reliance on infrequent and atypical collocations. It was also found that essay topic can have a significant effect on the use of L2 collocations. Further, mixed-effects models also revealed minimal individual variation among learners in terms of the production of the target sequences. Taken together, the findings from Garner and

Crossley (2018) and Siyanova-Chanturia and Spina (2019) provide a clear indication of how robust statistical techniques can provide the opportunity to arrive at a more comprehensive view of L2 phraseological competence and its development over time.

In sum, the evidence from the longitudinal explorations described in this section suggests that the investigation of L2 phraseological development hinges on considerations of multiple factors. This concerns various internal factors pertaining to learner characteristics (e.g. individual-level differences, language proficiency, L1 background, exposure), as well as external factors related to certain situational and linguistic parameters, such as the number of participants, time span, unit of analysis, the target language and register (spoken or written), and the methodological and statistical approaches adopted (also see Granger, 2019). It can therefore be argued that any systematic operationalization of L2 phraseological development should rest on careful consideration of such factors.

## 1.2 The present study

In the present longitudinal investigation, we sought to shed further light on the developmental aspect of L2 phraseological knowledge. Specifically, our main goal was to determine whether, and to what extent, L2 knowledge of verb-noun constructions changed as a function of time. The rationale behind the study stemmed from a number of gaps in the existing literature on longitudinal L2 phraseology. First, although large-scale longitudinal analysis of L2 phraseology has attracted more attention in recent years, longitudinal studies employing data from a large group of learners are still rare. As mentioned earlier, such studies are important in that they can lay claim to greater generalizability. Second, the overwhelming majority of longitudinal research in this area has focused on English as the target L2, save for a few exceptions (Siyanova-Chanturia, 2015; Siyanova-Chanturia & Spina, 2019; Spina, 2019; Yuldashev *et al.*, 2013). Accordingly, the study of other L2s has remained on the fringes of longitudinal L2 phraseology research. Finally, while advanced statistical techniques, such as mixed-effects modelling, have been shown to be more suited for the analysis of longitudinal corpus data (compared to traditional tests, such as ANOVA, *t*-test), very few longitudinal studies have used such methods to investigate L2 phraseological development.

In light of the above-mentioned gaps and the findings from previous research, the present study set out to expand the existing body of knowledge on longitudinal L2 phraseology by employing data from a large group of participants (comprising 175 learners), focusing on a relatively under-researched L2 (Italian), and utilizing a more rigorous and sophisticated statistical method (i.e. mixed-effects modelling) to analyse the development of learners' phraseological competence over time. The following section describes in more detail the material and methods used in the present study.

## 2 Data and Methodology

### 2.1 Corpus

The present study is based on an analysis of the Longitudinal Corpus of Chinese Learners of Italian (LOCCLI, https://www.unistrapg.it/cqpwebnew/). The LOCCLI is a part of speech (POS) tagged corpus, comprising 350 essays (c. 97,000 words) produced by 175 Chinese learners of Italian over the course of a 6-month language program at a university in Italy. The corpus contains two essays from each learner: one produced at the beginning (data collection 1) and the other at the end of the program (data collection 2). The reason for using only two time points was the logistics challenges involved in having a large group of learners write essays in computer laboratories. The LOCCLI also includes various metadata, such as learners' proficiency levels and the topics of the essays they produced. Proficiency levels were determined through a placement test conducted at the beginning of the program, using the Common European Framework of Reference for Languages (CEFR): A1 or beginner (n = 39), A2 or elementary (n = 86), and B1 or intermediate (n = 50). The learners were offered three comparable composition topics: (1) My first impression of Italy and Italians, (2) My hobbies: What do I usually do in my free time, and (3) My last holidays. It is important to note that the learners whose essays were included in the LOCCLI did not write on the same topic twice.

### 2.2 Procedure

As a first step, all instances of contiguous verb-noun (VN) combinations were automatically extracted from the LOCCLI by conducting POS queries (e.g. [pos="VER.*"] [pos="ART"]? [pos="NOUN"]) on the CQPweb user interface (Hardie, 2012). The rationale for focusing on VN combinations was threefold. First, the acquisition of VN collocations has been shown to be challenging for L2 learners (Laufer & Waldman, 2011; Nesselhauf, 2005). Second, very few studies have investigated the L2 development of these particular word combinations over time (Yoon, 2016 is a rare exception). Third, similar to English, VN combinations are very common in Italian, and so the L2 acquisition of these sequences can be important for learners of this language.

The extraction procedure resulted in a list of 3,173 tokens and 2,032 types of the target sequences. This list included both directly adjacent verb-noun pairs (bigrams, *prestare attenzione* 'pay attention', 714 tokens and 449 types) and verb-determiner-noun combinations (trigrams, *dire la verità* 'tell the truth', 2,459 tokens and 1,583 types). It is important to note that we extracted learner forms rather than more abstract categories such as lemmas (see Durrant, 2014 for a discussion). A manual inspection of the list was then conducted to identify orthographical errors. Two hundred and eighty-four sequences were found to include orthographical errors, all of which were corrected by a native speaker of Italian (since orthography was not an aspect of interest).

The second step was to determine the frequency of occurrence of the extracted sequences in a reference corpus. The reference corpus used in this study was Paisà (Lyding *et al.*, 2014). Paisà is a large, annotated corpus of contemporary Italian, comprising 380,000 web texts (c. 250 million words) extracted from 1,067 different websites. The rationale for selecting Paisà was that (a) the corpus is sufficiently large to allow enough repetition of the target configurations, (b) Paisà is carefully designed by its creators to represent contemporary Italian, and (c) the corpus is enhanced by a rich set of annotated linguistic information that enables advanced data retrieval (Lyding *et al.*, 2014).

Computer programs were written in Perl to automatically retrieve frequency data for the extracted sequences from Paisà. These frequency data included the frequency of each combination as well as those of its constituent words (e.g. *avuto* 'had', *problemi* 'problems', *avuto problemi* 'had problems', f(V) = 45035, f(N) = 39993, f(VN) = 383). These data provided the basis for the final step of the procedure, which focused on the computation of different collocation measures, each corresponding to a particular dimension of phraseological knowledge. These dimensions and their associated measures are explained in more detail in the following section.

## 2.3 Phraseological dimensions and collocation measures

Three key dimensions of phraseological knowledge were investigated in the present study: exclusivity, phrase frequency, and phrasal diversity. Each of these dimensions captures a unique aspect of L2 phraseological development and collocation knowledge (more on this in Sections 2.3.1–2.3.3). Triangulating phraseological patterns explained by these dimensions can help us obtain a comprehensive view of the learner phrasicon and its development over time. As detailed in the following sections, these dimensions are represented and defined by certain collocation measures.

### *2.3.1 Exclusivity*

Exclusivity is often described as the extent to which two words are strongly and exclusively connected to one another (Brezina *et al.*, 2015; Sinclair, 2004). This dimension can highlight the development of learners' awareness of semantic associations and interconnections between lexical items. Learners unaware of such associational information often tend to make facile assumptions regarding the semantic constraints of lexical items and produce semantically incompatible and communicatively inappropriate utterances (see, for example, Omidian & Siyanova-Chanturia, 2020 and Wray, 2002, for a discussion).

The strength and exclusivity of the association between two words can be statistically assessed by various *association measures* (see Gries & Durrant, 2019). Two particular association measures that have been widely used in phraseological research are *t*-score and MI score (also see Section 1.1.2). These metrics, however, have been criticized for their inherent bias towards raw frequency – with *t*-score favouring and MI score penalizing highly frequent collocations (e.g. Gablasova *et al.*, 2017). In the present study, we employed an alternative measure of exclusivity, namely, Log Dice (Rychlý, 2008; also see Brezina & Fox, Chapter 7 of this volume). Log Dice is a standardized association measure which, unlike *t*-score and MI score, neither favours nor penalizes high frequency. In addition, an attractive feature of Log Dice is that it has a theoretical maximum value (i.e. 14), which makes Log Dice scores remain stable and comparable across different parts of a corpus (Rychlý, 2008).

Log Dice scores in this study were calculated using Rychlý's (2008) equation:

$$\text{logDice} = 14 + \log_2\left(\frac{2f(xy)}{f(x) + f(y)}\right),$$

where $f(x)$ is the number of occurrences of word X, $f(y)$ the number of occurrences of word Y, and $f(xy)$ the number of co-occurrences of words X and Y.

### 2.3.2 Phrase frequency

This dimension focuses on the frequency of occurrence of lexical phrases as an indicator of their prominence among language users. The frequency with which collocations occur in an L2 has important consequences for their acquisition and learning. According to Ellis (2016), high frequency of certain linguistic items acts as an anchor for their entrenchment in the learners' mental system. In other words, the more typical a sequence is in an L2, the stronger it is entrenched in the learner's mind. Thus, the overall repetition of L2 collocations is likely to impact their production by learners. Absolute frequency is typically used as a measure of overall repetition in language. Absolute frequencies tend to follow a Zipfian distribution, which is often highly skewed. Skewness in data can produce some high-leverage observations by restricting the vast majority of data points to a limited range of observed values.

In this study, we used logarithmic frequency scores instead of absolute frequency to control for Zipfian distribution.

#### *2.3.3 Phrasal diversity*

The final dimension considered in the present study is phrasal diversity. Phrasal diversity can be defined as the range of phraseological sequences that surface in the learner's language production (see Paquot, 2019). This dimension focuses on the imbalance between the number of types and tokens of sequences produced by the learner. Therefore, it can be argued that phrasal diversity has the potential to shed light on the wealth of phraseological units that are at the learner's command. The degree of phrasal diversity in learner production could be assessed through various measures such as, type-token ratio (TTR), mean-segmental TTR, moving-average TTR, and so forth (see Jarvis, 2013). In the present study, the phrasal diversity of learner essays was calculated using Root TTR (RTTR, also referred to as the Guiraud index). RTTR is believed to mitigate the effect of text length on TTR. RTTR has also been found to be an appropriate index for measuring lexical and phrasal diversity at early stages of vocabulary acquisition (Vermeer, 2000).

RTTR was calculated for each text in the corpus using the following simple equation:

$$\text{RTTR} = \frac{\text{VN collocation types}}{\sqrt{\text{VN collocation tokens}}}.$$

### 2.4 Statistical analysis

Three analyses were carried out to examine the extent to which the above-described dimensions and their associated measures varied as a function of time in learner writing. The first analysis focused on exclusivity (Log Dice), the second on phrase frequency (logarithmic frequency), and the third on phrasal diversity (RTTR). In doing so, three separate scores, each corresponding to one of the three dimensions, were assigned to each student essay in the corpus. The scores for the exclusivity and frequency dimensions were determined by computing the mean of the Log Dice and logarithmic frequency scores[1] of the target combinations in each text. For the phrasal diversity dimension, RTTR scores were calculated for each text using the equation described in Section 2.3.3.

Regression analyses were then conducted using linear mixed-effects (LME) models. We opted for LME models because they account for individual variance among learners by including participants as random effects. LME models also offer advantages over traditional statistical tests (e.g. ANOVA) by handling multi-level data structures and possible dependencies among data points (see Schielzeth & Nakagawa, 2013). For instance, in the case of the LOCCLI, the corpus contains two texts for each of the 175 learners, who were taught by the same group of teachers in 17 different classrooms. Such a sampling design suggests that observations within classes are not necessarily independent of each other, since the performance of students in the same class might correlate as a result of teaching style or learning environment (see Linck & Cunnings, 2015). Ignoring such dependencies in data would run the risk of conflating their random effects with those of predictors, resulting in biased estimates and spurious significant results (see Gries, 2015).

Three LME models were built in R using the *lme4* package. Each model was built with a unique outcome variable, corresponding to one of the three dimensions. The following predictors and their interactions were included in the models as fixed effects: Time (data collection point 1 and 2) and Proficiency (CEFR: A1/beginner, A2/elementary and B1/intermediate), TOPIC (with three levels), and PriorExposure (the number of months spent in Italy prior to writing the first essay). The rationale for including the predictor TOPIC was to control for its confounding effects on the production of the target collocations. As Gablasova *et al.* (2017) argue, topic has the potential to influence the exclusivity and strength of learner collocations, and so the inclusion of this variable in our models allowed us to account for its possible mediating effects. We also added PriorExposure to our models to examine whether time spent in an L2 country would impact the development of learners' phraseological competence. Learners whose compositions were included in the LOCCLI had spent on average 1.7 months in Italy (ranging from 0.5 to 5 months, SD = 0.69) before writing the first essay. The variable PriorExposure was mean centred and included in the models as a continuous predictor (see Zuur *et al.*, 2009).

In order to model possible dependencies in our data, learners were included in the models as a random effect, by fitting a by-subject random intercept for each learner. The random effect of learners was also 'nested' within class to account for the random effects induced by the multi-level, hierarchical structure of our data.

The model selection procedure adopted a top-down stepwise approach, following Zuur *et al.* (2009: 120). Specifically, we started with a model that included a maximum number of fixed effects, and first explored random effects to find the optimal random effect structure justified by the data. Once we specified the optimal random structure, we explored fixed effects to specify the optimal fixed effect structure for each model.[2] At each step, log likelihood ratio tests were performed to exclude those random variables and fixed effects parameters that did not significantly contribute to model fit ($p < .05$). We then compared each of the final three models to a respective 'null' model that contained only the random effects. Following this, assumptions of the models were checked by producing various validation graphs. Finally, we checked for multicollinearity for the predictors in the final models using Variance

**Table 8.1** Descriptive statistics for LOGDICE, PHRASALDIVERSITY, and FREQUENCY at two time points

| Measure | Time point | Range | Mean | Standard Deviation |
|---|---|---|---|---|
| LogDice | Point 1 | –14.9–3.5 | –4.0 | 7.8 |
| | Point 2 | –13.7–5.9 | –4.3 | 8.0 |
| LogFrequency | Point 1 | –4.0–1.53 | –1.36 | 1.13 |
| | Point 2 | –4.0–2.27 | –1.29 | 1.25 |
| PhrasalDiversity | Point 1 | 1.0–4.8 | 2.8 | 0.7 |
| | Point 2 | 0.7–4.6 | 2.7 | 0.8 |

Inflation Factors (VIF): all VIFs were found to be smaller than 2 (see Zuur *et al.*, 2009: 387).[3]

## 3 Results

### 3.1 Descriptive statistics

A preliminary observation of the data for the three indices showed that LogDice and PhrasalDiversity measures decreased over the 6-month study period. Frequency was the only measure that increased in the second data collection. However, as can be seen from Table 8.1, these differences are very small.

### 3.2 Regression results

Tables 8.2–8.3 summarize the results of the three models with LogDice, Frequency, and PhrasalDiversity as dependent variables.

All the final models were found to be significant when compared to their respective null model (Table 8.2). The results of Model 1 (with LogDice as the dependent variable) showed a significant main effect of Proficiency (Cefr), indicating that Chinese intermediate (B1) learners of L2 Italian produced more strongly associated VN combinations than beginner (A1) and elementary (A2) learners (Figure 8.1) (also see Brezina & Fox, Chapter 7 of this volume). It is important to note that neither Time nor Topic was found to have a significant effect on LogDice scores.

Additionally, an examination of $R^2$ values showed that Model 1, as a whole, accounted for 24% of variance in the data (see the value for conditional $R^2$ in Table 8.2). It should be noted that conditional $R^2$ indicates the variance explained by both fixed and random effects in the model, while marginal $R^2$ explains the variance explained by only fixed-effect parameters (see Nakagawa & Schielzeth, 2013). Considering that the value of marginal $R^2$ for this model is very small, compared to that of conditional $R^2$, it can be argued that the majority of the variance in

**Table 8.2** Fixed effects of models with LogDice, Frequency and PhrasalDiversity as dependent variables

| Model | | Parameter | Estimates | Standard Error | t-value | Pr(>\|*t*\|) |
|---|---|---|---|---|---|---|
| Model 1 | LogDice | (Intercept) | −5.32 | .46 | −11.55 | <.001*** |
| | | Cefr A2 | .96 | .555 | 1.74 | .08 |
| | | Cefr B1 | 1.63 | .61 | 2.65 | <.01** |
| | | Marginal $R^2$ = 0.03 Conditional $R^2$ = 0.24 | | | | |
| | | Model 1 vs. Null Model ($\chi^2$ = 6.98, *p* = .02) | | | | |
| Model 2 | LogFrequency | (Intercept) | −1.47 | .20 | −7.17 | <.001*** |
| | | Cefr A2 | .37 | .18 | 2.06 | .04* |
| | | Cefr B1 | .54 | .19 | 2.73 | <.01** |
| | | Topic 2 | −.14 | .17 | −0.84 | .40 |
| | | Topic 3 | −.36 | .17 | −2.00 | .04* |
| | | Marginal $R^2$ = 0.03 Conditional $R^2$ = 0.26 | | | | |
| | | Model 2 vs. Null Model ($\chi^2$ = 12.79, *p* = .01) | | | | |
| Model 3 | PhrasalDiversity | (Intercept) | 2.14 | .15 | 10.41 | <.001*** |
| | | Time 2 | .36 | .14 | 2.41 | .01* |
| | | Cefr A2 | .31 | .14 | 2.14 | .03* |
| | | Cefr B1 | .64 | .16 | 3.96 | <.001*** |
| | | Topic 2 | .52 | .10 | 4.78 | <.001*** |
| | | Topic 3 | .16 | .11 | 1.44 | .15 |
| | | Time 2:Cefr A2 | −.43 | .17 | −2.51 | .01* |
| | | Time 2:Cefr B1 | −.54 | .19 | −2.81 | <.01** |
| | | Marginal $R^2$ = 0.11 Conditional $R^2$ = 0.38 | | | | |
| | | Model 3 vs. Null Model ($\chi^2$ = 46.44, *p* = <.001) | | | | |

**Table 8.3** Random effects of models with LogDice, Frequency and PhrasalDiversity as dependent variables

| Model | | Random effects | Variance | Standard Deviation |
|---|---|---|---|---|
| Model 1 | LogDice | τ00 Class:Learner | 3.11 | 3.19 |
| Model 2 | Frequency | τ00 Class:Learner | .33 | 0.57 |
| Model 3 | PhrasalDiversity | τ00 Class:Learner | .17 | 0.42 |

the data was explained by random effects (also see Siyanova & Spina, 2019). The results of random effects for Model 1 revealed considerable individual variation among the learners (taught in different classes) with respect to the LogDice scores of the collocations they produced (SD = 3.19, Table 8.3). Figure 8.2 provides a visual representation of this variation by plotting the random intercept effects of learners nested within class.

The model with logarithmic frequency as the outcome variable (Model 2) reported significant main effects of Proficiency and Topic.

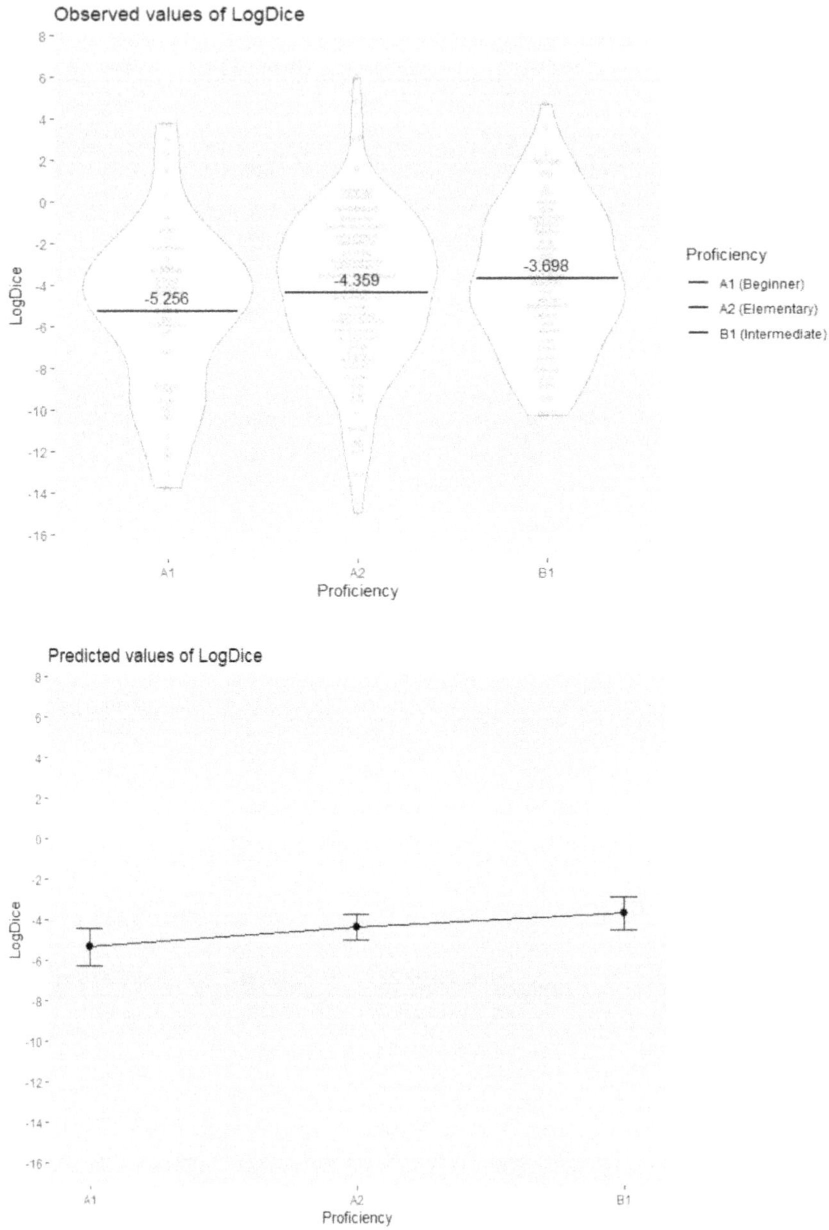


**Figure 8.1** Observed and predicted values of LogDice across CEFR levels

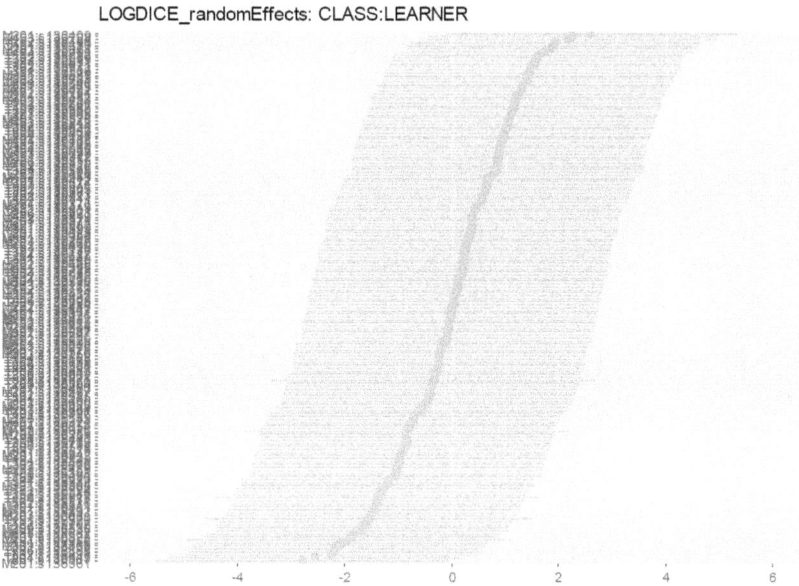


**Figure 8.2** Plot of random intercept effects on LogDice scores, with learner nested within class

As illustrated in Figure 8.3, beginner (A1) learners produced more infrequent VN combinations than elementary (A2) and intermediate (B1) learners.

With regards to the main effect of Topic, learners were found to make use of more infrequent VN combinations when writing the third type of essays ('My last holidays', e.g. *visitato un paesaggio* 'visited landscape', *vedere gli appartamenti* 'see apartments', *vedere la mostra* 'see the exhibition'), compared to the other two composition types (Figure 8.4). Further, similar to Model 1, the marginal $R^2$ for Model 2 was much smaller than conditional $R^2$, suggesting that the random-effect component of the model explained the majority of the variance in the data. The analysis of random effects for Model 2 also revealed variability among learners in terms of the frequency of the combinations used ($SD = 0.57$). However, the degree of this variation was lower than that observed for the LogDice measure (see Table 8.3).

The results of the model with PhrasalDiversity as the outcome variable (Model 3) showed significant effects for Time, Proficiency and Topic. The effect of Time interacted significantly with that of Proficiency (see Table 8.2). Since making inferences about main effects in the presence of an interaction effect could be misleading, we base our interpretation on the results of this interaction effect. As shown in Figure 8.5, the effect of Time on the diversity of the target collocations

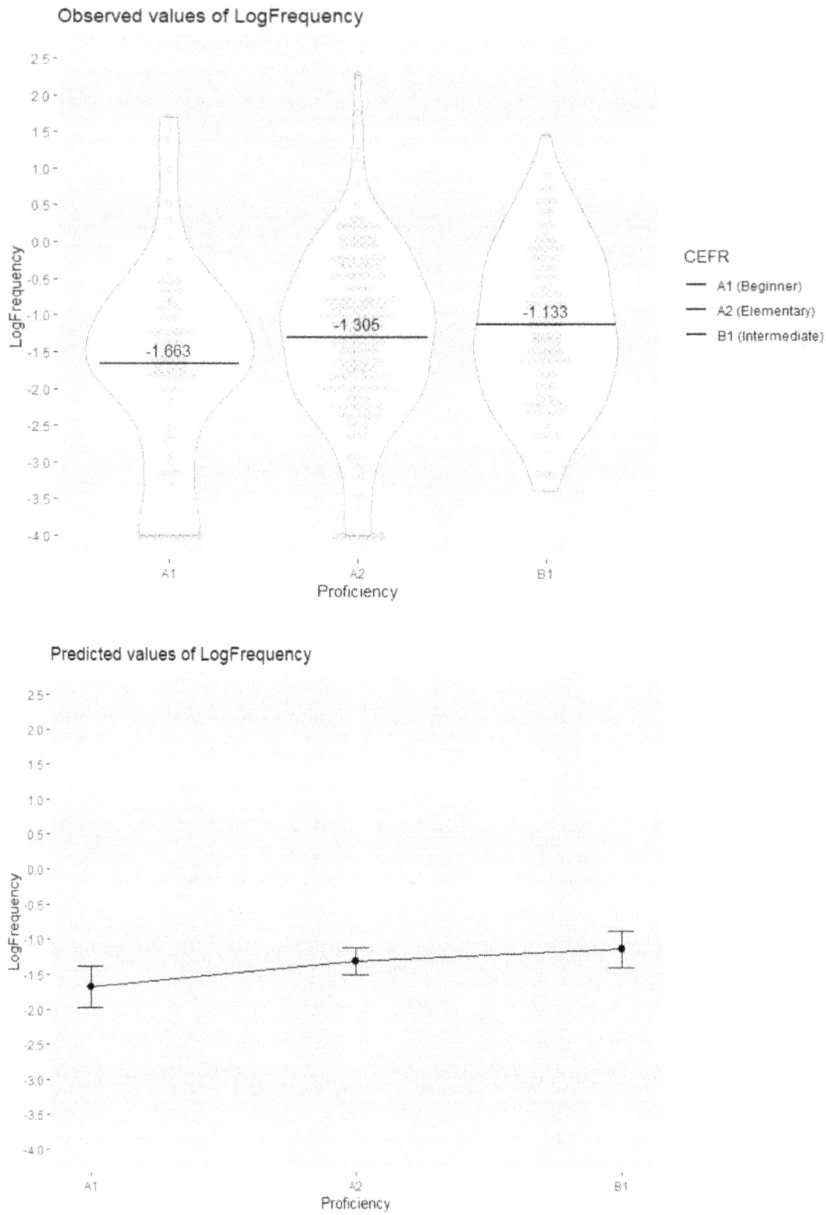


**Figure 8.3** Observed and predicted values of LogFrequency across CEFR levels

varies depending on learners' proficiency level. As can be seen, while intermediate (B1) learners in general used more diverse VN collocations in their essays than the other two CEFR levels, beginner learners (A1) are the only group that showed a longitudinal increase in the diversity

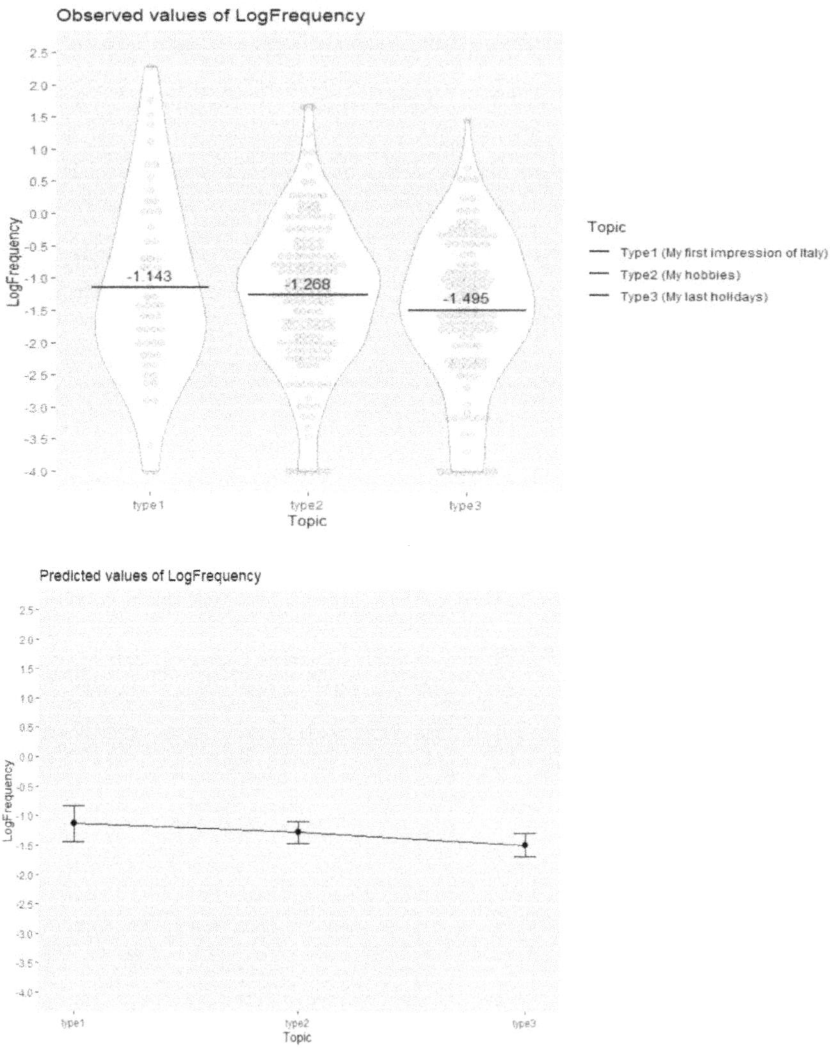


**Figure 8.4** Observed and predicted values of LogFrequency across essay topics

of the collocations they produced. This suggests that the longitudinal development of phrasal diversity may not necessarily be symmetric across all proficiency levels.

As regards the significant effect of Topic, the second type of composition ('What do I usually do in my free time') was found to contain the most diverse VN collocations (Figure 8.6). However, as can be seen from Table 8.2, the effect of Topic did not significantly interact with the other regressors, meaning that the effects of Time and

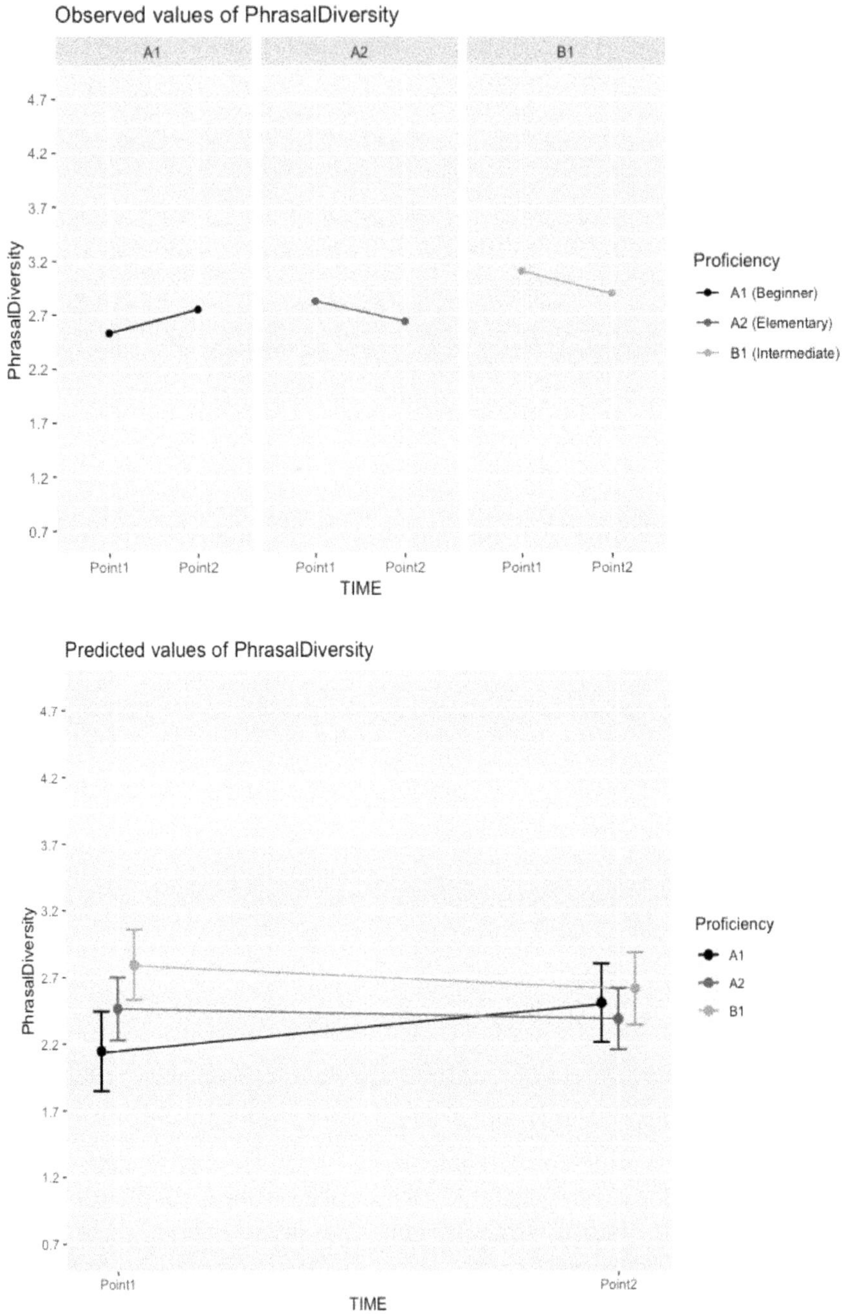


**Figure 8.5** The interaction effect of Time and Proficiency on PhrasalDiversity

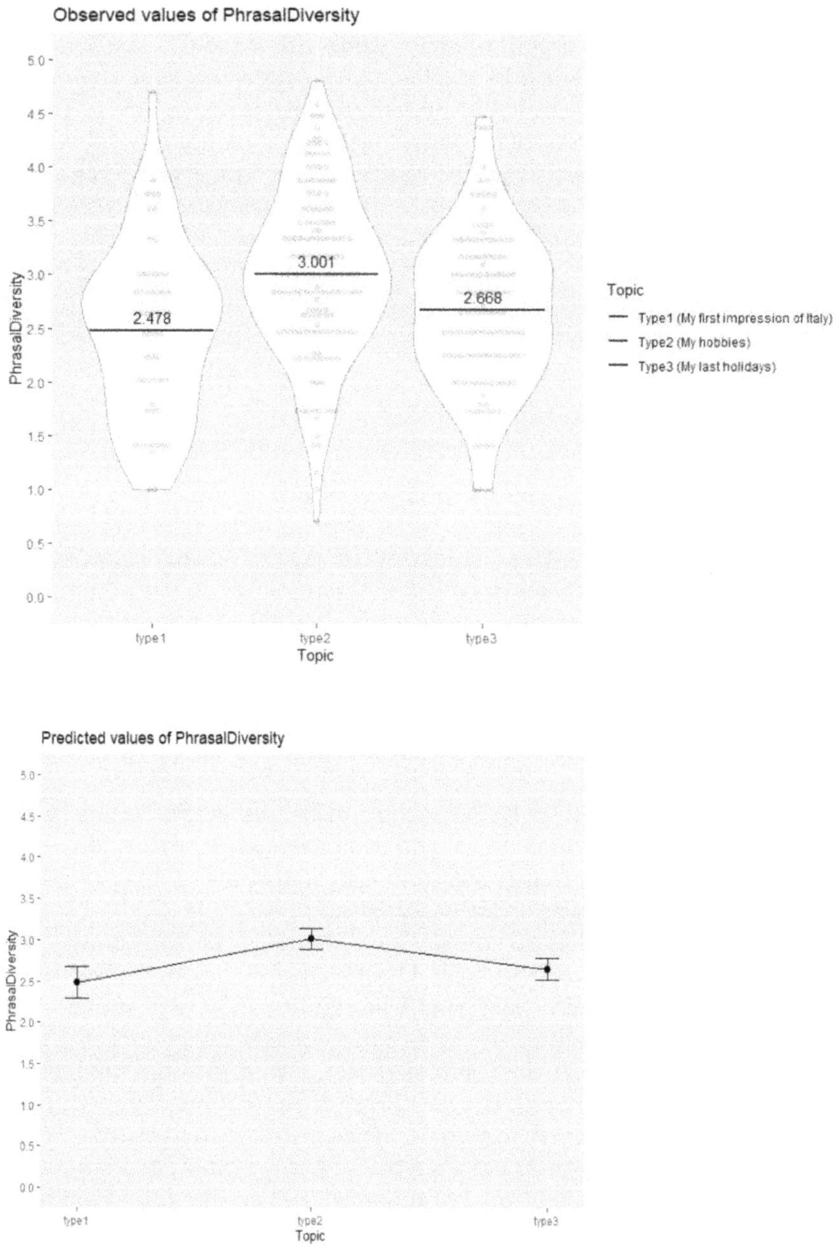


**Figure 8.6** Observed and predicted values of PhrasalDiversity across essay topics

Proficiency on PhrasalDiversity were not mediated by essay topic. Further, marginal and conditional $R^2$ values for Model 3 showed that while the variance explained by the fixed-effects parameters in the model was around 11% (marginal $R^2$), both fixed and random effects in the model accounted for 38% of variance in the data (conditional $R^2$). The analysis of random effects for this model also revealed some degree of variability among learners (SD = .42), although this variation was lower than that observed for LogDice and Frequency scores (Table 8.3).

Finally, the regressor PriorExposure was not found to be significant in any of the three models, either as a main effect or in interaction with the other three predictors.

## 4 Discussion and Conclusion

The present longitudinal study set out to investigate the development of L2 phraseological competence over a 6-month period. Our main goal was to determine whether, and to what degree, learners' knowledge of VN collocations changed as a function of time. For this purpose, we examined three key dimensions of phraseological knowledge, each assessed by a specific measure: exclusivity (Log Dice), phrase frequency (logarithmic frequency), and phrasal diversity (RTTR). Based on the data from a large longitudinal corpus of L2 writing and an L1 reference corpus, we conducted three separate LME regression analyses, each corresponding to one of the three dimensions. We opted to use LME models because they not only offer statistical advantages over traditional regression models (e.g. ANOVA), but also afford the opportunity to highlight possible individual variation among learners. We now discuss the findings that emerged from our analyses based on the three phraseological dimensions investigated in the study.

The first phraseological dimension examined in this study was exclusivity (as measured by Log Dice). Our descriptive results for this dimension revealed a very small longitudinal decrease in the Log Dice scores of VN combinations produced by learners over time. A closer inspection of the data revealed the use of certain infelicitous combinations (e.g. *cercano storia* '[they] look for history', *ho fatto pianto* 'I did crying', *avevo curiosità* 'had curiosity') by learners at the end of the language course. In constructing such word combinations, learners often tend to rely on grammatical rather than combinatorial mechanisms of the L2 (see Bardovi-Harlig & Stringer, 2017). This is, perhaps, because, as was mentioned earlier, learners' knowledge of word association does not develop in parallel with their general syntactic and vocabulary knowledge.

The results of our regression analysis for this dimension showed that the negative effect of time on the Log Dice scores of learner collocations was *not* statistically significant. These results corroborate the findings of Yoon (2016). Examining L2 development of English collocations, Yoon (2016), too, found a non-significant longitudinal decrease in the association strength of VN combinations (as attested by MI scores), indicating that time did not significantly impact the development of L2 association knowledge. Considering that the target L2 in Yoon (2016) was English, while we focused on Italian, the common pattern of results observed in the two studies is noteworthy. The non-significant impact of time on the exclusivity dimension in both studies suggests that not all learners demonstrated a decrease in the association strength of collocations they produced over time. In fact, in the case of our study, a closer examination of the data revealed that more than 45% of the learners showed modest or substantial improvement in terms of the mean Log Dice scores of the target combinations. This suggests that learners may vary considerably in their acquisition and development of collocational knowledge of VN dependencies. That is, while some learners may become attentive to the co-occurrence of certain verbs with certain nouns after a 6-month language course, others may need more time and instruction to reach this level of awareness. Previous case studies in this area have provided evidence that individual learners vary in their acquisition and use of L2 collocations, depending on variables such as language proficiency, L1 background, prior exposure to L2 and so forth (see Section 1.1.1). As Dörnyei (2009) argues, such individual difference factors have the potential to modify and personalize the overall trajectory of L2 acquisition processes. This is further supported by the results of our regression analysis, which revealed significant variation among learners based on their proficiency level, such that intermediate (B1) learners produced more strongly associated VN sequences than beginner (A1) and elementary (A2) learners. Our results also showed substantial random variation among individual learners, suggesting that the L2 acquisition and development of VN collocations can be highly idiosyncratic.

The second dimension that was investigated in this study was phrase frequency. Similar to the results of the exclusivity dimension, the effect of time on phrase frequency was not statistically significant. The results of our LME model for this dimension showed that the use of frequent VN combination varied as a function of proficiency, indicating that more proficient learners produced more frequent combinations than less experienced learners. These results appear to align with earlier studies that investigated the L2 acquisition and use of VN collocations. In a cross-sectional study focused on the L2 development of English VN collocations, Laufer and Waldman (2011) observed a significant relationship between the number of target collocations and learner proficiency, such that advanced learners produced significantly more typical and native-like VN collocations than beginning level learners. The model for this dimension also showed considerable individual-level variation in the learners' reliance on frequent VN combinations. However, the magnitude of this variation was considerably smaller than that observed for the exclusivity dimension. This finding implies that collocational strength of word combinations can be a stronger driver of individual learner variation than their frequency of occurrence. In addition, we observed that the use of frequent VN configurations significantly varied as a function of essay topic. Specifically, the data showed that Topic 1 ('My first impression of Italy and Italians') produced combinations with higher frequency values than the other two topics ('My hobbies: What do I usually do in my free time' and 'My last holidays'). This finding provides evidence in support of Gablasova *et al.*'s (2017) proposition that topic can potentially impact L2 collocation use and that researchers should account for the confounding effect of this mediating factor. Gablasova *et al.* (2017) demonstrated that composition topic can influence the exclusivity of word combinations, as measured by MI score. As the authors argue, this is due to the fact that MI tends to favour specialized and content-specific word combinations. Interestingly, among the three phraseological dimensions examined in this study, the exclusivity of the target combination (as attested by Log Dice score) was the only dimension that did not significantly vary as a function of essay topic. This indicates that Log Dice scores can remain stable across composition types and that, compared to MI, the Log Dice measure is less likely to be sensitive to the mediating effect of topic.

The third and final dimension pertained to phrasal diversity, as measured by RTTR. The results of our regression analysis showed that the effect of time on this dimension significantly interacted with proficiency, indicating that time affected learners differently depending on their CEFR level. More particularly, we found that while intermediate (B1) learners in general used more diverse VN collocations in their essays than the other two CEFR levels, beginner (A1) learners were the only group that showed a growth pattern in the diversity of the target combinations. In fact, the RTTR patterns for both elementary (A2) and intermediate (B1) learners indicated a decline over the 6-month period (see Figure 8.5). This drop in RTTR values over time indicates that the more proficient A2 and B1 level learners produced fewer distinct VN combinations and instead relied on the repeated use of certain phrases (*avevo fretta* 'I was in a hurry', or *leggere libri* 'to read books') in their writing at the end of the language course. In comparison, beginner (A1) learners were more inclined to experiment with combinatorial mechanisms of the L2 by creating new types of combinations (also see Spina, 2019). This seems to imply that, as learners gain more experience with the target language, they are more likely to become risk-averse with respect to using new types of collocations and prefer to rely on the ones they have already mastered. As Laufer (1998) argues, this is the point where the development and use of L2 items reach a 'plateau' beyond which there is little incentive for learners to produce high-stakes, novel, and infrequent words or word sequences (also see Daller *et al.*, 2013). This is consistent with the findings of Siyanova-Chanturia and Spina (2019), who also found that beginner learners were more likely to experiment with unusual word combinations in their writing than more proficient learners. Further, our results provide support to earlier case studies (Li & Schmitt, 2009, 2010), which showed that the diversity of collocations employed by proficient learners is likely to decrease as a function of time. Altogether, the observed interaction effect on the phrasal diversity dimension seems to reflect fundamental differences in the ways in which time and instruction can affect learners at different proficiency levels. The LME model for this dimension also revealed significant individual random variability among learners in their production of diverse VN combinations. However, the magnitude of this variation was smaller than the degree of the individual variance observed for exclusivity and frequency dimensions. These results suggest that patterns of individual-level variation can vary considerably depending on the phraseological dimension under analysis. The model for this dimension also reported that essay topic exerted a significant effect on the diversity of VN combinations, suggesting that the topic of texts has the potential to prompt learners to be more flexible and less conservative in their production of different types of word combinations (also see Vermeer, 2000 and Yu, 2009 for similar effects of topic on lexical diversity).

Finally, our analysis showed that the predictor PriorExposure never significantly affected the three dimensions, suggesting that short-term stays (in the case of the present study, from 0.5 to 5 months) in an L2 country may not have a profound impact on the L2 development and use of VN combinations. Previous studies in this area have expressed doubts about the significance of the impact of informal and naturalistic L2 exposure on collocation use. Focusing on verb-noun English combinations (*follow a trend, make money*), Nesselhauf (2005) observed that the length of stay (ranging from 0 to 7 months) in English-speaking countries did not contribute to an increased use of collocations and that it only slightly decreased the number of learner errors in the use of these sequences. Based on these results, Nesselhauf (2005) concluded that increased incidental exposure to the target language in an L2 country may not lead to dramatic improvements in collocational performance. Counter evidence to this conclusion, however, has been provided by other learner corpus studies (e.g. Groom, 2009; Waibel, 2008). For instance, Waibel (2008) demonstrated that long-term stays in an L2 country could have a substantial effect on learners' frequency of use of phrasal verbs. However, it is important to point out that the magnitude of this effect was particularly small for short-term stays (less than 5 months). Similarly, Groom (2009) found that ESL learners whose length of stay in an English L1 environment was more than 12 months made greater use of L2 collocations than those who had spent less than one month in an English-speaking country. This finding led Groom (2009) to conclude that, although immersion-based L2 exposure can be conducive to the acquisition of phraseological knowledge, it is clear that 'the process of L2 collocational development is likely to be a slow and occasionally painful one' (2009: 33). The implied corollary here is that, perhaps, incidental exposure to the target language would need to reach a 'critical mass' to bring about substantive change in L2 collocational performance. Further research is needed to explore this possibility.

Overall, our results showed that time was a significant predictor of only the phrasal diversity dimension, whereas the significant effect of proficiency was present on all three dimensions. Importantly, the findings of the present longitudinal exploration point to the conclusion that L2 phraseological development is a multifaceted process, that time is but one part of this process, and that language proficiency and other individual-level learner differences can influence the overall trajectory of L2 collocation development. Future longitudinal research on L2 phraseology could shed further light on such internal factors by adopting rigorous methods of data analysis that can yield the opportunity to expound upon both within-group and between-group variation in learner data.

## Notes

(1) It is important to note that, in order to accommodate the combinations that had a frequency of occurrence of zero in the reference corpus, a very small value (0.0001) was added to frequency values of all the extracted sequences prior to the calculation of the Log Dice and logarithmic frequency scores.

(2) Below are examples of the R code used for fitting the initial and final models:

```
fit1<-lmer(LOGDICE~TIME*CEFR*TOPIC*EXPOSURE+(1+TIME|CLASSID/STUDENTID), data = logd)
fitMain<-lmer(LOGDICE~CEFR+(1|CLASSID/STUDENTID), data = logd)
```

(3) The only VIF values that were found to be greater than 2 (ranging from 2.6 to 4.96) belonged to the interaction term and its components (Time and Proficiency) in the third model (Phrasal Diversity): interaction terms are often correlated with their components because they include these main effects (see Allison, 2012; Foster, 2013 for a discussion).

## References

Bahns, J. and Eldaw, M. (1993) Should we teach EFL students collocations? *System* 21 (1), 101–114.

Bardovi-Harlig, K. and Stringer, D. (2017) Unconventional expressions: Productive syntax in the L2 acquisition of formulaic language. *Second Language Research* 33 (1), 61-90.

Bestgen, Y. and Granger, S. (2014) Quantifying the development of phraseological competence in L2 English writing: An automated approach. *Journal of Second Language Writing* 26, 28–41.

Bestgen, Y. and Granger, S. (2018) Tracking L2 writers' phraseological development using collgrams: Evidence from a longitudinal EFL corpus. In S. Hoffmann, A. Sand., S. Arndt-Lappe and L.M. Dillmann (eds) *Corpora and Lexis* (pp. 277–301). Leiden & Boston: Brill.

Brezina, V., McEnery, T. and Wattam, S. (2015) Collocations in context: A new perspective on collocation networks. *International Journal of Corpus Linguistics* 20 (2), 139–173.

Cheng, W., Greaves, C., Sinclair, J.M. and Warren, M. (2008) Uncovering the extent of the phraseological tendency: Towards a systematic analysis of concgrams. *Applied Linguistics* 30 (2), 236–252.

Cowie, A.P. (1994) Phraseology. In R.E. Asher (ed.) *The Encyclopedia of Language and Linguistics* (pp. 3168–3171). Oxford: Oxford University Press.

Crossley, S. and Salsbury, T.L. (2011) The development of lexical bundle accuracy and production in English second language speakers. *IRAL-International Review of Applied Linguistics in Language Teaching* 49 (1), 1–26.

Curran, P.J., Obeidat, K. and Losardo, D. (2010) Twelve frequently asked questions about growth curve modeling. *Journal of Cognition and Development* 11 (2), 121–136.

Daller, M., Turlik J. and Weir, I. (2013) Vocabulary acquisition and the learning curve. In S. Jarvis and M. Daller (eds) *Vocabulary Knowledge: Human Ratings and Automated Measures* (pp. 185–218). Amsterdam: Benjamins.

Dörnyei, Z. (2009) Individual differences: Interplay of learner characteristics and learning environment. *Language Learning* 59 (S1), 230–248.

Durrant, P. (2014) Discipline and level specificity in university students' written vocabulary. *Applied Linguistics* 35 (3), 328–356.

Durrant, P. and Schmitt, N. (2009) To what extent do native and non-native writers make use of collocations? *IRAL-International Review of Applied Linguistics in Language Teaching* 47 (2), 157–177.

Ellis, N.C. (2016) Frequency in language learning and language change. In H. Behrens and S. Pfänder (eds) *Experience Counts: Frequency Effects in Language* (pp. 239–256). Berlin: de Gruyter

Gablasova, D., Brezina, V. and McEnery, T. (2017) Collocations in corpus-based language learning research: Identifying, comparing, and interpreting the evidence. *Language Learning* 67 (S1), 155–179.

Garner, J. and Crossley, S.A. (2018) A latent curve model approach to studying L2 n-gram development. *The Modern Language Journal* 102 (3), 494–511.

Granger, S. (2019) Formulaic language in learner corpora. Collocations and lexical bundles. In A. Siyanova-Chanturia and A. Pellicer-Sanchez (eds) *Understanding Formulaic Language: A Second Language Acquisition Perspective* (pp. 228–247). Abingdon: Routledge.

Granger, S. and Bestgen, Y. (2017) Using collgrams to assess L2 phraseological development: A replication study. In P. de Haan, S. van Vuuren and R. de Vries (eds) *Language, Learners and Levels: Progression and Variation* (pp. 385–408). Louvain-la-Neuve, Belgium: Presses universitaires de Louvain.

Gries, S.T. (2015) Statistics for learner corpus research. In S. Granger, G. Gilquin and F. Meunier (eds) *The Cambridge Handbook of Learner Corpus Research* (pp. 159–181). Cambridge: Cambridge University Press.

Gries, S.T. and Durrant P. (2019) Analyzing co-occurrence data. In M. Paquot and S.Th. Gries (eds) *Practical Handbook of Corpus Linguistics* (pp. 1–15). Berlin & New York: Springer.

Groom, N. (2009) Effects of second language immersion on second language collocational development. In A. Barfield and H. Gyllstad (eds) *Researching Collocations in Another Language* (pp. 21–33). London: Palgrave Macmillan.

Hardie, A. (2012) CQPweb – combining power, flexibility and usability in a corpus analysis tool. *International Journal of Corpus Linguistics* 17 (3), 380–409.

Jarvis, S. (2013) Capturing the diversity in lexical diversity. *Language Learning* 63 (supplement 1), 87–106.

Laufer, B. (1998) The development of passive and active vocabulary in a second language: Same or different? *Applied Linguistics* 19 (2), 255–271.

Laufer, B. and Waldman, T. (2011) Verb-noun collocations in second language writing: A corpus analysis of learners' English. *Language Learning* 61 (2), 647–672.

Li, J. and Schmitt, N. (2009) The acquisition of lexical phrases in academic writing: A longitudinal case study. *Journal of Second Language Writing* 18 (2), 85–102.

Li, J. and Schmitt, N. (2010) The development of collocation use in academic texts by advanced L2 learners: A multiple case study approach. In D. Wood (ed.) *Perspectives on Formulaic Language: Acquisition and Communication* (pp. 22–46). New York, NY: Bloomsbury.

Linck, J.A. and Cunnings, I. (2015) The utility and application of mixed-effects models in second language research. *Language Learning* 65 (S1), 185–207.

Lyding, V., Stemle, E., Borghetti, C., Brunello, M., Castagnoli, S., Dell'Orletta, F. and Pirrelli, V. (2014) The PAISA corpus of Italian Web texts. In F. Bildhauer and R. Schäafer (eds) *Proceedings of the 9th Web as Corpus Workshop (WaC-9)* (pp. 36–43). Gothenburg, Sweden: Association for Computational Linguistics.

Nakagawa, S. and Schielzeth, H. (2013) A general and simple method for obtaining R2 from generalized linear mixed-effects models. *Methods in Ecology and Evolution* 4 (2), 133–142.

Nesselhauf, N. (2005) *Collocations in a Learner Corpus*. Amsterdam: Benjamins.

Omidian, T. and Siyanova-Chanturia, A. (2020) Semantic prosody revisited: Implications for language learning. *TESOL Quarterly* 54 (2), 512–524.

Omidian, T., Shahriari, H. and Siyanova-Chanturia, A. (2018) A cross-disciplinary investigation of multi-word expressions in the moves of research article abstracts. *Journal of English for Academic Purposes* 36, 1–14.

Paquot, M. (2019) The phraseological dimension in interlanguage complexity research. *Second Language Research* 35 (1), 121–145.

Pawley, A. and Syder, F.H. (1983) Natural selection in syntax: Notes on adaptive variation and change in vernacular and literary grammar. *Journal of Pragmatics* 7 (5), 551–579.

Rychlý, P. (2008) A lexicographer-friendly association score. In P. Sojka and A. Horák (eds) *Proceedings of Recent Advances in Slavonic Natural Language Processing, RASLAN* (pp. 6–9). Brno, Czech Republic: Masaryk University.

Schielzeth, H. and Nakagawa, S. (2013) Nested by design: Model fitting and interpretation in a mixed model era. *Methods in Ecology and Evolution* 4 (1), 14–24.

Schmitt, N. (1998) Tracking the incremental acquisition of second language vocabulary: A longitudinal study. *Language Learning* 48 (2), 281–317.

Sinclair, J.M. (2004) *Trust the Text: Language, Corpus and Discourse*. London: Routledge.

Siyanova-Chanturia, A. (2015) Collocation in beginner learner writing: A longitudinal study. *System* 53, 148–160.

Siyanova-Chanturia, A. and Pellicer-Sánchez, A. (eds) (2019) *Understanding Formulaic Language: A Second Language Acquisition Perspective*. Abingdon: Routledge.

Siyanova-Chanturia, A. and Spina, S. (2019) Multi-word expressions in second language writing: A large-scale longitudinal learner corpus study. *Language Learning* 70 (1), 1–44.

Siyanova-Chanturia, A. and Omidian, T. (2020) Key issues in researching multiword items. In S. Webb (ed.) *The Routledge Handbook of Vocabulary Studies* (pp. 529–545). Abingdon: Routledge.

Spina, S. (2019) The development of phraseological errors in Chinese learner Italian: A longitudinal study. In A. Abel, A. Glaznieks, V. Lyding and L. Nicolas (eds) *Widening the Scope of Learner Corpus Research. Selected Papers from the Fourth Learner Corpus Research Conference* (pp. 95–119). Louvain-la-Neuve, Belgium: Presses universitaires de Louvain.

Vermeer, A. (2000) Coming to grips with lexical richness in spontaneous speech data. *Language Testing* 17 (1), 65–83.

Waibel, B. (2008) *Phrasal Verbs: German and Italian Learners of English Compared.* Saarbrucken, Germany: VDM Verlag Dr Müller.

Wray, A. (2002) *Formulaic Language and the Lexicon.* Cambridge: Cambridge University Press.

Yoon, H. J. (2016) Association strength of verb-noun combinations in experienced NS and less experienced NNS writing: Longitudinal and cross-sectional findings. *Journal of Second Language Writing* 34, 42–57.

Yu, G. (2010) Lexical diversity in writing and speaking task performances. *Applied Linguistics* 31 (2), 236–259.

Yuldashev, A., Fernandez, J. and Thorne, S.L. (2013) Second language learners' contiguous and discontiguous multi-word unit use over time. *The Modern Language Journal* 97 (S1), 31–45.

Zuur, A., Ieno, E.N., Walker, N., Saveliev, A.A. and Smith, G.M. (2009) *Mixed Effects Models and Extensions in Ecology with R.* Berlin: Springer.

# 9 Tracing Collocation in Learner Production and Processing: Integrating Corpus Linguistic and Experimental Approaches

Marco Schilk

## 1 Introduction

It has frequently been shown that much of language production contains the use of multiword units that have arbitrary selection criteria and may entail a level of semantic opacity in the sense that the meaning of the lexical combination is not restricted to the sum of the meaning of its component parts and its syntax-based constructional meaning (e.g. Cowie, 1998; Nattinger & DeCarrico, 1992; Wray, 2002). These semi-formulaic units include the combination of two single lexemes (collocation) as well as longer strings of lexico-constructional frames (Schmitt & Carter, 2004; Sinclair, 1991; Stefanowitsch & Gries, 2003). It is generally claimed that the ubiquitous occurrence of these combinations in production data, as shown, for example, in large language corpora, is related to a processing advantage of these combinations over combinations that are not co-selected but generated by means of grammar and the lexicon.

However, so far, this assumption is based on relatively little direct evidence, and research into the nature of the processing of collocations and larger multiword units is still only in its infancy (Ellis *et al.*, 2009; Ellis & Frey, 2009; Schmitt *et al.*, 2004). This is especially true when abstracting from monolingual speakers of English and including bilingual and multilingual speakers whose lexical activation process includes more than one linguistic system and should also include more than one co-selection network. Studies into second language processing of formulaic language only recently gained some pace as Conklin and

Carrol's (2018) state-of the-art report illustrates. Since the collocational range and co-selection criteria of lexical items differ between languages, focusing on second language speakers may not only be beneficial for an understanding of potential problems of the language learner but might also add to a general understanding of collocational processing.

In other words, if lexical selection and activation is influenced by co-selection (i.e. the activation of a specific item facilitates the activation of collocationally related items), second language speakers of English may display facilitation effects for collocations in their L2. Additionally, they may transfer the collocational structures of their L1 to their L2, a phenomenon that is frequently observed in the language production of language learners (Nesselhauf, 2005). These influences have long since been the focus of learner corpus research (LCR), where the phrasal focus, often adopted in this discipline, also underlines how learners not only deal with single lexical items and grammatical regularities but also – and perhaps to a stronger extent – with phraseological preferences that often define paradigmatic choices.

Granger (2015) points out this focus of LCR within contrastive interlanguage analysis (CIA) and the present volume is yet another example of the rich body of literature that now exists concerning these issues of bilingual phrasal preference:

> The dominant view of lexis in CIA has been phrasal rather than single-word based. The literature abounds in studies of collocations, colligations, lexical bundles and collostructions, which have considerably enhanced our knowledge of the L2 phrasicon. (Granger, 2015: 10)

In the preface to Granger and Meunier's (2008) book, Sinclair points out how 'traps for the unwary' (Sinclair, 2008: xviii) that exist for the learner in the form of 'false friends between pairs of languages' are also expected to exist at the level of the phrase. The difficulties that are encountered at this level are, however, harder to master for the learner and harder to describe for the linguist, as 'there are all sorts of differences in scope, range, connotation and usage conventions, and the influence of wider culture to take into account' (Sinclair, 2008: xviii). An oft-cited example in this context is how the information contained in the phrase *I want to marry you* may be conveyed by numerous alternatives, but that these alternatives would not be 'likely to be accepted as ordinary, idiomatic uses by English speakers' (Pawley & Syder, 1983: 196). As phraseological preferences differ between individual languages, language learners must navigate issues of cross-linguistic differences at the level of the word (Sinclair, 2008) as well as at the level of multiword or phrasal units. Additionally, language specific preferences in terms of collocation and larger phraseological units carry over toward preferences in co-selection of these larger units (Hunston, 2002: 175) and are thereby also influential for longer stretches of text. Considering that these preferences seem to have some psycholinguistic validity for individual speakers (as Wray's (2002) description of formulaic sequences suggests), learners and bilingual speakers operate with different language specific preferences at the level of language production as well as language processing (Schilk, 2020: 62).

While language production data of these speakers are represented in learner corpora, there are presently relatively few studies focusing on learners' collocational and phraseological processing. This chapter explores a number of theoretical and methodological avenues for the integration of those two levels by focusing on the use and processing of collocations by advanced learners of English. Being based on a larger work (Schilk, 2020), it highlights the areas of collocational interference in language production and collocational processing of learners in relation to their production data.

## 2 Collocations and Interference Collocations of Advanced Learners: Production

Collocation as part of the phraseological competence of learners of English has been the focus of attention for a relatively long time and a large body of literature now exists that describes how learners use different types of lexical combinations. Two main fields of interest in this regard have been quantitative comparisons of the use of specific lexical combinations by native speaker (NS) and non-native speaker (NNS) informants on the one hand (e.g. Gilquin & Shortall, 2007; Granger, 1998), and tracing innovation and interference in interlanguage varieties on the other (e.g. Nesselhauf, 2005). Most of these studies implicitly agree on the different types of functions that collocations may perform for speakers of any variety and variant (see, for example, Wray, 2002), which Nesselhauf summarizes as follows:

> (a) they play an essential role in language learning and acquisition;
> (b) they are essential for fluency in spoken and written language;
> (c) the use of prefabricated units supports comprehension;
> (d) prefabricated units indicate membership of a certain linguistic group.
> (Nesselhauf, 2005: 2)

She goes on to point out, that:

> two of the (...) functions are at least as essential for non-native speakers as for native speakers. Enhancing fluency through reducing processing effort must be of particular interest for non-native speakers, as they naturally need more processing effort to convey their intended message. (...) The third function, making comprehension easier, is doubtless of importance for every user of a language. (Nesselhauf, 2005: 2)

However, two points within this reasoning are not immediately clear and have been grounds for some debate. First, while it seems convincing that the use of (semi) prefabricated items should be advantageous for language comprehension, mere observations of frequency of production of specific combinations in the cumulative data of many speakers are not sufficient to substantiate claims on individual processing facilitation (see, for example, Ellis *et al.*, 2009; Schmitt *et al.*, 2004). Second, the influence of the two different language systems and their relationship to phraseological processing is, as of today, relatively unclear (see, for example, Siyanova-Chanturia *et al.*, 2011; Underwood *et al.*, 2004).

In the following, I will initially sketch out the production side of the matter at hand by focusing on typical collocational deviations produced by language learners as recorded in interlanguage corpora, such as the International Corpus of Learner English (ICLE) (Granger *et al.*, 2009) and the Louvain International Database of Spoken English Interlanguage (LINDSEI) (Gilquin *et al.*, 2010). The remainder of the chapter will then focus on the processing side by illustrating the experimental approach taken by Schilk (2020), and will discuss some of the results of this approach.

Collocations as a type of phraseological unit are usually defined within a double continuum of syntactic fixedness and semantic transparency. On the open/transparent side of this cline we find combinations that are only restricted syntactically and are usually analytically transparent, or in Sinclair's (1991) terminology, the slot-filler model on which the open-choice principle operates. Towards the fixed/opaque side of the continuum, combinations become increasingly semantically opaque as well as syntactically fixed. These are the combinations that are of specific interest to phraseological approaches, which could be described as models of description along Sinclair's (1991) principle of the idiom. Collocations are generally situated towards the middle of both clines; here, what Cowie (e.g. 1994) describes as 'free combinations' (*drink tea*), are situated more towards the free and transparent part of the cline, while what Cowie calls 'restricted collocations' are situated closer to the fixed and opaque side. Pure idioms could be seen as representing the extremely fixed/opaque end of the cline. Restricted collocations are especially problematic for learners of a language, since, although they themselves are relatively easily understandable, the selection criteria are largely opaque and language- or variety-dependent.

Using Halliday's (1966) framework of *item*, *set* and *collocation*, this can be illustrated for different contexts of cultures and languages. Halliday (1966: 150) uses the examples of *strong argument* and *powerful car* to illustrate the point of items such as *strong* being members of a specific set that also includes *powerful*. While some items within the set can be used in collocation with items of different sets, such as *argument*, others cannot and are instead used with items of different sets, such as *car*.

As Greenbaum (1974: 81) points out: 'synonyms may be separated collocationally because of restrictions to a language variety or style'. In the case of the L2 learner, similar expressions in the different linguistic systems at their disposal may, thus, differ in these arbitrary restrictions, which can be illustrated by using Halliday's example of *strong tea* as a restricted combination within a set that includes both *strong* and *powerful*. While in the English language hot beverages such as *coffee* or *tea* only collocate with *strong* but not with *powerful*, in German the collocational range includes both *stark* (strong) and *kräftig* (*powerful*). The differences in the collocational range of *strong* and *powerful* in English and German can even be taken somewhat further when using, for example, *ein starker Raucher* (a heavy smoker) in German. While substance abuse and overindulgence can be used with the adjective for *strong* in German, the item that would collocate in English is *heavy* (*schwer*), so that members of the set 'abusive/indulgent user' (smoker, eater, drinker, etc.) would collocate with a different and non-synonymous adjective in English.

The concept of an interference-based collocation can, therefore, be defined in terms of the collocational ranges of source and target lexemes. When treated in isolation, there are usually one or more target lexemes that differ in frequency, range of use and range of collocability. While learners of a language often have access to a set of possible target lexemes, they might lack a complete knowledge of the context these lexemes tend to be used in within the L2, and of the collocational range and co-occurrence likelihood of the item within the target language. They do, however, have this information for their L1 and may transfer this knowledge to the L2, although the collocational networks differ between the languages and the resultant lexical combination would seem unusual to a speaker not familiar with the bilingual speaker's L1.

Nesselhauf (2005) provides an in-depth description of collocational innovation and interference by advanced German learners of English. In an analysis based on the German component of the ICLE, she shows how these learners produce a large number of native-like combinations and collocations, but similarly produce many lexical combinations that are neither typically encountered in native-speaker corpora, nor judged as acceptable by native-speaker raters. Her approach is phraseological rather than quantitative in describing occurrences of innovative or transfer-based combinations regardless of statistical measures of typicality. This is necessary since the relatively small publicly available learner corpora that currently exist (Nesselhauf, 2005: 35) contain relatively few examples, making solid quantification difficult.[1] This is quite normal for studies into the combinatory preferences of content words in small corpora, although more recent studies are using increasingly refined methods to quantify lexical co-occurrence and dependencies even within relatively small corpora (see, for example, the use of dependency indices by Kyle & Eguchi, Chapter 6 of this volume). However, these procedures are largely dependent on comparing learner use represented in smaller learner corpora to larger native-speaker corpora, and are therefore better suited to measure native-like performance of non-native speakers than to trace interferences or innovations.

Focusing mainly on restricted collocations at the level of the verb phrase (i.e. verb-noun collocations), Nesselhauf (2005) identifies a relatively large number of combinations that are not typical of native speaker use and are rated as questionable or unacceptable by her native speaker raters. In the following, I will discuss three typical examples of interference-based verb-noun combinations represented in the German component of the International Corpus of Learner English (ICLE-GER) in more detail:

(1) *found + family*
[...] when you yourself will have ***?founded*** a ***family***, you will give your children as much love as you have [...] (ICLE-GER: GESA 5021)
(2) *get + baby*
[...] so when they ***?get*** a ***baby*** the woman should take one period of grace and the husband should also take one. (ICLE-GER: GESA 3017)
(3) *make + career*
[...] notions that life's purpose is to ***?make*** a ***career*** and to gather as much money and material goods as possible [...](ICLE-GER: GEDR 0017)

Example (1) is a typical example of a collocational transfer, where the different lexical items differ in their collocational range in the speaker's L1 and the target language. In German, the situation of starting a family is encoded with the verb *gründen* that can be translated as *found*. The collocational range of *found,* however, is different in English, where it is used in combination with nouns such as *company*, or cities/towns and their names but not with *family*. Here, the preferred verb would be *to start*. In the above example, the learner is aware of the meaning of *found* and that it is a translation of *gründen*, but is unaware of the different collocational restrictions between L1 and L2.

A similar situation is shown in example (2). The German expression for *having a baby* is *ein Baby bekommen*. Being an advanced learner, the informant does not fall into the 'false friend trap' of substituting the English *become* for *bekommen* but translates *bekommen* (receive, get) as *get*. While this is a likely translation for *bekommen* in a large number of cases, it does not follow the preferred collocational pattern in English (*have a baby*).

Example (3), finally, contains a further element that is problematic for many advanced learners. Similar to the situation in example (2), *make* (as well as *have*) is a highly polysemic verb that is often used in light-verb constructions, i.e. constructions in which most of the semantic load is carried by the noun, while the verb itself is relatively meaningless and used rather arbitrarily by speakers of different languages. Additionally, the polysemic possibilities of *machen* (as a cognate of *make*) are considerably wider in German than in English. The relatively fixed collocation of *Karriere machen* is now directly transferred to the cognate expression *make (a) career*, as the learner in question seems to be unaware of the collocational restrictions of *career*. In this case the situation is further complicated by the fact that there are circumstances in which combining the verb *make* with *career* is admissible and relatively frequent in English. A typical example would be the use of *career* as a part of a phrasal direct object when followed by an *of*-prepositional phrase (*make a career of V-ing something*).

These examples, as well as many others like them, show that L1 influence is very likely to play a role in the production of L2 expressions by learners, a notion probably attracting unanimous agreement. On the other hand, in a very large number of cases – likely the majority of them – learners at this level of proficiency produce typical native-like collocations. This shows that they are aware that L2 expressions are not simply translations of L1 expressions and that collocational preferences exist. However, it also seems to be the case that learners preferably use those native-like collocations that are similar, or have a direct translation equivalent, to their respective L1 combinations. An example of this would be the use of *severely punished* by francophone speakers due to its similarity to the French combination *sévèrement puni*, pointed out by Granger (1998: 151).

One issue in corpus-based studies is that while they only show what a number of speakers/writers produce, they do not tell us much about the reasons for these types of productions. A possible way of bridging this gap between what we know about their language production or performance and their competence, is to focus more strongly on the processing side. For example, the learner who produced example (1) might have been very well aware that the expression *to found a family* may not be the preferred expression (since they most likely did not encounter positive evidence of native-speaker usage of this combination) but, not knowing the preferred expression, settled on the preferred German combination as 'the next best thing'. As corpus data might not, therefore, be the best tool for finding explanations about the cognitive reality of individual speakers, experimental data may complement the findings produced by focusing on corpus data.

## 3 Collocations and Interference Collocations of Advanced Learners: Processing

There are a number of possibilities to investigate the levels of linguistic knowledge and competence that individual speakers possess.

First, it is possible to ask speakers directly. For the topic at hand, Gilquin and Shortall (2007) have shown that speaker elicitation can be used effectively to complement corpus findings by directly providing information about the speakers' linguistic knowledge. In the context of the present work, their first case study is of specific interest. Here they compare the use of collocations with the semantically light verb *make* as observed in the French component of ICLE to a fill-in-the-gap elicitation test where speakers similar to the ones represented in ICLE choose verbs in predefined contexts and report on their level of confidence in the respective choices. Similar to the results in Granger (1998), this elicitation test shows that the students perform much better with collocations that are congruent between their L1 (French) and their L2 (English) than they do where collocational preferences are incongruent between the languages. Results also imply a certain degree of avoidance of incongruent collocations in the corpora, since results in the elicitation tests point towards difficulties that were not apparent in the corpus findings. While these types of elicitation tests have a number of advantages, ease of applicability being one of them, the disadvantage here is that speakers can only inform the researcher about what they know they know, and competence below the level of conscious and explicit awareness cannot be assessed directly with elicitation methods (Schilk, 2020: 29–31).

Addressing processing below the level of conscious awareness usually requires some kind of experimental or behavioural data that use language data as the input, while specific physical reactions, such as reaction times, eye-movements or electroencephalograph (EEG) readings, are used as dependent variables that can potentially be interpreted as indicators of the speakers' linguistic competence. In other words, to gain insights into the cognitive reality of the speaker, experimental psycholinguistic methods are needed; or, as Ellis *et al.* (2009) point out:

> The analysis of whether word recognition and lexical access, semantic activation, and the process of production of speech are sensitive to collocations, formulas, and the more abstract schemata potentially derivable from them, is an empirical matter, one that falls into a different domain of investigation, that of psycholinguistics. (Ellis *et al.*, 2009: 91)

Typical psycholinguistic procedures that seem particularly well suited to shedding light on the questions raised in the previous sections fall into two categories. First, by measuring direct reaction times (e.g. in word recognition studies), speed of lexical activation can be assessed. This can be done by asking participants to produce a specific reaction (e.g. hit a button), or by focusing on more involuntary reactions (e.g. by tracing oculomotor events). Second, it is also possible to focus on physiological reactions that the participants are completely unaware of, by focusing on neurocognitive events (e.g. by using electroencephalographic or functional magnetic resonance imaging (fMRI) settings).

With respect to learner language data, there is a relatively large amount of work that uses more direct elicitation methods, while relatively few studies make use of more advanced psycholinguistic tools. A notable exception here is the work of Schmitt and colleagues (e.g. Siyanova-Chanturia *et al.*, 2011; Schmitt *et al.*, 2004; Underwood *et al.*, 2004) that shifts the focus of learner language research from observations of corpus-based language production towards the analysis of experimental psycholinguistic data. Underwood *et al.* (2004), as well as Siyanova-Chanturia *et al.* (2011), use eye-tracking to investigate differences between native-speaker and non-native speaker processing of formulaic language. Millar (2011) also uses an eye-tracking design to analyse reading processing of learner-based formulae. However, here the participants are native-speaker readers processing learner production data, rather than being learners themselves.

Underwood *et al.* (2004) focused mainly on differences between native and non-native speakers in terms of the number and duration of word fixations in relation to words being part of formulaic sequences. Here they found processing advantages for the native speakers that can be seen as indicative of a more formulaic storage of these sequences by the NS group. Siyanova-Chanturia *et al.* (2011) use a somewhat similar procedure to describe differences in the processing of idiomatic sequences, i.e. sequences situated further to the right of the fixedness-transparency cline mentioned above. They show, *inter alia,* that non-native speakers display longer fixation times overall and that the speaker groups differ in their treatment of idiomatic expressions: while the native speaker participants displayed 'a processing advantage for idioms over novel phrases, [...] L2 speakers process idioms at a similar speed to novel phrases' (Siyanova-Chanturia *et al.*, 2011: 251).

Regarding the second type of analysis described above (i.e. the use of electroencephalograph (EEG)/event-related potential-based (ERP) methods), there are even fewer studies focusing specifically on the processing of non-native speakers. A noteworthy exception is Hahne (2001), who compares brain potentials of Russian L2 learners and native speakers of German in relation to semantic mismatch, illustrating how these groups react differently to violations of semantic restrictions.

## 4 Combining Corpus-based Input with a Combined Eye-tracking – EEG/ERP Setting

### 4.1 Research questions

Considering the evidence from learner corpora and studies into language processing, we can formulate a set of basic observations and resulting questions. Studies into the production of collocations by advanced learners show that these learners use a large number of native-like collocations; at the same time, however, they produce a number of collocational deviations that are (at least partially) based on collocational interference from their first language. Combining these observations from language production with our knowledge of collocational processing then raises the following questions:

(1) Do advanced learners of English experience processing advantages for:
  (a) native-like collocations and/or
  (b) interference-based collocations?
(2) Do advanced learners process interference collocations differently from:
  (a) native-like collocations?
  (b) non-collocating semantically incongruous items?
(3) Do different groups of learners (e.g. intermediate vs. advanced learners) perform differently?

## 4.2 Data and methodology

Answering these questions, presents a number of methodological concerns. First, it is necessary to translate corpus-based examples into structures that are suitable for a more controlled experimental setting (see, for example, Schmitt *et al.*, 2004), which consequently raises issues of possibilities and limitations of such a combined approach. The current study uses corpus-based and corpus-attested examples as input stimuli for a combined eye-tracking/EEG experimental setup.[2]

Three types of input stimuli were created. The first of these types contains significant native-like collocations. These are based on high to medium frequency verbs and their nominal collocates as well as high to medium frequency nouns and premodifying adjectival collocates, which are extracted in a collocational analysis of the British National Corpus (BNC). Additionally, similar interference-based examples are extracted from two learner corpora (ICLE-GER and LINDSEI-GER). As these corpora are significantly smaller than the BNC, statistical significance of these examples cannot be established, so that these examples are corpus-attested (i.e. typical examples exist in the learner corpora) but their typicality is not quantified.[3] These two groups are complemented by a set of semantically incongruous combinations that follow the same syntactic design. These combinations include either a transitive verb that is not congruent with its direct object complement (see example (6) below), or a premodifying adjective that is similarly not congruent with its verbs (for example, constructions such as *a tasty house*, which are grammatically well-formed but semantically incongruous).

Significant native-speaker collocations were created based on lemmatized word lists based on the complete BNC data. High and medium frequency verbs were, for example, *tell* (ranked at number 24 of all lemmata in the BNC with 733,131 occurrences) as the most frequent verb and *declare* (ranked 330, with 6,096 occurrences) as the least frequent verb. Verbs were compared to the Cambridge English: Preliminary Wordlists (2012) to ensure that verbs were rated at a sufficiently low level of difficulty, making it highly likely that all participants are familiar with them.[4] Highly significant noun collocates were extracted based on a lemmatized log-likelihood ($G^2$) score within a (+5|–5) window. A similar procedure was applied to nouns and their adjective collocates. The selection of interference collocates was based on the deviant V + N combinations described in Nesselhauf (2005) as well as a set of similarly derived Adj + N collocates. Incongruent combinations were constructed based on base words with similar frequencies. Items in the constructed incongruous category were chosen from the same frequency ranges as the corresponding items in the native-speaker category and were also cross-validated with the aforementioned Preliminary Wordlists. Syntactically, all inputs were created as simplex sentences without subordination or major embedding for the reasons described in the following paragraph.

A major limitation of the combined eye-tracking/EEG approach is based on the fact that complete sentence inputs are necessary to record eye-movement and EEG data simultaneously. Accordingly, it is necessary to edit the (longer and structurally messier) corpus-derived examples to create experimental inputs of similar design and length. For example, the relatively complex sentence shown in example (1) is shortened to the simplified version in (4). Similar sentence types are created for the other input groups as shown in (5) and (6):

(4) I am ready to found a family.
(corpus-attested interference collocation)
(5) She lost her virginity at sixteen.
(corpus-based native-like collocation)
(6) Michelle did not really drink my question.
(constructed incongruous combination)

For each of the input types in examples (4)–(6), 15 inputs were created; Adjective + Noun combinations were created in a similar manner. Input stimuli were separated into ten areas of interest of equal size; for data interpretation the two areas of interest (AoI) that contain the lexical elements in question are referred to as AoI1 (verbs and adjectives) and AoI2 (nouns). For the EEG recording, three different temporal windows were selected: one second after stimulus presentation (–100ms to 900ms), as well as two identical windows after participants' first visits to AoI1 and AoI2.

Two different groups of German-speaking learners partook in the experiment: a less advanced group consisting of 17 first-year undergraduate students (BA-English) and a more advanced group consisting of an equal number of first-year graduate students (Masters for teaching English as a Foreign Language). The participant population in the experiment was comparable to the informants represented in the learner corpora used for the creation of the interference collocations (ICLE-GER and LINDSEI-GER). Participants were between 19 and 36 years old, the median age being 23 (mean 24); 27 participants were female. All participants were German L1 speakers, 5 of whom spoke an additional L1. Participants had undergone from 8 to 15 years of formal English education (median/mean 10 years). All students in the more advanced group had been studying in an English-speaking country for at least three months as a prerequisite of their degree.

Stimulus presentation and the recording of data were based on a relatively standard eye-tracking design. The measurement of eye-movements and EEG data was conducted in a sound-attenuated and dimly illuminated chamber (2 × 4 × 2.5m). The illumination of the chamber was adapted to the luminance of the screen. Viewing distance was 100cm. During experimental trials, EEG data were recorded using a 32-channel EEG system with active Ag-AgCl electrodes.[5]

## 4.3 Some evidence from eye-tracking

Results from the experiment described above show that a large amount of variation can already be observed when participants start focusing on the left-hand part of the combination in question. This may seem surprising, considering the fact that the status of the combination (i.e. native-like collocation, interference collocation or incongruous combination) only becomes fully transparent when speakers have processed both parts. However, this may be explained by the relatively short sentence length and the fact that stimuli are presented as full images containing the complete sentences. It therefore seems very likely that participants experience preview effects and are, at least partially, aware of the right-side items. This view is corroborated by the EEG/ERP data (discussed in Section 4.4).

Considering total fixation times within AoI1, the area of interest containing verbs and premodifying adjectives, Schilk (2020) attests a sentence condition main effect, but no further effects for word class or learner group. Figure 9.1 displays a graphic representation of predicted fixation times and illustrates this main effect. Native-like collocations are labelled as E, interference-based collocations as D and semantically incongruous combinations as EW.[6]

As can be inferred from Figure 9.1, predicted fixation times are shortest for the left parts of native-like collocations (E: mean: 283ms,

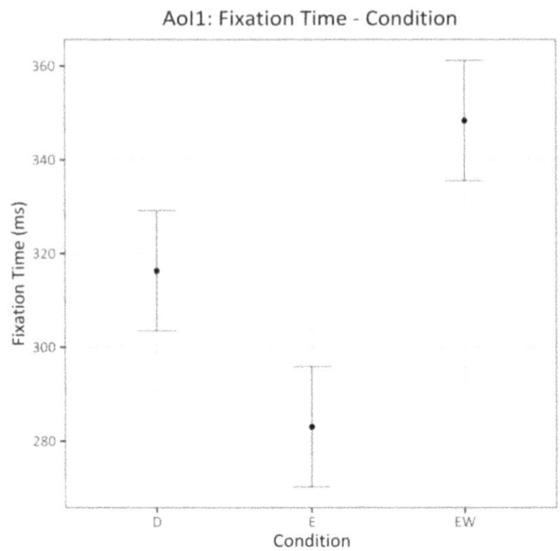


**Figure 9.1** Total fixation times, by sentence condition (Schilk, 2020: 126)

median: 274ms, SE: 8.5ms) and longest for the completely incongruous combinations (EW: mean: 343ms, median: 338ms, SE: 12.6ms), while, for interference collocation, fixation times range between the times of those two cases (D: mean: 316ms, median: 301ms, SE: 12.6ms). Error bars in Figure 9.1 are based on Fisher's least significant difference. By applying a more conservative Bonferroni-corrected post-hoc t-test, the difference between D (interference collocations) and EW (incongruous combinations) is not significant ($p = 0.065$).

This shows that participating learners experience clear processing facilitation for native-like collocations, compared to the incongruous combinations and the interference collocations, when focusing on the left item in the combination. While these items, in interference collocations, are processed slightly faster than the corresponding items within the incongruous combination, this difference does not hold up when applying conservative post-hoc testing. The overall results for this variable, therefore, match expectations. Learners – who are known to produce a large amount of native-like combinations – also profit from these in processing. Their interference-based knowledge of similar combinations in their L1 may assist in decoding interference collocations, which sets those (slightly) apart from incongruous combinations. Still, interference-based collocations are not the preferred alternatives for the relatively advanced learners, who seem to process typical English collocations significantly faster. This is in line with results from Wolter and Yamashita (2015), who fail to illustrate processing advantages of similar Japanese-based interference combinations over native-like collocations. Results from Wolter and Yamashita (2015) and from the present study therefore indicate that there does not seem to be a clear L1-based activation path for collocations in the case of advanced learners.

It is somewhat surprising, however, that no student group effects can be attested at this level. Reasons for this become clearer, when also focusing on the number of visits to the respective area of interest (AoI). Here a student group effect can be shown ($F = 5.25$, $p < .05$) that is based on the more advanced students revisiting the left part of the combination more frequently than their less advanced cohorts (Table 9.1).

Table 9.1 shows that BA students revisit AoI1 significantly less frequently than the students in the Masters program. This difference in revisiting AoI1 may be explained by a slightly different reading style of the two groups: while the less advanced participants generally only spend one visit to the initial AoI, the more advanced students spend slightly shorter times on initial visits but revisit this AoI in those cases where they are unsure about the combination's validity. By focusing purely on total fixation times, this relatively small effect gets blurred by stronger effects. This view is, however, supported by focusing on all variables jointly and is also corroborated by the EEG/ERP data. Table 9.2 provides an overview of the total data by degree course.

As shown in Table 9.2, fixation times are relatively similar between student groups, while first fixation durations are slightly longer for the less advanced students. At the same time, revisiting is more frequent for the students in the Masters program, compared to the Bachelors students.[7]

**Table 9.1** Revisits to AoI1, by degree course (Schilk, 2020: 135)

| Cond:DC | BA | MA |
|---|---|---|
| **D** | **AoI 1** | **AoI 1** |
| mean (ms) | 0.09 | 0.18 |
| median (ms) | 0 | 0 |
| SD (ms) | 0.26 | 0.38 |
| **E** | **AoI 1** | **AoI 1** |
| mean (ms) | 0.04 | 0.13 |
| median (ms) | 0 | 0 |
| SD (ms) | 0.19 | 0.33 |
| **EW** | **AoI 1** | **AoI 1** |
| mean (ms) | 0.13 | 0.31 |
| median (ms) | 0 | 0 |
| SD (ms) | 0.33 | 0.43 |

**Table 9.2** All variables, by degree course (Schilk, 2020: 160)

| | First Fix. Duration | | Fixation Time (ms) | | Fixation Count (#) | | Revisits (#) | |
|---|---|---|---|---|---|---|---|---|
| **BA** | **AoI1** | **AoI2** | **AoI1** | **AoI2** | **AoI1** | **AoI2** | **AoI1** | **AoI2** |
| mean | 230 | 267 | 315 | 315 | 1.13 | 1.09 | 0.09 | 0.03 |
| median | 216 | 244 | 303 | 303 | 1 | 1 | 0 | 0 |
| SD | 69 | 73 | 89 | 89 | 0.31 | 0.27 | 0.27 | 0.18 |
| **MA** | **AoI1** | **AoI2** | **AoI1** | **AoI2** | **AoI1** | **AoI2** | **AoI1** | **AoI2** |
| mean | 218 | 247 | 317 | 317 | 1.25 | 1.17 | 0.20 | 0.06 |
| median | 207 | 232 | 295 | 295 | 1 | 1 | 0 | 0 |
| SD | 53 | 78 | 105 | 106 | 0.42 | 0.36 | 0.39 | 0.22 |

## 4.4 Some evidence from EEG/ERP

For the current discussion, the results for two different event-related potentials are of specific interest. The first of these is the N100 component, a component with negative polarity that is displayed at a very early point in the electroencephalogram. Generally, this component is associated with initial attention and early lexical processing in terms of lexicality and word regularity (Sereno *et al.*, 1998). Due to its very early nature (i.e. only a tenth of a second after stimulus presentation), it is generally not associated with higher cognitive functions, such as conscious reflection on semantic content. In combination with other components, it may, however, be part of a larger cognitive complex, as illustrated in the following. The second ERP component under discussion is the N400 component, frequently described to be associated with semantic integration of mismatching or difficult items (see, for example, Friederici *et al.*, 1993; Hahne, 2001; Kutas & Hillyard, 1980). This later measure is thus more clearly associated with active semantic processing.

Different measuring points are used as time locks for EEG measuring. Initial recording takes place in the first second after sentence onset (–100ms to 900ms); two further recordings with identical temporal windows are initiated when participants first visit AoI1 and AoI2, respectively. In this chapter, the initial focus is on the N100 component in the EEG readings recorded immediately after the presentation of the (full sentence) stimulus.

Figure 9.2 shows the EEG readings at three central scalp positions (frontocentral = Fz, centrocentral = Cz and parietocentral = Pz), i.e. abstracting from potential hemispheric differentiation. Data are organized according to sentence construction (D = interference collocation, E = native-like collocation, EW = incongruous combination); EEG readings are shown as averages over student groups (degree course = DC). Negative polarities are displayed above O (zero), positive polarities below O. The temporal window is t = –100 – 900 ms after full

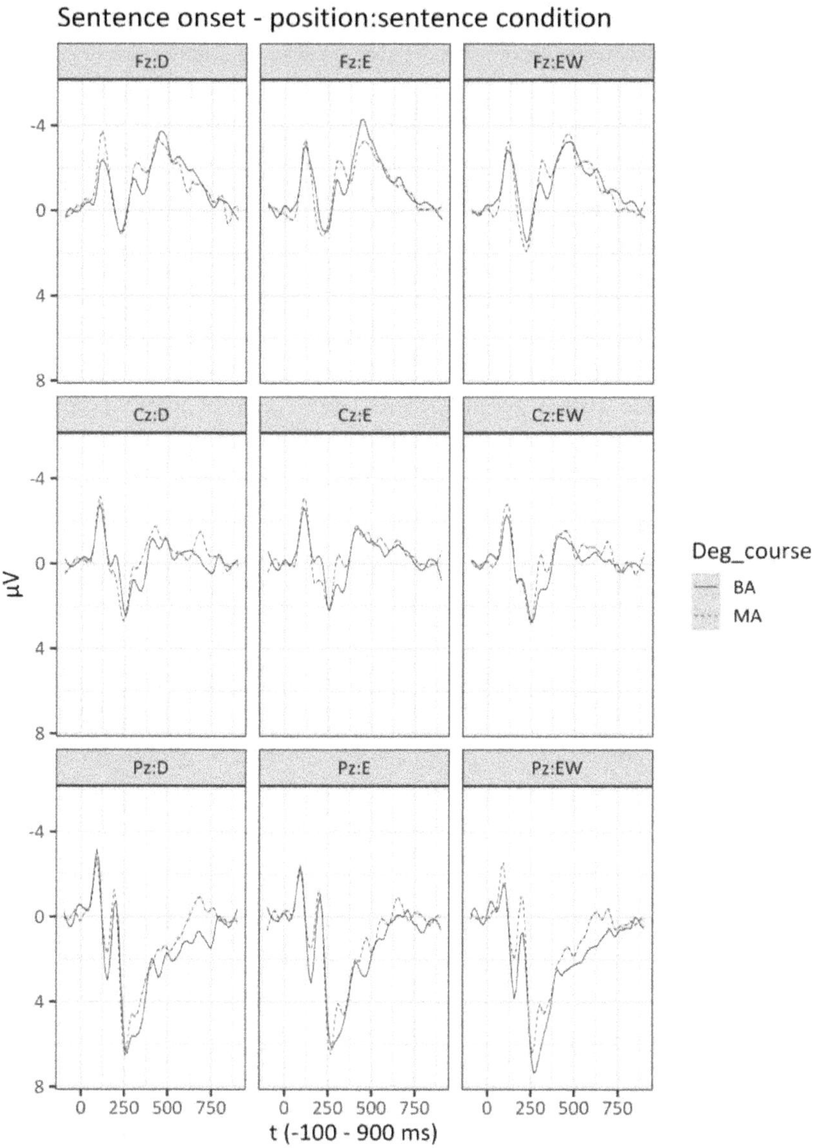


**Figure 9.2** EEG reading directly after stimulus presentation, by sentence condition and student group (Schilk, 2020: 183)

stimulus presentation, i.e. EEG readings depict the averaged electroencephalogram at the respective positions in the first second after stimulus presentation.

For the N100 component, clear differences between the student groups can be seen at the Fz position (similar differences are recorded at the Cz position, although somewhat less clearly). A repeated measures ANOVA identifies main effects for degree course and sentence condition as well as a degree_course:sentence_condition interaction. Conservative Bonferroni-adjusted post-hoc testing, however, does not corroborate the sentence condition main effect, as shown in Tables 9.3–9.5 (ANOVA, post-hoc test and descriptive statistics).

Overall, the more advanced students display higher negative amplitudes than their less advanced counterparts and this difference is particularly interesting when focusing on interference collocations. While these differences are significant for all within-condition/across student group comparisons (i.e. BA:D vs. MA:D, BA:E vs. MA:E and BA:EW vs. MA:EW), differences are strongest in the BA:D vs. MA:D comparison, with an amplitude difference of 1.15 μV. By accepting N100 as an indicator of initial attention to stimulus, two important interpretations are possible for this result. First, it is surprising that we find differences between the sentence conditions. Although these are not corroborated

**Table 9.3** N100 – Condition/Deg_Course (Fz) – ANOVA (Schilk, 2020: 185)

```
$ANOVA
       Effect DFn DFd          SSn       SSd          F            p p<.05         ges
1 (Intercept)   1  40 817.2767792 58.773431 556.221927 4.421567e-25     * 0.930040459
2          DC   1  40   9.0100430 58.773431   6.132052 1.760409e-02     * 0.127825110
3        Cond   2  80   0.5978135  2.703796   8.844063 3.387882e-04     * 0.009630497
4     DC:Cond   2  80   5.8958505  2.703796  87.223319 7.938359e-21     * 0.087510482

$`Mauchly's Test for Sphericity`
   Effect         W            p p<.05
3    Cond 0.2704807 8.446129e-12     *
4 DC:Cond 0.2704807 8.446129e-12     *

$`Sphericity Corrections`
   Effect       GGe        p[GG] p[GG]<.05       HFe        p[HF] p[HF]<.05
3    Cond 0.5781953 3.251986e-03         * 0.5845494 3.142242e-03         *
4 DC:Cond 0.5781953 4.767046e-13         * 0.5845494 3.637042e-13         *
```

**Table 9.4** N100 – Condition/Deg_Course (Fz) – Post-hoc test (Schilk, 2020: 185)

**Pairwise comparisons/*p*-value adjustment: Bonferroni**

| | | | | | |
|---|---|---|---|---|---|
| | | | | | BA |
| MA | | | | | 0.00 |
| | | D | | | E |
| E | | 1.00 | | | – |
| EW | | 0.10 | | | 0.07 |
| | BA:D | BA:E | BA:EW | MA:D | MA:E |
| BA:E | **<0.01** | – | – | – | – |
| BA:EW | <0.01 | 1.00 | – | – | – |
| MA:D | **<0.01** | **<0.01** | **<0.01** | – | – |
| MA:E | **<0.01** | **<0.01** | 1.00 | **<0.01** | – |
| MA:EW | <0.01 | <0.01 | <0.01 | **<0.01** | 0.25 |

**Table 9.5** N100 – Condition/Deg_Course (Fz) – Descriptive Statistics (Schilk, 2020: 185)

| Condition | Mean (μV) | Median (μV) | SD (μV) |
|---|---|---|---|
| BA | –2.28 | –2.39 | 0.71 |
| MA | –2.81 | –3.06 | 0.77 |
| D | –2.48 | –2.37 | 0.90 |
| E | –2.52 | –2.86 | 0.85 |
| EW | –2.64 | –2.82 | 0.59 |
| BA:D | –1.91 | –2.29 | 0.60 |
| BA:E | –2.42 | –2.79 | 0.84 |
| BA:EW | –2.51 | –2.71 | 0.54 |
| MA:D | –3.06 | –3.23 | 0.77 |
| MA:E | –2.61 | –2.93 | 0.86 |
| MA:EW | –2.78 | –2.87 | 0.62 |

overall, i.e. by abstracting from student groups in the interaction, these differences hold for some of the within-group interpretations, especially those related to D-condition sentences. This suggests that participants are subconsciously aware of a difference between interference collocations and the two other types of combinations. However, while the Masters students display significantly higher amplitudes regarding the interference collocations compared to the other combination possibilities, bachelor students display lower amplitudes in the same comparison. This leads to the second interpretation: that Masters students experience a peak in initial awareness when encountering transfer collocations, while BA students show relatively higher peaks for native-like collocations and incongruous combinations. Keeping in mind the very early temporal point, such a distinction is somewhat surprising, but it seems to be the case that the more advanced students are more aware of potential transfer stimuli. This may be due to the fact that those students are highly sensitive to L1 transfer, due to their advanced teacher training.

The results for the N100 component analysed in the recording at sentence onset are complemented by taking into account the data for the N400 component recorded at the point of latest recognition (i.e. recording time-locked to AoI2). At this point, participants have reached the nouns that are either complementing the verbs in the verb + noun combinations or build the head of the modified NP in the adjective + noun combinations. Therefore, the nature of the combination (i.e. native-like collocation, interference collocation or incongruous combination) should become obvious upon reaching this area, regardless of any preview effects. Figure 9.3 shows the EEG reading for the centrocentral position that was most relevant for the interpretation of an N400 component in the experiment. The upper panel in Figure 9.3 shows

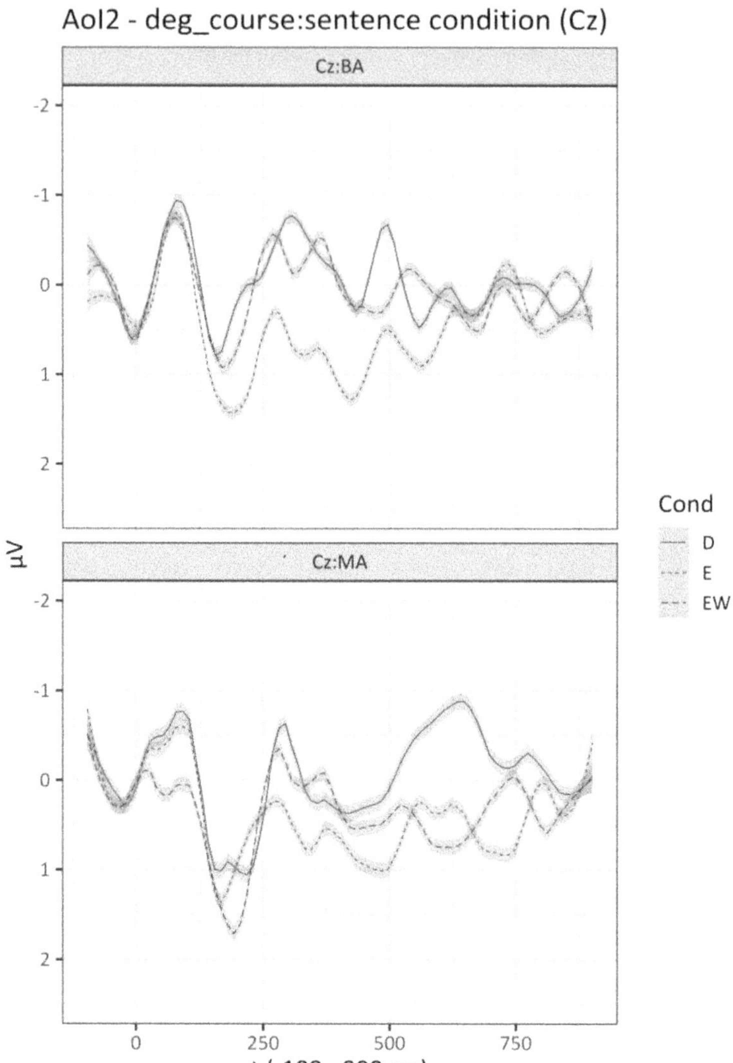


**Figure 9.3** EEG reading directly after stimulus presentation, by sentence condition and student group (Schilk, 2020: 271)

the readings for the less advanced group, the lower panel shows averaged readings for the more advanced students. Notably, amplitudes are lower at the reading within AoI2 when compared to the reading at sentence onset (similar to readings for AoI1, which are, however, not discussed in this selective overview). This general difference between the initial and the later reading is very likely influenced by the full stimulus presentation within the experiment.

As shown in Figure 9.3, Masters students display a late EEG peak at around 625ms after entering AoI2 (mean amplitude for the 550–700ms window: –0.68μV) for the interference collocations. This peak is not observed for the other combinations and it is also not displayed in the averaged EEG signature of the BA students. The morphology of the peak (slow onset, wide peak, sharper decline) is typical of an N400 EEG component. However, it is observed with a slightly increased latency and relatively low amplitudes.

As Hahne (2001) also observed delayed N400 latencies in the case of L2 learners, this delay may be typical of non-native semantic integration. Remarkably, this peak is not shown for the incongruous combinations, where higher semantic integration cost and surprise to unexpected stimulus would be more expected (although it is rudimentarily represented for the incongruous combinations at the frontal position). A plausible explanation, for the occurrence of this N400 component may be similar to the earlier explanation for the pronounced N100 component for the interference collocations in the case of the Masters students: while they profit from native-like collocations in a manner similar to native speakers, incrongrous combinations are relatively obvious in their erroneous nature. The interference combinations, however, may need a higher integration and separation of the two linguistic systems that are at the disposal of the participants. Additionally, all Masters students are English teacher trainees and are potentially quite sensitive to L1 transfers.

## 5 Discussion

As the experimental results discussed in Section 4 have shown, processing different types of lexical combinations is a highly complex process that may be further complicated for bilingual and multilingual speakers. It is, therefore, not surprising that simple initial hypotheses that non-native speakers and learners of English would be experiencing a facilitation effect in processing interference combinations are not fully corroborated. Rather, it seems to be the case that a number of different factors are jointly influencing collocational or combinatory processing. As suggested by the corpus data, the learners represented in the experimental approach all seemed to profit from frequent and typical native-like collocations. Fixations times for these collocations were overall shorter. However, it should be pointed out that, if we take the EEG data into consideration, non-native speakers do seem to treat these combinations differently than native speakers do. As Hahne (2001) points out, non-native speakers also display N400 components for typical native-like combinations and some of our results corroborate this finding (it is not possible, however, to discuss these parts of the analysis in this chapter). Clearly, more work that directly compares collocational processing of native speakers to the processing of non-native speakers is needed here.

Regarding interference collocations (and to some extent the incongruous combinations) an interesting picture emerges. Student groups seem to follow a slightly different reading style: while the less advanced students may follow a more sequential style, i.e. focusing on single words at a time, the more advanced students seem to produce a summary scan of the whole sentence that is represented in shorter initial fixations and a higher propensity for revisiting in the case of problematic items. These results are complemented by the EEG/ERP results. The Masters students display an early N100 peak that shows their increased attention to sentences containing interference collocations. Furthermore, these students also show a higher propensity for revisiting, which suggests that they may backtrack after encountering semantically problematic items. The delayed N400 component observed for the interference collocations (and to a far smaller extent for the incongruous combination) may serve as a trigger for those revisits. That is to say that the advanced students seem to be aware of the erroneous nature of the interference combination very early on, albeit at a level far below conscious awareness. At a later point (i.e. after the point of latest recognition) this low level 'suspicion' is confirmed by higher level functions (represented in the N400 component), which leads to backtracking to the initial item.

While this interpretation seems plausible, a number of caveats apply. First and foremost, this interpretation is not yet strengthened by data that focus on the exact times and directions of gaze movements, i.e. saccadic data. Presently, data show that those students revisit and that they display heightened semantic integration cost for interference collocations. Combining these observations suggests backtracking. There is, however, no conclusive evidence of such behaviour without analysing time and direction of gaze movements in addition to fixations. In order to meaningfully analyse saccade onset times and saccade directions, larger experimental settings would be needed. The relatively low number of participants does not allow for such a procedure: while a total of 34 participants is sufficient to analyse fixation data and averaged EEG readings, it is too small to generate signal-to-noise robust averaged groups for group-based interpretation of saccadic data. A larger number of participants would therefore be necessary to further substantiate claims on proficiency-based reading styles.

Finally, the combined eye-tracking/EEG analysis is not without specific setting-inherent problems. While such an approach is very well suited to use of the two different types of experimental data in a complementary fashion, it drastically limits the amount of text that can be included into single stimuli and also includes requirements related to stimulus-group averaging. This in turn limits the potential of using purely corpus-based stimuli, as such stimuli tend to be longer and often more complex. Such longer stimuli may be better suited to a moving window approach when considering EEG readings, while such an approach is not well suited for eye-tracking procedures. Similarly, more complex inputs are harder to group into similar stimulus types that data could be averaged over, since here same-type stimuli should ideally be relatively homogeneous, while stimuli should differ significantly across averaged groups.

## 6 Conclusion

In this chapter, and in the larger work it reports upon, I propose a combination of using learner corpus data and experimental data to describe both the performance and the processing of collocations by advanced learners of English. While corpus-based descriptions of phraseological structures, such as collocations and other semi-formulaic types of language, have become relatively popular over the last couple of decades, most analyses of language processing of such sentence types are limited to (often monolingual) native-speakers. This study describes one possibility of bridging this gap and, at the same time, identifies a set of methodological challenges for such research.

First, corpus data are often not very well suited for experimental analysis, as they include singular examples of language used by individual speakers. Finding patterns in such data is, of course, useful and may describe tendencies that specific groups of speakers follow. Using these results as input for experimental designs may therefore be beneficial in gaining insights into the cognitive behaviour of similar speakers.

However, corpus-derived inputs require a certain amount of adaptation to be successfully used in experimental designs. Especially in the current approach, which combines eye-tracking with electroencephalography, the adaptation of corpus data to experimental stimuli is necessary for several reasons. First, the eye-tracking approach requires relatively short sentences that fit within a single screen and can be divided into different areas of interest of similar size. For this reason, natural sentence complexity needed to be removed and the stimulus sentences were simplified and adjusted to a size that fit these requirements.

Measuring and analysing the EEG/ERP data, on the other hand, requires a dataset that can be divided into groups that are relatively homogeneous within the groups and relatively heterogeneous across groups. The reason for this is that, for the EEG/ERP analysis, it is necessary to average the data twice to generate meaningful signal-to-noise ratios. The first averaging is carried out within the stimulus groups. For the EEG/ERP analysis the different inputs within a group are considered repetitions of similar stimuli, which is an idealization of the actual linguistic data. With certain differences in word frequency and the possibility of individual familiarity with the items used in the stimuli, this is already a relatively strong simplification. Using purely natural corpus data would complicate this further, as not only lexical and semantic factors but also factors such as syntactic complexity would have to be taken into account. The second averaging needed for meaningful EEG results is related to the participant groups. Similar to the stimulus groups, the participants are considered to be relatively homogenous within their respective groups and heterogeneous across these groups. This may neglect individual participant-based factors that could be more easily integrated into an experiment type that only includes one of the two methods (i.e. eye-tracking or EEG).

Additionally, the individual L1-based components within publicly available learner corpora are relatively small and it is therefore sometimes difficult to isolate usage patterns that are typical of a large number of language learners. When it comes to the combination of specific lexical items, often singular examples are encountered that may, however, stand proxy for more general learner issues. Deriving such general interpretations from differentiated examples, however, is also not entirely unproblematic and is often based on intuitive interpretations. In turn, generating comparable groups of data for experimental approaches involves a number of steps that are increasing in their level of abstraction and may not necessarily reflect the 'real language' data we encounter in corpora.

As mentioned, not all results of the original experiment could be presented in this chapter. For example, and perhaps most importantly, some interactions between the different word-class based groups (V + N versus Adj. + N collocations) have not been discussed, although they are frequently shown in the larger study. In general, collocational salience for both learner groups seemed to be stronger for the combinations containing a verb and a noun that functions as a direct object complement of the verb than for combinations that consist of a premodifying adjective and a head noun. This effect was pertinent in both the eye-tracking analysis and the EEG analysis: in the analysis of the eye-tracking data, it could be shown, for example, that German interferences in the input were met with longer fixation times in the case of the V + N combinations, while these interferences were not reacted to as strongly in the case of the Adj. + N combinations (Schilk, 2020: 142–143). This effect also seemed to be somewhat stronger for the less advanced learners than for the more advanced learners, which became particularly apparent when considering the N100 ERP in the EEG-based dataset: here the more advanced students seemed to experience both input groups in a similar manner, while the less advanced group only reacted to potential incongruences in the case of the V + N combinations (Schilk, 2020: 174–177). This is in line with some of the results of studies focusing on the comparison of native-speaker and learner production data, where combinations of verbs and their direct object complements have a clearer influence on perceived learner proficiency than combinations of nouns and premodifying adjectives (see, for example, Chapters 5 and 6 of this volume).

While the present study and the larger work it is based upon could highlight some important developments in L2 learner language processing (in the sense that more advanced learners treat collocational preferences differently from their less advanced cohorts), closer insights into the cognitive realities of learner processing are necessary, in order to better understand the how and why of learner production. Here a stronger cooperation between psychologists, psycholinguists, corpus linguists and language teachers seems a strong desideratum, as it may improve our understanding of learner language far better than individual contributions can.

## Notes

(1) The amount of learner material available in corpora such as ICLE and LINDSEI has increased considerably since the publication of Nesselhauf (2005). However, this growth is mainly dependent on adding new L1 components, while the average component size is still comparably small, with approximately 225,000 words represented in each ICLE subcorpus and 100,000 words in each LINDSEI subcorpus.

(2) The difference between corpus-based and corpus-attested examples is mainly one of perspective: while corpus-based examples have been derived from the corpora by more direct corpus analyses that use the data as the initial input, corpus-attested examples are based on more intuitive observations of learner behaviour that is compared to corpus data.

(3) While there are approaches to statistical quantification of collocational use in small learner corpora (see, for example, Granger & Bestgen, 2014, or Kyle & Eguchi, Chapter 6 of this volume), these are mainly used for direct comparisons of learner data with native-speaker data represented in larger corpora. Thus, they can provide measures of native-like collocational proficiency of learners. However, these measures do not seem to be ideally suited to the identification of learner transfers, as these combinations are by definition only rarely encountered in native-speaker corpora (see also Schilk, 2020: 248–249).

(4) These lists (and their titles) are regularly updated/changed. Preliminary/Preliminary for Schools is the title of the 2012 version used. The current title is B1 Preliminary for Schools Vocabulary List. The updated (2020) version of the Cambridge English: Preliminary Wordlists is available at: https://www.cambridgeenglish.org/exams-and-tests/preliminary-for-schools/preparation/

(5) For a more detailed description of experimental design and input stimuli see Schilk (2020) pages 91–115 (input stimuli) and pages 105–110 (participant selection).

(6) Here, E refers to the combination being typical of English usage; D to a combination that would be typical in German (Deutsch) but is not in English; and EW refers to a combination that is semantically incongruous in English (simplified to being wrong in English (EW)).

(7) There are additional effects based on the different word class types of combinations: for example, BA students specifically focus long on adjectives in the Adj.+ N combinations. For the influence of these effects, see the full description in Schilk (2020).

## References


Conklin, K. and Carrol, G. (2018) First language influence on the processing of formulaic language in a second language. In A. Siyanova-Chanturia and A. Pellicer-Sánchez (eds) *Understanding Formulaic Language: A Second Language Acquisition Perspective* (pp. 62–77). New York, NY: Routledge.

Cowie, A.P. (1994) Phraseology. In R.E. Asher (ed.) *The Encyclopedia of Language and Linguistics* (pp. 3168–3171). Oxford: Pergamon.

Cowie, A.P. (1998) Introduction. In A.P. Cowie (ed.) *Phraseology: Theory, Analysis and Applications* (pp. 1–20). Oxford: Oxford University Press.

Ellis, N.C. and Frey, E. (2009) The psycholinguistic reality of collocation and semantic prosody (2): Affective priming. In R. Corrigan, E.A. Moravcsik, H. Ouali and K.M. Wheatley (eds) *Formulaic Language. Volume 2: Acquisition, Loss, Psycholinguistic Reality, and Functional Explanations* (pp. 473–498). Amsterdam: Benjamins.

Ellis, N.C., Frey, E. and Jalkannen, I. (2009) The psycholinguistic reality of collocation and semantic prosody (1): Lexical access. In U. Roemer and R. Schulze (eds) *Exploring the Lexis Grammar Interface* (pp. 89–116). Amsterdam: Benjamins.

Friederici, A.D., Pfeifer, E. and Hahne, A. (1993) Event related potentials during natural speech processing: Effects of semantic, morphological and syntactic violations. *Cognitive Brain Research* 1 (3), 183–192.

Gilquin, G. and Shortall, T. (2007) Reconciling corpus data and elicitation data in FLT. In M. Davies, P. Rayson, S. Hunston and P. Danielsson (eds) *Proceedings of the Corpus Linguistics Conference (CL 2007)* (pp. 12–27). Birmingham: University of Birmingham.

Gilquin, G., De Cock, S. and Granger, S. (2010) *Louvain International Database of Spoken English Interlanguage. Handbook and CD-ROM*. Louvain-la-Neuve, Belgium: Presses universitaires de Louvain.

Granger, S. (1998) Prefabricated patterns in advanced EFL writing: Collocations and formulae. In A.P. Cowie (ed.) *Phraseology: Theory, Analysis and Applications* (pp. 145–160). Oxford: Oxford University Press.

Granger, S. (2015) Contrastive interlanguage analysis: A reappraisal. *International Journal of Learner Corpus Research* 1 (1), 7–24.

Granger S. and Meunier F. (eds) (2008) *Phraseology: An Interdisciplinary Perspective*. Amsterdam: Benjamins.

Granger, S. and Bestgen, Y. (2014) The use of collocations by intermediate vs. advanced non-native writers: A bigram-based study. *International Review of Applied Linguistics in Language Teaching* 52 (3), 229–252.

Granger, S., Dagneaux, E., Meunier, F. and Paquot, M. (2009) *The International Corpus of Learner English. Handbook and CD-ROM, Version 2*. Louvain-la-Neuve, Belgium: Presses universitaires de Louvain.

Greenbaum, S. (1974) Some verb-intensifier collocations in American and British English. *American Speech* 49 (1), 79–89.

Hahne, A. (2001) What's different in second-language processing? Evidence from event-related potentials. *Journal of Psychological Research* 30 (3), 251–266.

Halliday, M.A.K. (1966) Lexis as a linguistic level. In C.E. Bazell, J.C. Catford, M.A.K. Halliday and R.H. Robins (eds) *In Memory of J.R. Firth* (pp. 148–163). London: Longman.

Hunston, S. (2002) Pattern grammar, language teaching and linguistic variation. In R. Reppen, S.M. Fitzmaurice and D. Biber (eds) *Using Corpora to Explore Linguistic Variation* (pp. 167–183). Amsterdam: Benjamins.

Kutas, M. and Hillyard, S.A. (1980) Reading senseless sentences: Brain potentials reflect semantic incongruity. *Science, New Series* 207 (4427), 203–205.

Millar, N. (2011) The processing of malformed formulaic language. *Applied Linguistics* 32 (2), 129–148.

Nattinger, J.R. and DeCarrico, J.S. (1992) *Lexical Phrases and Language Teaching*. Oxford: Oxford University Press.
Nesselhauf, N. (2005) *Collocations in a Learner Corpus*. Amsterdam: Benjamins.
Pawley, A. and Syder, F.H. (1983) Two puzzles for linguistic theory: Nativelike selection and nativelike fluency. In J.C. Richards and R.W. Schmidt (eds) *Language and Communication* (pp. 191–225). London: Longman.
Schilk, M. (2020) *Language Processing in Advanced Learners of English: A Multi-method Approach to Collocation Based on Corpus Linguistic and Experimental Data*. Amsterdam: Benjamins.
Schmitt, N. and Carter, R. (2004) Formulaic sequences in action. In N. Schmitt (ed.) *Formulaic Sequences: Acquisition, Processing and Use* (pp. 1–22). Amsterdam: Benjamins.
Schmitt, N., Grandage, S. and Adolphs, S. (2004) Are corpus-derived recurrent clusters psycholinguistically valid? In N. Schmitt (ed.) *Formulaic Sequences: Acquisition, Processing and Use* (pp. 127–152). Amsterdam: Benjamins.
Sereno, S.C., Rayner, K. and Posner, M.I. (1998) Establishing a time-line of word recognition: Evidence from eye-movements and event-related potentials. *Neuroreport* 9 (10), 2195–2200.
Sinclair, J. McH. (1991) *Corpus, Concordance, Collocation*. Oxford: Oxford University Press.
Sinclair, J. McH. (2008) Preface. In S. Granger and F. Meunier (eds) *Phraseology: An Interdisciplinary Perspective* (pp. xv–xviii). Amsterdam: Benjamins.
Siyanova-Chanturia, A., Conklin, K. and Schmitt, N. (2011) Adding more fuel to the fire: An eye-tracking study of idiom processing by native and non-native speakers. *Second Language Research* 27 (2), 251–272.
Stefanowitsch, A. and Gries, S.Th. (2003) Collostructions: Investigating the interaction of words and constructions. *International Journal of Corpus Linguistics* 8 (2), 209–243.
Underwood, G., Schmitt, N. and Galpin, A. (2004) The eyes have it: An eye movement study into the processing of formulaic sequences. In N. Schmitt (ed.) *Formulaic Sequences: Acquisition, Processing and Use* (pp. 153–172). Amsterdam: Benjamins.
Wolter, B. and Yamashita, J. (2015) Processing collocations in a second language: A case of first language activation? *Applied Psycholinguistics* 36 (5), 1193–1221.
Wray, A. (2002) *Formulaic Language and the Lexicon*. Cambridge: Cambridge University Press.

# Part 4: Postface

# 10 Phrasicon, Phrase, Phraseology

David Singleton

This volume's title contains the word *phrasicon*, which appears to have been first used in an English context in the 17th century but which is increasingly current in the terminology of corpus linguistics. By analogy with the reference of *lexicon* to a collection of words, *phrasicon* refers to the compendium of phrases associated with a given language or language variety, a given learner population or individual learner.

It is worth saying that the sense of the base term *phrase*, like that of *lexis*, is multiply interpretable, even (or especially) within linguistics. In syntax-focused discussion, for example, what is usually said about phrases concerns their components in terms of 'parts of speech' and their role in sentence-structure (noun phrases, verb phrases, etc.). On the other hand, as Howarth notes, people working in such areas as lexicology and lexicography think of phrases in terms of 'a "scale of idiomaticity", ranging from the most freely co-occurring lexical items and transparent combinations to [...] the most cast-iron and opaque idiomatic expressions' (Howarth, 1996: 32). What is clear (see Singleton, 2000: Section 4.3) is that the distinction between 'fixed expression' and compound word, certainly in a language such as English, can be a matter founded on arbitrary orthographic taste.

*Phrasicon* relates to the notion of *phraseology*, which in some of its definitions comes close to the same idea. Gledhill, for example, defines phraseology as follows:

> Broadly speaking, phraseology involves the study of formulaic sequences of words, including idiomatic phrases and proverbial expressions, which stand in contrast to other more prosaic constructions in the language in that they have a highly conventionalised form and frame of reference. (Gledhill, 2011: 5)

Even more broadly speaking, however, phraseology covers a very large multitude. Thus, its definition in the *Oxford English Dictionary* runs as follows:

> The selection or arrangement of words and phrases in the expression of ideas; manner or style of expression; the particular language, terminology, or diction which characterizes a writer, work, subject, language, place, etc.

The *OED* definition (or rather set of definitions) takes us some distance from the 'formulaic' flavour of Gledhill's. The opening gloss – the 'arrangement of words and phrases in the expression of ideas' – is broad enough to stand for what the lexico-syntax of language does generally, and the other two, while narrower, cover but go beyond formulaicity. I would wish to claim that, while formulaicity illustrates the processes underlying the 'arrangement of words', it needs to be conceived of fluidly, as in varying degrees characterizing *all* such processes to a greater or lesser extent, even when the outcome is not self-evidently formulaic.

It may be worth citing in this context Leśniewska's (2019) treatment of the problem posed by articles in English to learners of English as a second language. Her approach is phraseological, but in the broad sense, citing researchers such as Sinclair and Hoey. The former was of the opinion, let it be remembered, that 'many of those people who are professionally engaged in handling language have known in their bones that the division into grammar and vocabulary obscures a very central area of meaningful organization' (Sinclair, 1991: 137). Hoey, even more radically, stated that each of us 'constructs a grammar – leaky, inconsistent, incomplete – out of the *primings* we have for the sounds, words, phrases that we encounter' (Hoey, 2007: 31, *emphasis added*). Leśniewska's own results lead her to conclude that her participants 'were consistently more successful at using articles when they appear in word combinations that are frequent' (2019: 98), a finding that she explicitly relates to Sinclair's theorizing.

This line of thinking is very much in tune with recent understanding of the way in which second language grammar is established, on which Lantolf and Thorne have the following to say.

> From the perspective of emergent grammar … learning an additional language is about enhancing one's repertoire of fragments and patterns that enables participation in a wider array of communicative activities. It is not about building up a complete and perfect grammar in order to produce well-formed sentences. (Lantolf & Thorne, 2006: 17)

It also accords with the whole usage-based perspective on language knowledge generally:

> Language knowledge involves statistical knowledge, so humans learn more easily and process more fluently high-frequency forms and 'regular' patterns which are exemplified by many types and which have few competitors. Usage-based perspectives of acquisition thus hold that language learning is the implicit associative learning of representations that reflect the probabilities of form-function mapping. (Ellis, 2017: 130)

According to these perspectives, language 'rules', including syntactic rules, are based on structural patterns emerging from unconscious analysis of distributional characteristics of language input.

This is a simplification, of course, which leaves out of account the role of pedagogical grammar at school – as well as in homes where its dictums are relayed by parents who are intent on getting their children to 'speak properly'. With regard to second language learning, my own experience is that pedagogical rules and examples can sometimes actually inculcate resistance to the lessons of naturalistic data.

## Some Thoughts on Frequency

The authors in this collection seem to interpret *phrasicon* on the whole in the sense of 'compendium of phrases' and are basically interested in *phraseology* in Gledhill's earlier-cited definition of 'formulaic sequences of words ....in contrast to other more prosaic constructions in the language'. The phrases in question are interesting because of their recurrence, which raises the issue of frequency, a seemingly innocent, unproblematic concept, but one which is beset with all kinds of difficulties, no matter what definition of *phrasicon* we are working with or what kinds of word sequences are in question.

That giant of applied linguistics, Stephen Pit Corder, discussed the difficulties posed by the construct of frequency many decades ago (1973), before the advent of massive computerized corpora, and the points he makes hold good no matter how many million words a given corpus contains. It seems to me worthwhile to give a tiny flavour of the caveats he puts before us. They should perhaps appear somewhere as a 'health warning' in every frequency-based treatment of linguistic data.

One of the problems he mentions (1973: 215–217) relates to sampling. He himself is largely concerned with the use of word-counts as a basis for syllabus design, but what he says is relevant to the drawing of conclusions about the use of the relative frequency of words, collocations, phrases, sentences, etc., for any purpose whatsoever. His basic point is that the sample used should ideally be representative and that this is impossible for language use generally since we do not know – almost certainly cannot *ever* know – the global relative frequency of different sorts of language activity. More serious, perhaps, for scientific uses of corpora is his point that we are not in a position to categorize and precisely demarcate different varieties of language use.

Corder also addresses the problem of the units that are being counted:

> Even if we could establish some satisfactory criterion of similarity for sentence, phrase or word structures, we would still be faced ... with the problem of multiple meaning. One and the same surface structure may

have a number of interpretations, just as quite different surface structures may have similar interpretations. (Corder, 1973: 218)

The above small sample of the worries Corder had about the use of frequency data in applied linguistics and language teaching should perhaps give us pause. There is absolutely no question but that language corpora are very valuable resources, but, as the authors in this volume are very clearly aware, such resources always need to be handled with care. There is plenty of evidence that they treat the concept of corpus frequency in line with Corder's admonitions – stating without hesitation where the limits are to frequency-based interpretations, emphasizing the value of the contribution of qualitative insights, and conceding again and again that important elements of situations are not yet established.

## The Relevance of the L2 Lexicon

Much of my own work has been focused on the L2 lexicon (e.g. Singleton, 1999, 2000; Singleton & Little, 1991). As indicated in previous discussion, the lexicon and phrasicon are not categorically separate, because the class of words and the class of phrases run into each other. Many researchers indeed take the view that, as Sinclair implies (see above), there is no clear separation between the lexicon and what has traditionally been called grammar, never mind phraseology (cf., for example, Bates & Goodman, 1997; Paquot, 2015; Römer & Schultze, 2009).

My first foray into lexical research (with David Little) was concerned with how L2 lexical processing related to L1 lexical processing (Singleton & Little, 1991). At the time, the prevailing view was that there was a fundamental difference between the two (Laufer, 1989; Meara, 1978, 1980, 1984), that the L2 mental lexicon was qualitatively different from the L1 mental lexicon – more 'phonological' and more 'loosely organized'. Little and I presented some C-test-elicited data which called the above view into question, suggesting that the way in which words were processed depended not on the status (L1 or L2) of the language they belonged to, but, rather, on the degree of difficulty of the lexical task concerned. Our data further suggested a measure of interaction between L1 and L2 lexical processing. To sum up the message of the L2 lexical research in all my publications mentioned above, it is that lexical processing in the L2 is not essentially different from L1 lexical processing,

More lexical exploration occurred in my work on the age factor in L2 acquisition (e.g. Singleton, 1995, 1998; Singleton & Ryan, 2004). Maybe the first thing to be said in this connection is that, given good mental health, vocabulary acquisition in L2 as in L1 continues throughout life (Singleton, 1995: 12–13; cf. Pfenninger & Singleton, 2019). This clearly further supports the proposition of the similarity of L1 and L2 lexical processing.

In respect of the earlier sector of the age range, L2 research findings relative to lexis follow the same pattern as that set by findings regarding the acquisition of L2 morphosyntax. That is to say, short-term naturalistic studies and long-term formal instructional studies show adult and adolescent L2 beginners progressing more rapidly than children, and older children progressing more rapidly than younger children. Naturalistic studies show (on the whole but not inevitably) that the younger a start is made to L2 acquisition, the higher the level of proficiency that is likely eventually to be attained (Singleton, 1995: 13–22; cf. Pfenninger & Singleton, 2017; Singleton & Ryan, 2004). The fact that the lexical findings conform to the grammatical findings is a further indication of the lack of a clear lexico-grammatical divide.

## Reflections on the Chapters in the Present Volume

What follows is a brief *tour d'horizon* of the chapters in the book. It is not a collection of summaries but rather of personal reflections on dimensions of the individual pieces that struck me as particularly interesting, thought-provoking and valuable.

For Ebeling and Hasselgård the burning question is to what extent L2 phraseological choices have a contrastive dimension. Their quantitative comparison does identify differences between L1 and L2 novices, but these are not reflected in the contrastive analysis. Their comparison between the writing of novices and the expert writing in the published sources also yielded inconclusive results. However, a qualitative analysis showed similarities in lexicalization between L1 English novices and experts on the one hand and between L2 English and Norwegian L1 experts on the other. The importance of the qualitative angle in phraseological research comes through in these results.

Focused on the issue of phraseological competence and language assessment, Gyllstad and Snoder's chapter argues for the use of corpora in the context of language testing and assessment. They retail a study reporting on how it is possible to utilize data from the International Corpus of Learner English (ICLE) (Granger *et al.*, 2020) to inform test development, claiming that the potential for learner corpus data to inform the design of language tests in general constitutes an area ripe for investigation. Their results show how a combination of various corpus resources and a manual analysis of verb + noun combinations can provide an empirical basis for informing test item design.

Gilquin and Granger's chapter does for the passive what Leśniewska's (2019) book (see above) has done for English articles. The passive, like the article system, has traditionally been seen as a strictly grammatical matter – since long before Chomsky's (1957) portrayal of them as resulting from the transformation of active base structures. Corpus-based studies of the passive, however, have indicated that there is more to it than rules. On the one hand, the active/passive distinction is not a strict dichotomy but a gradient, ranging from verbal to adjectival roles for the past participle. On the other, the passive is clearly lexical: some verbs occur more often in the passive voice than others and the passive seems to be typically used in a particular set of phraseological units. As far as pedagogical implications are concerned, the authors conclude that learners should focus on 'which structures should be used with which words and in which contexts' (Salazar, 2014: 127).

In their contribution Rubin, Housen and Paquot start from the metrics of phraseological complexity proposed by Paquot in respect of L2 English (2018, 2019). In a partial replication study, they demonstrate the importance of the role of phraseological competence in the assessment of L2 Dutch. Under critical scrutiny here is the Common European Framework of Reference for Languages (CEFR) (Council of Europe, 2001) approach to language proficiency. The results and the discussion presented in this chapter yield the conclusion that phraseological competence is a significant contributing factor to the assessment of proficiency at the CEFR B1 and B2 levels and needs to be taken account of by the CEFR assessment machinery. This is certainly a very important probing of yet another deficiency in the CEFR (cf. Hulstijn *et al.*, 2010 – cited by the authors), thus not only providing research insights but pointing the way towards some much needed improvements in practice.

Kyle and Eguchi point out that the reaction to increased attention to lexical and phraseological competence in second language research has included a number of studies investigating the relationships between word-level, n-gram level, and dependency bigram level characteristics of learner productions, on the one hand, and productive second language proficiency, on the other. The results of their own preliminary exploration seem to show that dependency bigrams may be better indicators of phraseological competence than adjacent bigrams. It is extremely interesting that particular aspects of phraseology are found in the study reported by Kyle and Eguchi to be more to the fore than others in contributing to and betokening phraseological proficiency. The whys and wherefores of these relationships cry out for further investigation!

Brezina and Fox note that comparing L2 users with 'native speakers' is not without controversy, implying a dichotomy of NS/NNS rather than the possibility of a continuum of native/non-native learning. In any case, they point out that defining what a native speaker is poses real problems (Davies, 2003), citing Cook's (2007) view that the target for the L2 learner, including the way in which phraseological competence operates, should be the proficient L2 speaker. They also point to the need in phraseological research (as in SLA research generally) always to keep an eye on the qualitative dimension of results.

Omidian, Siyanova-Chanturia and Spina cite Granger (2019) in support of their statement that L2 learners' knowledge of multiword expressions is not as extensive as that of L1 users and that such learners tend to overuse a limited range of multiword expressions in their L2 production. They go on to regret, however, that this tends to ignore the dynamic dimension of the development of phraseological knowledge in an L2 (Paquot & Granger, 2012), which is addressed by their study. Their results lead them to the conclusion that phraseological development is affected by a multiplicity of interacting elements and that time is but one factor – language proficiency and other learner differences also influencing L2 collocation development. The treatment of the dynamic aspects of the second language learner's mastery of multiword expressions is very welcome; even late second language learners can become indistinguishably native-like (see, for example, Kinsella & Singleton, 2014) – presumably phraseologically as well as in other respects.

Schilk's chapter reports on a study based on the use of a combination of corpus data and experimental data to explore the use and the processing of collocations by advanced learners of English as an L2. This research found that different groups of learners display different reactions to reading corpus-based native-like collocations, L1-interference-based collocations and incongruous combinations. It also established, via eye-tracking and also EEG readings, that advanced learners differ from less advanced learners in reading style and language processing, specifically in relation to interference-based collocations. One has to agree with the author that insights into the cognitive realities of learner processing are highly desirable and with his plea for stronger cooperation between psycholinguists and corpus linguists.

## Concluding Remarks

The above short discussion begins by pointing to the cline of interpretations, from the narrow to the virtually all-inclusive, attaching to the umbrella terms – *phrasicon*, *phrase*, *phraseology* – associated with the subject-matter of the present volume. The cline in question characterizes not only the lay use of these terms but also their deployment in a scientific context. Sometimes, one and the same author may shift from a narrower to broader usage and back within the same text. Such shifting is not a feature of the writing in the present volume, which on the whole adopts a narrower interpretation of the terms in question. In fact, the broader implications of some of the findings could fruitfully have been explored further.

There follows a brief foray into the matter of the care that is required with the use of the concept of frequency. This draws on Corder's lively discussion of the topic dating from nearly half a century ago – but still very relevant. In general, the use of the notion of frequency is not treated with enough caution in applied linguistics, especially perhaps applied lexicology. It has to be said that the authors contributing to this volume, for their part, are very aware of the problems raised in Corder's discussion.

A personal note is sounded in the subsequent section, where I explore the connections between the study from the SLA perspective of the phrasicon and the investigation of the acquisition and processing of the second language lexicon, which is where a considerable portion of my own research, including some of my age-related research, has had its focus. My conclusions regarding the similarity of L1 and L2 lexical processing and the lack of a clear separation between lexicon and grammar are, I think, in tune with the spirit and content of this collection.

Finally, with regard to the studies reported and ideas discussed in individual chapters of this volume, as I indicate in my commentary, these are overwhelmingly of very sharp interest and make an enormous contribution to understanding and debate in this extremely lively domain. The range of topics and approaches included is impressive and attractive, and the various chapters do much to increase excitement about the role of the whole corpus linguistics enterprise in the L2 area. Particularly welcome is the virtually omnipresent concern to have an influence on the amelioration of second language teaching and testing conditions and materials. The desired outcome will, thanks to the impact of this publication, undoubtedly materialize.

## References

Bates, E. and Goodman, J.C. (1997) On the inseparability on grammar and the lexicon: Evidence from acquisition, aphasia and real-time processing. *Language and Cognitive Processes* 12 (5/6), 507–584.

Chomsky, N. (1957) *Syntactic Structures*. The Hague: Mouton.

Cook V. (2007) The goals of ELT; Reproducing native-speakers or promoting multi-competence among second language users. In J. Cummins and C. Davison (eds) *Handbook on English Language Teaching* (pp. 237–248). London & New York: Springer.

Corder, S.P. (1973) *Introducing Applied Linguistics*. London: Penguin.

Council of Europe (2001) *Common European Framework of Reference for Languages: Learning, Teaching, Assessment*. Cambridge: Cambridge University Press.

Davies, A. (2003) *The Native Speaker: Myth and Reality*. Clevedon: Multilingual Matters.

Ellis, N.C. (2017) Chunking in language usage, learning and change: *I don't know*. In M. Hundt, S. Mollin and S.E. Pfenninger (eds) *The Changing English Language: Psycholinguistic Perspectives* (pp. 113–147). Cambridge: Cambridge University Press.

Gledhill, C. (2011) The 'lexicogrammar' approach to analysing phraseology and collocation in EP texts. *La Revue de GERAS: ASP (Anglais de Specialité)* 59, 5–23.

Granger, S. (2019) Formulaic language in learner corpora. Collocations and lexical bundles. In A. Siyanova-Chanturia and A. Pellicer-Sánchez (eds) *Understanding Formulaic Language: A Second Language Acquisition Perspective* (pp. 228–247). Abingdon: Routledge.

Granger, S., Dupont, M., Meunier, F., Naets, H. and Paquot, M. (eds) (2020) *International Corpus of Learner English. Version 3*. Université Catholique de Louvain. Louvain-la-Neuve, Belgium: Presses universitaires de Louvain.

Hoey, M. (2007) Grammatical creativity: A corpus perspective. In M. Hoey, M. Mahlberg, M. Stubbs and W. Teubert (eds) *Text, Discourse and Corpora: Theory and Analysis* (pp. 31–56). London: Continuum.

Howarth, P. (1996) *Phraseology in English Academic Writing*. Tübingen: Max Niemeyer.

Hulstijn, J.H., Alderson, J.C. and Schoonen, R. (2010) Developmental stages in second-language acquisition and levels of second-language proficiency: Are there links between them? In I. Bartning, M. Martin and I. Vedder (eds) *Communicative Proficiency and Linguistic Development: Intersections between SLA and Language Testing Research* (pp. 11–20). Amsterdam: European Second Language Association.

Kinsella, C. and Singleton, D. (2014) Much more than age. *Applied Linguistics* 35 (4), 441–462.

Lantolf, J. and Thorne, S. (2006) *Sociocultural Theory and the Genesis of Second Language Development*. Oxford: Oxford University Press.

Laufer, B. (1989) A factor of difficulty in vocabulary learning: Deceptive transparency. *AILA Review/Revue de l'AILA* 6, 10–20.

Leśniewska, J. (2019) *Articles in English as a Second Language: A Phraseological Perspective*. Kraków: Jagiellonian University Press.

Meara, P. (1978). Learners' word associations in French. *Interlanguage Studies Bulletin* 3 (2), 192–211.

Meara, P. (1980) Vocabulary acquisition: A neglected aspect of language learning. *Language Teaching and Linguistics Abstracts* 13, 221–46.

Meara, P. (1984) The study of lexis in interlanguage. In A. Davies, C. Criper and A.P.R. Howatt (eds) *Interlanguage* (pp. 225–235). Edinburgh: Edinburgh University Press.

Paquot, M. (2015) The lexis-grammar interface in learner language: From learner corpus data to applications. Paper presented at the Second Language Research Forum, Atlanta, October.

Paquot, M. (2018) Phraseological competence: A missing component in university entrance language tests? Insights from a study of EFL learners' use of statistical collocations. *Language Assessment Quarterly* 15 (1), 29–43.

Paquot, M. (2019) The phraseological dimension in interlanguage complexity research. *Second Language Research* 35 (1), 121–145.

Paquot, M. and Granger, S. (2012) Formulaic language in learner corpora. *Annual Review of Applied Linguistics* 32, 130–149.

Pfenninger, S.E. and Singleton, D. (2017) *Beyond Age Effects in Instructional L2 Learning: Revisiting the Age Factor*. Bristol: Multilingual Matters.

Pfenninger, S.E. and Singleton, D. (2019) A critical review of research relating to the learning, use and effects of additional and multiple languages in later life. *Language Teaching* 52 (4), 419–449.

Römer, U. and Schultze, R. (eds) (2009) *Exploring the Lexis-Grammar Interface*. Amsterdam: Benjamins.

Salazar, D. (2014) *Lexical Bundles in Native and Non-native Scientific Writing: Applying a Corpus-based Study to Language Teaching*. Amsterdam: Benjamins.

Sinclair, J. (1991) *Corpus, Concordance, Collocation*. Oxford: Oxford University Press.

Singleton, D. (1995) Introduction: A critical look at the Critical Period Hypothesis in second language acquisition research. In D. Singleton and Z. Lengyel (eds) *The Age Factor in Second Language Acquisition* (pp. 1–29). Clevedon: Multilingual Matters.

Singleton, D. (1997) Learning and processing L2 vocabulary. *Language Teaching* 30 (4), 213–225.

Singleton, D. (1998) Age and the second language lexicon. *Studia Anglica Posnaniensia* 23, 365–376.

Singleton, D. (1999) *Exploring the Second Language Mental Lexicon*. Cambridge: Cambridge University Press.

Singleton, D. (2000) *Language and the Lexicon: An Introduction*. London: Routledge and New York: Oxford University Press.

Singleton, D. and Little, D. (1991) The second language lexicon: Some evidence from university-level learners of French and German. *Interlanguage Studies Bulletin* 7 (1), 61–81.

Singleton, D. and Ryan, L. (2004) *Language Acquisition: The Age Factor*. Clevedon: Multilingual Matters.

# Index


Academic writing (prose, texts) 11, 26, 33, 36, 42–43, 74–76, 79–80, 83, 154–155
Accuracy 51, 101, 168, 170, 181
Adjectival modifier 104, 106, 108–111, 113–114, 118, 122, 124, 131, 140, 145, 147
Adverbial modifier 104, 106, 108–111, 113–114, 117–118, 122, 124, 131, 140, 145, 147
ANOVA 160, 163–164, 184, 188, 198, 222
Assessment 12, 14, 49–50, 52, 63, 66–68, 74, 101–105, 109–110, 117, 120–124, 147, 239–240
Association index 129, 135, 137, 140, 143, 146
Association measure 15, 52, 55, 67, 103, 106, 134–135, 182, 187
Association score 11, 129, 144, 147, 182
Association strength 14, 16, 52, 68, 117, 126–127, 129–137, 140, 143–144, 146–147, 182, 199

Bigram 15, 123, 126–127, 129–140, 143–148, 167, 172, 181–183, 185, 240
British Academic Written English corpus (BAWE) 25, 27, 28–29, 31–33, 37–42, 44–45, 48
British National Corpus (BNC) 8, 54, 68, 75, 84, 146, 154, 182, 215–216

Cluster analysis 89, 91, 96
Collocate 91, 159, 165, 170
  Adjectival collocate 154, 161–163, 215–216
  Verb collocate 55–67, 215
Collocation (*see also* Interference collocation)
  Adjective-noun collocation 13, 15–16, 53, 64, 130, 135, 138–140, 143–144, 148, 152–174, 180, 182, 216, 223
  Restricted collocation 153, 171, 209, 211
  Statistical collocation 6, 10–11, 52, 102, 153, 171
  Subject-verb collocation 15, 76, 135, 138–139, 143, 148
  Verb-noun collocation 10, 14, 16, 49, 52–55, 59, 64–66, 68, 154–155, 171, 179, 181–182, 184–186, 188, 190, 193–195, 198–201, 211, 223, 239
  Verb-adverb collocation 15, 130–131, 135, 138–140, 143, 145, 147–148
  Verb-direct object collocation 13, 15, 104, 106–110, 117–119, 122, 126, 130–131, 135–136, 139–140, 143–145, 147, 212, 228–229
Collocational processing 154–155, 207–208, 215
Collocational range 207, 210–211
Common European Framework of Reference for Languages (CEFR) 51, 65, 96, 101–105, 110–111, 113–116, 119–124, 130, 153, 157, 185, 189–192, 194, 200, 202, 240
Complexity measure 103–116, 120–121, 122, 124
Contrastive Analysis (CA) 14, 25–28, 32–33, 35, 38, 42–44, 239
Contrastive Interlanguage Analysis (CIA) 10, 14, 26–27, 29, 31–32, 38, 43, 207
Corpus of Contemporary American English (COCA) 54–64, 68, 129–131, 133–135, 146, 182
Correlation 51, 110, 137–141, 144, 146, 148, 162, 169
Cross-linguistic influence (CLI) 14, 53, 59, 61–63, 68

Cultural Identity in Academic Prose corpus (KIAP) 25, 27–29, 32–34, 37–45, 48

Dependency bigram 15, 126–127, 130–147, 240
Dependency relation 9, 15, 106, 109, 130, 135–137
Discourse 3, 8–9, 11, 14, 26, 30–31, 33, 35, 41, 73, 75, 79, 92–93, 168, 178

Electroencephalogram (EEG) 16, 213–217, 219–221, 223–228, 241
Elicitation 7, 17, 78, 213–214
English as a Foreign Language (EFL) 14–15, 67, 72–74, 80–83, 85, 88–90, 92–96, 154, 217
English as a Second Language (ESL) 14–15, 72–74, 80–83, 85, 88–90, 92–96, 201, 236
Error 10, 51, 53, 63, 66, 72, 79, 106, 119, 154, 170, 186, 201
Event-related potential (ERP) 214, 217, 219–220, 226–227
Experimental data (approach, study) 7, 9, 16–17, 78–79, 155, 206, 209, 212–217, 225–229, 241
Exposure 15–16, 18, 80, 82, 86, 89, 127–128, 154, 170, 181, 183–184, 189, 198–199, 201–202
Eye tracking 7, 16, 155, 214–217, 226–228, 241

Grammar (grammatical, grammaticality); *see also* Lexico-grammar) 3, 5, 14–15, 41, 44, 51, 64, 72–78, 82, 86, 95, 101–104, 106–108, 110, 120–121, 123, 130, 135, 144, 156, 182, 198, 206–207, 215, 236–237, 239, 242

Idiom (idiomatic, unidiomatic, idiomaticity) 3–6, 8, 10, 12, 25, 28, 30, 43, 51, 60, 65, 74, 78, 91–94, 102, 118, 123, 152–153, 155, 171, 178, 207, 209, 214, 235
Integrated Contrastive Model (ICM) 14, 25–27, 32, 43
Interference 52, 53, 208, 210, 211, 215
 Interference (-based) collocation 16, 210–211, 215, 217–218, 241, 208, 212, 216, 220, 222–223, 225–226
Interlanguage 10, 25–27, 43–44, 208–209
International Corpus of Learner English (ICLE) 9, 12, 14–15, 49, 51, 53–68, 82–96, 209–211, 213, 215, 217, 229, 239

Learner corpus research (LCR) 7–13, 17–18, 29, 52, 207
Lemma (lemmatization) 54–58, 60, 62, 84–85, 106, 108, 110–111, 113, 115, 120, 133, 135, 138–139, 144, 148, 159, 186, 216
Lexical bundle (bundle) 3, 6, 10–14, 28–29, 31, 36, 52, 76, 80, 102, 123, 129, 178, 181, 207
Lexical complexity; *see also* Phraseological complexity 104, 107–108, 110, 120–123, 172
Lexical diversity; *see also* Phraseological diversity 66, 103, 106, 107–108, 120, 146, 201
Lexical proficiency; *see also* Phraseological proficiency 63, 126–132, 140, 143, 147
Lexical sophistication; *see also* Phraseological sophistication 15, 60, 103, 108, 126–127, 140, 146
Lexico-grammar (lexico-grammatical, lexis-grammar) 3, 13–14, 72–73, 87, 93, 95, 126, 130, 239
Linear regression 15, 137, 139
Log Dice 16, 67, 163–165, 167, 170, 173, 187–188, 198–200, 202
Longitudinal learner corpus 171, 179, 185, 198
Longitudinal study (design, research); *see also* Pseudo-longitudinal 7, 12–14, 16, 53, 80, 154–155, 171, 178–184, 194–195, 198–199, 202
Louvain Corpus of Native English Essays (LOCNESS) 53–61, 63, 68, 83–92, 96

Mental lexicon 102, 178, 238
Multiword unit (expression) 3, 7–8, 206–207, 241
Mutual Information (MI score) 6, 10–11, 15–16, 52–62, 65–67, 103–104, 107, 109, 115, 117–119, 129–130, 134–136, 143, 161–171, 173, 180, 182, 187, 199–200

N-gram; *see also* Bigram 14, 25–26, 28–45, 123, 127–132, 143–144, 155, 169, 240

Overuse 11, 63, 65, 80, 86, 91–93, 153–154, 178, 241

Part-of-speech (POS) tagging 9, 83, 106, 130, 133, 235
Passive 14–15, 32, 42–43, 72–88, 91–96, 107–108, 111, 113, 115, 121–122, 239–240
Passive gradient 73, 76–78, 84
Passive ratio 15, 73, 75, 82, 85–92, 94–95
Passive voice 72, 74–76, 83, 85, 94, 240
Adjectival passive 72, 77–78, 84–85, 87, 94
Phraseological competence 15, 17, 102–103, 105, 120, 123–124, 129–131, 146–147, 155, 168–172, 179–181, 183–185, 189, 198, 208, 239–240
Phraseological complexity; *see also* Lexical complexity 15, 101, 105, 108–110, 114–117, 120–124, 168, 240
Phraseological development 102, 154–155, 171, 173, 181, 183–184, 186, 202, 241
Phraseological diversity (phrasal diversity); *see also* Lexical diversity 103–104, 106, 108–109, 117, 121–122
Phraseological indices 13, 15, 138–139, 147
Phraseological knowledge 16, 152, 168–170, 179–181, 183–184, 186, 198, 202, 241
Phraseological measure 12, 103, 109, 114, 116, 120–122
Phraseological proficiency; *see also* Lexical proficiency 129, 131, 147, 240
Phraseological sequence 25, 44, 73, 76, 81–82, 91, 94, 188
Phraseological sophistication; *see also* Lexical sophistication 103–104, 106, 109–110, 115, 121–122, 153
Phraseological unit 3–4, 9–10, 12–13, 17, 52, 55, 59, 72, 102–103, 105, 109, 117, 119–120, 123, 130, 144, 154, 171, 178, 180, 183, 188, 207, 209, 240
Predictor 15–16, 110, 112–113, 115–117, 120, 128, 134, 137–141, 143–144, 146–147, 149, 157, 163, 183, 189, 198, 201–202
Proficiency (language proficiency, proficiency level); *see also* Lexical proficiency, Phraseological proficiency, Writing proficiency 10–17, 49–53, 63–65, 79, 90, 94, 101–103, 105, 107, 110, 117, 120–132, 140, 143–147, 153–173, 181, 183–185, 189–191, 193, 198–202, 212, 226, 229, 239–241
Pseudo-longitudinal design 13–14, 16

Random effect 188–191, 193, 198
Reference corpus 11, 54–55, 106, 109, 117, 119, 127–128, 130, 133, 135, 144, 149, 158, 182, 186, 198, 202
Register 6, 11, 34, 41, 60, 68, 72–77, 156, 167, 184
Regression 110, 112, 137, 144, 190
Linear regression 15, 137, 139
Regression model (modelling, analysis) 13, 15–16, 109–113, 117, 119–120, 138, 188, 198, 200
Replication 15, 94, 101, 103, 105, 122, 173, 240

Speech (spoken) 6, 8–9, 13, 15–16, 35, 45, 54, 68, 77, 94, 140, 152–153, 156–158, 166–168, 170–173, 178, 181, 183–184, 208–209, 213
Spoken BNC2014 corpus 15–16, 152, 153, 157–158, 160–162, 164, 167, 173
Syntactic complexity 66, 107, 115–116, 121–122, 146, 168, 228

Task 9–10, 12–13, 52, 65, 78–79, 104–105, 120, 127, 132, 147, 157, 159, 238
Teaching 3–4, 6, 65, 92, 94–95, 101, 147, 154–156, 178, 189, 238, 242
English Language Teaching (ELT) 73–77, 217
Testing (test) 7, 12, 14, 49, 50–53, 59, 63–65, 67–68, 101, 134, 185, 213, 239, 242
Test of English as a Foreign Language (TOEFL) 15, 128, 132, 137–140, 146, 149
Topic 9, 39, 41, 45, 60, 66, 87, 92, 105, 123, 127, 152, 157, 162–163, 170, 172, 183, 185, 189–191, 193, 195, 197–198, 200–202
Transfer 12, 14, 27, 59, 63, 80, 93, 154, 170, 173, 207, 210–212, 223, 225, 229
Trinity Lancaster Corpus (TLC) 15, 152–153, 156–159, 161, 164, 167–169
T-score 6, 10–11, 15, 55, 65–67, 155, 169, 180, 182, 187

Type-token ratio (TTR) 103–104, 108–111, 113–114, 117, 119, 124, 166, 188, 198, 200

Underuse 11, 15, 72, 79–80, 85–87, 93–94, 153–154
Usage-based perspective (view) 81, 86, 89, 94, 236

Varieties of English for Specific Purposes Database (VESPA) 25, 27–29, 31–33, 37, 39–42, 44–45

Writing proficiency 15, 101, 126–127, 130–132, 140, 143

For Product Safety Concerns and Information please contact our EU Authorised Representative:

Easy Access System Europe

Mustamäe tee 50

10621 Tallinn

Estonia

gpsr.requests@easproject.com

www.ingramcontent.com/pod-product-compliance
Ingram Content Group UK Ltd.
Pitfield, Milton Keynes, MK11 3LW, UK
UKHW021836150926
8656IPUK00003B/10

*9781788924856*